The
Politics of
BANKING

GEORGE S. ECCLES

The
Politics of
BANKING

GEORGE S. ECCLES

Edited by
SIDNEY HYMAN

Copyright © 1982 by The University of Utah
Published by The Graduate School of Business, University of Utah

Library of Congress Catalog Card Number 82-50635
ISBN cloth 0-87480-208-3
ISBN paper 0-87480-209-1

To my wife Dolores (Lolie)
To my brother Marriner
and
To my beloved profession of banking

Contents

V   THE STRUGGLE TO GOVERN

Foreword

I first met George S. Eccles while preparing a biography of his brother, Marriner S. Eccles, who dominated the Federal Reserve Board when he was its chairman or member between 1934 and 1951. I knew how the two brothers as relatively young men—though Marriner was the senior of the pair by ten years—laid the foundations of the First Security Corporation, a pioneer multibank holding company. I also knew that the striking growth of First Security in the Intermountain West dated from 1945 when George became its Board Chairman and Chief Executive Officer. Yet beyond such surface details, there was not much more that I knew about him. My encounters with George amounted to a handshake between the brackets of a hail and farewell.

The case changed in the late 1970s when I began work on a fifty-year history of First Security, later published as *Challenge and Response*. Aside from the right of access to source material, I needed George's help in getting at meanings which were not carried on the face of raw facts and figures. In the course of many meetings extending over the length of a year, he responded in generous measure to every request I made and every question I posed.

All the while, of course, he was daily engaged in managing the affairs of a banking empire. When their immediate demands on his attention broke into our sessions, he would have me sit by while he disposed of a critical piece of business by speaking a few words. Then, without a moment's pause for breath, he would resume our conversation where it had been left off. He seemed to bear himself in the high style of a patriot king riding at the head of troops in battle—to embrace difficulties with the pride of a master. Though George at the time was in his late seventies, the weight of his years rested lightly on his shoulders. It was hard to imagine any circumstances when he would ever show fatigue. It was harder still to imagine that he would ever be forced to open his door to an ambassador of death.

The more time I spent with George, the more it was brought home to me that his concerns—and the theme running through what he had to say—were in no way limited to the affairs of the First Security Corporation. He was as much if not more concerned with the profession of banking, of where it fit in the wide world of national and international political economy. It was in character for him to respond with a firm "Amen," when once, during our conversations, I recalled Alfred North Whitehead's remark that "a great society is a society whose men of business think greatly of their functions."

This is not the place to dwell on his diverse efforts to promote the cause of "economic literacy" in the Intermountain West and elsewhere. It is the place to say that the idea for the present book about the politics of banking surfaced at an advanced stage of our frequent talks about the specific functions of bankers. He then voiced the hope that after the history of First Security was completed, something might be gained on the side of understanding if he ventured a book of his own about banking itself, written from the perspective of six decades of experience with the management of financial resources. He stressed the importance of placing the subject of banking in its historical and political context, saying that history and politics—as the source of law—often predetermine what can or cannot be done in banking, without regard to the kind of decisions "pure economics" would dictate.

Still, as he was carrying a heavy load of work—all the heavier in view of an increasingly distressed economic and political environment—he observed that he could not unaided produce the kind of book he had in mind. He could amass the necessary documentation, sift the wheat from the chaff, provide the connective tissue linking a cause to its effect, suggest areas for further research, formulate draft pages for further development. If I was prepared to work with him in the role of an editor, distilling and refining further what he placed in my hands, he was willing to proceed with a projected book about the politics of banking. I welcomed his proposal, and the deed was done.

The months when we worked together—sometimes in Salt Lake City, sometimes through correspondence, sometimes through lengthy telephone conversations—ran concurrently with external events that brought the structure of American banking under heavy siege and shook the foundations of the American economic order and that of the world around it. All this required successive revisions of draft chapters to keep abreast of swift moving changes.

Suddenly, however, in the spring of 1981, when George was in the eighty-first year of his life, his eyes began to fail. The affliction made him dependent on his long-time aide, Ms. Julia Cottrell, for a reading of material related to the gestating book. Yet he remained committed to the completion of the project. Later, in the fall of that year, when he learned that he was in the grip of a remorseless kind of cancer, his commitment to his book was invested with a passionate urgency. Though wracked with pain, or isolated in a hospital for surgery, or debilitated by post-surgery treatments, he kept in close touch with me. His voice at the Salt Lake City end of our telephone conversations grew progressively weaker, but he was in full possession of his immense analytical powers, and his comments on points of detail in the draft chapters of the book that were read to him, retained their cogency and mathematical precision.

On the morning of January 20, I was in Chicago awaiting the passing of an hour in the time zone difference before placing a call to George in Salt Lake City. I meant to tell him that I had just received the first batch of page proofs for *The Politics of Banking* from the University of Chicago Printing Department, and would be mailing them to him at once. In the hour of waiting, there was a telephone call from Salt Lake City. Mason Smith, a First Security officer, was at the other end of the line. He informed me that George had died at 5:30 A.M. I later learned something else from David Gardner, President of the University of Utah. At midnight on January 20 when Gardner received word that George's vital signs were failing rapidly, he raced to his friend's bedside, found him awake, and assured him that his book would be published exactly as he wanted it to be. George reached for Gardner's hand, and with his last strength clutched it in a sign of gratitude, then loosened his grip and fell back on his pillow. It was his last conscious gesture.

It remains for me to say that I am indebted to the individuals who joined in my own race against the absolute of time itself to provide a dying man with the evidence that the book on which he had spent his final energies would see the light of day. Foremost among these is David Gardner who brought the manuscript to the attention of a review committee at the University of Utah, which then recommended its publication under the imprimatur of that university's Graduate School of Business. In a sequel to this decision, I owe a debt to the personnel in the University of Chicago Printing Department who, in their respective ways, cleared the track so that the manuscript could appear in print a short three months after the text was turned over to them. These were Gerald N. Davy, the general manager of the Printing Department, Cynthia C. Susmilch, the art director, Kathryn Krug handling the editing, and both Everett Conner and Stuart M. Gross on the customer service side of operations.

Sidney Hyman
Chicago, March 15, 1982

Preface

George Stoddard Eccles was an outstanding banker, a talented applied economist, and a widely respected public policy advisor on national and international financial affairs. His great work, however, was the development and guidance of First Security Corporation, a pioneer bank holding company and the leading financial institution headquartered in the Intermountain West. The ultimate measure of the excellence of the man should therefore probably be made in terms of his performance as a corporate chief executive officer. Chief executives of major corporations can be judged by the financial results achieved, a point of view with which one feels sure Mr. Eccles would agree. Close associates can also observe and judge qualitative performance in the essential chief executive roles of personal leader, organizational leader, and strategist. A very good chief executive would presumably be one who ranked high on both financial and qualitative grounds. What additional quality, then, makes a great chief executive? I believe it is the quality of *perspective*—the ability to get above the noise level of ongoing events, to see through the traditional mythology of the corporation and its industry, and to form clear and independent judgments about the capabilities of the firm in relation to the environment in which it lives and expects to continue to live.

The credentials of George Eccles as a great banker and chief executive do not stand in need of further proof to the legion of his colleagues, competitors, and friends. For those less fortunate individuals who did not know him, this book, *The Politics of Banking,* communicates unmistakably his vision—his *perspective*—and testifies eloquently to his place in management history as one of the truly great chief executives.

Banking is the keel of the ship of business, and money in usable form, the product of banking, is the current in which the ship makes its way. If one were to select a single line of business as the stage for a study of the general problems of the chief executive—the field which business educators call Policy—that line of business would have to be banking. The study of Policy, mirroring the activity pattern of chief executive life, is increasingly preoccupied with the interaction between the corporation and society at large, usually represented by government. Policy is becoming, to an increasing extent, Politics.

George Eccles has offered *The Politics of Banking* as a management text in banking business policy and, necessarily to this purpose, as a history and analysis of public policy related to banking. It is a rare experience to open a book on a topic apparently so prosaic as business policy and find in it high drama, set on the central stage of the nation's economic life.

Along with the need to be concerned more and more with public matters seemingly unrelated or even antithetical to the economic thrust of the firm, today's chief executive must live with rates of sociopolitical and technological change unprecedented in history. Rapid environmental change creates uncertainty, equivalent to risk or, in Eccles's more sensitive human term, ambiguity. No segment of economic life is undergoing more rapid and fundamental change than the financial services industry. George Eccles led his bank through "recurrent national disasters, a global war and two major regional wars, depressions, recessions, inflation, along with revolutionary changes in science, technology, and in social and cultural attitudes." One concludes from his book, however, that he believed that the largest changes were still to come—and probably sooner rather than later.

Ironically, it is deregulation which is the cutting edge of change causing the uncertainty and ferment which currently plagues the banking industry. The historical roots of bank regulation, the economic theories which have affected banking through monetary policy, the changes in Federal Reserve structure and procedure, and the competing interests which have shaped the banking laws are all described in this book in highly competent technical detail. The philosophical detachment shown will undoubtedly surprise readers unfamiliar with the Eccles family trait of independent thought. It is impossible to write about social, political, and economic events, however, without expressing the values which emerge from a general point of view about life and the way the world works. Mr. Eccles has written: "as no man should be the judge of his own case, with the judging reader in mind, the honest thing to say is that the text does indeed have a governing perspective." His perspective is one which most educated people whose careers have been spent in finance, commerce, or industry will share. No one will be in doubt about where George Eccles is coming from, but most readers will be deeply impressed with the scrupulous fairness which is manifest in his treatment of the antecedents and the political contexts of banking regulation.

George Stoddard Eccles died January 20, 1982. He was not sure then, nor can any of us be sure now, exactly what the face of commercial banking will look like in January, 1992. It is unlikely, however, that one could find a better background analysis from which to interpret and predict the ongoing and future course of events than *The Politics of Banking*. This book will stand out among the many monuments Mr. Eccles leaves, including those which reflect his generosity to higher education in Utah. The faculty and students of the Graduate School of Business of the University of Utah have gained both from their professional association with George Eccles and from his financial support. In 1978, we collaborated with First Security Foundation in publishing *Challenge and Response,* a history of First Security Corporation written by Sidney Hyman. Mr. Hyman has edited the present volume with consummate literary skill reinforced by his firm grasp of economics and banking.

The Graduate School of Business is immensely proud to serve as publisher of *The Politics of Banking*. The foremost objectives of business education are to train managers and professionals of the highest competence and to contribute to the permanent body of knowledge about applied economics and management. In publishing George Eccles's book, we serve both of these high objectives.

JAMES HAMILTON GARDNER
Salt Lake City, March 1982

I

THE ENVIRONMENT OF BANKING

1. Why This Book?

ON THE NATURE OF BANKING

In an ideal world, banking would be an exact science, comprised of universally true laws. Then, too, bankers who mastered those laws would be spared the strains of risks and uncertainties. As long as their practical decisions conformed to what was universally true, they would always gain the profitable ends for which they were framed.

In the real world, bankers *do* in fact share a common core of knowledge, rules, and conventions—which can be taught—and from which they take their bearing. In the absence of that common core, they could not speak the same language of interaction. With it, they can govern their conduct on the basis of reasonable expectations about what their opposite number will do—or, at least, can anticipate the general repertory from which responses to their own actions will be drawn.

None of this, however, makes banking an exact science. It is not like physics whose dynamics are the same in China as in the United States. Banking—like man-made law, politics, ethics, and history—belongs to the family of the judgmental sciences. It has its techniques, swims in a sea of facts, has its lore about cause and effect relationships. Yet when the chips are down and bankers must choose between a yes or no, what will sway what they will ultimately say? A mathematical table for predictions? Maybe. The choice is more likely to be swayed by their judgments of inexact things—assessments of past performance, estimates of dangers and opportunities, the felt needs of the time, the imperatives of public policy, the inconvenient prejudices of common humanity.

In all this, moreover, the way individual bankers react to things that cross their lines of vision can never be an immaculate process where "pure logic" is divorced from the raw surge of life itself. Their reactions are bound to be influenced in some degree by the personal experiences which set the lens for their perceptions.

If so, then the reality here is the source of another judgmental variable in the conduct of banking—because personal experiences can be as bad a teacher as they can be a good one. In financial matters, no less than in politics, love or war, people can be ambushed by the illusion that future success will be theirs if they repeat over again everything that led to a past success, or do everything the exact opposite of what led to a past failure. The lessons of experience count for good or ill depending on whether they help us "see and see ourselves seeing," or predispose us to seek in the case before us only what we want to find in it, and find only what we are looking for.[1]

RESUME

In stressing straight off the judgmental nature of banking, my motive springs from what needs to be said about the book now in the hands of the reader. In offering an analytical account of the politics of banking, I have tried to stay within the four corners of what the evidence will support. Yet as no man should be the judge of his own case, with the judging reader in mind, the honest thing to say is that the text does indeed have a governing perspective. It is a perspective shaped by more than six decades of personal experience in all aspects of commercial banking and its development, and in the general management of financial resources. It is awkward to use the stilted "I" of a "resume" in accounting for those experiences, yet the use will be terminated with all due deliberate speed.

To start with, upon graduating in 1921 from the School of Business at Columbia University, followed by an apprenticeship in the Irving Trust Bank of New York, I became an executive in a bank in Ogden, Utah. Then, between 1925 and 1928, I joined my older brother, Marriner S. Eccles, and our family business associate, Marriner Browning, in forming a pioneer multibank holding company, the First Security Corporation. At a time when branch banking was almost universally barred by state laws, the holding company's constituent banks were initially confined to the northern tier of Utah, to the contiguous southern tier of Idaho, and to an adjacent corner of Wyoming. In those days, when communications seemed primitive compared to what they have since become, the physical extent of First Security's network of banks was by deliberate design limited to cities that could be reached by an overnight train ride from Ogden.

Though every bank in that network was assailed by the Great Depression, all emerged intact from the ordeal without the loss of a cent of depositor funds. More than that, in a movement *against* history, First Security increased the count of its constituent banks during the Great Depression in the act of acquiring—incident to emergency rescue operations—certain strategic but gravely endangered institutions from their former owners. Later, with concurrent changes in federal law, and in Utah and Idaho state banking laws, First Security banks in Utah were reorganized in 1934 under a national charter as a state-based branch-banking system. They were simultaneously reorganized in Idaho as a state-chartered branch-banking system, but were eventually brought under the cover of a national charter. For want of any new legislation in Wyoming to permit branch banking, First Security institutions in that state remained unit banks.

After 1934 when my brother Marriner was called to Washington where he served for seventeen years as the Chairman and member of the Federal Reserve Board, the management of the family's banking interests in the Intermountain West devolved upon me. Eventually, in 1945, I became the President and chief executive officer of First Security Corporation, the parent holding company, while continuing as President of the First Security Bank of Utah. With later corporate changes, I relinquished the presidency of that bank but remained the Chairman and chief executive officer of the holding company—now one of the dominant financial institutions in the Intermountain West, itself one of the swiftest growing regions in the nation. At the same time, I have been a director of nonbanking corporations, such as the Union Pacific Railroad, Utah International Mining, Amalgamated Sugar, Texasgulf, four insurance companies, and Aubrey G. Lanston & Company, a major dealer in government securities.

During this time I was necessarily drawn into frequent policy discussions with legislators and regulatory authorities at national and state levels of government—necessarily, because of the posts held in professional organizations of bankers. These included service as President of the Association of Reserve City Bankers, President of the Association of Registered Bank Holding Companies, member of the Government Borrowing Committee of the American Bankers Association (an advisory body to the Secretary of the Treasury), and member of the National Advisory Committee on Banking Policies and Practices (an advisory body to the U.S. Comptroller of the Currency). Finally, starting in the late 1940s with work as economic advisor to the Marshall Plan, and subsequently as chairman of the Vienna meeting of the International Monetary Conference, entwined public concerns and private interests led to close personal contacts with a worldwide network of commercial and central bankers.

Standing alone, however, the stilted "I" of this resume conveys no sense of the *context* for the personal experiences that were just detailed. It is necessary to add, therefore, that during the past six decades, the conduct of banking unfolded in an environment hit by recurrent natural disasters, a global war and two major regional wars, depressions, recessions, inflation, along with revolutionary changes in science, technology, and in social and cultural attitudes. It was a time as well of achievements in communal life which eclipsed even those associated with Golden Ages of the past.

Either way, good or bad, few things remained in the same place for very long. The terrain special to banking—as to any other province of business— was strewn with the debris of firm beliefs and practices that were overrun by events and ground into the dust. Orthodox economic theories and doctrines were snapped like matchwood when hit by irrepressible forces. Laws enacted in the public interest either failed to gain their laudable ends, or in the name of "regulation" frequently spread a contagion of trouble over the very institutions they were intended to safeguard. Mounds of reports and statistics meant to serve as a luminous basis for "control" often hid the very truths they purported to reveal. Prophecies, whether of apocalyptic doom or salvation, were alike proved false. There were also repeated instances, both ironic and baffling, where the problems of success were as great as the problems of failure. All such experiences shaped my outlook on banking, account for my motive in writing this book, and set its focus.

PROSPECTUS

This is not a "how to do it" manual, setting forth general maxims for certified success in banking. No general maxim from the time of the Seven Sages of Greece onward has ever prevented a single folly in banking, and none by itself has ever lit up from within the exact way to apply broad principles to the specific features of cases in banking. The form and substance of this book take their character from three audiences I have in immediate view.

The first consists of prospective readers for whom banking in times past seemed to be some sort of occult exercise by a tribal shaman. Now, however, signs abound that they are all the more mystified by the commotions whirled by rival financial institutions, each with its own strangely named new attempts to attract depositor funds for use in connection with their respective institutional investments and loans. Things standing so, I want to chart as best I can the course of the historical forces that have come to a head in the current tumult in the financial world—along with the new problems they pose, and the terms of the disputes over proposed solutions to them. In agreement with Justice Holmes's view that "a page of history is worth a volume of logic," I want to set the current upheavals in the financial world in their historical context, to help general readers—in their diverse personal relationships with various financial institutions—see where *they* fit into the contemporary picture.

The second audience among the three is comprised of students of banking in colleges and universities, whether at the undergraduate or graduate levels of course work. They are certainly not lacking in instructional materials. The mound of these towers very high. A while ago, however, I was forcefully struck by a gap in the mound—this, after surveying a representative group of leading textbooks on banking with an eye to their possible use in connection with bank officer training programs. With one notable exception, the authors of the recommended textbooks were not banking practitioners, and the one exception was flavored with irony. Its author, upon becoming a top executive in a major New York bank, had the melancholy distinction of being swept up in judgmental practices that brought the bank to the brink of a financial precipice.[2]

All the other recommended textbooks were the work of academic economists who set their sights on certain instructional goals and reached them in fine style. If they read at vital points like typographical misprints, it was not because the authors or editors were at fault. It was because events themselves, moving on a very fast track, raced beyond the existing conditions when the texts went to press. So much so, as to make the boundary lines between commercial banking and a sweep of other financial enterprises as indistinct as lines drawn in water. In fact, the very term "bank" has now lost its traditional meaning, and is in need of a redefinition.

The gap I alluded to a moment ago lay between the two general classes of books prepared by academic economists. Each, to repeat, served an important instructional purpose, beyond any fair ground for complaint. The point is that one portion of the total consisted of texts designed for under-graduate introductory courses where the focus was usually on the mechanical routines of banking, and on the related routines of central banking. The other portion consisted of texts designed for advanced or graduate courses which usually focused on sophisticated econometric models and associated theories about the dynamics of money, credit, investment, interest rates, fiscal policy, and so on. What was missing from the total was any text of manageable size that conveyed some sense of the inner life of banking—the throbbing pulse of its *politics*.

The third audience set for these pages is the one perhaps most in need of knowledge about the politics of banking. It is comprised of junior per-sonnel in bank-sponsored training programs, and of middle level managers destined for the various institutes the banking profession sponsors on special aspects of banking. The future of any bank as a continuing enterprise depends on how well these are prepared to assume increased and increasing respon-sibilities. Yet over the years, one recurrent reality has often been brought home to me. It is that bank personnel with promising natural endowments who can deal effectively with problems *defined for them* by top executive management, often stammer when it comes to discovering *on their own* the existence and nature of the problems in which they are encircled.[3] Junior personnel tend to be so engrossed in mastering the nuts and bolts of a particular bank, and middle level managers tend to be so absorbed in daily operations bearing on their prospects for advancement, that they often have no surplus energy left to "step outside themselves" and reflect on what banking itself in all about—where it stands and where it is trending.

RESTATEMENT OF PURPOSE

Based on all the general appraisals I have so far made, my paramount aim in this book can be restated as follows. I want to guide the general reader, the academic student, the novice banker, and the middle level bank manager past the mechanical routines of commercial banking which they know by heart. I want to place them at the desk of the chief executive officer of a commercial bank so that they can see from *within* how the politics of banking looks from that internal perspective. Especially how it looks to the chief executive officer who functions in the context of a bank holding company, now the dominant form for the management of bank financial assets. I want to show the banking practitioner at work in an environment shaped by the invisible hand of history and by the outcome of political contests in the dim past—exposed at every turn to competitive clashes among rival interests—pushed in different directions by technological imperatives—subject to minute regulatory constraints—straining and sometimes succeeding in having the constraints eased. I also want to show the banking practitioner poised midway between logical forms of knowledge as in mathematics, and the intuitive forms of knowledge as in the creative arts—a mixed intellectual economy combining elements of fact with elements of the imagination, the objective calculus of risks with the subjective calculus of the will to take risks.

On top of all else—and this repeats for emphasis what was touched on already—I want to bring the reader abreast of the changes overtaking the world of banking, and of the arguments about how best to meet the problems change always brings. Every age is, of course, an age of change. Yet in a retrospect of the six decades of my own experience in banking, alterations in the structure of banking, starting in the 1960s, have gone forward at an accelerating speed and in an ever widening reach beyond comparison with anything known to bankers now alive.

Banking still remains a business central to all other individual, family, and corporate efforts in a profit *and* loss system. Banking institutions themselves depend for their legitimacy on the extent to which they constructively serve the needs of society to the satisfaction of society. But this does not suggest that they stand in place of government. They don't, can't, and shouldn't. Rather the cardinal problem of government today vis-a-vis banking specifically, and business generally, is the problem of *governance*—with all that the term implies by way of fairness and the exercise of responsible power by both public and private authorities. It is to decide anew as Edmund Burke put it in his own day, "what matters should be directed by public wisdom, and what should be left as far as possible to private exertion."[4] It is to draw up anew and distinguish anew the Agenda of government, from its Non-agenda.

CAVEATS

Two difficulties intervene between the objectives of this book and its attainment. The first and obvious difficulty is that bankers and banks come in all sizes and shapes. Hence it is impossible to be grammatically exact in speaking of them in the singular, or to account for each particular difference they exhibit. All one can do is try to deal with common elements amid their diversity, and then find refuge in Plato's disarming remark: "What I am about to tell you may not be exactly true, but something very much like it is.'' The second difficulty recalls the old saying that you can't step in the same river twice. The next time, it is a different river. So, too, with present-day banking. As you try to say what it is about, it is in fact undergoing a change both in the materials that act on it, and in the way bankers deal with the materials.

Still, events in banking do not occur in a vacuum. They have a *past*, and they move toward the future—slowly or swiftly—by way of the present. Subject to all the limitations that inhere in a book addressed to a reality that is constantly on the move, it is possible to draw a picture showing how American banking reached its present point, its perennial conflicts, its present concerns, how it goes about doing its business, its worries and divisive debates.

At the time of this writing, many issues related to banking are the subjects of sharp disputes in Congress—and the issues include those thought to have been settled yesterday. It is a risky business, therefore, to try to lip-read the terms on which all the disputed issues will be finally resolved—if they are ever conclusively resolved. Hence a final cautionary note. It is that any statements made regarding the outcome of current controversies related to banking are only conjectures based on probable reasoning.

2. Concerning the Obvious

Some truths about banking are as obvious as air, and perhaps for that reason, are, like air, often overlooked. To start the enumeration, God did not bring forth banking on the sixth day of creation, and then sit for a portrait commissioned by bankers. Banking, in other words, does not exist in nature. It is man-made. Like most man-made things, its means and ends are ceaseless topics for dispute. All the more so because, under capitalism, the "money creating" and the "money destroying" functions of private banking—the first through loans and the second through collections—impinge on functions usually reserved for the state. In the disputes over those functions, some theorists uphold the vision of an ideal banking system that will operate automatically in obedience to impersonal economic laws; others insist that public intervention in the banking system is indispensably necessary at every point to prevent private abuses of powers that have major public effects.

In any case, the ways of American bankers and banking have been attacked from one generation to the next, starting in the hour when the American Republic was still in its swaddling cloths.[5] In 1794, for example, John Taylor of Caroline, a close political ally of Thomas Jefferson, judged American banking to be "only a fraud whereby labour suffers the imposition of paying an interest on the circulating medium." A decade later, he raised the pitch of his attack: "In the history of our forefathers we recognize three political beasts, feeding at different periods upon their lives, liberties and properties. The beasts called hierarchical and feudal aristocracy, to say the worst of them, are now the instruments of the third—viz., of banks." Ex-President John Adams was of the same mind. "Our banks," so he wrote in 1819, "have done more injury to the religion, morality, tranquility and prosperity and even wealth of the nation than they can have done or ever will do good."

Later, during the Jacksonian era, Senator Thomas Hart Benton added his own distinctive flourish to the attack on banks, saying: "Are men with pens sticking behind their ears to be allowed to put an end to this Republic? . . . All the flourishing cities of the West are mortgaged to this money power. They may be devoured by it any moment. They are in the jaws of the monster . . . One gulp, one swallow, and all is gone." An Ohio newspaper offered an editorial variation on Benton's theme: "There is not a single bank in the United States that is much better than a den of thieves seeking an opportunity

. . . to rob the people. How disgusting, then, is the hypocritical jargon of the bank lackeys and slaves about the character of good banks and sound banks. Humbug! How can GOODNESS come out of HELL?''

THE SECOND TRUTH

Banking has theories which help organize knowledge about the ways of the banking business. It has trade schools which offer useful introductions to the mechanical routines of banks and banking. It has high-speed techniques for making and recording transactions, all necessary to preserving the differences between ''mine'' and ''thine.'' It has professional organizations which speak to the operational problems of banking. It has a high quality financial press which tracks every political and regulatory breeze likely to affect banking. Yet the whole of this—the theories, the trade schools, the mechanical routines, the professional organizations, the financial press—are only the tools of banking. Left in their own kit, they build nothing. What is built with them depends on the interaction among the things comprising the personal circumstances of a banker and his environment at the moment of decision.

This is all the more true because bankers, as individuals, are not like a family of identical twins. They are more like figures in paintings by Peter Brueghel where all sorts of odd people do all sorts of odd things.[6] In those paintings, some figures saw wood and some bake bread. Some hawk fish and some just stare out of windows. Some carouse and some lie in the shade of a tree asleep. Some fly kites and others wash dirty laundry in a brook. Without pressing analogies too hard and too far, the same variety is present in the banking picture. Its figures subdivide broadly into groups of commercial bankers, mortgage bankers, mutual savings bankers, building and loan bankers, acceptance bankers, investment bankers, international bankers, and central bankers. Within each of these broad categories, they also subdivide into many species.

At the present time, for example, there are 14,710 commercial banks in the United States. Yet the legal setting in which the individual commercial banker works varies from one context to the next. His institution can be a unit national bank which is automatically a member of the Federal Reserve System. It can be a unit state bank which voluntarily ''elects'' to be a member of the System. It can be a unit nonmember state bank, or a branch of a national or state bank, or a one-bank holding company, or a multibank holding company.

Viewed from the standpoint of its physical setting, the bank may occupy the greater part of a skyscraper in a major ''money center'' or ''reserve city.'' It may be a lead regional bank with a network of affiliates in different states. It may be a ''country bank'' housed either in a one-room building opposite the village green or even in a trailer parked in a shopping center.

These days, it may also be an American branch of a huge foreign bank headquarters in an overseas metropolis.

Then again, in the grouping of banks according to deposit size,[7] the institution may be among the 3,781 banks with deposits ranging between $20 million and $50 million. At the next distinctive level on an ascending slope, it may be among the 8,340 middle-range institutions whose average deposits are roughly $100 million. At yet another distinctive level, it may be among the 132 banks whose deposits are in excess of $1 billion. Still higher, it may be among the nation's fifteen largest banks, starting with the Mellon Bank with deposits of $11.34 billion and soaring upward to the apex of the pyramid occupied by Manufacturers Hanover with deposits of $39 billion, Chase Manhattan Bank with deposits of $57.17 billion—and Citibank and Bank of America which vie for the No. 1 position with deposits in excess of $90 billion.

Hence a particular bank may have a great or small impact on the Federal Reserve Board's attempts to regulate the nation's money supply—depending on how "monetary aggregates" are defined. A textbook revelatory case in point occurred in October 1979, coincident with the Federal Reserve Board's new anti-inflation program, featuring new curbs on the growth of the money supply. Within an eleven-day period, two erroneous "M-1" reports the Board received from Manufacturers Hanover Bank of New York grossly distorted the money supply statistics for the month—starting with a $3.7 billion overstatement discovered on October 18, followed by a $900 million overstatement discovered on October 29. Plainly, no one country bank filing an M-1 report could by itself be the source of a $4.6 billion aggregate error in computing the nation's money supply.

THE THIRD TRUTH

Banking depends for its success on accurate cost-benefit analysis—or in plain English, on rational judgments. Banking is also a "calculating" business in that no one can actually count costs and benefits without actually counting. In its largest sense, however, banking is no mere arithmetic drill for an "indifference machine." It is a way of looking at things, a complete part of everything. The greater the responsibilities vested in individual bankers within the structure of a banking organization, the greater the demands on what they must know. They may be specialists about some things, but they must also have the informed knowledge of a generalist about all else that impinges on the conduct of banking. In addition, they must be capable of making their special and general knowledge fit the most changeable phenomenon in the world—the needs and wants, the desires and resources of human beings.

Still more. The moment bankers move past the purely routine realms of banking—the moment they enter into a discretionary realm where they have some sort of say regarding the use of institutional resources—they deal with values as the rival of values. In that discretionary realm, bankers cannot be as detached as an anthropologist looking at primitives. They are personally a part of the heats and ferments that go with the social organization of economic activity. These heats and ferments inhere in the concerns bankers have with the factors of safety for their depositors and for the profits on which all else depends. It is only through a balance between safety and profits that there can be fair returns to investors in bank stocks, favorable judgments by governmental examiners and bank security analysts, attractive employee benefits and career opportunities, rewards for managerial skill, and more risk-taking in the cycle of loans and collections incident to orderly economic growth.

THE FOURTH TRUTH

Everything said so far can make for anxious days in banking, frustrating days, tiring days. But it also makes banking an infinitely complex and intriguing intellectual venture. For in direct or indirect ways, bankers deal with what moral and political philosophers call "distributive justice"—with the question, posed against the background of scarce resources, of how far the needs and wants of one person are to be gratified against those of another, or left ungratified in favor of another. They deal with questions of social choices—of what goods and services are to be produced, and in what proportion. They deal with questions bearing on the organization of production—of getting done the things settled upon as most worth doing. They deal with questions of distribution—of how the fruits of production are to be apportioned among the members of society. Not least of all, they deal with questions of how the social structure can be maintained and improved.

To speak of banking as an infinitely complex and intriguing intellectual venture does not argue that all bankers see their activity in that light. In fact, more than a few bankers would become defensive if the term "intellectual"—used as an adjective or noun—were applied to their own person. They view themselves as practical men and women of action who deal only in hard facts which make for "bottom line" profits in quarterly or annual reports. Yet the unease some bankers have with the term "intellectual" is hard to square with the great changes that have occurred in the educational background of leaders of American finance.

In the early 1900s, most banks, like most other business enterprises, were fairly modest in size, and were managed mainly by men with little formal education beyond grammar school, or at the most, high school. Where banks in particular were concerned, they were often managed by men who had begun as messengers, starting young, and who then rose to the sucessive posts of teller, bookkeeper, cashier (the key executive in country banks), vice president, and then president. They grew up with an institution, and seldom left it for a rival institution—an action thought "treasonable." They held their cards very close to their chest, and were subject to only casual demands for "public disclosure" of how they played them. They thoroughly understood the technical operations of their bank, but gave little thought to the interaction between their bank and the society around it. The Great Depression, in which the banking system—led by the Federal Reserve System—collapsed, became the bell that tolled for them.

Since then, as banks in common with other corporations have grown more complex—and as they are subject on every front to crisscrossing demands and counter-demands—bank executives can scarcely take their bearings from the aphorisms of *Poor Richard's Almanac* or from weather predictions in the *Farmer's Almanac*. Nor do they. With the growing interdependence between local and regional economies, between regional and national economies—and among national economies—banking decisions require a grasp of almost limitless political, legal, social, economic, and cultural variables. On the same grounds, senior and middle level bank executives insistently demand ever sharper analytical tools that can be used in examining and formulating business policies. Today, with steadily diminishing exceptions, college educated bank executives deal across the table with college educated executives at the heads of other corporate business enterprises.

Today, also, the time chief executive officers of banks and their principal lieutenants directly spend on the business of lending and collecting is often but the time left over from their preoccupation with other matters. Aside from their expected involvement in civic work, they must meet with federal and state regulatory officers. They must provide materials for "audits" focused not merely on the financial transactions of the bank but on its personnel policies under equal opportunity legislation. They must prepare for and participate in meetings with security analysts and stockholders. They must negotiate the necessary financing which precedes their own lending. They must consult at every turn with legal counsel as to what acts are permissible under ever-changing legislation, administrative rulings, and judicial opinions. They must decide questions about what to computerize and where to computerize. They must initiate training programs for personnel who will carry forward new services offered by a bank. In fact, it sometimes seems that it is only in the spaces between the raindrops of these torrential claims on attention spans, that chief executive officers of banks and their key lieutenants can focus their thoughts on the "regular" transactions of the banking business.

All such imperative demands on the intellectual resources of a bank's senior management would be difficult enough to meet even in a context where units of value were stable and exhibited themselves in clear forms. Today, nothing or very little of the sort is true. Today, the whole environment for banking is in flux—as the chapter following indicates.

3. *Banking: A World in Flux*

CROSSCURRENTS

Major efforts to deregulate aspects of financial institutions picked up momentum during the Carter Presidency, and the momentum has been carried forward under the Reagan Presidency. The details later. Yet suppose you were the chief executive officer of a bank with a primary responsibility for insuring that all the transactions in any and every corner of your institution complied with all the laws and rules applicable to them. Would you conclude that all the moves toward deregulation of financial institutions pointed to an emergent future where only Adam Smith's "invisible hand" set the metes and bounds to the operations of your institution? Hardly. One day's reading of incoming official pronouncements by monetary and credit authorities would tell you that what "the Lord giveth, the Lord taketh away." That is, for each gesture entailing the deregulation of financial institutions, another gesture entailed a new set of regulations.

A single example may help fix this point. On April 1, 1981, the Federal Reserve Board published a proposed new version of its Regulation Z, dealing with the terms for truth in lending.[8] Its commendable motive in doing so sprang from the fact that in the years since the enactment of the truth-in-lending law, the Board and its staff had issued 1,500 individual interpretations centered on various features of the legislation. So to ease the burden of compliance with Regulation Z, the staff of the Board was assigned the task of reducing the accumulated commentary to a more coherent and unified form; compliance with the results would become mandatory on April 1, 1982. The yield of the effort so far is this. In an earnest attempt to simplify the burden of compliance in the matter at issue, the staff now seems likely to add 159 pages of new regulations for bank managers to comply with. And that bulk covers only one letter in the whole alphabet of Reserve Board regulations.

LAW AND ADMINISTRATION

Leaving authentic deregulations out of account for the moment, the passing years have witnessed a continuous law explosion at both the federal and state levels of government, all adding new layers of legislation and administrative regulations onto banking. The additions, moreover, go far beyond the old concern with financial solvency. The new laws and rules reach into virtually every aspect of a bank's performance—in a range from employment policies, to truth in lending, to equal opportunities for access to credit, to mandated reinvestment in community development. True, American business as a whole is subject to a complex harness of regulations, often without regard to the size of the enterprise. Yet the regulations special to banking *as* banking, are in *addition* to those applicable to business generally. By the start of the 1980s, bankers were denied even a fig leaf to cover their judgments and transactions. Public disclosure of virtually everything they did in the banking business was mandated by law.

In estimating what it costs a good-sized bank to comply with government regulations, statistics advanced by one authority tend to make war on the statistics advanced by another. Yet without trying to put too fine a point on the matter, many chief executive officers of banks would probably agree that the approximations made in 1979 by Professor Jerome Darnell of University of Colorado on behalf of the United Bank of Denver—a $2 billion institution—have at least the flavor of truth.[9]

Professor Darnell concluded that (1) total direct and indirect costs of satisfying government regulations in 1979 amounted to 33.2 percent of before-tax bank income and 47.5 percent of after-tax income; (2) direct labor costs represented 10 percent of total wage and salary payments, with the typical bank employee devoting an average of 48 minutes out of every eight-hour day to satisfy regulatory requirements; (3) while the preparation of periodic reports constituted only about 10 percent of the total direct cost of compliance, the lion's share of the direct costs—entailing a heavy drain on officer and managerial time—consisted of the energies that went into trying to understand the regulations and in formulating policies and procedures congruous with them. But the key conclusion Professor Darnell reached concerned the *merits* of the regulations. It was that only 20 percent of the reports the bank filed with governmental bodies were considered essential to sound bank management, and that another 20 percent were viewed as desirable but nonessential. As for the remaining 60 percent of the forms, they were judged to be completely nonessential.[10]

Meanwhile, more laws applicable to banking have increased the vulnerability of banks to intermural conflicts among the different regulatory agencies with their separate mandates and sometimes clashing rules. Can you imagine the pain and bewilderment of Albert Payson Terhune if he were bitten by his favorite collie while patting it on the head? If so, then you can understand the mood of a bank executive who scrupulously tries to keep his institution in the right with one regulatory agency, yet on that very count places it in the wrong with another. The case may be changed in some measure for the better by the work of the Federal Financial Institutions Examination Council, a fairly new agency designed to formulate common rules and criteria applicable to all financial institutions subject to federal regulation.

At the same time, more demands for more public disclosures by banks have not been confined to public authorities. Banks are also subject to mounting disclosure demands by *private* bodies. These include security analysts, the national board which establishes standards for the profession of certified public accountants,[11] public interest lawyers, and single interest consumer groups. In the experience of bank executives, it sometimes seems that these private bodies—and especially those claiming to be the conscience of the public—can be more imperious than public authorities in their demands for full disclosure.

To keep the full picture in perspective, this is the place to say that some of the restrictive federal and state regulatory barriers against the branching and geographical expansion of banks have been eased.[12] In 1950, for example, only 1,241 banks operated branches. Today, over 6,000 banks have more than one office. In 1950, the total of all branches in the nation was less than 5,000. Today the total approximates 35,000. In 1960, eighteen states prohibited full-service branch banking. By the end of 1979, the number had dropped to twelve. At the same time, inflation-engendered worries about the health of a number of banks and their takeover by foreign institutions added to the political pressures for the easing of McFadden Act barriers to interstate banking. Measures now before the Congress—though strongly resisted— would authorize interstate banking in emergency situations where the Federal Reserve would allow a domestic out-of-state holding company to acquire a bank or bank holding company in receivership, or a bank holding company controlling a bank in receivership.

Besides the foregoing, regulatory lines which fixed distinctive prices for commercial banks on the one side, and other financial intermediaries on the other, are to be phased out of existence in the future under the terms of the 1980 Depository Institutions Deregulation and Monetary Control Act. Where markets in particular are concerned, institutions which used to be restricted by laws and rules to defined spheres of protected activity now present an increasingly "homogenized" picture. As former restrictions are eased, savings and loan associations, mutual savings banks, and credit unions now offer financial services which used to be the special preserve of commercial banks—as is true the other way around. Moreover, all in turn face increasingly brisk competition from sources not usually included in traditional lists of financial intermediaries. These include major brokerage houses with their offerings of "money market funds" and the equivalent of "checking accounts," consumer credit companies such as American Express, and giant merchandising establishments such as Sears, Roebuck and Co.

MANAGEMENT

The device of the operating bank holding company has been in existence since the 1920s, but it emerged in the 1960s as the dominant institutional form for the management of bank financial resources. At the same time, as an offset to the existing barriers against branch banking across state lines, the legal structure of the bank holding company permits its nonbank affiliates to expand bank-related activities well beyond the boundaries of a particular state—a process facilitated by the computer as a tool of management. The tool itself is still in its costly experimental stage. Though it has not as yet produced all the science fiction results envisioned in the 1960s, its effects on banking to date have been very great indeed. The computer revolution has had a major impact on points of deposit, on the transfer of funds, on consumer credit, on the entire check-clearing process, on accounting, on record keeping, on the storing and retrieval of information, and on management's capacity to determine the actual cost benefits of particular banking operations and services.

In one respect, the computer's effect on banking resembles nothing so much as the dual character of the Devil—who is both a tempter and tormenter. This is because the very existence of the computer has inspired more demands by government regulatory agencies for more reports from banks. With the proliferation of bank laws and regulations, senior executives in banks are ceaselessly taxed by the need to retrain their personnel in the fine points of new rules which go beyond the familiar concerns with the integrity of loans and safety for depositors. At significant operating costs, these open-end retraining programs often go forward each day or night of the working week, and, not infrequently, on weekends.

In fact, if a European or Japanese banker on a tour of the United States wandered into a series of large buildings without knowing that they were banks, it would not be surprising if his first impression was that these were law schools. In one place after another, he would find bank personnel being formally instructed in the latest legal wrinkles on the permissible terms for loans under new anti-inflation programs, or under social programs related to affirmative action, equal opportunity, truth-in-lending, consumer protection, and community development. In between the rustle of pages being turned in thick tomes of instructional material, he would also hear the lecturing training officers dwell on the heavy punitive costs to banks if they were found not to be in compliance with the fine points of the new laws and rules.

To round out this summary account of the major changes in banking that logically fall under the heading of "management," something should be said about the new emphasis senior bank managers are now placing on planning and control systems for their institutions. Formal profit planning and control were for many years recognized as vital managerial tools in most manufacturing industries, but it was only in recent years that commercial bankers became interested in the subject. This is not to say that they were without any kind of system for planning and control. After the model pioneered long ago by the Irving Trust Bank of New York, bankers, for example, learned to subdivide their allocations of lines of credit according to classes of business. Yet the need for capital budgets, cash flow projections, and operational plans—all the submissions a bank might require of a borrower—seemed to most bankers to have no applicability to them.

Attitudes among bankers in this head began to change in consequence of all the other major changes that impacted on them—changes in the balance sheet, in the growth rate of loans, in the way banks acquired their funds, in the retail segment of the market, in profit margins, and so on and on. In consequence, the new emphasis in banks of any appreciable size is now on profit center accounting and on the "cost center." A profit center or cost center—or group of cost centers—have the responsibility for revenue-producing activities in addition to cost control. The planning function is a handmaiden of this responsibility. With an eye focused on the external controls of legislation and regulations, planning is addressed to such matters as the profitability of and market reactions to free checking, lines of credit, charge cards—the more so, when being competitive may decrease profit margins on bank services.

In the nature of the case, planning is not a task that can be done at random. It requires the active leadership and sustained support of a bank's executive management. Only they can really provide the parameters within which departmental personnel—in their respective profit and cost centers—can proceed with the detailed work of planning. In military terms, however, this is only *tactical* planning. The objective of *strategic* or long-range planning is to enhance the bank's ability to increase not only the growth of its assets, but the *returns* on them.

The housewife may do her strategic planning by reading a horoscope, the man at the race track window by a prior reading of the *Racing Form*. This is not the place to ask if all chief executives of banks are better futurists than these two. It is the place merely to indicate the contingent elements that enter into long-range planning for a bank.

The elements group themselves into different but related kinds of forecasts. *Forecasts of economic conditions and other external influences*—GNP growth, federal and state budget positions, Federal Reserve policy, interest rate assumptions, rates of inflation, corporate expenditures, projected rates of consumer savings, tax legislation, local economic conditions. *Forecasts from the standpoint of financial and operational factors*—deposit size and mix, loan portfolio, capital structure, income from trust fees and other service charges, liquidity, income tax management. *Forecasts from the standpoint of organization and manpower*—manpower requirements to meet growth objectives, management development and training programs, salary structure, employee benefits and personnel policies, revision and creation of internal accounting systems. *Forecasts from the standpoint of facilities and equipment*—projected costs of computer systems, effects of new automated systems, space requirements, and new branch cities. *Forecasts from the standpoint of marketing*—new corporate and personnel services, share of market objectives, degrees of types of advertising desired, desirability of promotional campaigns and their costs, along with their permissibility under existing regulations.

VOCABULARY

A remorseless inflation whose rates and duration are unprecedented, and whose consequences are reflected in the heightened interest sensitivity of bank-held funds, has gone hand in hand with other revolutionary developments that have either issued from or affected bank management. These include marked changes in the character of the bank deposit structure, with a substantial increase in new types of savings and time deposits, and with a new emphasis on retail banking and various forms of consumer credit. They include the introduction of new financial instruments, along with the extension of credit by the creation of marketable time drafts in the form of an acceptance instead of the traditional promissory note. They also include the profound shift of emphasis in which "liability management" has become as critical to profitable large-scale bank holding company operations as "assets management." These, and a web of related developments, have brought into serious question the authoritative definitions of "money" used in the conduct of monetary policy, and have spurred the formulation of new definitions corresponding to the new realities of how and where money is held, whether in a "traditional" form or as "near money."

The explosion in the very vocabulary of banking since the start of the 1960s comments on new financial techniques invented by bank managers, on the new roles of their respective financial institutions, and on the extent to which the managers of public credit have also joined the search for hidden pools of funds.[13] In mortgage and real estate finance, for example, there are now variable interest rate mortgages, graduated level-payment mortgages, project loans, private conventional and government-guaranteed Government National Mortgage Association (GNMA) pass-throughs, a GNMA futures market, mortgage-backed bonds, tax-exempt issues to finance private residential housing, and real estate investment trusts. Corporate finance has been marked by the advent of medium-term notes, industrial revenue bonds, floating-rate notes and bonds keyed to various indices, the distribution of bonds in Eurodollar markets as well as borrowing in foreign currency, leveraged buy-outs, back-to-back loans, and a massive volume of lease financing.

In municipal financing, the innovations include tax-exempt anti-pollution bonds, pre-refunding and advance-funding obligations, and a proliferation of municipal revenue bonds—meaning those secured not by general tax revenues, but by municipal income from sources such as highway tolls, parking fees, or airport license revenues. In the federal agency sector, the past twenty years witnessed the new market securities introduced by the

Government National Mortgage Corporation and the Federal Home Loan Mortgage Corporation, the Federal Financing Bank, and the Private Export Funding Corporation, and the issuance of money market paper by various agencies.

In the U.S. government market, the "auction" technique for financing has replaced the "rights offering." In the 1950s for example, there were only the weekly auctions of three- and six-month bills. Currently, the Treasury finances all major sectors at regular intervals—monthly offerings of two-year note issues, quarterly sales of four- and five-year notes and fifteen-year bonds, along with one-year and cash-management bonds, foreign currency dominated Treasury obligations, Treasury futures, and so on.

THE MONEY MARKET

In the 1950s, the money market was virtually static in its dynamics. It revolved around a weekly bill auction, and a moderate issuance of commercial paper, mainly by finance companies. Even bankers acceptances, a traditional money market obligation, had little life in the 1950s. In contrast to the picture of the recent past, the money market by the start of the 1980s was crowded with the commercial paper offerings by nonfinancial corporations, bank holding companies, and even savings and loan associations—while bankers acceptances stood at $47 billion. The negotiable certificate of deposit (CD) had not been conceived in the 1950s, but in 1979 its outstandings totaled $90.6 billion. What is more, the negotiable CDs have current offshoots which include the variable rate CD whose rates can be changed every thirty days, the Yankee, and the Eurodollar CD.

In the 1950s and early 1960s, the information needs of managers of trading desks in the money markets were neither extensive nor well organized. The managerial task of monitoring monetary policy at the time was relatively easy. Monetary policy changed infrequently, perhaps once or twice a year, and the focus was on free or nonborrowed reserves and not on a multiple of reserves and monetary aggregates. By the end of the 1970s, transactions in money market instruments depended on detailed market knowledge and interrelationships, complex communication links with traders and clients, along with the *anticipatory* information about new financing volume, dealer positions, calculations on soon-to-be released economic indicators, estimates for the weekly money supply data, projections of daily Federal Reserve operations, estimates relating to near-term dollar strength or weakness.

The household sector itself acquired a high order of financial sophistication, starting perhaps in 1959 when the public first began to flirt with offerings in security markets that yielded more than savings accounts. The nature of the development led to the invention of a new descriptive term—

"disintermediation"—standing for the withdrawal of funds from traditional financial intermediaries. It was in 1959 that savings were first withdrawn on a massive scale from banks and channeled into U.S. government "Magic Fives"—a five-year Treasury note with a coupon of 5 percent. Subsequently, household savings were attracted to new instruments that came into the market. These included money market funds, municipal bond funds, closed-end corporate bond funds, money market certificates of deposit pegged to the six-months bill rate, and Negotiable Order of Withdrawal (NOW) accounts.

FOREIGN DIMENSIONS

The new impact on banking of scarcity in natural resources, and the shifts of capital from the industrially developed nations to the treasuries of the oil-exporting nations has worked its way backward into the whole order of the American economy. In one direction, it cast major American banks in the vulnerable position of engines "recycling" the deposits they receive from the Organization of Petroleum Exporting Countries (OPEC) into private bank loans to the governments of Less Developed Countries (LDC). In another direction, it intensified the internal American cross-tensions engendered by the struggle against inflation, and the demands for funds to finance rising social expectations, by the scramble for funds in the private sector, and the federal government's massive operations in money markets to finance and refinance the public debt.

Meanwhile, the Eurodollar (or petrodollar) has become an increasingly important source of funds for American banking, and American and foreign banks have increased their competition on each other's home grounds. Since the 1880s, foreign banking organizations have been present in the United States, and since the first decades of the twentieth century, there has been an American banking presence abroad. During the 1970s, however, both have expanded greatly. As of January 1980, for example, there were over 900 branches of American banks conducting a dollar denominated business in offshore locations.[14] At the same time, 11 percent of the commercial and industrial loans made in the United States were made by foreign banks through their 325 American subsidiaries.

The expansion just mentioned has gone hand in hand with a rising dispute over aspects of the foreign takeover movement in banking, and especially over U.S. banking laws and policies as they affect the nonfinancial interests of foreign banks and bank holding companies. Under the Federal Reserve's current interpretation of the 1970 Bank Holding Company Act, foreign corporations that are extensively involved in nonfinancial commerce—manufacturing, wholesale and retail trade, shipping—may buy major U.S. banks even though domestic bank holding companies are explicitly barred from engaging in such nonfinancial activities.

In March 1979, for example, the Federal Reserve Board approved the holding company application of the Hongkong and Shanghai Bank (HSBC) to acquire control of the Marine Midland Bank of Buffalo, New York, whose deposits of $13 billion made it the twelfth largest bank in the U.S. The acquisition was approved in full knowledge of HSBC's direct or indirect ownership position of more than 25 percent in hundreds of nonfinancial firms that engaged in such diverse activities as airlines, carpet trading, commodities trading, film production, food packaging, insurance, pharmaceuticals, printing and publishing, limestone quarrying, shipping, telecommunications, and timber production. In fact, it was fair to ask whether HSBC was a conglomerate instead of a bank. No U.S. corporation engaged in such businesses could under existing law own a U.S. bank, and no domestic holding company could itself engage in any of the indicated lines of activity. On this ground, attempts have been mounted in Congress to correct the legal tilt that favors foreign corporations as against domestic bank holding companies.

THE CULTURAL AND SOCIAL ASPECTS OF INFLATION

For many years after the start of the 1950s, inflation was both minimal and cyclical in nature. It characteristically rose in the advanced stages of an economic expansion cycle and then fell quickly during the subsequent business recession and early recovery. For example, inflation rose to an annual rate of 3.4 percent during the final four quarters of the economic recovery that ended in the summer of 1957, and then slowed to 0.9 percent during the subsequent recession. Again, inflation averaged 1.7 percent in the last year of the economic expansion that ended in April 1960, and then slowed to 0.6 percent in the subsequent recession. Since the end of the 1960s, however, the pattern was different. Every cyclical low and high in the inflation rate was above the preceding cyclical trough and peak, and inflation persisted at high rates even when the economy cooled.

The fundamental change in the nature of inflation fostered new attitudes among Americans toward their government and toward the individual economic and financial decisions they faced. In previous inflationary contexts, Americans tended to behave in ways that may have been socially beneficial but didn't benefit them personally over the long run. Whenever inflation heated up, they saved more. They assumed that an overheated inflationary economy might soon be followed by a slowdown. Their savings would then come in handy, and in fact, the savings themselves might also dampen inflation. Yet a point was subsequently reached where many Americans doubted that effective anti-inflation measures would ever pressed to the hilt. They expected not a reversal of the menacing upward secular trends in the rate of inflation, but at best, only temporary relief.

The consequences, visible to bank executives, were these: Under a compulsion to fend for themselves, many Americans rushed to test every conceivable hedge against inflation. As investors, they tried to guess what favored instrument's turn would come next. They wanted to seize and to exploit it before the crowd caught on to the existence of the hedge—though the net effect of such activity intensified rather than relieved the total problem. Nor was the behavior of firms markedly different from that of individuals. Firms that wished to raise capital had no choice but to expect and to accept the mercurial verdicts of a market riven by inflation. If short-term investment for the purpose of quick gain is a definition of "speculation," then the "speculator" of a former day became the "prudent" fiduciary agent—such as a pension fund manager—legally bound carefully to guard assets in a highly volatile world.

Meanwhile, the rush among individuals to acquire tangible hedges against inflation—land, houses, gold and silver—contributed to undermining the traditional savings and investment processes. In fact, many did more than simply draw down their savings accounts or sell bonds and stocks. To finance the comfortable patterns of life to which they had recently grown accustomed, they also "monetized" their assets. They took the accumulated equity in their homes, jewelry, and other assets and converted it to ready cash. A family, for example, might sell a house for $100,000, pay off $25,000 of an outstanding mortgage, and then temporarily bank $75,000. If it then bought another $100,000 house and took out a new mortgage for $50,000, the owner was left with $25,000 of free cash to spend any way he wanted.

An estimate made by Morgan Guaranty indicates that in the foregoing ways, homeowners alone raised about $50 billion a year in the mortgage market to keep up their spending. Alan Greenspan, in a concurring view,[15] argued that the translation of home ownership equity into cash available for consumer spending was perhaps the most significant reason why the economy in the last half of the 1970s was consistently stronger than expected. As a corollary, the weakening in home prices would cause a significatnt deterioration in the consumer balance sheet.

Consumers who were not in a position to "monetize" any assets continued to borrow and to sustain through grants of credit their existing standards of creature comforts. Going hand in hand with this was a substantial deterioration in the quality of credit, though the deterioration could be masked by the nominal growth in income, profit, and credit market accommodations. Yet the fact that debt was increasing at an extraordinary pace while productivity was falling meant that new debt was financing inefficiencies, consumption, and not enough wealth-creating projects. As usual, however, it was hard to say precisely where and when the marginal debt would get into trouble. Marginal credits would be exposed if inflation were harnessed and reduced, whereas if inflation were accelerated, it would hide marginal credits longer. Anyway, the increase of participants with poor credit quality would enhance the ultimate risk to the economy and to credit markets.

THE RADICAL EXPANSION OF CREDIT

Computations made by Henry Kaufman of Salomon Brothers show that total market debt outstanding at the end of 1958 was only $720 billion. By the end of 1969, it totaled $1.4 trillion. A decade later, or at the end of 1979, it totaled an estimated $3.8 trillion.

At the same time, the burgeoning growth of credit in individual sectors of the economy was even more striking than the general picture suggested. Among the key areas of demand for credit, mortgage debt grew from a total of $192 billion in 1959 to $443 billion in 1969 to an estimated $1.3 trillion in 1979. The volume of outstanding corporate bonds increased from $84 billion in 1959 to $178 billion in 1969 to $455 billion in 1979. As a matching piece to the debt growth, financial assets surged upward. In 1959, for example, the total assets of life insurance companies and commercial banks were respectively $135 billion and $192 billion. At the end of 1979, assets were $576 billion for insurance companies and $1.2 trillion for commercial banks.

Another perspective on the expansion of the credit market can be gained by glancing at the dollar volume of credits outstanding during two years— 1964 and 1978—each of which fell in the fourth year of an economic recovery, though the dates were fourteen years apart. The overall increase in credit market debt was $61 billion net in 1964, compared with $397 billion net in 1978. In terms of gross volume of financing, new corporate bond issuance in 1964 totaled $10 billion, an amount now offered in less than three months. The gross new volume of long "tax exempts" in 1964 was $10.5 billion. In 1978, it was $39.2 billion, or nearly four times as large. The federal government and its agencies borrowed publicly a mere $3.2 billion net in 1964, whereas its net borrowing in 1979 was roughly nineteen times greater.

THE ORDEAL OF THE FEDERAL RESERVE BOARD

In its managerial role for a quasi-central bank, the Federal Reserve Board since late 1974 tried through a policy of "practical monetarism" to promote economic stability. But the best intentions of the monetary authorities, coupled with those of the fiscal authorities, failed to attain that objective. For one thing, the moment there was a significant increase in unemployment, the politics of unemployment generated pressures for an expansionist fiscal policy or a relaxation of a restrictive monetary policy before secular inflation was actually brought under control. For another thing, fiscal and monetary authorities both mistakenly thought that they had considerable leeway in policy formulation. Without giving due weight to the subversive force of the new and intransigent elements in the dual inflation and energy picture, their acts seemed rooted in the belief that traditional policies for dealing with a recession-recovery period were warranted. In any event, national policy missed its timing.

In response to massive unemployment, for example, fiscal policy starting in 1975 was stimulated too much and for too long. It ignited a consumer spending boom and thwarted the building of a financial base conducive to business capital formation. Federal spending increased annually by 12 percent during the economic expansion that began in 1975, which was far greater than expenditures growth in previous periods of recovery. When the inflation rate rose to 7.7 percent in 1978, federal expenditures (including off-budget outlays) were still allowed to increase by 12.5 percent, a rate exceeded only six times in the previous twenty-five years. The federal budget deficit at the time was equal to 22.6 percent of the Gross National Product—compared with between 18.5 percent and 20 percent in earlier comparable periods—though the nation in 1978 was in the third year of an economic expansion.

Meanwhile, there were shortcomings in the conceptual tools for conduct of monetary policy. Among other things, the statistical benchmarks the Federal Reserve used to gauge the growth of the money supply had become increasingly outmoded by structural changes in the nation's financial system. Thus, while the Federal Reserve defined its money-supply target along the classical lines of currency, demand deposits, and to some extent time deposits, firms, households, and even governments hardly distinguished between money and credit—and in many transactions viewed them as being indistinguishable. For another thing, structural changes in the financial system undercut the Federal Reserve's ability to control financial intermediaries. Financial intermediaries could escape the disciplining impact of credit policies through an arbitrage spread where they passed on increased interest rates to themselves to sources representing the final demands for credit.

The effect on lending institutions was to encourage them to persist in aggressive lending policies—policies that could be sustained over a long period only by accelerating an increase in the money supply, with a consequent stimulant to further inflation. This was the picture that prevailed when the Federal Open Market Committee and the Board of Governors of the Federal Reserve Board met all day Saturday, October 5, 1979. The result—a new anti-inflation program announced at a press conference held that night by Federal Reserve Board Chairman Paul Volcker—was followed in subsequent months by more announcements and by more legislation that opened up a strange new world for most bankers and managers of financial assets.

The nature of the case will be returned to eventually after a range of other things are set in place, starting with the subject of the next chapter. The subject concerns the distinction *and* the relationship between *applied* economics and *pure* economics, and their meaning for bankers.

4. Where Banking Fits in the World of Economics

THE GREEKS HAD A WORD FOR IT

In its original form as *economie*, the word "economics" was derived from the Greek terms *oikos* meaning house, and *nomos* meaning law. It thus signified the wise and legitimate rule of a household for the common good of the entire family. Applied economics, which is the realm of banking, comes closest in meaning to the original term *economie*. It began in the infancy of civilization, and at an early hour developed forms of money and forms of markets, along with mores, folklore, rules, techniques, and institutions by which men struggled to provide for the needs of life. Institutions which performed some of the functions of a modern bank also surfaced in remote antiquity.[16] Moreover, public policies based on insights into economic principles—including those which had a direct bearing on functions now associated with banking—can be deduced from the surviving records and laws of ancient civilizations.[17] Yet the formal theories we identify with pure economics, and the subset among them which pertain directly to banking, though gestating by the end of the seventeenth century, did not officially come to birth until the publication in 1776 of Adam Smith's *Wealth of Nations*.[18]

PURE ECONOMICS: CORE IDEAS

The core ideas which lay close to the heart of the classical form of pure economics remain to this day the source of a mystical homesickness for many American bankers, as for other businessmen. This is not the place to argue the question whether they could in fact "go home again"—or would be happy if they actually got there. It is the place to touch on four core ideas central to the classical form of pure economics. They entailed the following contentions: First, the motive force in the economic system is a rational self-interest which guides people as by an "invisible hand" (and not by conscious design) to serve the common interest. Second, the invisible hand regulates the economic system through the competition of many firms in each line of production. Third, because of the impersonal regulatory power of competition, regulation by the state should be as small, unobtrusive, and inexpensive as the requirements of the common defense against domestic and foreign enemies would allow. Fourth, because competition and the market bring the best economic results, the enlargement of both is a goal ardently to be

pursued: the greater the trading area, the greater the opportunity for specialization; the greater the opportunity for specialization, the greater the
competition, and from there, the stronger the market.

Consumer sovereignty

Of a piece with the foregoing was the concept of "consumer sovereignty"
which some latter day or neo-classical economists associated with the meaning of "liberty," as well as a Darwinian view of social evolution. Its core
idea was that it was in no way incumbent upon a state to be a moral or
paternalist censor, stopping individuals before they walked into a cul-de-sac
of economic folly where they alone would be the trapped victim. More
directly, it was not the responsibility of the state to regulate economic choices
individuals made—what to do with their personal resources, how much to
spend or save, and if to spend, for what and at what price. Individuals must
be free to decide these matters according to their personal character, knowledge, and judgment. Those who made wanton use of their freedom would
fall by the wayside, not being fit to survive. Those who used their freedom
with prudent restraint would prosper and would also transmit their virtues
to their descendants. Through some such natural selection process, "consumer sovereignty" would insure the survival of the fittest, and thus
strengthen the moral fabric of society as a whole.

Later concepts

It is scarcely necessary to say that development in economic theory did not
stop with the core ideas of the classical economists. The proliferation of
subsequent theories that directly or indirectly influenced the conduct of
banking branched and flared in every direction. They included theories about
the "real bills doctrine" (of which more will be said in a later place), theories
about central banking, theories about the gold standard, theories about the
quantity theory of money, theories about fiscal policy and taxation, theories
about monetarism which have added new dimensions to the old theory about
the quantity theory of money, theories about interest rates, theories about
investments.

But there is more to this business of economic literacy than the magisterial theories. These days, even the banker who works in a fly-speck place
on the nation's map is inundated by an incoming tide of economic data that
may bear on his institutional or personal decisions. Except for weekends
and official holidays when mail is not delivered, no day seems complete—
or to have happened—unless it brings to the banker's desk more economic
data in more government documents, in studies commissioned by professional organizations, in the reports of the financial press—newspapers, mag-

azines, newsletters, bulletins of money center banks, appraisals by security analysts, and so on.

It was not always so. In an earlier day—say, for example, the 1920s—bankers were mainly concerned only with conditions in their immediate service area. Local crops were good or bad. Local prices were up or down. Local factories were hiring or laying off men. Local merchants were placing new orders or were buckling under a glut of inventories. Few bankers took into account or tried to keep abreast of what theoretical economists were saying about prospects facing the economy as a whole. They did not factor into their own judgments the estimates these sources of professional opinion made about national employment, national income, debt structures, the money supply, private investment expenditures by sector, consumer savings and purchases, expenditures by state and local governments—and the quantitative or qualitative effects these matters had on the national economy.

Today the picture is radically different. Bankers, along with other businessmen, not only track these details, but keep their ears tuned to what theoretical or other professional economists have to say about what the details mean. More than that, they welcome the professional economists as featured speakers at meetings of bank associations. They engage their services as consultants. They employ them to direct the research department of a sizeable bank, and to write monthly economic bulletins sent by such a bank to a wide circle of customers or subscribers.

So far, so good. But there is a question to be asked. Are the theoretical or other professional economists at grips with the same problems that daily besiege bank executives? If the question were spoken, there would be no pejorative ring in its sound. It is here asked because, paradoxically, it contains within itself the genetic seed of a defense of the theoretical economist in the very act of distinguishing the latter's vocation from that of a banker's.

In defense of theoretical economists

After several decades of basking in the sun of public awe, theoretical economists came to have a bad press by the end of the 1970s. They were criticized for their sharp disagreements on how to cope with the energy problem, and for their equally sharp disagreements on how to resolve the dilemma of sustained inflation and concurrent unemployment. They were criticized for being wrong in predicting the onset of the latest recession and its severity, and for their manifest uncertainties when asked to predict when the latest recession would end. Yet is it possible to imagine a world that could be explained and governed by a single economic theory, or one in which economists themselves would not be in sharp disagreement? To ask the question is to answer it in the negative. We can expect much jostling, shoving, arguing and uncertainties among theoretical economists because the world itself is inexhaustibly queer.[19]

Other sciences have their sharply divisive problems, but the public is less aware of them. Astrophysicists, for example, have been debating whether the universe will go on expanding indefinitely or will collapse into one big black hole in forty billion years. A 5 percent error in measuring the rate at which quasars are receding could spell the difference, though the dispute has not captured headlines. Even so, the questions astrophysicists face are nothing compared to those of theoretical economists. The latter face a world of conflicting classes, nationalisms, ideologies, always in transition from one state to another, of mercantile, industrial, and managed economies in all their varieties.

Some think it best to explain that capitalist profits are a reward for abstinence from consumption; others think it best to explain that profits are a reward for waiting, rather than abstinence. Some playfully prefer the sunspot theory of business cycles, and others seriously deny that business cycles are possible. One camp warns: you have sinned, go back to the competitive model; break up large corporations and unions before it is too late; dismantle the government bureaucracy; let the invisible hand do its work or be scourged. The other camp replies: it is too late to go back; big institutions are the facts of modern life, and even if you wanted to break them up, it would take a revolution to do it. We have bitten the apple of knowledge of large organizations and can't disgorge it; we had better finish the apple and learn how to control the organizations we live in. Some stress arrangements where resources will be allocated by the market, while others favor allocations made by public intervention. The marketeers stress the allocative efficency they see in the things comprising the outer ring of the "economic doughnut." The interventionists stress the size of the hole, standing for such things as social costs and breakdowns in the distribution system.

It is both necessary and proper for theoretical economists to argue these questions. Let them be interventionists or free marketeers, fiscalists, monetarists, or gold bugs. Let them make claims to the effect that they fulfill their functions solely by engaging in a rational science of the choice of means, regardless of the means at hand or the end to which they are applied. Let them confine themselves to solving sophisticated mathematical puzzles, or to formulating interesting generalizations about the celestial mechanics of a hypothetical universe. Let them also justify their pursuit of theoretical knowledge for its own sake—when they advance a method for testing the efficiency of all conscious actions or for explaining in a hindsight view "what happened." In an inexhaustibly queer economic world, many vocabularies are needed to gain even an intimation of where the truth might lie. At the same time, it is important to bear a simple point in mind. It is the difference between the vocation of professional economists in the realm of Higher Economics, and the vocation of bankers in the realm of Lower or Applied Economics with its disorderly, intractable aspects of daily economic life.

CONFRONTATIONS

Today, as in ancient times, the realm of applied economics is the great stage where all of us—regardless of age, tastes, and aptitudes—act out every day within ourselves the endless confrontation between the opposing forces of wants and needs, plans and resources, consumption and savings, supply and demand, desires and a chance to fulfill them. We live that confrontation each time we choose a specific means and apply it toward the hoped-for specific end we have in view.

All the while, different kinds of bankers and banks are among the financial intermediaries which function on the stage of applied economics with its limitless individual dramas. They are the vehicles through which the funds of an original saver and ultimate lender on one side of the counter are transferred to the ultimate borrower and user on the other side. In the process, with its risks and uncertainties, they must try to earn a profit—an objective that sometimes falls through a crack in the floor because of an obsession with bigness for its own sake—or because *profit* itself is sometimes taken to be a dirty word not fit for the ears of children.

Yet banks could not stay in business for long, at least not *as* banks, if they tried to operate without profits. The profits bankers seek inhere in their functions as financial intermediaries. The funds they need are acquired through the demand or time deposits of savers for which they pay an implicit or explicit interest. They also acquire funds through their purchase of various forms of nondeposit funds in the money market on which they must also pay interest. They then use the money acquired either to make loans on which borrowers must pay interest, or to buy for themselves financial assets such as bonds, mortgages, or government securities with yields that will hopefully exceed what *they* have to pay in interest on deposit funds or those they borrow in the money market. Banks profit when their income from the loans they make or the assets they buy exceeds what they have to pay for the money they use.

Each borrower from a bank also hopes to profit in a tangible or intangible way from what he does on the basis of a loan. Each borrower also runs the risk of a miscarriage between his initial aim and the final result. But the individual borrower's risks are compounded in the case of the lending bank by the number of borrowers it has on the books. If bank executives could control from start to finish the course of every choice they made—either as lenders or as borrowers for their own relending needs—their work in the realm of applied economics would be as void as drama as the work of a man running an elevator in a one-story building. It would be a thing of automatic gains and no losses. In point of fact, the choices bank executives make in the realm of applied economics are made far away from the suburbs of Utopia where risks are unknown.

The risks bank executives run—as they live with doubt and yet decide—entail many slippery imponderables. The decisions they make in contexts which seemed constant can be undercut by the impact of new realities that are unstable and fluid. They can be undercut by the advent of a new competitor or a new technology, by disasters of nature, by a deflation in the general economy or by a spurt in the spiral of inflation. They can also be undercut by an election outcome, a revolution or war overseas, a new law enacted by Congress or by a state legislature, a new opinion by a state or federal court, a new rule or policy promulgated by a regulatory agency.

THE VIEW FROM BEHIND A BANKER'S DESK

The conduct of banking in the realm of applied economics stands to the realm of pure economics as engineering stands to physics. The two share a common frontier, and developments on the one side can influence those on the other. But they differ in their inner life and in the factors they must take into account. They differ again in their constraints, and in their respective responsibilities for the effects they produce.

The theoretical economist, for example, may be a source of insights into how the banking system as a whole works over a tract of time, just as the physicist may be a source of insights concerning the stresses in bridge-building.[20] But it is not the direct function of the theoretical economist to decide how a specific banker will use the financial resources at his command in a specific context, any more than it is the function of the physicist to decide if a particular bridge shall be built over a particular river. The decision here is for a banker himself to make, in the light of the knowledge he draws from countless sources—including the sources of economic theory—and subject also to the harness of legal constraints that need not be at the forefront of the theoretical economist's calculations.

Place yourself, for example, on the policy committee of a bank, empowered to make organic decisions affecting the operations of the institution. All members of the committee live intimately with concurrent lines of responsibility to the depositors of the bank, to its stockholders, and to the community at large. But what degrees of emphasis should be assigned to each of these when the policies of a bank are being framed and carried out? A policy focused solely on safety to depositors can lead, by the route of excessive caution, to sharply reduced returns to stockholders, and to a sharp cutback on the bank's contributions to community development. Conversely, a high order of risk taking in lending policy, focused on more returns to stockholders and extensive community development, can weaken the structure for safety to depositors. The costs for being wrong on either side of the policy equation can bear heavily on the individual bank.

No such sharply focused decisions are the daily lot—and the daily hazard—of the theoretical economists. Except for those who have evolved "master theories" that directly influence the fiscal and monetary policies of government, and through government, banks, the consequences of being wrong are personal. They are confined to the loss of an economist's prestige in his profession. The costs are seldom spread as a contagion of adverse effects throughout a community.

Again, if you sat at the desk of a banker and dealt with a customer facing you on the other side, you would quickly discover that unlike the theoretical economist, you are not dealing with a hypothetically "abstract economic man" who behaves in a dispassionately rational way in pursuit of his personal interests, wants and needs.[21] You are dealing with a person whose interests are neither confined solely to the desires for pecuniary profit—an implicit or explicit assumption found in the constructs of some theoretical economists—nor are they confined solely to the narrow sphere of self. Starting with the single person, the concept of "interests" can include a desire for a sense of personal worth, for attention, for independence, for security, for friendship, for social utility, for knowledge. It can move outward from the single person to become family interests, corporate interests, class interests, benevolent interests, ethnic or cultural interests, national interests. The more the concept of interest expands, the more it moves beyond the province of pure economics and encroaches on the province of ethics and politics.

Nor is this all. In facing a stream of customers on the other side of your desk in the bank, you would quickly discover the nonrational face of wants—that people may want what they don't need, and need what they don't want, that wants never remain constant but are always changing. Moreover, in real life, wants are not merely the product of the economic system in general, but can be specifically influenced by advertising where adroit "puffing" can make a product more desirable to a purchaser and consumer. Adam Smith and the classical economists, in advocating freedom of access to the market, paid little or no attention to *personal influences* as a serious factor in economic relations. But as a banker behind the desk, dealing with the realities of applied economics, you would be forcefully struck at every turn by the importance of *personal influences* in every species and size of economic transaction. You would also be struck forcefully by current political realities which place banking practitioners under constraints more akin to the canons of medieval economics than to the classical theoretical economist's vision of a free competitive market.

Bank executives who have had extensive experience with these constraints know that public intervention and not "perfect competition" in a free market dominates the stage on which they move. They know that the source of public intervention is not always traceable to a government agent motivated by some sort of abstract notion of right. The source is often if not more often traceable to the successful efforts of one class of private financial institutions to secure the kind of regulations that would place a competing class of private financial institutions at a competitive disadvantage—that is, to prevent the market from actually being "free."

Veteran bank executives, at least those not addicted to self-centered advocacy, know something else. It is that the object of public intervention is not all of one piece. It varies from one case to the next. The object may be to provide safeguards against a repetition of past disasters or scandals, to restrict the risks of competition, to insure the safety of depositor funds and the integrity of bank operations. It may be to channel community funds toward particular economic activities, to govern the range of "consumer choices," to set in place the manipulative levers for monetary policy. It may also be to promote by legislation and administrative ruling certain ethical, social and political values that are absorbed in the collective phrase, "the general welfare."

The meaning in all of this is written large in the history of public intervention in American banking, whether by legislation, administrative rulings, or judicial opinions. It is a history predicated in large part on assumptions about market *failures*—about the inability of financial markets unaided to police the soundness of banks, to channel the flow of financial resources in efficient and fair ways, to exert an appropriate restraining influence on banking operations and risks. In consequence, and contrary to the preconditions implied in the classical economist's concepts of "perfect competition" in a "free market," banks cannot be born without government approval. They cannot die or voluntarily go out of business unless regulators permit. They cannot locate new offices or change the site of existing facilities without prior governmental approval. They cannot buy or sell anything on a proscribed list of objects. They have been subject to government imposed ceilings on the prices they can charge for their output or pay for their input.

THE FACES OF PRIVATE REGULATION

More will be said presently and later on about the substance and reach of public regulation, along with recent or current moves in the direction of "deregulation." But to keep the subject in proportion, it is worth pausing here long enough to develop a point that was alluded to in an earlier place. It is that there is a private as well as a governmental side to the regulation of banking, just as there are also conditions where the two sides tend to merge.

As to this last, a bank, for example, may be guided in its decisions by the advice of its legal counsel who, in turn, has previously consulted lawyers on the legal staff of government regulatory agencies. Then again, a private professional organization such as the Financial Accounting Standards Board, following a strong nudge from a government regulatory agency such as the Securities Exchange Commission, may issue new rules governing the manner in which certified public accountants make their calculations. Yet these rules, which bear the imprimatur of only a private professional organization, can have large public consequences when applied to bank accounting.

Of the many other facets of the private regulatory apparatus, there is space here to mention only several more. One entails the reports made by private organizations of bank security analysts regarding a bank's management practices and financial condition. The public dissemination of these reports can, for good or ill, have major effects on both the value of the bank's stock, and on its borrowing powers in money markets. Another and related aspect of the case—whose force must be experienced directly in order to be fully appreciated—entails comparisons between the performance of banks of comparable size. Such comparisons are ceaselessly drawn and publicized by bank analysts in the financial press. When they show that a particular bank's performance is consistently below par for other institutions in its class, the private regulatory consequences can be a fundamental change either of policy or of management, or of both in a single stroke.

Over the years, private organizations of bank security analysts—in a matching piece to similar efforts by government regulatory agencies—have devised or proposed various statistical models for use in grading the financial performance of banking institutions.[22] Two arbitrary judgments, however, have unavoidably haunted the design of the favored model. One is the judgment made regarding the factors in a performance that *should* be measured—such as earnings growth, return on assets, asset leverage, and price/earning ratios. The other entails the *relative weight* to be given to the factors assessed. The nature of these prior decisions can skew the results of the grading process that follows, and it would be wrong to assume automatically that the "scores" they yield amount to Revealed Truth.

A final element in the private regulatory apparatus. Call the element "prestige"—or the natural human desire of bank managers to merit and possess the respect of others in their profession. It is not quickly attained, and like the factor of "benevolence" in economic decisions, is not easily measured. Yet veteran bankers know from direct personal experience that within the four corners of the law, many things become possible or impossible for bank managers depending on their standing in the eyes of the profession. Judgments made of their personal talents and character can make the difference when a yes or no response to a telephoned request is of fateful importance in transactions which must be completed in a race against the absolute of time itself—with no pauses for the preparation of detailed documents, or for rounds of conferences.

"Bigness" can make for raw power in banking. But the kind of "prestige" being alluded to here as an element in the private regulatory apparatus has relatively little to do with the physical size of a banker's institution. It is a product of observed behavior in correspondent relationships, exchanges at meetings of banker associations, reports of economic performance in concrete situations, evidence of innovations that open on new opportunities for profitable services, contributions to the economic literacy of a community, and so on.

These criteria are in the air wherever bankers gather for confidential "shop talk" and professional assessments. On such occasions, they are known to give the highest marks for competence to bank executives who are not household names nationally, are seldom if ever mentioned in the national press, but are well known inside banking circles. On the other hand, their judgments of certain senior executives in leviathan banks in the nation's money centers is sometimes cast in words that would not be libelous but would nonetheless be kept out of a family newspaper. What is more, the judgments the profession makes in line with its own order of values sometimes prove the same as those *subsequently* made by directors of a leviathan bank—as in instances where they engineered the resignation or retirement of highly visible senior executives.

THE FACES OF PUBLIC REGULATION

The public regulators of banking are not limited to those acting on behalf of the federal government. They include those acting on behalf of each of the state governments. Yet again, within the federal government, they are not confined to the Federal Reserve Board and to components of the Federal Reserve System which carry out Congressional policies embodied in various banking laws. Other regulators of banking who carry out Congressional laws within their respective jurisdictions include the Treasury Department, the Comptroller of the Currency, the Federal Deposit Insurance Corporation, the Securities Exchange Commission, the Federal Home Loan Bank Board, the Anti-Trust Division within the Department of Justice, the Federal Trade Commission, the Consumer Credit Protection Agency, the Federal Housing Administration, the Veterans Administration, the Small Business Administration, the Department of Education (in the case of guaranteed student loans). All these are subject to the will and oversight of Congress, and to the higher will and oversight of the courts.

Among the federal agencies, there is a division of labor regarding the institutions they regulate and the aspects of banking they regulate either on their own or in conjunction with other agencies. Bank advertising, for example, is within the jurisdiction of the Federal Trade Commission, while the Federal Housing Administration has jurisdiction over the rates of interest banks can charge on government insured mortgages. The Federal Home Loan Bank Board, for its part, has the primary responsibility to regulate savings and loan associations, and at the same time, shares with the Federal Deposit Insurance Corporation certain regulatory responsibilities affecting mutual savings banks.

Further, the Federal Reserve Board and the Comptroller of the Currency have separate or overlapping jurisdictions depending on the nature of the banks in question or their functions. But the supervisory regulations they individually or jointly enforce have an extensive reach. Among other things, they cover the organization and chartering of banks; periodic examinations of banks and of the steps required of bank management to correct worrisome conditions found through such examinations; review and analysis of periodic reports of income and dividends. They also cover the rendering of counsel and advice on bank operating problems when requested, especially by smaller banks; terms for approving proposed changes in the scope of corporate functions exercised by individual banks or of proposed changes in their capital structures; authorizations of branches; approval of bank mergers and consolidations; and the regulation of bank holding companies.

Even under ideal circumstances, no banker is thrilled to have bank examiners walk into his institution and closet themselves with bank records for days on end. These time-consuming visits, to be sure, are seldom stormy. More often, they are marked by exquisite politeness. Yet an undercurrent of tension tends to run through them—on the examiners' side when their questions suggest an intention to lean over backwards in order to stand up straight as a scrupulously honest factfinder and appraiser; on the banker's side when he believes that the bank policies being questioned by examiners are safe and wise policies for *his* bank, whatever else they might be for some other bank under some other management in some other community.

A current example of these cross-tensions are the examination procedures used by regulators which make it difficult for banks to undertake tax-loss planning in handling their bond accounts. If a bank sells bonds that have depreciated in value and uses the proceeds plus the tax savings to reinvest, the regulators say the bank has impaired its capital to the extent of the loss. Yet if a bank does not sell its depreciated bonds, the regulators say the bank's portfolio is in good shape and its capital is not impaired. In reality, both the bank and the regulators know that if the funds are really needed, the bank cannot get book value back by selling the bonds. Many banks also know that they can markedly improve their earnings by the indicated "tax swaps," yet hesitate to take them because of the regulators' attitude toward the immediate losses that are involved, and the lower capital position that results.

When regulators themselves are asked why a bank's capital must be considered impaired if the bank does a tax swap and sells depreciated bonds—while no capital impairment is involved if the depreciated bonds are simply held—regulators answer that they have no choice under present laws. At the same time, they—and many bankers as well—fear that if the law is changed, it might be changed so that banks would periodically have to mark all bonds to market value. This would be a disastrous development for the banking industry because unlike stocks, bonds are subject to a money risk as well as a credit risk. When interest rates rise, bond prices fall, whether or not the bonds are of top quality. The result of forcing banks to mark all bonds to market whether sold or not when interest rates rise would wipe out the entire capital position of many banks, and would have a punishing effect on any bank with fixed investments of longer than a few years in maturity.

Where the Federal Reserve Board in particular is concerned, its regulations of member banks—designated by letters—have literally run through the alphabet from A to Z, and are now well into another round of the alphabet starting with AA. At the same time, truth-in-lending legislation and its regulations move directly against the grain of the classical economists' assumptions concerning "consumer sovereignty." That legislation and its related regulations proceed on assumptions of their own: one, that the market fails to disseminate the information consumers need; and two, that public authorities must act the part of a father-protector of consumers imperilled by their ignorance. Similarly, affirmative action, equal opportunity, and community reinvestment legislation, and their associated regulations assume a market failure in the matter of equal and equitable access to the distribution of goods, services, and financial resources. Hence public authorities must intervene to protect the consumer and the community against discrimination—even by imposing a tabu on conventional questions banks would ordinarily put to applicants for loans.

It is true, of course, that along with much else, the assumptions about market failures do not go unchallenged. In fact, the vigorous challenges—reinforced by the thrust of current events—account for such openings toward freer marketplace competition in banking and among other financial institutions as have occurred in recent years. Neo-classical critics of government intervention argue that competition in *most* instances is a more demanding regulator with a strong orientation toward efficiency than any government agent can possibly be. In the same vein, they also argue that competitive markets provide more timely adjustments to changing conditions than any process entrusted to legislation, rule-making, or amendments to existing rules.

Amid what is said on either side of the argument about market failures, veteran bank executives might pass some personal judgments in which they distinguished between necessary regulations which actually serve their express purposes, and those which amount in practice—despite their commendable aims—to a misfit as bizarre as a cupful of ambrosia mixed into a plate of sauerkraut. Veteran bank executives might also voice their profound unease over the efforts of special interest groups to pressure banks to do whatever the special interest group demands. The executives, on their part, may insist that they cannot lawfully meet such demands under existing regulations. But to little avail. They might still find themselves a fixed target for hot cries about their "lack of social consciousness" and "indifference to the general welfare."

In any event, among the personal judgments veteran bank executives pass on the different acts of public intervention in the banking market, if there would be one common idea on which they would all agree, it would most likely take the form of this piece of categorical advice to young bankers standing on the threshold of a career. It is that before they make any decisions involving the "pure" market factors of risk, uncertainty, and profit, they should remember that in the beginning *is* regulation—shaped by the invisible hand of history, a living force more real than anything they can physically measure in a computer print-out.

II

THE INVISIBLE HAND OF HISTORY: THE PAST AS PRESENT

5. The Dual Banking System: A Ten-Minute American History Lesson

ASSUMPTION

A group of young bankers drawn from different nations of Western Europe are on an introductory tour of the United States, sponsored by a government agency in Washington. The escort officer from that agency has arranged for the group to visit many banks, large and small, along the route of the tour. At every stop, executives of host banks have explained the practices of their respective institutions. Some prove the same as those adhered to by the institutions in which the visiting bankers work, and some are different. *Your* bank is the next scheduled stop on the itinerary. But in advance of the time when the group is due to arrive on the premises of your institution, you receive a telephone call from the escort officer. This is what he says:

The one thing that continues to mystify the young European bankers in my charge is the existence of what they have been told is America's dual banking system. There are no equivalents to it in their own experience. I've tried to explain that the existence of the dual banking system, like much else, is a product of American federalism. But that doesn't mean very much to them, because few members of the group come from countries organized along federal lines. And even in the countries which are so organized—West Germany and Switzerland—banks tend to be part of a single national system, many with branches that cross all internal boundary lines. So, when the group meets with you, can you focus your remarks on the dual banking system—to explain how it came into existence, its features, and the arguments that have always haunted its presence? If you agree to do this, try to be brief. Say ten minutes of talk in all. We are on a tight schedule.

You agree with the request, and, in due course, the visiting group does show up at your bank. By then, you have managed to compress more than one hundred and fifty years of American history into the allotted ten minutes. You can't dwell on every turn and return of the story. But perhaps your summary account could read along the following lines, broken down into minutes.

ONE MINUTE

In the early years of the American Republic under the U.S. Constitution, the federal government made two attempts to establish a national bank, each with branches of its own in the larger cities of the nation. The initial attempt, the First Bank of the United States, was launched in 1791 but was terminated in 1811 when Congress refused to renew its charter.[1] The institution in ques tion subsequently secured a state charter in New York and continued to operate as a state bank. The next attempt, the Second Bank of the United States, was launched in 1816, and, in the years ahead, had twenty-eight branches in all. The second attempt became a victim of the politics of the Age of Jackson as it unfolded in the 1830s. On the eve of the hour when the charter of the Second Bank was due to be renewed, President Jackson vetoed a Congressional attempt to insure the survival of the institution. Congressional friends of the institution lacked the legislative strength to override the veto, and the Second Bank expired with its charter.[2]

The First and Second Banks had both been assailed on much the same ground which proved fatal to their existence. It was charged that the Congressional charter which brought them to life was "unconstitutional" because the act violated the right of states to prohibit as well as to establish banks. That is, a national bank with powers and sub-branches that crossed state lines amounted to a usurpation of the chartering power which, so it was claimed, the Constitution reserved to the states alone. Of a piece with this, it was charged that the national banks—as *corporations*—concentrated in the hands of their managers an instrument of "monopoly, usury and favoritism" which held the rest of the nation "in thrall."

These outcries, however, tended to spring from a cause unrelated to any high ground of "principle." More often than not, they stemmed from the managers of state-chartered private banks who chafed under the discipline imposed on their institutions by the operations of either of the two national banks Congress had chartered. Specifically, among private banks of the day, deposits were not an important or conspicuous feature, and, in any case, were dwarfed in importance by bank notes. The notes which circulated as the money banks lent borrowers comprised much the greater part of the total amount of currency in circulation. In a fast-growing country, the powerful and hopeful demands for loans led in their own way to an overextension of credit. It was in the general interest, therefore, to impose restraints on expansion of credit before it reached extremes from which recovery was bound to be costly and painful. It turned out that such restraints were automatically imposed by the Bank of the United States.

As the depository of the government, with branch offices in the chief seaports and commercial centers, it constantly received from collectors of revenue the notes of private banks with which import duties were paid to the government. Upon receiving these notes, the Bank of the United States promptly called for their redemption in gold and silver by the banks of issue in an attempt to restrict the overextension of credit and to protect the economy from inflation. Though the Bank would ease the pressure for prompt redemption in periods of panic and deflation, the managers of the state-chartered private banks strongly objected to any restraints on their lending powers in the periods between boom and bust.

ANOTHER MINUTE

Between the death of the First Bank of the United States and the chartering of the Second Bank, and especially after the death of the Second Bank, state-chartered private banks had the banking field to themselves. Yet it would be misleading to suggest that governmental authority left these early institutions with untrammeled freedom to do what they pleased. State legislators hesitated about the specific conditions under which they would permit banking, but they had no doubts about their right and need to impose conditions of some sort. It was widely agreed that the banking function without express authorization from the sovereign power was both improper and impractical—because banks, being imbued by their nature with monetary powers, were in a peculiar sense responsible to the state. Thus, at an early hour, different states enacted legislation to restrict or prohibit banks from issuing notes in denominations below a certain amount. At the same time, banks were required to submit reports of their condition to public officials. Also, though the details varied from one state to the next, the principle was established that states could impose restrictions on bank liabilities in ratio to paid capital, as well as on the size of bank loans in ratio to assets.

Other regulations, the product of various state legislatures between 1802 and 1816, were not so mild. As if in an early prefiguring of aspects of current banking, the regulations reflected the will of ascendant political and social forces bent on turning the conduct of banking to their own sectarian interests. In Massachusetts, for example, the grant of bank charters was subject to the condition that a certain proportion of their loans should be agricultural, be secured by a mortgage, and run for at least a year. Connecticut's regulations provided that banks "at all times" accept subscriptions to their capital by schools, churches, and charitable institutions, the stock not to be transferable but to be redeemed for the subscribers on six months' notice. Maryland made the renewal of certain charters conditional upon investment by the banks in a company formed to construct a turnpike westward to Cumberland. Pennsylvania required that its state banks—forty-one were in existence at the time the legislation in question was enacted—should flat-out lend one-fifth of their capital "for one year, to the farmers, mechanics and manufacturers" of their districts. The spirit of the law is reflected in today's Community Reinvestment Act.

Whatever the nature of the regulations the different states imposed on the private banks they chartered, the laws—with some exceptions—were framed in ways that left so many loopholes open for abuses, as to suggest that public authorities had abdicated all responsibility for banking practices. Some things, however, shine more brightly when viewed against a dark background. So it was with the positive innovations in two state banking systems of the time—both of which were destined to affect the national banking structure of the future.

One of the innovations, known as the Suffolk System after the bank of that name in Boston, offered itself as a "mini central bank" for a regional network of individual local banks in New England.[3] Based on a certain proportion of their deposits held to their account at Suffolk, they were provided with "clearinghouse" services, the benefits of "central reserves," and the efficient management of bank notes when they were issued and redeemed. The Suffolk System surfaced in 1818 and lasted until 1858. Its key concepts were incorporated in the National Bank Act of 1863, and, still later, in the Federal Reserve Act of 1913.

The second important innovation of the period was a bank insurance plan known as the New York Safety Fund. Created in 1829 under the terms of a law enacted by the New York state legislature, the Fund was the great-grandfather of the Federal Deposit Insurance Corporation (FDIC) authorized by Congress in 1933. Each state-chartered New York bank was required by law to subscribe a certain proportion of its capital to a common insurance fund administered by the State Comptroller for the protection of all depositors. If the monies of this Fund sank below a certain level when they were used to pay off the depositors of a failed bank, levies were made on the surviving banks to restore the Fund to its former level.[4] The existence of this insurance scheme was among the leading reasons why New York banks were the first nationally to resume payments in specie which had been suspended everywhere during the Panic of 1837. It was that fact, in turn, which henceforth established the city of New York as the nation's preeminent financial center.

THIRD MINUTE

Prior to the Panic of 1837, state banks secured their charters through special enactments of state legislatures—an arrangement marked by instances of corruption and sleazy deals. Yet the demands for reform met with no responses from state legislatures until the plague of bank failures during the Panic of 1837 fueled a full-scale revolt over the abuses associated with the grant of bank charters by state legislatures.

New York's legislature was the first to respond to the new cry for reform when it passed in 1838 the "Free Banking Act"—a measure which served as a model for similar legislation that was presently enacted in other states. The text of the New York law deftly hopped over the usual objections that banks *as* corporations were monopolies—this, by asserting that they should be viewed as "associations," not as "corporations." Hence any respectable group of people could form a banking association without let or hindrance by public authorities. The title of right to perform banking functions under some sort of new-style charter would be theirs, as long as they conformed to the provisions of the Free Banking Act.

The free banking laws were hailed as one of the notable glories of the Age of Jackson. They breathed defiance to the old-style "chartered monopolies," reshaped the idea of the corporation, and proclaimed a new democratic concept of free enterprise and laissez-faire. But the local results of state banking laws enacted on the New York model differed widely. In some instances—Indiana, Louisiana, Missouri, Ohio, and Virginia are examples—the laws laid the basis for successful state banking systems, each served by its own "central bank" with expressly authorized branches. But in the greater number of instances—Alabama, Florida, Illinois, Kentucky, Mississippi, Michigan, and North Carolina are examples—the results ranged from bad to dreadful. Taking the country as a single whole, it is hard to understand how the laws for free banking ever merited the popular applause which greeted them. The many free banking systems became engines for banking chaos, especially in connection with banknote issues, which then comprised the greater part of the circulating medium.

Another negative development went hand in hand with the foregoing. Prior to the free banking laws, private bankers had exercised a common law right to establish branches. With the enactment of the laws, existing branch-bank systems came under the protection of "grandfather clauses" and were not disturbed. Moreover, as noted a moment ago, the new laws in some states created central banks and expressly authorized them to establish branches. In general, however, public policy in the Age of Jackson was hostile to the formation of large, privately owned regional banking institutions. Instead, the strongest encouragement was everywhere given to the organization of small unit banks. The more these continued to multiply after 1838, the more they added to the rising flood of state bank notes as a currency which varied from place to place in every respect—in design, size, material, in degrees of protection to the noteholder and of limitations on the total issue.

A point was reached, for example, where about 1,600 state banks issued in all approximately 10,000 different kinds of notes—most of which, except for those of New England and New York banks—had only local circulation. Counterfeiting was rife, and every financial house equipped itself with some sort of scanning device to spot bogus notes. Even in the case of genuine notes, the uncertainty regarding their true value at redemption compelled the further extension of the system where notes were discounted when used in transactions at points distant from their place of origin—assuming they were accepted at all. This was the woeful state of the currency at the start of the Civil War, and for the first two years of that conflict.

A HALF A MINUTE

After a quarter of a century lapse, the federal government resumed its national monetary responsibilities when Congress passed and President Lincoln signed the National Bank Act of 1863.[5] The motivating factor did not spring from a demand for banking and currency reform but from the need to generate more funds for use in financing the Civil War. The Act provided that "national banks"—so designated in federal charters granted them by the Comptroller of the Currency—would issue notes on the security of U.S. government bonds they pledged in Washington, D.C., with the comptroller. The notes would be in uniform, standard denominations, and they could be redeemed along procedural lines pioneered in New England by the Suffolk Bank of Boston, thus giving the nation a currency that circulated everywhere at par. The National Bank Act also incorporated a distinctive feature of New York's Free Banking Act of 1838. Unlimited national banks could be established on condition that the organization of each satisfied certain legal requirements, subject to the general oversight of the comptroller.

Tested by the immediate motive for its enactment—namely, the need for more funds to finance the war effort—the National Bank Act was a disappointment. It had been expected that the newly chartered national banks would buy great quantities of government bonds so that they could then proceed to issue larger volumes of bank notes. But the expected, as usual, didn't happen. Great quantities of bonds were not bought.

In the first place, the purchases of government bonds by national banks were limited by the Act to 5 percent of their capital. In other words, they could only buy bonds in relationship to their size, and most national banks were small. Second, by the time the Act was passed, the deposit business of banks exceeded and was growing more rapidly than their note circulation—with a corresponding decline in their desire to be issuing sources of notes. Further, it was expected that national charters would be so attractive that state banks would rush to transform themselves into national banks. Nothing of the sort occurred—not even after a 10 percent federal tax was slapped on state bank notes. The tax didn't touch existing state banks that had no note circulation; besides, it was wrongly assumed that note circulation was essential to banking. Faced by the tax, state banks which had issued notes relinquished their circulation and continued to function simply as banks of deposit.

A MINUTE AND ONE-HALF

During the life cycle of the First and Second Bank of the United States, one could see in outline the rudiments of a dual banking system comprised of state banks and national banks. But it was from the National Bank Act of 1863 that banks based on national charters or state charters took deep roots as a distinctive feature of American banking. American banking henceforth evolved as a system of systems—one national, and the other as varied and numerous as the states in the Union.

It was also from this time forward that other distinctive aspects of American banking acquired their form and force. For one thing, it was repeatedly said that state banks must not be forced against their will to become members of the national banking system. When they joined the system, it was only when they "voluntarily elected" to do so. Second, the National Bank Act of 1863 spurred the development of a unique correspondent relationship among American banks of diverse size, location, and legal status. In the practice of the matter, the correspondent network comprised the equivalent of a private "reserve system" in which the large banks performed functions on behalf of the correspondent smaller banks, paralleling those of a governmentally created reserve system.

The foregoing to one side, the actual administration of the National Bank Act promoted substantial improvements in banking practices, particularly with respect to the currency. National bank notes circulated at par throughout the nation, and noteholders were fully protected by the provisions for redemption. To that extent, the Act created a "safe" currency. But the improved picture also had a dark underside. The absence of a central bank with power to influence and control the flow of money and credit created the preconditions for recurrent financial stringencies and frequent bank failures—a topic that will be returned to in a moment. What merits attention right here is an early interpretation of the Bank Act of 1863 which had far-reaching implications for the future of branch banking in the United States.

If branch banking had been generally permitted in America (other than in its form during the life of the First and Second Bank of the United States), the evolution of American banking organizations might have paralleled the case in Western European countries which moved from unit to nationwide branch banking. In contrast to the Western European pattern, however, American banking institutions were set on a course which shifted from extensive multi-office or branch banking to extensive unit banking even beyond the picture prevailing in pre–Civil War years. The sharp change of course was not set by Congress. It was set by the legal construction which early comptrollers placed on a few words in the text of the National Bank Act of 1863.

The Act itself did not explicitly prohibit branches. In fact, the question of branch banking was not even raised during the congressional debates on the bill. As amended in 1864, the Act simply stated: "And its [the bank's] usual business shall be transacted at an office or banking house located in the place specified in its organization certificate." Comptrollers of the day construed the words "office" and "space" to mean only a single brick and mortar entity, and accordingly, would not permit national banks to have branches. With federally chartered banks limited to one-office institutions, any expansion of branch banking would have to develop within the four corners of state systems.

Again the expected didn't happen—though an 1865 amendment to the National Bank Act expressly permitted state banks seeking national charters to retain their branches. Authentic branch-banking systems prior to the Civil War were mainly centered in the Southern states. But these were either destroyed by the Civil War and the reign of the carpetbaggers, or met their end in yet another way. Authorities in the Southern states—in their postwar hostility to anything associated with "Washington"—dissolved their branch-banking systems rather than permit their conversion into national banks. On the other hand, in pre–Civil War years, members of the major branch-banking systems in the North operated in ways resembling independent banks. They were in a position to and generally preferred to enter the national system as unit rather than as branch institutions.

Still other factors helped entrench unit banking at the heart of the American financial system. The continuing outcry against "monopoly power" along with the fear of "bigness" comprised the political mortar used by some bankers to raise high protective walls around their unit banks. They were protected by federal rules which restricted national banks to a single office. They were protected by legislation in almost all states which explicitly prohibited branch banking of any kind. Eventually, however, legal means were discovered to circumvent the legal barriers standing in the way of what expansionist bankers wanted. It was the almost universal ban on branch banking which gave rise toward the end of the nineteenth century and the first decades of the twentieth to "group banking," whether in the form of "chain banks" or, ultimately, bank holding companies.

Two more minutes

Aspects of the National Bank Act of 1863 which contributed to recurrent financial crises and frequent bank failures included the following points of detail. First, the volume of currency did not expand or contract in response to the changing needs of the business community. Rather, the maximum volume of national bank notes—the workhorses of the currency—remained rigidly tied to the capital of the national banks. Second, and relatedly, the security requirements of the national banks—expressed in the securities they pledged with the Comptroller of the Currency in Washington—were more clearly linked to the fiscal operations of the federal government than to the level of economic activity.

Further, by the terms of the Act, national banks were required to hold reserves in proportion to their deposits, depending on whether the bank was located in central reserve cities (New York, Chicago, or St. Louis), in a reserve city (meaning a significant financial center), or was a country bank (meaning one located elsewhere than in a central reserve or reserve city). All this, however, fostered a "pyramiding" process where reserves were concentrated in the central reserve cities of Chicago and St. Louis, and particularly in New York. In periods of monetary stringency, the mechanics of the pyramiding process invited a war of all against all.

Typically in such periods, when interior banks called on their reserve city correspondents for cash, the heavy withdrawals from New York City banks prompted the latter to demand repayment of their loans to interior banks. To meet the demand, the interior banks squeezed their own debtors for the repayment of loans due, often forcing them to liquidate their goods and commodities at ruinous prices. Debts that could not be collected regardless of the means used left interior banks vulnerable to deadly runs. At the New York end of things, meanwhile, banks also demanded repayment of call money loans made to brokers active in security markets. The immediate result was a forced liquidation of securities, a sharp decline in their prices, and the weakening of commercial loans originally made when backed by the same securities at higher prices. Starting with the liquidity crisis of 1873, the pattern just sketched was duplicated in all the ensuing panics.

Between 1863 and 1907, the American economy was afflicted by five distinct liquidity crises, known by the years of their onset—1873, 1884, 1890, 1893, and 1907. Those in 1884 and 1890, when compared to the others, were classified as minor. They neither severely disturbed businesses and banks, nor lasted long. The crises of 1873, 1893, and 1907 were something else. In intensity and duration, these were major disturbances.

Each liquidity crisis was generally followed by calls for reforms of a national banking system whose existing rigidities did little to forestall and much to spur the onset of troubles. It was clear that the national banking structure, comprised of a multiplicity of autonomous banking units, must have some sort of internal coordinating mechanism. It was also clear that banks, like other enterprises, must have some place where they could occasionally borrow funds to tide them over immediate strains on their resources. With each economic recovery, however, the movements for reform lost their immediate urgency. So it went from one crisis to the next, until the pattern was changed in the aftermath of the panic of 1907.

The panic itself had a strange genesis.[6] It began with a speculative boom straight across the board of the New York Stock Exchange. By the fall of the year, American speculators, having exhausted native sources of funds for their operations, turned to European sources. These were tapped by means of "clean bills"—a name derived from the fact that they represented an advance of European funds against stocks held in New York without involving a commercial operation. Used in conventional ways, clean bills were indispensable tools of finance. But their speculative use was apparent by the end of 1906 when available data showed that London alone had provided almost a billion dollars in excess of normal American borrowing—all of which provided more fuel to the engines generating the Wall Street boom. More billions from European sources fed those engines during the winter and spring of 1907.

In June 1907, however, the Bank of England stopped rediscounting the clean bills of American borrowers from British financial institutions—the object being to stop the speculative abuses with this form of credit. Transoceanic and transcontinental consequences immediately followed. British institutions began to pressure New York banks for repayments of loans, and New York banks began to pressure interior banks who were their debtors. The credit squeeze within the United States was all the more painful because American crops had not been harvested, and a great many debtors were in no position to meet the immediate demands on them.

Credit was so tight by late August that New York City could not sell its bonds. Weeks of uncertainty were climaxed by a stock market crash on October 16, 1907. Five days later, in New York, the National Bank of Commerce announced that it would no longer honor checks drawn on the Knickerbocker Trust Company. Knickerbocker Trust, one of the largest and most respected institutions of the day, was promptly hit by a run and was forced to close. One run led to another as interior banks withdrew their funds from New York banks, six of which alone (under the pyramiding system) held three-fourths of all interior bank deposits in New York. On the New York Stock Exchange proper, with banks demanding repayment of loans to brokers, stocks continued to be dumped for what they could bring. Yet there were few buyers. By October 24, the price of call money had bounded upward to dizzy heights, until the day when none was to be had at any price, not even at 100 percent. To stem the rampage of disasters sweeping through banks and the financial community at large, a "legal holiday" was declared in New York on November 2. The back of the panic was eventually broken through ad hoc stabilization measures, but the nationwide economic malaise that followed persisted in the years leading up to the election of 1912.

Public sentiment at last seemed ready to support suggestions on how the nation could forestall repetitive debacles apparently brought on by a shortage of currency. The congressional response came on May 30, 1908, in the form of legislation that compromised the approaches of Senator Aldrich of the Senate Banking and Currency Committee, and of Representative Vreeland of the counterpart House Committee. The legislation provided for an emergency currency in times of stress, *and* for a thorough investigation of the nation's monetary and credit structure. The latter provision contemplated the formation of a National Monetary Commission empowered "to inquire into and report to Congress at the earliest possible date practicable, what changes are necessary or desirable in the monetary system of the United States or in the laws related to banking and currency."

The Commission's work, carried on for four years by congressmen and by experts in particular fields, served as the basis for a bill introduced into the Senate in January 1912 by Senator Aldrich. Its stated objective was to "permit the formation of an association of all banks of the country . . .

instead of having a large number of isolated unit banks working only in favor of their own interests and largely against the interests of all other banks."

The details of the Aldrich bill can be passed over, because the measure was not even reported out of the Senate Banking and Currency Committee. It was introduced at a time when the "money trust" inquiry was in full swing in Congress, leading to spin-off attacks on the Aldrich bill as being "almost exclusively a banker's measure." Moreover, as a "Republican measure," its fate was doomed when the political complexion of Congress changed in consequence of continuing economic stringencies. The House became Democratic after the 1910 congressional elections, followed in November 1912 by the election of a Democratic president, Woodrow Wilson. The banking problems of the country gravitated into new hands, those of Rep. Carter Glass of Virginia, Chairman of the House Banking and Currency Committee.[7]

The Federal Reserve measure which Rep. Glass introduced into the House in 1913 incorporated aspects of the Aldrich bill. But on the Senate side, Senator Owen of Oklahoma, who sharply disagreed with the Glass bill, prepared his own measure. The battle that ensued within the Congress, within the American Bankers Association, in the press, in the academies, and in the nation at large, was mean, nasty, and protracted, but finally produced the Federal Reserve Act of 1913. In its original form, the System was not an authentic central bank on any European model. It was the sum of all the political compromises forged in the thick of battle as the Reserve Act moved through Congress. Hence few of the divisive issues present at its creation faded away forever. As time went by—a year, a decade, a generation—a particular issue could remain as inert as a sword in a scabbard. But then, with a turn in the economic or political environment, there would be a flash of unsheathed steel, and old conflicts would be resumed in new forms.

The Reserve System formed in 1913 was *not* expressly related to any of the things currently associated with national economic policy—not to "full employment," or "orderly economic growth," or "stable prices." The main object was to avoid money panics and recurrent credit stringencies that had plagued the nation. At the same time, however, the Reserve Act preserved inviolate the preexisting "dual banking system." That is, banks that held national charters from the Comptroller of the Currency automatically became members of the Reserve System, but could contract out of the System upon surrendering their charters as national banks and converting themselves into state-chartered banks. State-chartered banks, for their part, were at liberty *not* to be members of the System. They became members only when they voluntarily "elected" to do so.

In other respects, the Reserve System was strongly tilted toward the decentralization of operations, with only unavoidable arrangements for centralized activities. Thus a regional credit pool was established within each of the twelve autonomous Federal Reserve Bank districts, along with an interregional check and currency clearing system. Each member bank domiciled within an autonomous Federal Reserve district subscribed to the stock of the district bank on a prescribed formula based on its capital. It would receive a modest return on the profits earned by the Reserve Bank in the region. Also on a prescribed formula, each member bank earmarked a portion of its own reserves to be held at the district bank. Though classifications of directors for each district bank included individuals not directly engaged in commercial banking, the member commercial banks had effective "majority control" of each Reserve Bank and decided its policies.

Member banks could bring their commercial paper to the Federal Reserve Banks in the area, and, at a rediscount, gain from the Reserve Banks the means to supply temporary, seasonal, and emergency needs of banks so that they could take care of customers who wanted credit and currency. Paper "eligible" for discount was "short-term liquid paper," generally with due dates limited to ninety days.

As representative of the public interest, the Federal Reserve Board in Washington was not vested with command over the system. Its powers were confined to a "supervisory role" expressed in general directives toward which it hoped the system would point its decisions. Open market operations were little understood and not provided for, perhaps because the public debt at the time the Reserve System was created stood at less than $1 billion. The real control over the system's operations was entrusted to the impersonal, pervasive, automatic, and impartial workings of the gold standard.[8] It was assumed that the mechanics of the standard, and not any arbitrary decisions made by human beings, would determine the amount of currency and bank credit that could be made available to the economy at any given time. That assumption was undercut soon after the system became operational. With the outbreak of the First World War, the gold standard was abandoned by virtually all parties in the war, thus rendering useless this automatic determinant of economic conditions.

Some of the compromises made to secure the enactment of the Federal Reserve measure would reveal their full costs to the nation's banking system at the start of the 1930s. Others, as suggested already, would be a fixed cause for conflict up to the present hour. To give but one example, the legislators who favored a Reserve System that would be a central bank in fact, and not in name only, insisted that every commercial bank must join the system. All must be members without regard to the factor of size, or whether they were national banks chartered by the Comptroller of the Currency, or banks chartered by state authorities. On the other side, legislators who spoke for the resisting battalions of state banks insisted that mandatory membership in the Reserve System would lead to a "concentration of power in Washington" and an "end to the dual banking system." They also insisted that a unified national banking system would enhance "the monopoly power of the Big Banks" and, to a commensurate degree, threaten with extinction the small unit banks that were "locally controlled" and "responsive to the needs of the local community."

In the upshot, the defeated advocates of mandatory membership consoled themselves with the belief that the advantages of membership would soon become so clear that most state banks would voluntarily elect to join the system. The will to believe, however, did not force the proof of its truth—no more than it did in 1863 after the passage of the National Bank Act when it was believed that the advantages of being chartered as a national bank would be so compelling that all state banks would apply for national charters. With the creation of the Federal Reserve System, the larger among the state-chartered banks did become members. Most of the small state banks—and they comprised in the aggregate a majority of all commercial banking institutions in the nation—remained nonmembers. Yet the system of correspondent relationships previously noted in connection with the National Bank Act of 1863 was extended still further under the Federal Reserve Act's dispensation for the dual banking system. That is, to provide for the institutional needs of nonmember state banks, their correspondent relationship with member state banks or with national banks took on the character of a "private reserve system," separate from but with functions paralleling those of the publicly enacted Federal Reserve System.

At critical moments in subsequent American history, attempts were made to have all state-chartered banks become members of the Federal Reserve System. At the time when the Federal Deposit Insurance Corporation was created, for example, the law originally provided that the insurance coverage provisionally granted nonmember state banks should be withdrawn unless they joined the Reserve System by a specified date. The deadline was subsequently extended on three occasions, only to be dropped entirely in the end. It was realized that to withdraw the coverage from the nonmember banks could lead to panic-driven runs on these banks which most likely would close many of them. At a still later hour, the costs of maintaining non-interest-bearing reserves with the Federal Reserve system, under conditions of high inflation and high interest rates on the funds banks needed for their operations, led to the migration of many member banks out of the Reserve System. In the case of the national banks who did so, they surrendered their national charters in favor of state charters. The effect worked in its own way to infuse new life into the dual banking system—until the picture was modified in 1980. But that's another story, with no time left to tell it here. The ten minutes are up.

6. Remote Seeds for Homogenized Competition

Suppose you were a commercial banker the day before the Federal Reserve Act became law in 1913. Suppose, next, you were asked on that day to name your main institutional competitors. What would your answer be? Mutual savings banks, savings and loan associations, and credit unions were in existence at the time. Yet it is highly unlikely that you would have named any of them. It is far more likely that you would have pointed to other commercial banks—national or state chartered—as your main competitors.

Now leap ahead sixty-seven years to the day prior to April 1, 1980, when the Depository Institutions Deregulation and Monetary Control Act became law. Suppose again that as a commercial banker you were asked to name your main institutional competitors. Once again you would point to other commercial banks. But this time around, you would not stop with them. You would extend your list of competitors to include mutual savings banks, savings and loan associations, credit unions, insurance companies, department stores, giant merchandizing establishments such as Sears and Penney's, issuers of credit cards such as American Express, brokerage houses, pension funds, personal finance companies, sales finance companies—and in some areas, direct-lending government agencies, as well as the Treasury of the United States.

You would go on to note how institutions originally formed for a special purpose were trying to offer a broad array of financial services, while other institutions appealed to courts or to legislatures to bar or severely restrict the scope of that attempt. You would note the lengthening of the maturity of assets held by financial institutions, a great resort to volatile sources of funds, a growing use of substitutes for currency and checks, a growing tendency among "nonfinancial firms" to provide financial services, a marked attempt by locally rooted firms to achieve geographical diversification. You would also note how financial institutions were trying to break out of the accumulated web of laws and regulations in order to adapt to changing competitive circumstances for the delivery of financial services. Wherever you looked, the direction in which events were moving at an accelerating pace increasingly pointed to the homogenization of financial activity in America—a process in which bank and nonbank institutions offered competitive financial services previously forbidden to some, on turf previously forbidden to others.

How did this all come about? How and why did aspects of the homogenization process ultimately receive the sanctions of law in certain provisions of the Depository Institutions Deregulation and Monetary Control Act which President Carter signed on April 1, 1980? The full story, told in one place, would by its length fatigue the reader. What follows here, then, are only the opening episodes focused on the formative years of three financial institutions in particular—mutual savings banks, savings and loan associations, and credit unions.[9] Their respective developments, taken together, write large a repetitive experience in the history of American finance. Each of the three was originally formed to serve an important market need not being met by commercial bankers of the day. Each, as time went by, also expanded its functions and then used the lawmaking and regulatory process in an attempt to build a legal wall around its share of the market—while commercial bankers, for their part, tried to breach that wall.

MUTUAL SAVINGS BANKS

A mutual savings bank, as legally defined by the Supreme Court of the United States, is an institution "in the hands of disinterested persons, the profits of which, after deducting the necessary expenses of conducting the business, innure wholly to the benefits of the depositors, in dividends, or in reserved surplus for their greater security." As such, the American form of the institution is descended from late eighteenth century European savings banks, which were strongly supported by the clergy and influential leaders such as Daniel Defoe, David Ricardo, Jeremy Bentham, and Robert Malthus.

In the United States, following the receipt of reports of a mutual savings bank that was successfully organized in Scotland in 1810, prominent civic figures—James Savage of Boston, De Witt Clinton of New York, and Condy Raguet of Philadelphia—took the initiative in organizing such banks for their respective communities. Their motive can be directly ascribed to a "market failure" on the part of other financial institutions of the day, for there was no organization which really welcomed the savings of the man of little or moderate means. Commercial bankers, being almost exclusively preoccupied with the work of discounting commercial and industrial paper, did not even consider it a paying proposition to accept the common man's savings as a deposit. So his small savings were hidden in his home or were entrusted to a shopkeeper or other business proprietor who owned a strongbox.

To provide greater safety and an inducement to thrift, mutual savings banks initially had the character of a philanthropy, sponsored by wealthy business and professional men with the paternalistic objective of managing "the savings of mechanics, laborers, servants and others." The present-day names of some of these banks—Five Cents Savings, Dime Savings, Dollar Savings—suggest that they originally obtained most of their funds from small individual savers. As such, the first mutual savings bank in America to be accorded governmental recognition was the Provident Institution for Savings in Boston, chartered by the Commonwealth of Massachusetts on December 13, 1816. The first mutual savings bank to accept deposits, however, was the Philadelphia Savings Fund Society, which opened for business on December 2, 1816. Today these two institutions rank close to the top of the nation's one hundred largest savings banks.

The services initially provided by mutual savings banks were well received by the public, and others were soon formed—two more in 1818, and four more the year after that, including one organized by Clinton in New York. In the following decades, the rate of growth continued to accelerate until slowed first by the depression of 1873, and then by the depression of 1907, at which time there were 678 mutual savings banks. The numbers then began to decline through the process of liquidation or consolidation, but the growth in the number of depositors and in the dollar amount of the deposits continued at a rapid pace. In 1970, on the eve of a fundamental change in the competitive position of mutual savings banks, the 482 mutual savings banks in the United States and its possessions served more than 28.3 million depositors and held assets of $106.7 billion. Individual accounts averaged just a shade over $3,400—though there was no restriction on their size. The institutions themselves ranged in size from those with deposits of $4 million to twenty-one whose deposits were between $1 billion and $3.4 billion.

These figures would change by the end of the 1970s, when the number of mutual savings banks shrank to 463, while their total assets increased to $158 billion. But almost all mutual savings banks were still to be found in places where they began and had their early growth—the New England and Middle Atlantic States of New Hampshire, Massachusetts, Connecticut, New York, and Pennsylvania. Elsewhere, six other states—Alaska, Indiana, Minnesota, Oregon, and Wisconsin, plus Puerto Rico—had at least one mutual savings bank, but thirty-three states and the District of Columbia had none. Of the total number of mutual savings banks, three-fifths were in New York and Massachusetts alone, and of the industry's total deposits, 54 percent were in mutual savings banks located in New York. The figures explain why Massachusetts and New York were the nurseries for the post-1970 developments in the mutual savings bank industry—and the place as well where the greatest headaches were felt because of the way inflation impacted on mutual savings banks.

Savings banks traditionally offered a wide range of savings choices, including passbook accounts; a varied list of special high-yield accounts including time, special notice, bonus, systematic savings, and others; and such special purpose accounts as school savings and Christmas and vacation clubs. The funds themselves were traditionally channeled into mortgage loans and government bonds. After the end of World War II, however, the mutual savings banks began to move step by step toward the goal of providing a full range of financial services to their depositors. The nature of the great breakthroughs that occurred, starting in 1971, and their effects on commercial banks, will be noted in a later place.

SAVINGS AND LOAN ASSOCIATIONS

On January 3, 1831, a group of citizens assembled at Thomas Sidebotham's Inn at Frankford, Pennsylvania—now a part of Philadelphia—where they drew up the articles for the Oxford Provident Building Association of Philadelphia County. This was the first cooperative home-financing society in the United States, though the model had existed in England for over a half century. The idea spread, and soon there were many similar neighborhood associations where families of limited means could generate sources of credit that would enable them to buy or build a home of their own. Here was an activity that fell outside the interest of both the commercial and mutual savings banks of the day—even when they faced no legal barriers to their participation in lending programs related to home ownership.

By 1890, savings and loan associations were in operation in every state and territory of the nation, though the 5,600 then in existence were called by various names: cooperative banks, homestead associations, building and loan associations, savings associations, and later, savings and loan associations. Along with an increase in their number, savings and loan associations came under closer public scrutiny and regulation by the states in which they were domiciled. The years between 1920 and 1930 saw their resources increase some 250 percent as a result of pent-up demands for housing after World War I, and the economic prosperity of wage earners who had previously been able to save very little. The late 1920s found a thriving and speedily growing group of local, state-regulated associations whose competitive impact was being felt by other financial institutions.

By that time also, the associations had altered their original character— namely, groups formed to accumulate the savings of members until each could obtain a home construction loan. Under the initial arrangement, they were single-purpose mutual institutions, limited to the same group of participants. When all the loans were paid off, the purpose for which a society was formed was accomplished, and the society was liquidated. As the movement spread, however, the service function of the societies ceased to be confined to members who bought shares and obtained loans. The societies began to solicit savings from nonmembers and to make loans to nonmembers in order to put idle funds to profitable use.

The evolutionary changes along these lines reached a point where saving and borrowing functions were completely separated, and participation became unrestricted. In this form, the associations became permanent corporate entities, soliciting savings from the general public and merchandizing funds to any potential borrower who wished to buy or build a home. Moreover, with their permanence and increased size, the associations could no longer be run directly by members as was true initially. In place of part-time amateur managers, they employed full-time aggressive, promotional-minded men with excellent political connections at all levels of government.

The onset of the Great Depression found most savings and loan associations in relatively sound condition. After a year of pressure, however, mortgage delinquencies increased and withdrawals became widespread. Congress responded to the call for help. In the last months of the Hoover Administration, it passed the Federal Home Loan Act of 1932 as a means for strengthening the entire savings and loan system.

The terms of the Act—stated in the present tense—provide for a central reserve credit agency for savings and home financing institutions similar to the Federal Reserve System's structure for commercial banks. To this end, a Federal Home Loan Bank System is comprised of eleven regionally located banks whose capital comes from the subscriptions of member associations. Each regional bank is governed by a board of directors, answerable to the Federal Home Loan Bank Board in Washington. Each regional bank can borrow money and issue obligations when necessary. Each can invest funds in government securities and make deposits in banks or trust companies. Each, above all, can extend loans to its member associations on the security of first mortgages in order to provide liquidity or expanded credit when these are needed in a particular area.

In the first year of the New Deal, the savings and loan system was further strengthened when Congress passed the Home Owners Act of 1933—a measure which provided for the federal chartering of savings and loan associations when they were initially formed or when they converted from state charters. Either way, the Home Loan Bank Board was the designated regulatory agency for all federally chartered institutions. It was empowered to supervise their operations, conduct examinations, and to grant charters on the basis of a community's need for an association and the ability and integrity of its prospective management.

It was also in the first year of the New Deal that two provisions of the Banking Act of 1933—better known as the Glass-Steagall bill of 1933—which directly affected commercial banks, worked by indirection and in the long run to strengthen the competitive position of the savings and loan associations as against commercial banks. One of the two barred the payment of interest by commercial banks on demand deposits. The other vested in the Federal Reserve Board the discretionary right to establish ceilings on the interest rates member banks could pay on savings and time deposits—the heart of what came to be known as Regulation Q. In the second year of the New Deal, the competitive position of the savings and loan association was further strengthened when the National Housing Act of 1934 authorized the creation of the Federal Savings and Loan Insurance Corporation (FSLIC) under the Home Loan Bank Board.[10] Through it, savings and loan associations were provided with a deposit insurance scheme similar to the coverage the new Federal Deposit Insurance Corporation provided commercial banks.

More will be said in a later place about the circumstances leading to the 1933 ban on the payment by commercial banks of interest on demand deposits, and on the issuance by the Federal Reserve Board of Regulation Q. What needs to be noted right here is this. At the time these two regulations became law, it would have been hard to find anyone who foresaw their immense consequences. But from the mid-1950s onward, the two regulations were at the center of an increasingly intense political tug-of-war between the managers of commercial banks (and their government allies) and the managers of the savings and loan associations and other thrift institutions (along with *their* governmental allies.)

CREDIT UNIONS

A group of people + a common interest + pooled savings + loans to each other = a credit union. If a financial institution has just two of these four features, it is not a credit union. If it has three, it is not one either. It takes all four elements. For a credit union is a cooperative self-help thrift and loan society composed of individuals bound together by something such as a common employer, membership in a labor union, a church, a fraternal order, or residence in a well-defined geographic area. "Members" purchase "shares" resembling savings accounts, and each in turn may borrow from the association—a privilege not extended to nonmembers. Income from these loans and other investments provide funds from which members are paid dividends.

The earliest credit unions were organized in Germany in the mid-1800s as self-help societies (as opposed to charitable institutions) in order to encourage thrift in the working classes and to provide credit on reasonable terms. The first credit union in the United States was organized in 1908. Today, state-chartered credit unions are usually regulated by the state's department of financial regulation, along with banks and savings and loan associations.[11] Federally chartered credit unions are regulated by a separate regulatory agency, the National Credit Union Administration (NCUA). A federal share insurance program, similar to the FDIC for banks and the FSLIC for savings and loan associations, was not available to credit unions until 1970. At that time, the National Credit Union Share Insurance Fund was established under the administration of the NCUA, with the maximum amount insured for any shareholder being the same as the limit set under the FDIC and FSLIC.

As was said a moment ago, the common bond is the central concept of the credit union movement. No other financial institution starts life with such restrictions on its growth. A commercial bank, for example, may be subject to limits on the number and locations of its offices, but there are no restraints on the number of depositors or borrowers who can do business at the bank. Common membership bonds, however, particularly if based on economic ties, may pose awkward problems. Layoffs, strikes, the bite of inflation, or poor income years for a plant or an occupational group can cut savings inflow or cause outflows as well as increase loan demand. Alternatively, overtime and high income years can boost savings inflow and cut loan demand. Plant closings or relocations can also put a quick end to the credit union because of the loss of the field of membership. While the common bond requirement continues to limit the geographical area served by credit unions as well as their potential membership, rules for eligibility have been markedly liberalized over the years. So much so, that looser definitions of occupational entities such as shopping centers and office buildings have been used to allow formation of credit unions.

The whole of this trend toward a liberalization of the common bond requirement has had competitive consequences of no small import for commercial banks and other financial institutions. It has also engendered objections particularly from executives of banks and other financial institutions. The latter, for example, contrast the relative ease and small investment required to start a credit union with the time and large sums of money involved in starting a bank. They observe further that as a credit union grows, it takes on the character more of a business than of a cooperative organization. Further, credit unions receive many direct and indirect subsidies from their sponsoring organizations and members. Officers, except for the treasurer, serve without salary, while the sponsoring organization often provides free office space, clerical help, and payroll deduction services. Still further, credit unions presently pay no federal taxes and generally pay little state taxes except on real property.

There are additional advantages credit unions have, particularly in the field of consumer savings and lending. Unlike other lenders, the fact that a credit union official has direct personal knowledge of the borrower, or a previously established customer relationship, reduces the costs of collecting information on the applicant. At the same time, payroll deductions made to pay off the loan reduces collection costs for occupational credit unions. Further, though consumer loans typically have a higher default rate than do other loan categories, credit unions are better placed than other financial institutions to keep the defaults at a fairly low level. The cooperative nature of the credit union acts as an incentive for the individual to repay his loan, and the credit union can use group pressure to encourage repayment. This reduces the costs of attempted loan collection, or the charge-off of the uncollected balance of the loan. All this is to one side of how credit unions have lately come to perform functions and to offer services in direct competition with commercial banks.

7. The Banking System
in the 1920s

The operations of the Federal Reserve System, starting in 1914, did not fundamentally alter the preexisting picture of the nation's country banks. Aside from the fact that the overwhelming majority among them continued to be state-chartered nonmember banks, they were in most instances adjuncts of other businesses. The leading stockholder was often a merchant who had engaged in banking as part of his retail operations. Though he might hold the title of president, the "cashier" he employed was generally the person who actually managed the bank's day-to-day operations. Institutional practices were seldom standardized. Extreme differences in interest rates were commonplace. Distinctions were drawn between lines of credit available to individuals, but they were rarely drawn—or even understood—in the case of different kinds of business activity. Clearinghouse differences were settled by an actual exchange of gold and currency, and the cashier used gold for many other transactions. Surviving veterans of the process still tell in a kind of dreaming awake way, how as young bank employees they chained bags of gold to their bodies and moved between banks incident to their work in settling accounts.[12]

In agricultural areas, loans and their due dates were geared to the agricultural cycle, starting with springtime planting, and extending to the fall when crops were harvested and marketed. In the cities, loans were geared to what has since been called "wholesale credit"—meaning, in the main, commercial enterprises such as the general store, warehouse, granary, or creamery. Retail credit such as is now associated with the broad pattern of consumer needs was under a strong tabu. The automobile, for example, was coming into ever wider use. But a banker was thought to be eccentric or reckless if he even considered making a loan for the purchase of an automobile—a general attitude which left the road clear for automobile manufacturers to create their own captive finance companies.

Prior to 1916, national banks were not permitted to make home mortgage loans. Even after that restriction was lifted, state laws limited the loans to the narrow kind of home mortgage financing carried on by state banks, insurance companies, or mortgage loan companies. The near universal rule, sealed in law, restricted banks and insurance companies to a maximum loan of 50 percent of the appraised value of a home, and limited to five years the life of a loan made by a national bank, and to ten years by an insurance company. Few people could make a down payment of 50 percent on a new home, and pay for the balance within five or ten years. Most of them took out second and third mortgages payable in installments, at high interest rates and with due dates extending beyond the life of the first mortgage.[13]

THE LEGACY OF THE FIRST WORLD WAR

In the United States, even before the outbreak of the war in Europe, each village and each town as a matter of local pride and economic promise wanted its own general store, its own creamery, granary, warehouse, and its own bank. High prices following the clash among Europe's belligerent powers, starting in August 1914, seemed to assure a bright future for all locally based enterprises along American byways.

By the time America itself entered the First World War, the proliferation of small country banks encouraged the proliferation of enterprises which, under normal circumstances, would have been submarginal. The demand for food products when prices were inflated triggered a boom in the price of land, leading to the cultivation of fields that could not be profitably farmed when prices declined and the demand for products declined. Local bankers, meanwhile, extended credit to young men which enabled them to purchase land, equipment, and stock on the basis of loans whose "soundness" depended on the continuance of inflated prices. Aside from extensions of such credit to inexperienced one-crop "instant" farmers, they also helped veteran farmers finance sharply expanded purchases of cattle, sheep, and hogs for feeding. If local bankers thus played a vital role in meeting the immediate wartime need for more food, the full price which they and others paid came later. It came in the form of an economic disaster, followed by the ecological disaster of the "dust bowl."[14]

In retrospect, it is easy enough to say that the independent unit bankers on Main Street should have buffered themselves against trouble by diversifying the character of their loans. At the time in question, however, they were in no position to do so. Their resources and their ability to provide financial assistance were largely tied to the welfare of the nearby and undiversified small area they served. When the ventures common to the area were hit by the sharp decline in agricultural prices at the end of the First World War, the same event crippled the power of local bankers to help stabilize the local economy.

At an earlier hour—1917—the Federal Farm Loan Board had been created to supervise the financial operations of what eventually became an agricultural conglomerate consisting of twelve intermediate credit banks, fifty-two joint stock land banks, twelve federal land banks, and 4,670 National Farm Loan Associations with assets in excess of $2 billion.[15] But its scatter-pattern approach to the banking side of agriculture can be sensed from the administrative picture the Board showed in 1927–28 when a belated attempt was made to remedy a decade of mismanagement. It was discovered at the time that the records of the Board were virtually useless. Its minutes, containing policies and rules for the previous decade, were an unbound heap of paper without an index. Bylaws of banks and associations in the farm loan system were missing from the files of the Board. The Board itself had no general counsel, and the land banks differed widely in what they approved as collateral for farm loan bond issues. Delinquent mortgages had been accepted as security. Farm loans had been improperly granted on cut-over timberland. Accounting methods were often chaotic. Interest charges on mortgages were often higher than the law allowed. Rampant nepotism and conflicts of interest had gone unchallenged. In several spectacular cases, major units of the farm loan system which had been given a clean bill of health by examiners of the Farm Loan Board went into receivership shortly afterward.

The one government agency that did in fact help ease the transition from war to peace was the War Finance Corporation (WFC), created during the war to help finance industries contributory to the defense effort. Under the leadership of Eugene Meyer—who later became the chairman of the Federal Reserve Board in the depths of the Great Depression, as well as the architect of the original Reconstruction Finance Corporation—the WFC, with congressional approval, was converted after 1918 into an instrument to ease the transition of the economy from wartime to peacetime conditions. All other wartime agencies as well as controls had been dismantled within a month after the Armistice, and the WFC stood virtually alone to cope with the consequences of the global upheaval in all units of value.

The capital at the disposal of the WFC was limited to $500 million, but it effectively served American agriculture, in particular, in two ways. First, it helped fill a glaring breach in the agricultural finance mechanism of the day as it pertained to breeder loans to livestock men. Managers of national banks and state member banks were reluctant to make breeder loans. The paper they entailed, with their long maturity dates, could not be discounted at the Federal Reserve Banks under the rigid and prevailing canons for eligibility. Things standing so, until Congress authorized the creation of a system of intermediate credit banks to be capitalized by the government and financed by tax-exempt borrowing, the WFC stepped in with its own resources and took the first mortgages representing breeder loans that adventuresome bankers were willing to make. Second, the WFC helped brace the nerve of people who had formerly financed the export of American agricultural products to overseas markets, but had held back from resuming their activities when European currencies fluctuated widely after the Armistice. They resumed the financing of agricultural exports only on the assurance that the WFC would underwrite any losses they might incur due to the instability of European currencies.

In the early spring of 1920, however, at a time when President Wilson's protracted illness caused policy initiatives to gravitate to the hands of his cabinet members, Secretary of the Treasury David Houston—who had previously been Secretary of Agriculture, and before that president of the University of Texas—ordered the WFC to cease operations.[16] It was, he said, a war agency, and the war had been over for more than sixteen months. Eugene Meyer, to no avail, warned against the consequences if operations were stopped, and the warning materialized at harvest time.

Farmers who had borrowed from the banks when agricultural prices were high at the start of the planting season could not repay their loans when the glut of the harvest—and the sudden absence of an overseas market—drove prices down precipitously. From 1919 to 1920, for example, potatoes which had brought $1.50 per hundredweight dropped to 31 cents. Steers declined from $120 to $20 a head, and sheep declined from $20 to $3 a head. Similar sharp declines occurred in everything from sugar beets to dairy products. In the thirteen-state cotton-producing South, the costs of harvesting the crop often exceeded the market price for a pound of cotton—a bitter economic fact that contributed to the postwar resurgence of the Ku Klux Klan. In the great granary states of the Middle West, corn and wheat lay in the bins because farmers could not sell in a demoralized market without making themselves bankrupts.

Even when banks renewed loans to hard-pressed and over-extended farmers, the effect merely postponed the inevitable liquidation of marginal enterprises. Credit without a reduction in costs or an increase in income might help farmers "hang on" for a while—but at the price of weakening the lending bank further.[17] When farmers could not repay their loans to country banks, the latter could not meet their obligations to their depositors or to city and eastern banks from whom they had borrowed. The conditions compounded the preexisting instability of many country banks, and lent new force to a wave of failures among them. Between 1919 and 1921, one half of all country banks that existed on the eve of America's entry into the First World War failed.

Between March 1921 when the WFC resumed operations and the summer of 1924 when the agency was finally liquidated, the WFC was involved in many emergency operations—including the consequences of a severe drought that imperilled the livestock industry throughout the West from the Canadian to the Mexican borders. But it could not, unaided, remove all the causes for the failure of 5,711 banks between 1921 and 1929 with total deposits of $564 million, and with substantial loss to depositors. Most of these banks were small, under-capitalized institutions, geared to one-crop agriculture and located in communities of less than 3,000 people—and in many instances as few as 200 people. They were thus all the more vulnerable not only to the sharp drop in agricultural prices and the value of farmlands, but to the consequences of three other concurrent events extending over the length of the 1920s.

THE BUSINESS REVOLUTION OF THE 1920S

The first of the three events was the postwar shift of the population from the rural countryside to the cities. The second event, related to the first, was the rise of all-weather roads and the marked increase in the use of the automobile, which made it convenient for the farmer to shop and bank in the larger cities. The third event was related to the preceding two. It was the impact on the small unit bankers of the business revolution of the 1920s.

One aspect of that revolution was the consolidation of 7,000 independent manufacturing firms in one of the greatest merger waves in American history—long before the term conglomerate came into popular use. Another aspect was the displacement of the individual retail grocery, drug, clothing, and other stores by the nationwide chains—with thousands of outlets in the aggregate. The effect of the chain movement not only took away from local banks a profitable outlet for the use of their funds in financing the once independent merchants, but also hit the banker in a vulnerable spot—his deposit volume.[18]

The process which hit him worked like this. The receipts taken in by local units of the chain system were deposited in the local banks, but were not left their long enough to be profitably employed by the bank. As soon as the deposit was made, it was transferred from the bank by draft, wire, or check to the central institution. The bank had the costs of handling the account, collecting the checks, and making the transfer, but with very meager balances to compensate for it. In the majority of cases, the balance was so small that the account was handled by the local banker at a loss—either because the banker didn't want to lose the account to his competitor or because he had not analyzed his costs and didn't know that he was losing money. It was only after many exhortations and much educational work through committees of the American Bankers Association, that banks began to ask for, inaugurate, and get service charges for the services they rendered the chains.

Meanwhile, the revolution in American business and the failure of many thousands of small, under-capitalized banks in the 1920s established the preconditions for a consolidation movement among the surviving banks. Because branch banking was almost universally barred by state law, the consolidation movement took one of three forms: the outright merger into a single institution of two or more banks; the acquisition of separate banks which continued to function as autonomous units in a banking chain; or the spread of the bank holding company movement which saw ninety-seven companies in operation by the end of the 1920s.

Different motives animated the parties to the different forms of group banking.[19] In the specific case of bank holding companies, for example, some were created for investment purposes only, or for what seemed to be the sole purpose of speculating in bank stocks, or in order to act as agents in the purchase and sale of country bank stocks. Some were formed to provide an overhead staff organization that could efficiently and economically provide the units in the multibank holding company with services each had previously performed separately—auditing, advertising, purchasing, credit inspection, and so on. Others were formed in anticipation of a much-talked-about prospect—that the pervasive ban against branching national and state banks would be lifted. The thing to do in the meantime was to acquire control of banks which would function as unit banks, and not as part of an integrated system under central direction. They would be converted into branch banks when and if the legal impediments were removed. Yet another motive lying behind the formation of bank holding companies was the protection of correspondent relationships that were threatened by the expansionist acquisition programs of rival or "outside" interests.

THE MCFADDEN ACT

In an ideal view of the case, larger banks or the various forms of group banking made possible the pursuit of better credit policies and a greater diversification in the lines of credit that were actually extended. The *real* did not, of course, always correspond to the ideal. But the effects of the consolidation movement produced a statistical picture that looked like this. In June 1923, there were 30,178 banks of all kinds in the United States with total resources of $54 billion, and with capital funds of $6.8 billion. Five years later, there were 26,213 banks with total resources of $71.5 billion and capital funds of $8.8 billion. In other words, with 3,965 fewer banks, resources had increased by $17.5 billion and capital funds by $2 billion.

Meanwhile, however, all forms of group banking—branch banking, chain banking, and bank holding companies—were the subject of extensive and increasing acrimonious debates in Congress and in the banking business generally. Unit bankers tried to secure from Congress an outright legal ban on any kind of group banking. They claimed that while the collapse of a unit bank might damage a particular community, the disasters consequent upon the mismanagement and failure of any type of *group* banking were widespread. Second, they claimed that group banking, in contrast to locally controlled unit banks, eliminated competition and stiffened access to credit in local communities. Third, they claimed that group banking made it possible to control an inordinate volume of banking funds by controlling a small amount of investment funds in a bank holding company. Finally, they claimed that there was built-in potential for dangers in the case of bank holding

companies whose operations extended to fields of business not closely related to banking.

Against the background of all such lines of argument, Congress passed
the McFadden Act of 1927. The Act was virtually silent on the subject of
bank holding companies but dealt mainly with the branching rights of national
banks and member state banks of the Federal Reserve System. Thus it
granted permission to member banks of the system to have home city
branches where state law permitted, but prohibited any further extensions
by member banks of rural or outside branches, regardless of state law.
Further, state banks which came under national charters either by conversion
or consolidation were required to relinquish any out-of-town branches established after the McFadden Act became effective.

So viewed, the Act was a mirror image of sharply conflicting interests.
Congress, on the one side, had to concede something to national banks that
wanted the same right to branch that state banks might have under state law.
On the other side, it dared not concede too much. It must protect some
20,000 smaller banks against what was thought to be a threat to their independence. In the upshot, the McFadden Act in some respects liberalized
the provisions of federal law regarding the branching of national banks. But
in other respects, it permitted *less* branching expansion inside the Reserve
System than was possible for nonmember state banks. The grounds were
thus laid for a protracted conflict over the McFadden Act itself, with successive phase lines down to the present day.

THE ECONOMY AT THE CLOSE OF THE TWENTIES

By 1929, the worst phase of the postwar agricultural depression had passed
into history. Many pockets of instability—some purely economic, and some
institutional—remained. Though the collection of economic data was still in
a very primitive state, the balance sheet of economic progress drawn up in
1929 showed an immense sweep of achievements in the preceding nine years.
In the 1920s, for example, the national wealth was increased by the addition
of approximately $100 billion in physical properties. A cross-country net-
work of new roads was built to service an automobile industry that had more
than doubled its output. The system of oil production and distribution was
greatly increased to meet the needs of the automobile. The entire public
utility industry grew at a swift pace. In addition, the physical facilities of
religious, educational, and social institutions—along with those of the cities
and states—were greatly improved or expanded.

Further, and this needs to be said again, consumer price levels had
declined in the 1920s, while the national income and money supply had
increased by about 40 percent over the nine years ending in 1929. Labor
productivity was substantially greater than the normal trend, and there was
little unemployment. In the public sector, the federal budget of $4 billion

was not only balanced, but the budgetary surplus that regularly occurred allowed four major reductions in federal income taxes on the eve of elections. At the same time, $8 billion in total federal debts incurred in connection with war-related costs were paid off, with this result: whereas the federal debt stood at $1 billion in 1914 and $27 billion in 1920, by 1929 it had been reduced to $19 billion. There was virtually no competition between the governmental and private sector for savings, and very little governmental intervention in the free enterprise system. In the emblematic case of national banks, they seldom had to look to the Comptroller of the Currency before making their major decisions. They were required only to inform the comptroller of what the decisions were after they were made.

The status of central banking

Where the Federal Reserve Board was concerned, it seemed to serve more as a place for the dignified retirement of its members, than as a central bank regulating the flow of money and credit in the economy. The real levers of power in the Reserve System were in the hands of the governors of the twelve regional Federal Reserve Banks—led by Benjamin Strong, the governor of the New York Federal Reserve Bank.

The way this latter development came about was of itself an instructive comment on the free-wheeling nature of the regional Reserve Banks. Briefly, under the Federal Reserve Act of 1913, the statutory head of each Federal Reserve Bank was the chairman, chosen by action of the Federal Reserve Board in Washington. The Act did not even mention the position of governor of a Reserve Bank. The position was entirely extra-legal, born of the practical need for a chief executive officer competent to oversee the daily operations of a Reserve Bank. That officer, titled governor, owed his place to an election by the directors of each Reserve Bank—which meant, in practice, an election by private bankers who comprised a majority of the board. As for the Federal Reserve Board in Washington, its appointive powers were limited to the chairmanship of the bank. It could neither approve nor disapprove of the individual chosen to serve as governor—though in the daily operations of a Reserve Bank, the chairman was subordinate in importance to the governor—known since 1935 as the president of the Reserve Bank.

While other governors of Federal Reserve Banks tended to confine themselves to local and regional matters, the power of the New York financial community gave a national and international reach to Governor Benjamin Strong's operations. When acting on behalf of the New York Federal Reserve Bank, he dealt directly with the President of the United States and the Secretary of the Treasury, not with the Federal Reserve Board in Washington. Similarly, it was Strong who spoke for the Federal Reserve System in matters of interest to European banks in an era when their great central banks were each personified in and dominated by a single individual.

Montague Norman meant the Bank of England; Emile Moreau, the Bank of France; Hjalmar Schacht, the German Reichsbank.[20]

When these men came to the United States with serious business to discuss—whether in connection with the system for the repayments of debts and reparations, with the devaluation or the stabilization of their currencies— they rarely called on the Federal Reserve Board in Washington, except for a round of ceremonial handshakes. They headed straight for the New York Federal Reserve Bank and put their case to Governor Benjamin Strong. They knew he had the courage and personal force to achieve a policy consensus among the governors of the other eleven Federal Reserve Banks in the nation. So it went until his untimely death in October 1928—which was the eve of the hour when he would be needed the most.

It had been Strong, for example, who took the lead in pioneering arrangements bearing on the conduct of open market operations. When the Federal Reserve System was created, the effects of its open market operations were little understood, perhaps because they were on a very small scale. The public debt in 1914, as noted a moment ago, was less than $1 billion. At the end of the First World War, however, it gradually became clear to the autonomous Federal Reserve Banks, to the Federal Reserve Board, and particularly to Benjamin Strong, that when they bought and sold government securities connected with the $27 billion public debt, they were not engaged in a self-limiting action. They directly influenced not only market conditions but the reserves of member banks. The reserves, in turn, influenced the volume of deposits, the deposits determined the volume of loanable funds that could be made available by the commercial banks, and the volume of loanable funds influenced the minutest operations of the economy. These chain reactions, once set in motion, were national in their effects.

In the face of these realities, Federal Reserve bankers concluded that the principle of regional autonomy must be modified so that the purchase and sale of government securities could be nationally coordinated through some sort of "open market" investment committee. There followed a decade-long evolutionary process without foundation in law, but whose institutional aspects were simply improvisations that went unchallenged.

The evolutionary process started in 1922 with the creation of an informal body—the Governor's Committee on Centralized Execution of Purchase and Sales of Government Securities. This was followed the next year by the creation of a new committee known as the Open Market Investment Committee of the Reserve System. Membership was limited to the governors of the New York, Boston, Philadelphia, Cleveland, and Chicago Reserve Banks—and with no representatives drawn from the Federal Reserve Board itself. At the same time there was established a Federal Open Market Investment Account, operated by the New York Reserve Bank under the committee's supervision. The governor of the New York Reserve Bank was the dominant influence over this account, though from a legal standpoint the actions of the committee as a whole were subject to the approval of the Federal Reserve Board and the individual concurrence or participation of each of the other Reserve Banks. A further alteration in the composition of the committee—though not in its operational principles—was made in March 1930. The name of the committee was changed to the Open Market Policy Conference. Though its membership had been expanded to include all twelve governors of the Reserve banks, the execution of policy decisions was entrusted to a five-man body formed of the bank governors who comprised the previous Open Market Investment Committee.

All this, to repeat, had no basis in law, nor would it acquire that legal status until Congress passed the Banking Act of 1933—better known as the Glass-Steagall bill. Even so, as will soon be shown, the new legislation left untouched the dominant power of the governors of the Federal Reserve Banks in the strange set-up for conducting open market operations.

THE GREAT CRASH

Any adequate treatment of the Great Crash in the fall of 1929, followed by the onset of the Great Depression, would have to take into account the foreign as well as the domestic causes for the event. The foreign causes included, for example, the consequences of the Versailles Conference decisions regarding German reparations on which the repayment of allied debts to the United States depended. Included also were the way American private banks financed German reparations payments, the way German banks used American bank loans to finance speculative ventures, the collapse of major German and Austrian banks,[21] and the rush of Europeans to withdraw gold from the United States—causing the New York Federal Reserve Bank's percentage of the nation's gold reserve to fall below the legal limit.

Equally complex domestic causes helped trigger the crash and the depression. To take an arbitrary starting point, the high levels of employment and economic activity in the United States in the last half of the 1920s were sustained by a 50 percent increase of private debts outside the banking system, representing loans made possible by the large growth of savings by corporations and private individuals in the upper income groups. The funds involved in this exceptional expansion of private debt outside the banking system—at high interest rates—went into mortgage debt on housing, office and hotel construction, consumer debts, broker's loans, and foreign debts.

Meanwhile, on a nationwide basis between June 1927 and September 1929, Federal Reserve data for 141 index cities[22] showed that bank debits increased from $53.6 billion to $82.4 billion; bank loans increased from $37.4 billion to $90 billion; while loans to stockbrokers on securities increased from $3.5 billion to $8 billion—a fact reflected in the doubling of common stock prices. These figures, when viewed alongside today's debt structure for an economy with a gross national product in excess of $2 trillion, seem small. But they reveal their full magnitude when viewed in the context of the 1927–29 economy whose gross national product was roughly $90 billion. The combined stimulant to spending from these two causes—the sharp expansion of both private debts and bank loans—could only be short-lived. If current income from the national product had been spread more evenly—if there had been less savings by business and the rich and more income in the lower groups—the economy would have been more stable. If, for example, the $6 billion that corporations and wealthy individuals had loaned for stock market speculation had been distributed to the public in the form of lower prices and higher wages, the economic collapse that began at the end of 1929 might have been checked by a safety net short of the back-breaking abyss.

When credit was no longer available, debtors were forced to curtail their consumption in order to apply the margin saved to the reduction of outstanding debts. Prices then fell with the reduction of demand, leading, in turn, to increased unemployment, further decreases in consumption, more unemployment, a further drop in prices. Earnings were wiped out, forcing rigid economies in the wages, salaries, and work hours of those who *were* employed. By the time the bottom of the abyss was hit, one-third of the entire population was unemployed, and the national product was slashed by 50 percent. Still, at the bottom of the abyss, the aggregate debt burden when measured not in dollars but in current values and income, representing the ability to pay, was greater than ever before. Fixed charges, such as taxes, railroads and other utility rates, insurance and interest charges, clung so close to the 1929 level and required such a portion of the national income to meet them, that the amount left over for the consumption of goods was not sufficient to support the population.

On the canvas of the national picture just drawn in broad strokes, two specific developments in banking merit attention right here. Both were long in the making before they came to a head in the late 1920s. Both were to have a decisive effect on aspects of New Deal banking legislation—and from there, on the shape of banking in the decades that followed, as well as on the struggle to reshape the laws for its governance. Of the two specific developments, one saw the erosion of the line between commercial and investment banking. The other saw the payments of interest by money center banks on major kinds of deposits which produced a new version of the "pyramiding of reserves."

THE MOVEMENT AWAY FROM THE REAL BILLS DOCTRINE

American bankers, like their English counterparts, long professed their devotion to the commercial banking real bills doctrine—which held that the main role of commercial banks was to make short-term, self-liquidating loans for the purpose of financing industry and trade. The underlying assumptions of that doctrine—that an adherence to short-term, self-liquidating loans would result in just enough money and credit to support the "needs of trade"—sounded in a provision of the 1913 Federal Reserve Act that the credits which Federal Reserve Banks extended to commercial banks must be secured by "eligible paper."

Still, at an early hour in the development of American banking, there was a disconnection between what American bankers actually did and the catechism about the real bills doctrine they piously repeated. That is, long before the Great Depression finally consigned the doctrine to the trashbin crammed with economic theories, the demand for credit in a swiftly developing nation produced marked departures from the orthodox tenets. The enormous needs for new fixed investments could not be met solely by imports of European capital. In the absence of other American financial institutions that could close the gap between domestic demand and supply, American commercial banks were early called upon to provide a significant portion of the long-term credits business demanded. Yet a narrow interpretation of the National Bank Act of 1863, as made by the Comptroller of the Currency, prohibited national banks from underwriting or dealing in the securities of entities except those of the federal government.

With this limitation on their powers in the investment field, national banks were placed at a marked disadvantage in competition with state commercial banks, trust companies, and private banks in servicing large corporate clients. By the end of the nineteenth century, state commercial banks and state trust companies—not being subject to what was just said about the comptroller's ruling—were firmly established in the investment banking field. At the same time, however, a corner of that field was opened up to commercial banks by a series of judicial decisions. That is, courts began to interpret the National Bank Act in ways that allowed national banks to *invest* in state, municipal, and corporate bonds.

The start of the twentieth century saw Comptrollers of the Currency engaged in strained attempts to make the law and public policy square with the raw surge of the newly emergent industrial regime—while banks, in response to that same surge, tried to escape the existing grip of the comptrollers. In 1900, for example, the comptroller permitted national banks to underwrite and deal in municipal and corporate bonds to the extent that they were entitled to invest in them. But with a 1902 ruling by the comptroller, national banks were prohibited from underwriting and distributing corporate equities. To circumvent the restriction, national banks followed the lead taken in 1903 by the First National Bank of Chicago. They organized state-chartered affiliates for the conduct of their security activities. They were all the more inclined to do this after the end of the First World War, following the growth of a national market in which people of even modest means invested in corporate securities, and when the corporations themselves—being flush with funds due to a swift growth in their earnings—began to cut back on their short-term borrowings from banks.

Commercial bankers who had survived the plague that carried off thousands of banks between 1919 and 1921, and many hundreds in the recession year of 1924, were brought face-to-face with a sticky question. The institutions they managed experienced a rapid growth in their deposits. But how could these funds be put to profitable use under conditions in which the market for short-term commercial loans had shrunk? To compensate for the loss of their traditional short-term lending business, many bankers did either or both of two things on the basis of their growing deposits. In one direction, they increased their loans to business with maturities of more than one year. In another direction (subject to regulatory constraints), they increased their purchases of corporate, utility, and municipal bonds, and hesitantly pressed a little deeper into the dark continent of consumer and mortgage lending. All the while, however, the commercial loan proportion of total bank loans declined from 71 percent in 1923 to 54 percent in 1929. The proportion of total bank earnings due to commercial loans declined from over 50 percent in 1923 to 39 percent by 1929, while the commercial banks' share of total credits in the national economy steadily eroded.

Many commercial bankers now set out to reverse the downward trend by expanding their securities activities either directly or through their securities affiliates. Moreover, the preexisting legal barriers standing in their way were substantially reduced in 1924 by a ruling of the Comptroller of the Currency favorable to the purposes of the commercial bankers. After that, the barriers were entirely removed by provisions of the 1927 McFadden Act which explicitly authorized national banks to underwrite investment securities. In consequence, by 1929 commercial banks and their affiliates were underwriting over half of the new security issues reaching the market. They appeared to have made the transition from narrowly focused short-term business lenders in the true bill tradition to general financial institutions.

Still—

At a time when a significant segment of the public failed to see the difference between investments and speculations, but cared only for "get rich quick" prospects, a number of major commercial banks grossly abused their newly granted legal right to underwrite offerings of securities. As long as "profits" were readily harvested, few beneficiaries were found—or heard—who decried the tainted basis of the harvest. Later, however, the previously obscured ways some major commercial banks abused their underwriting privileges were laid bare on the stage of congressional investigations extending over the post-Crash years of 1931–33. The angry call for revenge that now rose on all sides led to restrictive laws that shackled saints and sinners alike among commercial banks. Of this, more later.

EFFECTS OF INTEREST PAYMENTS ON DEMAND DEPOSITS

A cause-and-effect relationship developed between interest payments on demand deposits, and the perils that went with the pyramiding of reserves.

The root of the matter dated from the hour when a provision of the Federal Reserve Act of 1913 altered a provision of the National Bank Act as amended in 1864. Because the latter Act set the same reserve requirements on time and savings deposits as on demand deposits, national banks did not actively compete for the first named class of deposits. The picture changed, however, when the Federal Reserve Act of 1913 reduced the required reserve on time and savings deposits below the required level for demand deposits. National banks now competed vigorously for time deposits even though the shift away from demand deposits increased bank interest costs.

Two benefits seen by commercial bankers at the helm of such national banks offset the higher interest costs. First, in recession or depression contexts, time deposits were more stable than demand deposits—a factor of no small importance to commercial bankers in planning their loan policies. Second, in a period of strong credit demands, the lower effective reserve requirements on time and savings deposits meant an enlarged base for credit expansion. A set of figures, placed side by side, reveal through the force of contrast, the extent of the actual shift from demand to time and savings deposits. In 1899, deposits in the latter categories amounted to only 18 percent of all bank deposits. By 1929—or three decades later—they comprised 44 percent of the total.

Not all bankers welcomed this line of development. Many—and especially country bankers—loudly complained about three particular aspects of the case. The first was that the more bank interest costs were increased by the brisk competition for time and savings deposits, the more their own institutions were caught in a tightening profits squeeze. Further, in direct consequence of that squeeze, and in order to offset the rising costs of "excessive rate competition," they were forced against their will to add to their portfolios more risky high-yield assets. Second, because the large and profitable city banks could outbid the small country banks in the competition for time deposits, what they absorbed to themselves reduced the basis on which the country banks could make the loans their local customers needed. Third, the large and profitable city banks could exploit their competitive advantages over country banks because, in the nature of the case, they alone had the effective means to pay interest on certain kinds of demand deposits.

The city banks paid interest on the demand deposits owned by other banks, on the bank balances of large corporations, on the balances of non-bank financial institutions, and on those of wealthy individuals. They also paid interest on the demand deposits of governmental units, subject to state law requirements. But among all these, what excited the greatest controversy was the interest paid on interbank deposits. Critics who zeroed in on that practice argued that even under "sedate" conditions, the flow of funds from country banks to larger interior banks, and from there to the major money center banks, entailed a pyramiding of reserves that made the nation's banking system vulnerable to periodic liquidity crises. Divorced from all else, this was bad enough. As things stood, however, the pyramiding of reserves enabled the major money center banks to increase their extensions of call money credits to speculators on the stock exchanges.

This line of criticism came to be shared by Federal Reserve authorities in the early days of 1929, when the continued rise in speculative fevers threatened to break all known economic thermometers. In a first attempt to block the means by which major money center banks converted interbank deposits into call money loans, Federal Reserve authorities tried to promote clearinghouse agreements entailing a reduction in the interest rates paid on interbank deposits.[23] Moves made in this direction, however, led to a countervailing reaction on the part of interior banks. Interior banks, when faced by the loss of interest on interbank deposits, took more of the raw funds involved for use in making their own direct loans in the securities market.

When this became apparent, Federal Reserve authorities, in a new tactic, tried to curb the speculative purchases of securities by interior banks—this, by trying to get New York banks to reduce their own security loans to the interior banks and to raise their own agency fees. This, too, was soon doomed to failure.

Something *did* survive the attempt. It was the memory of how interest payments on demand deposits had promoted stock market speculation. Just as there would be a backlash against commercial bank abuses related to security underwriting, the backlash against interest payments on interbank deposits would lead to restrictions on all commercial banks—those innocent of any previous abuse as well as those who were guilty as charged. What was remembered in the hour of reckoning is sketched in what follows below.

THE SOUTH SEA BUBBLE: 1929 VERSION[24]

In yet another attempt to check the speculative fevers, the Federal Reserve Board on March 26, 1929, announced that Federal Reserve Banks would no longer grant credits to member banks that directly or indirectly financed speculations. Coupled with the announcement was an earnest plea addressed to all banks to reduce their loans where the collateral entailed speculative securities. Nine days later, Treasury Secretary Andrew W. Mellon issued a press statement which was intended as a warning, but the language used had the ring of a shrewd money-making suggestion—soon fated to be the object of derisive laughter. "The present situation in the financial market," Mellon said, "offers an opportunity for the prudent investor to buy bonds. Bonds are low in price compared to stocks." He added that he fully agreed with the Federal Reserve Board's move to restrict credits for speculative purposes.[25] The next day, March 16, Governor Roy A. Young publicly appealed to the nation's bankers for voluntary cooperation with the Board's move.

By March 27, partly as a consequence of the foregoing, interest rates on market loans for speculative securities rose to a high of 20 percent per annum. But at the very moment when it appeared that this would put a brake on speculators, the National City Bank of New York, on the initiative of its chairman, Charles E. Mitchell, suddenly offered large credits to the stock market.

Senator Carter Glass bitterly attacked Mitchell for "slapping the Reserve Board in the face and treating their policies with contempt and contumely." Other national figures echoed Glass's sentiments. Just as many, however, resented the Federal Reserve Board's efforts to check any increases in stock market credit. The resentful, moreover, were not limited to the magnates among the bankers and brokers on Wall Street. The Board's efforts were also anathematized by Chairman Louis T. McFadden of the House Banking and Currency Committee, by other congressional hierarchs, and by influential newspaper publishers.

On April 3, 1929, the Federal Reserve Board returned to the contest with a new announcement. Unless banks supported a program of voluntary restriction of credit for speculation, the Board would "adopt other methods to influence the situation." When the statement seemed to fall through a crack in the floor, the New York Federal Reserve Bank broadcast its own proposal to check speculation. It publicly recommended that the discount rate on commercial loans be raised to 6 percent—a very high figure for the day. The echo of the recommendation still hung in the air when it was publicly rejected by Governor Young. The Federal Reserve Board, he said, would not approve such action—an action that would "penalize legitimate business in the act of getting at speculators." He again called on banks voluntarily to cease supplying speculative credit—and thus spare the whole country the penalties that would follow if the discount rate were actually increased to 6 percent.

To judge from the nonresponse, "voluntarism" had been dropped from the national dictionary. In early June, President Herbert Hoover tried to put his own cooling hand to the forehead of the speculative fever. He instructed the Justice Department to mount a drive to prevent bucket shops and tipsters from using the mails to stimulate speculation.[26] The drive, focused in New York City, closed down fifty such establishments. When the body count was conveyed to the White House, President Hoover voiced the hope that the exposure of the bucket shops to public scrutiny would awaken the public to the hazards of speculation. By mid-June, that hope proved as futile as a project to make a crab walk straight. Domestic and foreign sources, attracted by high prevailing rates, rushed forward with money for the call loan market, leading to a new surge of speculation. In August, the Federal Reserve Board, though still reluctant to penalize legitimate business, raised the discount rate to 6 percent as the only remaining way to bring things under control.

Stock speculation, meanwhile, was worldwide, and European central banks which had long helped fuel the activity concluded that they could no longer do so. In parallel actions, they ordered a sharp rise in European discount rates. The result was a September collapse of stock prices in eight or nine European countries—and for extra measure, in South America and Australia as well. It fell to the London stock market, which ranked second only to New York in world importance, to close the lid on the financial coffin. And so it did when the spectacular failure of a leading speculator brought all transactions on the London exchange to a full stop.

On the American side of the Atlantic, a few days of "weakness" in early October 1929 led to a panic fall of stock market prices on October 23 and again on October 26 and 29. Alternating declines and partial recoveries followed until November 13. "Wall Street may sell stock," chirped the *Saturday Evening Post*, "but Main Street is buying goods." Others grinned with the billboards which announced (as if in a retrospective on an event in the dimming past): "Wasn't the depression terrible?"

If the man on Main Street thought all would be well again once the wave of panic selling was checked, his amateur opinion was shared by the certified "experts" comprising the nation's business and intellectual leadership— Professor Irving Fisher, the noted monetary authority on the faculty of Yale; Charles E. Mitchell of the National City Bank of New York; Thomas W. Lamont of J. P. Morgan and Company; Stuart Chase, the popularizer of economic ideas; Alfred P. Sloan, president of General Motors; William Butterworth, president of the United States Chamber of Commerce; William Green, president of the American Federation of Labor; the editors of the *New York Times*. All these and more like them predicted that once the "lunatic fringe" was shaken out of the market, stock prices would resume their steady upward climb, and industrial conditions would again stabilize on their fundamentally sound basis.[27]

Yet within thirty days after the major break in late October 1929, the value of listed securities shrank by $30 billion. Within two and one-half months of the break, broker loans made mostly to individual speculators were sliced from almost $8 billion to $3.5 billion. Those who owed this money were necessarily forced to reduce their bank deposits or borrow elsewhere. Bank debits to individual accounts in 141 index cities decreased in three months from $95 billion to $60 billion, though loans did not decrease. At the same time, the stock market crash created panic conditions in the market for farm products. In the October weeks of the crash, wheat, for example, fell 17¢ per bushel and cotton, $7.50 per bale. Farmers who had not sold all their products were heavily in debt for the loans they had contracted to sustain the agricultural cycle. A sudden drop in prices along with the calling of loans forced vast quantities of commodities onto the market through liquidation to pay the loans, thus forcing prices down even further.

Yet these details were merely the shadows cast in advance of other events on the move. Bonds and mortgages could no longer find enough subscribers. Prospects for new construction began to evaporate. The employment index of the Department of Labor showed a 12 percent decrease from 98.3 percent in mid-October, to 86 percent ten weeks later. Factories cut back on production, and the ranks of the unemployed were swelled further. Purchasing power went into hiding. Business enterprises caught with inventories for which there were no effective buyers were driven to the wall. Mortgages on homes and farms were headed in the direction of foreclosures because the people involved lacked the means to keep up their payments.

As the days became weeks, and the weeks months, more business bankruptcy cases clogged court calendars, more hunger riots flared in the cities, more bread lines grew long, more robberies filled police blotters, more proposals for recovery sounded on all sides. No plan for redemption was too futile or absurd to be given consideration by the same men who in prosperity took every offer of advice as a personal insult, but in adversity sought counsel from every source.

8. The Bank Holiday: The Invisible Scar

Concerning President Hoover

When the Great Crash was followed by the Great Depression, President Hoover apparently believed that the responsibilities of the central government, *as* government, were in no way different in degree or in kind from those of other agencies in the nation at large—state and local governments, businesses, banks, trade associations, and individual entrepreneurs. The central government could only help prod and coordinate what *other* hands did in connection with national and local relief programs.

President Hoover's approach to the Great Depression perhaps becomes more understandable, as Professor Herbert Stein has argued,[28] when viewed in the light of the relatively small size of the federal budget in the 1920s. Total federal expenditures were then but a fraction of the gross national product; the percentage of federal purchases of goods and services was an even smaller fraction of the total national purchase, and the federal percentage of total national construction was microscopic. The federal government was not then a machine that constantly generated new programs or expanded old ones—a machine that lent itself to emergency increases of expenditures merely by advancing the date when plans already in the governmental fiscal pipeline would take effect. Only a major change on the revenue or the expenditure side of small budgets could make a significant dent in the national economy. So it was not unnatural for President Hoover to conclude that he could achieve the best results not by trying to manipulate federal government expenditures, but by trying to stimulate the expenditures of state and local governments and of private firms.

Meanwhile, on the eve of the very hour when Europe's financial structure collapsed, Eugene Meyer was appointed by President Hoover to succeed Roy Young as governor of the Federal Reserve Board. Meyer's credentials as a public servant, and, previously, as a far-seeing investment banker on Wall Street, marked him as a man of outsized abilities. He had watched with mounting alarm the course of the speculation rampant on Wall Street, though his warnings of the storm ahead were seldom heeded by the persons to whom they were addressed. He also was increasingly alarmed by the way in which the Versailles structure of debts and reparations spread its rot outward from Central Europe to France and England, to the growing peril of the American financial institutions that were financing the spread. He was convinced that no cures—such as the Young Plan or a "standstill" moratorium on debts and reparations—could stop the rot.

Meyer dwelt on that point during his first meeting with President Hoover following his appointment as governor of the Federal Reserve Board, and capped his remarks with an urgent suggestion. It was that Hoover call an international conference where he would offer a drastic cut in Allied war debts to the United States, in return for which, the governments owing those debts would agree to drastic cuts in the reparations they demanded from Germany. Hoover compressed his dour reaction to the suggestion into a single sentence: "There's been a lot of propaganda about debts and reparations, and I'm not listening to it."

The interview came to an end on that somber note, and a shaken Meyer returned to the Treasury Department building where the Federal Reserve Board was then quartered. He called the board members to a special meeting, related what had transpired at the White House, and gave his appraisal of what was in prospect. Records of the meeting quote him as saying: "The Board will soon find itself fighting a rear-guard action in a general retreat. The most we can hope for is that the retreat will be orderly."[29] The hope was but a dream that soon became a nightmare.

THE CHANGED PATTERN OF BANK FAILURES

Total net bank failures between 1930 and 1933 included 773 national banks with deposits of $721 million and 3,604 state banks with total deposits of $2.03 billion. Many failed when sound loans became uncollectable amid the general economic collapse. Still others failed because regulatory agencies mindlessly administered narrow rules for liquidity and eligible paper, and thus withheld from hard-pressed but solvent commercial banks extension of credit from Federal Reserve banks. At the same time, masses of unemployed depositors used up their savings in a struggle to survive. Vast numbers of bankruptcies forced bankers to write off their loan losses, and soon exhausted their reserves. Legislation and regulations prohibiting branch banking prevented small institutions from pooling their resources for their more efficient use. Bankers, on their part, tried to strengthen their defensive position—only to worsen their common lot. They pulled in outstanding loans, hesitated to grant new loans, and began to shift an ever-larger proportion of their resources to more stable government bonds and securities. There were also many searing instances where the weak felled the strong—where banks that might have survived the general economic collapse were fatally stricken when their depositors caught the contagion of panic from runs that closed nearby weak banks.

Each casualty had elements unique to itself, but the 1930–33 failures differed fundamentally from those in the 1920s. They were not confined to scrub oak institutions scattered in remote places. In the dimensions of the day, they included some of the largest redwood trees of the banking business nationally. Two of these, the New York–based Bank of the United States, and the Philadelphia-based Bankers Trust Company, collapsed within days of each other in December 1930.

The Bank of the United States was a privately owned state bank, with 400,000 depositors, but, in the popular imagination, it was wrongly thought to be a financial instrument of the United States government. With its failure, the wild impression was broadcast that the credit of the United States government collapsed with it. Moreover, its $200 million in deposits exceeded the combined deposits of the 484 banks that failed nationally in the fiscal year ending June 30, 1928—and again exceeded the combined deposits of the 551 banks that failed nationally in the next fiscal year ending June 30, 1929. As for the Bankers Trust Company of Philadelphia, its deposits of $450 million were more than twice those of the Bank of the United States. Taking the two banks in combination, their $650 million deposits in all were greater than the combined deposits of the 1,035 banks that failed in the two fiscal years preceding June 30, 1929.

Two years later, the moribund state of the automobile industry precipitated the failure of two Detroit-based bank holding companies—Guardian Detroit Group and Detroit Bankers Company. Their importance in the context of Michigan's banking structure can be sensed from a single statistic. On the eve of their collapse, the two in combination controlled more than 55 percent of all state bank resources in the state, and over 80 percent of all national bank resources.

It was not until early 1932 that efforts were made to stabilize or revive the banking system through the intervention of governmental measures. In some instances, the results comprised the margin of survival. In others, the results were calamitous. The first of the measures, passed by Congress and signed by President Hoover in January 1932, saw the creation of the Reconstruction Finance Corporation (RFC) under the chairmanship of Charles Dawes, who had returned to the Continental Bank in Chicago upon the expiration of his term of office as Vice President of the United States under President Calvin Coolidge.[30] The enabling legislation for the RFC gave it the authority to make loans to banks and other financial institutions as well as to railroads. It could also aid in the liquidation of banks and buy the stock of a reorganized bank. In support of these purposes, the authorized borrowing power of the RFC was initially set at $1.5 billion.

A second governmental measure designed to help banks was known as the Glass-Steagall bill of 1932. As enacted on February 27 of that year, the measure empowered Federal Reserve banks to loan money to member banks that lacked eligible paper or securities. Member banks, subject to specified restrictions, could do their borrowing on the basis of their assets. The measure also allowed Federal Reserve banks to use the "obligations" of the United States government as collateral for Federal Reserve notes. The intended effect was to ease the previously rigid constraints of law on the capacity of the Federal Reserve banks to control the flow of credit, and enlarge the scope for their discretionary judgments in the matter. Then there was the Emergency Relief and Construction Act of July 21, 1932, which increased the RFC's borrowing powers from $1.5 billion to $3.3 billion. A portion of the enlarged funds was to be allocated to the states as loans for the support of local relief work to be secured by various forms of state obligations.

Some self-destructive features, however, were entwined with the positive aspects of these programs. On the positive side, for example, the RFC by midsummer of 1932, had sharply reduced the pace of bank failures. Its loans to more than 5,000 financial institutions approached the $1.3 billion mark, and it helped to liquidate or reorganize several hundred other banks. Yet in making its loans to faltering banks, the RFC demanded as collateral the best assets the banks possessed, leaving these banks as vulnerable as before to any worsening in the economic climate. The RFC viewed itself as a governmental counterpart to a commercial bank, whose outlay of loans were to be repaid. But the banks most in need of money were those least likely to be able to pay it back on the conventional terms for commercial banking.

The most deadly aspect of the picture was a provision of the Emergency Relief Act requiring the RFC to release to Congress the names of the banks to which they had loaned money. When the publication of these names began in August 1932, the inclusion of a bank's name on the list was construed as a sign of its weakness. Two results often followed. One was a run on the bank. The other was that banks in need of help from the RFC were fearful of borrowing from it even to the extent of $1. As if the picture as it stood were not grim enough, it became grimmer still in January 1933 because of the backstage craftsmanship of John Nance Garner, the Democratic Speaker of the House of Representatives and Vice President–elect. He was the driving force behind a House resolution requiring the Clerk of the House to make public all loans to banks the RFC had extended in the six months *prior* to August 1932.[31]

The Glass-Steagall Act, to return to it, should have helped stabilize imperilled banks through loans on ineligible assets. But the flow of Reserve Bank funds under the Act still encountered so many regulatory obstacles as to amount to little more than a faint trickle in the dry bed of a creek. In fact, it was not until 1935 that a frontal assault was successfully made on the whole concept of "eligibility" and "liquidity," and more rational criteria for Reserve Bank loans to member banks were adopted.

THE BANK HOLIDAY

Though the events leading to the final collapse of the banking system were long in coming, the climactic episodes date from Thursday morning, March 2, 1933, when George L. Harrison, in New York, sent a jarring message to

Eugene Meyer and to Secretary of the Treasury Ogden Mills.[32] The foreign and domestic drain of gold, he said, had reduced the New York Federal Reserve Bank's percentage of the gold reserve below the legal limit. Hence he would "no longer take the responsibility" for running the New York Federal Reserve Bank "with deficient reserves in the absence of legal sanctions provided for by the Federal Reserve Act." When the Federal Reserve Board, joined by Secretary of the Treasury Mills, replied that it was reluctantly ordering a thirty-day suspension of the legal gold reserve requirements set by law, Harrison countered with a message that the suspension would solve nothing. The New York Federal Reserve would still have to pay out gold and currency to hoarders. The best course, he said, would be to declare a national bank holiday, which "would permit the country to calm down and allow time for the enactment of remedial legislation."

The initiative in declaring such a holiday could only come from President Hoover, but by now he had retreated into his own grief and was not accessible to Mills and Meyer. The pair, on being blocked at the door of the White House, returned to Harrison with a suggestion that he ask Herbert Lehman—who had succeeded President-elèct Franklin D. Roosevelt as governor of New York—to declare a bank holiday in that state. Harrison rejected the suggestion, saying that even if Lehman agreed to the request, the New York Federal Reserve Bank would still have to pay out gold to foreigners. Besides, to halt all banking operations in New York, the nation's financial center, would make it impossible for the banking system to function in the rest of the United States.

Another set of actors now added their voices to the confusion. Representatives of the Clearing House Banks of New York called on Governor Lehman to voice their strong opposition to a bank holiday. Such a holiday, they said, "would hurt their prestige." They "would rather stay open and take their beating."

Meanwhile, the directors of the New York Federal Reserve Bank adopted a resolution requesting the Federal Reserve Board in Washington to urge President Hoover to proclaim a nationwide bank holiday on Saturday, March 4. Governor Meyer at the Washington end of things replied that he needed no such "galvanic needle" from New York. On behalf of the Board, he had desperately tried from one hour to the next to reach President Hoover for that very purpose, but to no avail. So now, in the final steps of the dance macabre, Harrison joined the New York state Superintendent of Banks and representatives of the New York Clearing House Banks in a conference at Governor Lehman's home in New York City. Here he reversed his earlier opposition to a state bank holiday and declared his support for such a move. The Clearing House representatives, for their part, agreed to cooperate if Lehman declared a bank holiday in New York, but they wanted "the record to show" that they neither sought nor directly requested the action. Lehman declared the holiday effective March 4. Similar actions were taken by the governors of Illinois, Massachusetts, New Jersey, and Pennsylvania. On March 4 the Federal Reserve Banks remained closed, to complete the most absolute shutdown of banking facilities in the nation's history.

In Washington, many persons in the inaugural day crowd who had gathered to pay homage to the new leader—and to be the first in line for whatever jobs were available—found that they could not cash checks to pay for food, hotel bills or transportation home. Two days later, on March 6, when President Roosevelt proclaimed a national bank holiday, his action amounted to an *ex post facto* ratification of the bank holiday that was already in effect everywhere through forty-eight state proclamations.

III

THE CONTINENTAL DIVIDE OF TIME

9. The Legacy of the New Deal

PROCRUSTEAN BED

The same generation that was directly hit by the collapse of the nation's banking system was also the one that framed the legislative controls designed to forestall any similar event in the future. The legislative controls themselves, framed mainly in the first two years of the New Deal, continued with but two significant additions—the Bank Holding Company Act of 1956, and the 1970 Amendments to the same act—to be *the* organic legislation in the banking field until an historic new measure became law in April 1980. In the interval, the *political* history of American banking since the mid-1950s was in large part written by the clash between two camps. One was comprised of forces that would seal in perpetuity the special benefits they derived from the letter of the laws enacted between 1933 and 1935. The other was comprised of forces for whom those laws had become a Procrustean bed which they must escape in order to meet the challenges of new events on the move.

STOP-GAP MEASURES

The Emergency Banking Act of 1933, though drafted in great haste for a short-run purpose, and approved on March 14, provided a sensible procedure for dealing with all the banks closed by the holiday.

Under the procedure, all banks were divided into three classes. Class A banks—and they comprised 50 percent of the nation's banks—were institutions that were solvent and not endangered. They could immediately reopen upon being licensed to do so by the Federal Reserve Board, by the Comptroller of the Currency, or by state officials if they were nonmember banks. Banks grouped in Class B—and they comprised 45 percent of those closed by the holiday—were deemed to be endangered, weakened, or insolvent. But they contained potentially salvageable material; after an interval needed for their reorganization, they could be and were reopened subject to the approval of the newly formed Federal Deposit Insurance Corporation. Class C banks—or the remaining 5 percent of the total—were insolvent and would stay closed. They would be liquidated with an eye toward returning some portion of the depositors' money. A parallel attempt would be made to salvage something from the many thousands of banks that had failed in the months prior to the collapse of the banking system as a whole.

While the Emergency Banking Act of 1933 brought the banking system out of shock, it was not meant to get at the causes of the banking disaster in order to prevent such disasters in future years. The latter objectives comprised the heart of the Banking Act of 1933—again popularly known as the Glass-Steagall bill—which became law on June 6.

The terms of the new Glass-Steagall bill provided for major and minor changes in the governing structure for American banking. As such, they drew on the findings of successive congressional investigations of the banking system held in the years between the Crash of 1929 and the intense liquidity crisis of 1933. Of these investigations, the one conducted by Ferdinand Pecora, counsel for the Senate Banking and Currency Committee, focused on the securities activities of banks and their affiliates in the 1920s. What the Pecora investigation unmasked sent shock waves rippling across the nation, and the anger that went with the shock was no transient thing. It will be seen in a moment that it accounted for the restrictive features that were incorporated into the Banking Act of 1933. First, though, a word about other features of the legislation.

OPEN MARKET OPERATIONS

The Banking Act of 1933 for the first time gave express legal recognition to the conduct of open market operations. Under the renamed Federal Open Market Committee, these operations were to be conducted by a committee comprised of the twelve governors of the regional Federal Reserve Banks, designated annually by their respective boards of directors. The twelve were to meet periodically in Washington to perform the functions authorized by law.

The new law, however, did not touch the fundamental weakness that marked the previous history of open market operations. While no Reserve bank could engage in open market sales or purchases unless it conformed to Federal Reserve Board regulations, the 1933 Act preserved its right to *refuse* to participate in the sales and purchases the Open Market Committee recommended. The arrangement made for administrative chaos. The Federal Reserve Board, which was ultimately held responsible for policy, could not initiate open market operations; it could only ratify or veto the policies initiated by the Open Market Committee. The committee could initiate policy but could not execute it. The boards of directors of the individual Reserve banks, who took no part in forming policy, had the power to obstruct it. With over one hundred individuals responsible in varying degrees for the conduct of open market policy, a more effective way to fragment responsibility and to encourage inertia and indecision could scarcely be devised.[1]

FDIC

By creating the Federal Deposit Insurance Corporation, the Banking Act of 1933 designed its most durable achievement. The underlying concept was not by itself something new under the sun of American banking. As related earlier, the prototype for a bank deposit insurance scheme dated from the New York Safety Fund, established by the New York state legislature in 1829. Moreover, from the 1880s onward, approximately 150 different versions of a bank deposit scheme were introduced into Congress, only to die in a pigeon hole.

A feature in the original FDIC legislation, however, pointed to the possibility that a last chapter would be written to the long and tortured history of the dual banking system. By the terms of the original legislation, national banks, being automatically members of the Federal Reserve System, were covered by FDIC insurance, as were state-chartered member banks. Nonmember state banks, however, were granted FDIC coverage on condition that they join the Federal Reserve System within an indicated period. If they failed to join within the time set, the FDIC insurance provisionally granted them would be withdrawn. It seemed that the carrot and stick arrangement would bring all state-chartered banks into the Federal Reserve System, the more so because the number of nonmember state banks that failed during the depths of the Great Depression were more than three times greater than the number of national banks that failed.

As noted previously, there were three extensions of the grace period, but at the end of the third, an amendment to the FDIC eliminated entirely the threat of a denial of FDIC coverage that hung over the head of nonmember banks. It was argued that if the coverage granted were withdrawn, the effect could trigger runs on the banks involved. The immediate effect of the amendment itself was to give a new lease on life to the dual banking system. In the long run, however, a judgment made by Milton Friedman and Anna Schwartz in their monumental work, *A Monetary History of the United States*, commands assent. It is that the FDIC has contributed far more to the stability of the American banking system than has the Federal Reserve.

THE DIVORCE BETWEEN COMMERCIAL AND INVESTMENT BANKING

Though the Pecora investigation's disclosures about the abuses of banks and their affiliates in the securities field stirred public wrath, none of the abuses were strictly illegal. At least none led to criminal indictments and convictions of the involved bank officials. In football terms, the conduct of these officials amounted to "broken field running" through loopholes in existing laws. The consequences, however, were far from being small. They adversely affected banks and their affiliates in any one or all of several ways.[2]

These included "very prevalent" borrowing by the affiliate from the bank; security sales by an affiliate to its bank or other affiliates under repurchase agreements, or their purchase by the affiliate from the bank in the same manner; the purchase of securities by its bank to relieve the affiliate of excess holdings; more liberal lending by the bank to customers on issues sponsored by the securities affiliate in order to support their distribution; retailing securities, including maintaining corps of salesmen and branches in states other than that in which the affiliated bank operated; functioning as assets realization companies to take over from affiliated banks doubtful or nonliquid assets; providing a medium for supporting the stock of affiliated banks.

Further, they included injury to the goodwill of the bank if depositors suffered substantial losses on securities purchased from the bank; undesirable wide fluctuations in the price of the affiliate's bank stock through purchases and sales of the stock by the securities affiliate; unwise commitments made by the banks in the knowledge that in case of need the commitments could be shifted to affiliates and thus removed from the bank's condition statement; the reciprocal tendency of securities affiliates to expect the parent banks to back them when they assumed commitments less cautiously than would private investment bankers; and the way the responsibilities of fiduciary activities were compromised by banks with both a trust department and a trust company.

All such details which were part of the story of major banks that failed served to amplify the insistent call for a separation of commercial from investment banking. The result was the separation mandated by various sections of the Banking Act of 1933 applicable to national banks or to state banks, and by other sections which outlawed bank security affiliates.

While the Banking Act of 1933 seemed unequivocally to restrict the securities activities of banks, the separation of banks from securities markets was not absolute. Bankers were expressly permitted to buy and sell securities, including equities, at the order of customers for their accounts. They were also allowed to purchase some types of debt securities for their own portfolios and to underwrite Treasury issues and general obligation bonds of state and local governments—meaning bonds secured by regular tax revenues. The bill did not explicitly mention the authority of banks to serve as advisors to investment companies or other institutional investors. Nor did it prevent banks and trust departments, as fiduciaries or agents, from managing the assets of individuals or corporations, including the purchase and sale of both debt and equity securities.

In the three decades following the enactment of the 1933 banking legislation, Congress made some fifteen specific amendments to its ban on the security underwriting activities of commercial banks. To gain the benefits of commercial bank marketing, participation, or competition, Congress, for example, made commercial banks specifically eligible to underwrite bonds for government agencies such as Tennessee Valley Authority (TVA), the Washington Metro System, the World Bank, and the Export Import Bank. Also, in the Housing Act of 1968, Congress made commercial banks eligible to underwrite and deal in housing, university, and dormitory revenue bonds.

It remains to be added that in the same three decades after the banking crisis of the thirties, commercial bankers neither chafed under the existing legal restrictions on their securities activities, nor had a compelling motive to challenge them. During the New Deal years, for example, the market for new securities was nearly moribund. During the Second World War, wartime regulations restricted the scope of the securities market as a whole. In the years after the end of World War II, government securities in the portfolios of banks—amounting to 50 percent of the total holdings in some cases—enabled banks to profit from a swift and broad expansion of their loan activities in all directions. But by the start of the 1960s, the picture changed. The new scramble for funds to meet a continued surge in loan demands, an intensified competition among banks and between banks and nonbank financial institutions for sources of profits, and a somewhat more relaxed regulatory environment provided a motive where some banks were ready to test the 1933 legal limitations on their securities activities.

TWIN BIRTHS: NO INTEREST ON DEMAND DEPOSITS AND REGULATION Q

Though the severe and long depression following the 1929 collapse was due to many interacting domestic and foreign factors, survivors often singled out interest rate competition for deposits as a major contributing cause of the financial debacle. The authors of the 1933 Glass-Steagall bill shared that view, and wrote their convictions into Section 11 of the bill which flatly prohibited the payment of interest on demand deposits: "No bank shall directly or indirectly by any device whatsoever pay any interest rate on any deposit which is payable on demand." The Act also laid the basis for the formulation by the Federal Reserve Board of Regulation Q, under which the Board established interest rate ceilings member banks could pay on time and savings deposits. Its legal authority to do this was made even more explicit two years later in a provision of the Banking Act of 1935 which read:

The Board of Governors of the Federal Reserve System shall from time to time limit by regulation the rate of interest which may be paid by member banks on time and savings deposits, and shall prescribe different rates for such payments on time and savings deposits having different maturities or subject to different conditions by reason of different locations, or according to the varying discount rates of member banks in several Federal Reserve districts.

The ban on interest payments by commercial banks on demand deposits ruffled few feathers during the post-1933 years of the Great Depression when bankers began to swim in excess reserves but with only a limited loan demand on which they could earn any kind of interest. Nor were many feathers ruffled during the war and immediate postwar years when bankers had no difficulty meeting their loan demand on the basis of their reserve picture.

It was only at the start of the 1960s that a factor mentioned a moment ago—an intensified scramble for funds by all financial institutions—coupled with new cash management techniques by major corporations, broke the long calm of commercial bankers. They now began to agitate for the right to pay interest on demand deposits as a magnet that would pull back to their banks the corporate funds that had been withdrawn from them. As the contest over that right—to grant or withhold it—grew in intensity, savings and loan associations strongly resisted any concession to commercial bankers that would strengthen their competitive bid for loanable funds.

As for Regulation Q, the initial rates the Federal Reserve Board established in 1933 did not press with any severity on the rates member banks were actually paying on time and savings deposits. Even when a Regulation Q reduction in the permissible rates was made for the first time in 1935, few member banks were forced to reduce what they were actually paying. To the contrary, many did not even take advantage of the maximum levels permitted under the new regulation. The same bland condition prevailed during the first two decades of the regulation—during the depression years, because the loan demand was so small while excess reserves were high, and in the immediate postwar years, because banks could finance a sharp increase in loans from the proceeds from the sales of U.S. government securities that had accumulated during the war and for five years after V-J Day under the Treasury's debt management policies. Even as late as 1950–56, when Regulation Q rate ceiling for savings deposits was 2.5 percent, the average rate paid by commercial banks on time and savings accounts ran from 0.9 of 1 percent in 1950 to 1.6 percent in 1956.

In that same period, the average rate paid by savings and loan associations on savings accounts was approximately 1.5 percent higher than the commercial bank rates—a fact that contributed to the dramatic growth in deposits at savings and loan associations relative to their growth at the commercial banks. Many commercial bankers remained disinterested in competing for savings deposits that were gravitating towards the savings and loan associations, for they continued as before *not* to pay rates at or near the regulatory margin. On the other hand, bankers who wished to compete for savings deposits bumped up against the Regulation Q ceiling, and the thud hurt. Their pained cry eventually found the Federal Reserve Board sympathetic. When the Board adjusted the ceiling upward, effective January 1, 1957, competition-minded bankers moved their rates up to the new Regulation Q height, and mounted strong promotional efforts to attract more time and savings deposits.[3]

With each upward adjustment in Regulation Q ceilings, there was also an upward adjustment in the rates the savings and loan associations could pay. Each time, also, the disparity was justified on the grounds of social policy. It was argued that the legal differential which gave the savings and loan associations a competitive advantage in attracting funds was fully warranted because the added funds went into more mortgages that enabled more people to acquire homes of their own. The whole of the argument here, however, was recast when its frame was engulfed by raging fires of inflation. The nature of the new case, and its consequences, will be treated in a later place.

GROUP BANKING: ESPECIALLY BANK HOLDING COMPANIES

Another provision of the Glass-Steagall bill authorized national banks to open branches—not at will, but on terms which at least eased the restraints on forms of group banking dating from the McFadden Act of 1927. In the hearings on the draft Glass-Steagall legislation, spokesmen for unit banks attacked branches, chains, or bank holding companies with arguments that varied little from those they used in 1924–27 leading up to the McFadden Act. What's more, even when the Glass-Steagall bill was law, unit bankers in control of the American Bankers Association (ABA) pushed through a resolution in 1934 calling for a legal ban on all forms of branch banking— and the resolution remained the official position of the ABA for the next nineteen years. It was not until 1953 that a determined group of strategically placed bankers—members of *both* the Reserve City Bankers Association and the ABA—led the successful drive which saw the ABA reverse the categorical anti-group-banking stand it had taken in 1934.[4]

Where the Glass-Steagall bill itself was concerned, the case *for* group banking was strengthened by statistical evidence bearing on the comparative mortality rates of group banks and unit banks during the depths of the depression.[5] The evidence presented at the hearings did not say that group banking was disaster proof. It did say that group banking had a greater power to resist the onslaughts of a drastic deflation than did unit banks. During the critical years 1930–31, for example, the rate of failure among ninety-seven different groups, embracing 578 banks in all, was two out of ten, while the rate of failure among all unit commercial banks was five out of ten. Further, group failures involved less than 15 percent of group bank resources, compared with more than 20 percent for all commercial banks.[6]

The most commonly cited reasons why the *possibilities* for survival were greater for group than for unit banking ran along the following lines. Group banking, in contrast to the unit bank, could provide more adequate credit facilities to any community, irrespective of the small capitalization of the local unit; could better handle fiduciary and other types of business not ordinarily handled in volume by small unit banks; could offer sounder credit and investment through diversification and more efficient analysis and investigation and less promotional interests; could staff the various units with better trained and more efficient personnel; could institute more uniform and efficient systems of records; could provide superior executive management, especially for the small units, through zone supervisors and head office reviews; and finally, could achieve operating economies through group purchasing, banker's blanket surety bonds, counsel, and various other services.

The extent to which these *possible* sources of strength for group banking became *real* sources varied from one case to the next. Taken in the aggregate, however, the many local contexts in which banking groups withstood the onslaughts of the depression, while nearby unit banks were shattered, pointed up a moral for the architects of the Glass-Steagall bill. The bill, as enacted, lifted the 1927 McFadden Act restriction which confined the branching of national banks to the city where the head office of the bank was located. Henceforth, national banks could establish and maintain branches anywhere in a state on terms coequal with those the states gave to their respective state banks. If state law, for example, permitted the branching of state banks throughout a state, national banks would have the same statewide branching right. If state law banned the branching of state banks, national banks would come under the same ban. A number of state legislatures, for their part, were presently influenced by the same factors that swayed Congress at voting time on the Glass-Steagall bill. The result was a doubling between 1933 and 1936 in the number of states where branch banking was permitted, the increase being from nine to eighteen states.[7]

Where bank holding companies in particular were concerned, Congress, through the Glass-Steagall bill, rejected a death sentence for such companies demanded by spokesmen for unit bankers. It embraced the view set forth in the report of the Senate Banking and Currency Committee which called for the *regulation* of bank holding companies by the Federal Reserve Board. "Such companies," so the report read, "have in some parts of the United States become well rooted, and the difficulty of eliminating or abolishing them in any effective way is similar to the difficulty of eliminating or abolishing the affiliates of city banks. It is, therefore, thought best to attempt the control or oversight of these companies."

The Banking Act of 1933 devised a simple method for bringing under federal supervision a bank holding company which included a member of the Federal Reserve System as a constituent bank. Holding companies subject to regulation had to register with the Federal Reserve, which, in turn, was empowered to grant or to withhold the permits the respective company needed to vote their stock in choosing directors of their affiliated banks. In taking its own stand, the Board was to consider the public interest at stake, the financial condition of the applicant, the general character of its management, and the likely effect the grant of a permit would have on the affairs of each subsidiary member bank. Once granted, the Board could still revoke a voting permit if any holding company affiliate violated any provision of the Banking Act of 1933.

The 1930s were a time of retrenchment for bank holding companies. Federal Reserve Board data indicated that while ninety-seven groups with 978 banks were in operation in 1931, only fifty-two groups with 479 banks were in operation five years later.[8] The most obvious reason for the shrinkage was the failure of bank holding companies in the trough of the depression. Other reasons were more subtle. For one thing, the use by bankers of the holding company device to outflank legal barriers to branching lost much of its motive force when the Banking Act of 1933 permitted national banks to establish branches to the extent that states permitted such rights to state-chartered banks—as increasing numbers of them did. For another thing, during the economically depressed years of the New Deal, the average investor's skepticism toward bank shares made the raising of capital both hard and costly.

Again, though the deposits and liquidity of major existing banks had by 1936 begun to *exceed* their 1929 levels,[9] the low earnings of most banks prevented the accumulation of funds through retained earnings for use by their managers in buying more banks for cash. An exchange of bank shares between sellers and buyers remained as an alternative to cash purchases, but prospective sellers took a dim view of any such exchanges following the 1929–33 catastrophe. Lastly, bankers themselves hesitated to form any bank holding company under conditions where storm signals fluttered in the political air—as in 1935 when Congress passed the Public Utility Holding Company Act, and again two years later when President Roosevelt called for the elimination of *all* holding companies.

The provisions of the Act concerning bank holding companies remained for more than two decades the fundamental law in the governance of these banking entities. The provisions would, however, also be the subject of protracted controversies for the length of those decades. Successive bills would be introduced into Congress; successive initiatives would be taken by governmental regulatory agencies; and successive administrative hearings would be held within the agencies with variable objectives in view—to change the fundamental law, to attack the proposed changes, and to defend them. So it went from one season to the next until the whole of the controversies was provisionally resolved by the Bank Holding Company Act of 1956.

10.   More about the Shape
of Things to Come

PREVISIONS

Besides the Banking Act of 1933, the early New Deal years saw the enactment of other organic measures that profoundly affected the conduct of banking in the emergent future.[10] Of these added measures, two in particular merit notice right here. One was the National Housing Act of 1934, which revolutionized the field of home mortgage financing and, at the same time, set in place the makings of a competitive advantage favorable to savings and loan associations as against commercial banks. The other—with its focus on central banking—was the Banking Act of 1935, which provided the Federal Reserve Board in Washington with some of the effective means it actually needed to control Federal Reserve policy, and particularly the conduct of open market operations. These in turn were followed by the problems of "excess reserves" caused by an influx from Europe of "hot money," the nature of the 1937 recession amid the depression, and the early decisions regarding the financing of the rearmament effort which set in place the machinery for an engine of inflation.

THE NATIONAL HOUSING ACT OF 1934

When a commercial banker today scans the contents of his bank portfolio, he is likely to find—more often than not—that federally insured home mortgages comprise a substantial portion of his bank's assets. If he is also old enough to have experienced at first hand the commotion raised by commercial bankers over the National Housing Act of 1934, he is likely to be embarrassed by his memory of the event. And with good reason.[11] For commercial bankers, and especially those with close ties to major insurance companies, were nakedly hostile to a measure which in subsequent decades provided them with very profitable credit instruments. What's more, their initial hostility worked in its own way to compel the political managers of the housing measure to give the savings and loan associations the loan insurance scheme they wanted—and with consequences that eventually led commercial bankers to crowd the mourners' bench.

At an early hour in White House discussions about how to revive the economy, attention was focused on a housing program as a means to the end in view. Almost a third of the unemployed were in the building trades, and housing was the most important element in those trades. A program of new home construction launched on an adequate scale would not only provide employment for building trade workers, but would spur the forward movement of the economy as a whole.[12] In March 1934 after much discussion within the Administration, Marriner Eccles, who had but recently come to Washington as an assistant to Secretary of the Treasury Henry Morgenthau, led a conceptual breakthrough to the following effect. If idle privately held funds were to go to work, then the housing program being talked about must be private in nature, and financed by creditor institutions of the communities where individuals lived. Every kind of creditor agency with idle money on its hands should have a right to participate in the program.

The provisional consensus reached within the Administration in support of the key concept was expressed in the draft legislation for the National Housing Act of 1934. Title I of the Act, which provided for an insurance scheme for Federal Housing Administration (FHA) home improvement loans had fairly clear sailing in Congress. It was different in the case of Title II. Its new terms, applicable to small home construction for owner occupancy and to large-scale rental housing by corporations, amounted to a sweeping revolution in the traditional terms for mortgage loans that prevailed in virtually every state in the union. It offered an arrangement where a high percentage of the appraised value of a home could be covered by a single mortgage, coupled with a reduction in interest rates, and an extension of the maturity date so that mortgages could be amortized through fixed monthly payments in small and equal amounts.

It was recognized that private interests would never support the housing program on the radical new basis unless they could rely on some sort of government protection against loss. The nature of the guarantee that was wanted was expressed in the FHA's celebrated insurance principle.[13] In its original form, the FHA would insure mortgages up to 80 percent of the appraised value of a new home and lot whose total appraised value was not more than $16,000 on a single family unit. Interest rates would not exceed 5 percent, plus an insurance fee of 1 percent, making a total of 6 percent on the unpaid balance of the mortgage. The insurance fee would go into a fund for use in taking up defaulted mortgages if a lender foreclosed on the property and delivered title to the FHA. If the fund, plus the proceeds from the resale of foreclosed properties, was not enough to cover the costs of all defaulted mortgages, then the FHA would issue 2.5 percent bonds to the lender, guaranteed by the government and payable three years after the mortgage matured. The insurance fund would be privately created. The government would merely guarantee that losses would be made up through the use of public credit. The same terms applied to large-scale rental by corporations as to small home construction for owner occupancy, except that the builder had to secure FHA approval for his rental schedules and dividend payments.

Upon the public unveiling of the draft bill, executives of large commercial banks made common cause with executives of large insurance companies in mounting a bitter attack on Title II.[14] Some were animated by an honest conviction that the commercial banking system should not be encouraged to engage in any kind of long-term mortgage financing. Others were animated by a different kind of conviction. In their view, the depression would soon end, permitting a return to the old mortgage practices of the past—even though those practices had been fatal to the creditor agencies themselves, had ruined debtors, and had dried up opportunities for building and for the employment of construction workers.

Within the administration, the strongest attack on Title II was mounted by John Fahey, Chairman of the Home Loan Bank Board, the "roof" governmental agency of the federal savings and loan associations. Fahey insisted that the draft housing measure must provide savings and loan associations with an insurance scheme comparable to the FDIC for commercial banks. Banks insured by the FDIC, he said, could get public savings funds at very low rates of interest and could lend them profitably on the contemplated FHA mortgages. In the absence of a comparable insurance scheme, savings and loan associations would have to pay high rates of interest for savings and, hence, would be forced to lend their funds at rates higher than those permitted by the draft FHA Act. This would unfairly throw the mortgage business to banks.

Meanwhile, outside the administration, Building and Loan League lobbyists and their Congressional allies appeared to have enough political strength to scuttle the FHA measure as a whole unless their loan associations got the government-created insurance program they wanted. President Roosevelt could do political sums. At his express direction, a Title IV was added to the FHA, creating the Federal Savings and Loan Insurance Corporation (FSLIC) under the Home Loan Bank Board. A member association belonging to the FSLIC was to pay an annual premium, originally set at one-quarter of 1 percent of share accounts and creditor liabilities. In return the FSLIC was to insure all share accounts up to $10,000 in the event of default of the organization and proclamation of such default by a competent authority.

The premiums the savings and loan associations paid into the FSLIC were subsequently reduced from the initial one-quarter of a percent to one-eighth and then to one-twelfth of a percent. Managers of the associations could thus offer a higher return on savings than commercial banks with what seemed to be equal safety. Slowly throughout the remaining years of the depression, but at an accelerating rate after the Second World War, they could invest in mortgage loans virtually all the savings entrusted to them by nonmembers as well as by members of an association. They were not subject to the constraints of the Federal Reserve Board which applied directly to member banks, and they also benefitted from federal tax laws which placed but a light burden on their profits. They must be credited with an immense contribution to the cause of individual home ownership[15]—from one decade to the next until the end of the 1970s when the fundamental picture was changed by the impact of a raging inflation, and many savings and loan associations found themselves in a painful bind.

One more aspect of the original FHA measure remains to be touched on here. Title III of the FHA legislation authorized the creation of national mortgage associations which could buy up mortgages, large and small, and issue bonds against them in denominations that could be purchased by investors anywhere. It was hoped that through such national associations, fluidity could be given to the whole of the mortgage market, and investment funds could move across state lines from areas where they were in excess to those where they were in short supply. No financial group in a position to do so, however, undertook to organize any such association. Executives of large banks and of insurance companies probably reasoned that if they did not buy up any FHA insured mortgages, the whole of the housing program would fall through. Then when the depression "automatically ended," there would be a return to former customary conditions of high mortgage rates and short maturity dates.

The congealed inertia in the matter shown by private sources did not, however, govern the outcome. To help the housing program get off the ground despite the intense opposition to it, the RFC organized a Federal National Mortgage Association as provided for in the FHA law. Now known as "Fannymay," after the initials FNMA, it promptly provided a market for the insured FHA mortgage loans. Smaller banks of the day, particularly in the Intermountain and Far West, had pioneered the actual making of FHA loans, while the major initiative in the matter was taken by the California-based Bank of America. In time, executives of large financial institutions elsewhere belatedly awoke to the fact that their intransigent opposition to the whole of the mortgage scheme was pointless—that the FHA loan was in fact a desirable and profitable investment, though by the end of the 1970s the forces of inflation drove the fixed FHA mortgage onto the hooks of a complex lending problem.

THE BANKING ACT OF 1935

Patchwork amendments had been made to the Federal Reserve Act of 1913 in the two decades following the actual creation of the Federal Reserve System. But the Banking Act of 1935—at least in the draft form given it by Marriner Eccles, the newly appointed Chairman of the Federal Reserve Board—ventured a fundamental change in the structure and center of power within the system. The long and fierce battle over the Act ran concurrently with legislative contests over two other significant measures—the Social Security Act and the National Labor Relations Act. These measures had such direct and immediate personal implications for most Americans that most were aware of their importance. The Banking Act of 1935, however, dealt with seemingly impersonal and "technical" matters of but small interest to the public at large. It required a tutored observer to grasp the extent to which the terms of the Act could have a pervasive and critical effect on the everyday life of the American economy.

Walter Lippmann was one of these. He commented at the time that "in the whole long list of bills before the Congress, the one that has by far the greatest possibility for good or evil, the one that may affect most powerfully the economic and political fortunes of the whole nation, is the banking bill. . . . Compared with this bill, every other bill before the Congress is relatively unimportant." H. Parker Willis, a Columbia University professor, who had been a technical advisor to Carter Glass in the drafting of the original Federal Reserve Act, agreed, but saw only evil in the bill. He called it "the worst and most dangerous measure that has made its appearance for a long time—perhaps at any time in American history."

The Banking Bill of 1935, as enacted, conceded many things to the opponents of the bill in draft form—not the least of whom was Senator Carter Glass. Yet despite the many concessions that were made, the measure marked a major advance in the direction of authentic central banking. Among important but secondary points of detail, the bill gave legal expression to the fact that the governor of the Reserve bank was in fact *the* chief executive officer. Henceforth, though these officers would be appointed by the board of directors of each Federal Reserve Bank, the appointment would be subject to the approval of the board of governors of the Federal Reserve System. Second, under the old law, the Federal Reserve Board could increase or decrease the reserve balances of member banks during a declared emergency only if five members of the board and the president of the United States approved. Under the new law, the board, by an affirmative vote of four members, and without the prior declaration of an emergency or the approval of the president, could change requirements for both demand and time deposits of member banks within specified limits set by law.

Another significant change involved the old question of "liquidity" and "eligibility," in connection with paper that could be discounted in connection with Reserve Bank loans to member banks. As previously noted, under the original Federal Reserve Act, the discount privilege was restricted to short-term commercial loans and government securities. Reliance on that kind of liquidity had not protected the banking system from the disaster of 1930–33. On the contrary, it contributed to the disaster. If a single bank wished to protect itself against good loans going bad in a depression, its portfolio would have to consist of super-liquid, open market paper. It could then pay off all its deposits at a moment's notice—even though the national income was cut in half. But it could not adequately perform its duty to serve the community as a middleman-investor of a substantial portion of the community savings.

Even as late as October 1934, when the total paper eligible for rediscounting privileges within the meaning of the 1913 Federal Reserve Act came to little more than $2 billion annually, the total was substantially reduced by the exacting hand of the "eligibility" provisos that were still in force. Banks could not live on the interest from so small a volume of loans, and any attempt to do so would obviously sharply curtail the scope of banking. The more credits bankers refused—and their decisions would be influenced by the extent to which their loans were eligible for discount as well as the rediscount rate—the more a dominant role in the credit field would go by default to other agencies, including the government. It would not be until the recession of 1937–38 that attention was fully shifted away from liquidity and centered on "sound assets," but the Banking Act of 1935 took an important step in that direction. It granted permanent authority to any Federal Reserve Bank, under the regulation of the board of governors of the Federal Reserve System, to make advances on any "satisfactory assets," as well as on eligible paper, to any member bank. Restated, it bestowed liquidity on all satisfactory assets, making them an eligible basis for borrowing at the reserve banks in time of need. In this way, bankers were encouraged to concentrate their efforts on keeping these assets satisfactory and sound, and to pay less attention to the calendar date when a note was to mature.

But the key provision of the Banking Act of 1935, and the one that was most fiercely contested, involved the structure of the Federal Open Market Committee. The old committee, comprised of twelve governors of the Reserve Banks, was replaced by a new-style federal open market committee comprised of the seven members of the Federal Reserve Board plus five annually chosen representatives of the twelve Federal Reserve Banks. Meetings of the Open Market Committee were to be held in Washington at least four times a year at the request either of the chairman of the board of governors or of any three committee members. Further, the law for the first time required the Open Market Committee to maintain an accurate record of its transactions, to record the votes cast on every open market policy question, with the Federal Reserve Board submitting to Congress annually a full report of all such decisions. Above all—and this was the heart of the matter—the new law established the principle that open market operations would henceforth be established in Washington by a responsible public body, and not by one centered in New York and responsible to no one in particular. The actual arrangement here fell far short of the ideal, yet it would have been impossible to provide any kind of coherent management for the financing of the Second World War if it were not for the changes previously instituted by the Banking Act of 1935.

EXCESS RESERVES

Throughout the New Deal years the growth of excess reserves in banks, with no outlet for profitable loans to private enterprise, made the cost of money very cheap. Yet this fact did not mute the cry rising from Main Street bankers who, because of their numbers, generally control the offices of the

American Bankers Association and shape its public stand on banking policies.[16] Though investments in government securities were among the few profitable outlets for the idle funds in their banks, some elected officials of the ABA called for an embargo on the purchase of government securities issued in connection with the deficit financing program.

In their view, Federal Reserve banks used the money of *private* banks when they bought government securities, hence it was only right that the executives of private banks should have some say about how and where that money was invested. It somehow escaped their notice that Reserve banks did not in fact use existing money to buy government securities. They created new money for the purpose, thereby increasing the reserves and the reserve funds of private member banks—just as the latter lost deposits and reserve funds when Reserve banks sold securities. Nonetheless, many Main Street unit bankers continued to assail the New Deal's spending program on the ground—contrary to fact—that it was promoting the conditions for a "dangerous consumer price inflation like the one preceding the 1929 crash." They seemed not to remember that the consumer price index had been declining throughout the 1920s.

Polemics to one side, a development of the time was a valid object of concern to the Federal Reserve Board, Federal Reserve Banks, the Treasury, and to reflective bankers at the head of major institutions—S. Parker Gilbert of Morgan Guarantee is an example—who were not addicted to bombast and bluster. Specifically, starting in late 1935, the excess volume of bank reserves already on hand was being swelled by a heavy influx of gold to America, due in part to the Treasury's gold-buying price, and in part, to Europe's unstable political and economic conditions. It was feared that this influx could become the basis of a potential expansion of bank credit of such proportions that the Federal Reserve would lose all control or influence over the supply and costs of money. Opinions were divided, however, over what should be done to reduce the excess reserves. Some people within the Reserve System, within the Treasury, and in banking circles advocated selling a portion of the Federal Reserve holdings of government securities. Others advocated an increase in the reserve requirements of member banks.

When the issue landed on the agenda of the Federal Open Market Committee on December 17–18, 1935, no immediate decision was reached. Follow-up studies by the Federal Reserve Board indicated a wide geographic distribution of excess reserves among banks. Even if reserve requirements were increased by as much as 50 percent, the remaining excess in most banks would still be beyond the needs of business and would provide more than an adequate basis for legitimate credit expansion. On the other hand, the longer action was delayed, the more interest rates would drop under the pressure of the excess reserves. More banks would then try to overcome that decline by increasing the volume of loans and investments. It would thus be more difficult to deal with any inflationary consequences that might develop—since any later order for a substantial increase in required reserves would lead to painful liquidation of holdings. Timing was central to any decision made in line with the Board's studies.

Banking opinion remained divided on what should be done, with an apparent preponderance being opposed to any increase in the required bank reserve. On the other hand, it was expected that the adherents to the neo-greenbacker views, popularized by Father Coughlin and Congressman Lempke, would attack any increase in the required bank reserves as being "restrictive," "deflationary," and typical of the "money changers" with their "passion for higher interest rates." Nonetheless, with President Roosevelt's backstage assent, the Federal Reserve Board on July 15 ordered a 50 percent increase in the reserve requirements of member banks, effective August 15, 1936. The $1.79 billion in excess reserves that was actually siphoned off merely eliminated what was superfluous to the needs of the economy. Reserves were still so large and well spaced that executives of all but a few member banks met the August 15 order either by using their balances with the Reserve banks or by drawing on their excess balances with correspondent banks.

This, however, was far from being the end of the matter. As the months went by, the problem of excess reserves grew more acute. By November 1936, total bank deposits and currency—the most liquid resources at the disposal of the public—exceeded their 1929 level. Concurrently, because of mounting war threats in Europe, increasing numbers of Europeans liquidated investments in their own countries, bought dollars, and invested them in American stocks and bonds. As the gold equivalent of these dollar purchases flowed into the United States, the Treasury, after taking possession of the gold, deposited the equivalent in gold certificates in the Federal Reserve System. These foreign funds—"hot money" in Roosevelt's phrase—continued inexorably to swell the already high level of excess reserves.

The existence of the excess did not by itself lead to a more active use of the existing money supply. But it was estimated that if the excess were used as fully as in the past, it would form the basis for an expansion of $15 to $20 billion in deposits. Even if reserve requirements were increased to the full amount permitted by law, the remaining excess would still form the basis for a potential credit expansion of more than $7 billion without further action by the Federal Reserve Banks. It was against this background that several decisions were made whose effects—or lack of effects—on the recession of 1937–38 remain to the present day a subject of debate among professional economists and economic historians.

Once again, the Treasury and Reserve System were both concerned over a potential runaway expansion of credit because of the unchecked growth of excess reserves. But once again, opinions within and between both institutions were divided on how to meet the danger. Proposals agreed to one day became unstuck the next, only to be revived and modified a day later. So it went until early December 1936, when the Treasury staff hit upon a relatively simple plan to divorce the management of the domestic monetary system from the effects consequent upon the settlement of international balances of payments.[17] The staff proposed that as the Treasury's Stabilization Fund accumulated gold by converting foreign exchange to bullion, it would use dollars to buy gold from the fund, but would not follow the usual procedure of depositing counterpart gold certificates with the Federal Reserve Banks. The gold instead would be segregated or "sterilized" in a special account in the Treasury's General Fund, and this would prevent the incoming gold from entering bank reserves and expanding the credit base. It was agreed that this was better than the alternative policy of continually increasing reserve requirements—a "practice that would drive member banks out of the Federal Reserve System." The sterilized "gold would be available for export to countries which, in time of war, would sequester the American securities owned by their nationals, sell them on the American market, and take home the gold thus obtained."

Though the sterilization policy was put into effect at the end of 1936, the fears of a runaway expansion of bank credit continued to be fed by the ceaseless influx of gold from Europe and the consequent increase in excess reserves. At the meeting of the Federal Open Market Committee on January 26, 1937, the Reserve Bank presidents on the committee agreed that the money market, as judged by the low level of short-term interest rates in relation to long-term rates, was "abnormally and dangerously easy." Later in the day, when the discussions within the committee spilled over into a separate meeting held by the Board of Governors, the Board decided to order a 33⅓ percent increase in the required reserve. Secretary of the Treasury Morgenthau now complained that the decision would leave less than $600 million in excess reserve. When it was observed in reply that the amount would still be more than the Reserve System had had in predepression years, Secretary Morgenthau and his advisors feared that the contemplated increase would increase the costs of Treasury financing by making money tighter. A compromise resolved this clash of views. On January 30, 1937, the Board publicly announced a 33⅓ percent increase in the required reserve, but added that the increase would be made in two steps. One-half of the increase, or 16⅔ percent, would take effect on March 1, and the remaining half would take effect on May 1.

At no time after the second increase in reserve requirements went into effect on May 1, 1937, were the Reserve System's excess reserves less than $500 million over and above legal requirements—a figure, to repeat, that exceeded the size of the excess reserves that sustained the boom of the twenties. The final increase in reserve requirements, however, coincided with the peak in the economic expansion which had been underway since 1933, and which was followed by a contraction. On this account, it would be claimed that the recession of 1937–38 was primarily due to the cumulative effects of the August 1936 increase in reserve requirements and the increase of March 1 and May 1, 1937.

THE RECESSION OF 1937–38

The claim just alluded to was stressed, for example, by Milton Friedman and Anna Jacobson Schwartz in their influential book, *A Monetary History of the United States, 1867–1960*. They contended that the 1937–38 recession and the severity of the decline were largely due to the indicated increase in reserve requirements. According to their calculations, the result was a decrease in the stock of the money supply, tightened money rates, and a slowdown in the flow of credit to the economy.

Economists who took a different tack contended that the downturn in production did not develop until three months after the final increase in reserve requirements went into effect—while private credit did not begin to contract until the end of 1937, or sometime after the recession was underway. In short, the private contraction of credit was an *effect* of the recession, and not a *cause* of it.

The fuller case made by the Federal Reserve Board itself regarding the causes for the recession, emphasized *fiscal* instead of *monetary* factors—as revealed in the contrasts drawn between the years 1936 and 1937. Briefly, when the government in 1936 was expending substantial funds on the recovery program, private business was also increasing its activity, and a soldier's bonus of $1.7 billion was paid. This increased the 1936 cash deficit of the Treasury to more than $4 billion, or the government's net contribution (after taxes) to consumer disposable income. Meanwhile, the heavy influx of gold from Europe, the increased demands for American raw materials by European powers that were rearming, war fears, and disturbed labor conditions at home combined to trigger a major inventory boom. There was a desire in all quarters to convert money into things in the belief that costs of goods were going to rise higher. Many business interests feared they would have difficulty in getting deliveries, so they placed orders not only for current but for future needs. This spurred a further rise in prices, and the speculation in inventories grew to over $4 billion in 1937.

While this was taking place in the business world, the government in 1937 was *reducing* consumer disposable income by almost $4 billion—in contrast to its 1936 increase by $4 billion. For one thing, the new Social Security law that went into effect in 1937 entailed the collection of $4 billion in social security taxes, no part of which was disbursed in benefits—though the tax pulled potential buying power out of the pockets of the very people most likely to spend the money if it had not been taxed away from them. Second, no soldier's bonus of $1.7 billion was paid in 1937 as it had been in the previous year. These combined factors resulted in a $66 million federal cash surplus for the first nine months of 1937 in contrast to the large deficit in 1936. Most significantly, *the consumer disposable income in 1937 contracted by an amount roughly equal to the inventory that had been accumulating.* In the absence of consumer purchasing power upon which the speculative growth of inventories had been based, the inventories were dumped on the market in a drastic deflation, and the conventional pattern of a recession was reenacted.

It was the 1937–38 recession that finally made a New Dealer out of President Roosevelt, in the sense that he no longer reluctantly accepted unbalanced budgets as a temporary expedient, but came to view planned government deficits as an instrument of economic policy.[18] The American financial world has never been the same since Roosevelt's conversion was set forth in the text of his 1939 budget message.

It was also against the background of the 1937–38 recession that a circle of graduate students in economics at Harvard, MIT, and Tufts worked on Professor Alvin Hansen of Harvard—one of the senior academic economists of the day—and converted him to their own newly received creed based on the 1936 publication of John Maynard Keynes's *The General Theory of Employment, Interest and Money.* The manifesto they jointly issued in support of Keynesian concepts presently made a grand tour of economics departments at American universities, to seal the imprint of Keynesian doctrine on the pages of "required textbooks."

MISPERCEPTIONS

In 1940 when the American rearmament program got underway in earnest, many young apostles of Keynesianism came to Washington as economists on the staff of defense agencies during the rearmament period, and, then, of wartime agencies. Some such as Walter S. Salant and Gerard Colm grasped fairly quickly the economic implications of the rising flood of spending for defense. It was that the problem now to be faced differed fundamentally from the one during the years of the Great Depression. It was not to reflate the economy by pumping out dollars to be used by dollar-short consumers in overcoming their underconsumption. Under emergent conditions where goods and not dollars would be in short supply—where too much money would in fact be chasing too few goods—the new problem was to control inflation by inducing consumer savings instead of spending, and by tax increases where the government would recapture the highest proportion of the income generated by its own defense expenditures. Other young Keynesians, however, were slow to grasp the existence of the new problem, perhaps because they continued to see things from the perspective of depression experiences, when doing too much hardly seemed possible and when the questions of how much to do and what instruments to use were not critical.

It would be wrong to imply that this second group of young economists exerted a decisive influence over the way the Treasury Department actually managed the financing of the defense and then the war effort. Many other forces—within the Department and in the world around it—had a strong hand in shaping the Treasury's program. The significance of the second group of young economists who came to Washington in 1940 is that they were destined in time to play a leading role in shaping a "public philosophy" as it concerned economic policy. Even President Richard Nixon would give voice to the existence of that public philosophy when he remarked, "We are all Keynesians now."

11.   The Legacy of the Economics of Armageddon

A HANDFUL OF STATISTICS

In March 1933 when Franklin D. Roosevelt was inaugurated as president, the United States public debt stood at $22 billion. The figure represented the unpaid costs of the First World War and the deficits accumulated by the Hoover Administration despite its efforts to balance the budget in the depths of the Great Depression. In the eight years and eight months between Inauguration Day 1933 and the eve of Pearl Harbor, the national debt rose from $22 billion to about $48 billion. But in one year of actual war, the public debt was increased by $50 billion, or a sum exceeding the total deficits the nation had incurred in the preceding twenty-five years. By V-J Day, war expenditures of approximately $389 billion left the nation with a public debt of $280 billion, or nearly six times what it was on the eve of Pearl Harbor.[19]

As of December 1941, the ratio of the entire debt of the nation stood at one-fourth public to three-fourths private. By the end of 1945, the ratio stood at two-thirds public and one-third private. There was a striking symmetry between the latter figure and those bearing on the way the war was financed. The Federal Reserve Board, joined by other elements in the Reserve System, repeatedly urged that the American war effort be financed, as in England and Canada, two-thirds by taxation and one-third by borrowing. The emphasis on taxation would reclaim for the government a substantial proportion of its expenditures on the war effort and, at the same time, reduce inflationary pressures. The Federal Reserve Board recognized the indispensable need for a "stable" government securities market in which the Treasury could conduct its extensive war financing. To this end, it came forward with certain technical procedures designed to insure the existence of such a market, but without paying the price of the abuses that went with a policy of a "pegged" market. The Reserve Board's proposals, however, fell on deaf ears. Policy makers in the Treasury managed the financial side of the war effort in ways which seemed to exclude any consideration save one—to insure the immediate dollars-and-cents success of their successive war-loan drives.[20] The practice of the matter generated inflationary pressures that could only be restrained by direct controls while the war was on, followed by a flash flood of inflationary rises in prices the moment direct controls were removed.

That potential was visible in some comparative statistics. During 1941–45, only 30 percent of bank deposits were loaned out. The remainder went into the purchase of government securities bearing an interest rate of 2.5 percent. At the same time, commercial banks paid only 1 percent on the first $5,000 of passbook savings, and reduced the rate to 0.5 percent on savings over $5,000. More to the immediate point, while in 1920 demand deposits in the banks were less than $25 billion, at the end of 1944 there were in excess of $100 billion. In 1920, corporations and individuals held less than $20 billion in government securities. At the end of 1944, they were in excess of $80 billion, with an added $48 billion held by banks. In 1920, the total liquid assets in the hands of individuals and businesses were approximately $45 billion. At the end of 1944, the total was approximately $200 billion. Yet the relatively small volume of liquid funds after the First World War led to one of the worst credit inflations in American history up to that time.

THE DAM BURSTS

As the war neared its end, there were marked differences of opinion regarding the economic challenges the nation would have to face with the coming of peace. Would the challenge be on the side of inflation or deflation? Some of the most talented young Keynesians—Paul Samuelson and Robert Nathan being among them—predicted that the immediate postwar years would be marked by a cataclysmic return to depression-time conditions of massive unemployment. They therefore urged that plans be prepared, according to the Keynesian prescription, for a massive spending program that would hold an otherwise drastic deflation in check. They somehow failed to construe the meaning of the steady rising curves of liquidity visible on Federal Reserve charts.

When the harness of wartime controls was removed at breakneck speed after V-J day, the extraordinary liquidity of the economy, coupled with an extraordinary demand-pull, made for a classical inflation where too much money chased too few goods and services. Everyone wanted everything that had not been within reach during the fifteen preceding years—ten of depression, and five of war. Except in the gray and black market, however, virtually everything was in short supply. The immediate result was a price inflation where many prices in the fifteen months between August 1945 and November 1946 exceeded the aggregate increase in the five years between 1940 and V-J day.

Meanwhile, the Federal Reserve's role in monetary policy remained a captive of the Treasury's approach to its vast postwar refunding operations—the same approach that governed the Treasury's management of wartime finance. The Federal Reserve, against its will and judgment, was compelled by the Treasury to support the market for government securities at pegged prices and low interest rates, though the effects expanded bank reserves, expanded bank credit—and led to price inflations as increased demands pressed on supply shortages. The Federal Reserve did not question the need to provide proper support for the Treasury's vast refunding operations in the security market. The problem it faced was how to provide that support without adding to excess bank reserves and the inflationary expansion of credit.

The solution it first proposed at the end of 1945 was subsequently revived from time to time. The solution contemplated a "special reserve" that would apply to all banks receiving demand and time deposits, insured and uninsured banks, member and nonmember banks of the Reserve alike. All banks covered by the proposed plan would be required (in addition to their regular reserves) to hold a special reserve consisting of United States obligations such as Treasury bills, certificates, and notes, or, at the option of the bank, cash or its equivalent. The power to impose and vary the special reserve requirement—subject to a maximum amount fixed by statute—would be vested in the Federal Open Market Committee and would be limited by law to a three-year period.

Members of the Federal Reserve Board believed that the plan would give the Reserve System a working tool to support government securities, and, at the same time, restrain credit. By partially separating government financing from private financing, the low rates on the former would not determine the rates on the latter. Restraint on private lending could be imposed by substantial increases in the discount rate of the Federal Reserve Banks. Nor would the plan deny income to the banks, as would be the case if further increases in reserve requirements were authorized. Banks would get some return on short-term securities which the Reserve System would lock up.

Some banking leaders opposed the special reserve on the ground that it was impractical, socialistic, drastic, or not strong enough to achieve its expressed objective.[21] Others considered the plan unnecessary. They claimed that banks themselves, as a matter of ordinary business prudence, had a vital interest in preventing excessive credit expansion. It was observed, in reply to the claim, that "ordinary prudence" had no real meaning as long as banks, with their excess reserves, could readily meet unlimited private credit demands which were vigorously sustained by the very inflation they contributed to. Nor could bankers refuse safe credit demands of individuals whose requests for loans, taken separately, were based on legitimate credit needs. The rub was, that in freely accommodating legitimate credit demands, the banking system expanded bank deposits and added to the money supply. Under prevailing conditions of continued shortages of labor and materials, an increase in the aggregate outstanding volume of credit extended to individuals or to business did not increase *total* production. It merely increased the demand for goods and services with inflationary consequences.

The Federal Reserve's case for the special reserve was coupled with its opposition to the tax reductions that had been made after the war, when the fight against inflation called for fiscal measures that would create large budgetary surpluses. In a statement made in the name of the Federal Reserve Board, Chairman Marriner Eccles observed that "the need for action on the monetary and credit front would be reduced to the extent that needed action was taken on the far more important front of fiscal policy." Where, he asked, were the "budget balancers" who decried government deficits during the drastic deflation and massive unemployment of the Great Depression? Why were they strangely silent when a balanced budget, to be attained by higher taxes on a booming economy, was imperative in the postwar years? How could deficits be justified when industrial production promised to surpass its wartime peak, and when employment was steadily rising—54 million jobs in 1945, 57 million in 1946, and 60 million in 1947?

In the fall of 1947 when President Harry S. Truman called a special session of Congress to deal with the acute inflationary pressures of the hour, it briefly appeared that he would advocate the proposal for a special reserve. At the last minute, however, Treasury Secretary John Snyder was instrumental in eliminating the proposal from the previously prepared draft message on inflation scheduled for submission to Congress. Subsequently, the inflationary picture went from bad to worse, and especially after America was drawn into the Korean war. In the six months between June 1950 and the start of 1951, the cost of living rose 7 percent, wholesale prices 17 percent, wholesale farm prices 22 percent, textile products 32 percent, and basic raw materials 50 percent.

These increases were not due to the arms program or to an excess of government spending over receipts. The volume of arms production was still relatively small, while the federal government's receipts exceeded expenditures by almost $2 billion. The price rise was mainly due to two interrelated factors, of which the first was the increased use of the *existing* excessive supply of money. Second, the existing supply was greatly expanded because the Federal Reserve was still being forced to support the government security market in line with the Treasury's cheap money policy. This entailed continued purchases by the System of government securities from nonbank as well as from bank investors, and the result was an abnormal and swift growth in bank credit. In the last half of 1950, the banking system expanded its loans and investments by 20 percent—almost $10 billion—while concurrently increasing by 8 percent the money supply in the form of deposits.

The cold statistics of a hot inflationary spiral dominated the domestic economic picture by the end of 1950. In January of 1951, the picture exploded in a bitter Treasury–Federal Reserve conflict when Secretary of the Treasury John Snyder—speaking against the background of a grim turn of events in the Korean conflict—unilaterally announced that the Federal Reserve would continue to support the existing pattern of rates for government securities. The Federal Reserve made no such commitment, not before the Snyder speech, nor afterward in an emergency meeting held in the White House with President Truman and members of the Federal Reserve Board. There followed a protracted uproar lasting until early March, and culminating in the celebrated "Accord" between the Treasury and the Federal Reserve—negotiated with the assistance of Senator Paul H. Douglas.

As an aspect of that Accord, the Federal reserve agreed to commit itself to support the pegged market for government securities up to the limit of $440 million dollars—and no more. The whole of the amount was spent in only three days. The Federal Reserve thus lived up to the terms of the Accord and cited the terms when the dismayed Treasury officials asked for continued support. The request was refused, and there was nothing more the Treasury could do about the matter. Henceforth, the Federal Reserve ceased to be a party to the system of pegged prices, with their inexorable inflationary consequences.

THE STATUS OF COMMERCIAL BANKING: 1945–53

The ceaseless re-funding of the public debt dictated the conscious control and management of money by government authorities. That was a fundamental fact of life for bankers and banking. In other respects as well, both were confronted by a new world. Previously, in the trough of the Great Depression, the main problem for commercial bankers was to convert frozen assets and imperilled investments into liquid funds. In the New Deal years, it was to find profitable outlets for idle funds. In the war years, it was to support war-loan drives, and to help finance productive enterprises contributory to the war effort.

After V-J day, despite the doubts and fears engendered by the advent of nuclear weapons and the onset of the Cold War, the years 1945–63 saw an immense surge upward in the American standard of living and in the expansion of its economic plant. The vast pools of liquid savings formed during the war could be tapped by consumers to buy things not previously within their means. To meet the effective demand, business enterprises borrowed funds to modernize plants, to replenish inventories, or to launch new ventures which capitalized on war-induced scientific and technological advances. Many business ventures owed their birth to the new mobility of the nation's population.

Other developments cut across these. Following the low birth rate during the depression and war, the years 1945–53 saw the peak of family formations with an associated "baby boom" and its economic effects—the need for more clothing, more food, more toys, more schools (starting with the primary grades), more teachers and teaching materials, and more home and real estate developments in the suburbs. Housing construction more than tripled, with proportionate increases in the output of durable consumer goods. The wartime spur to labor-saving devices meant more leisure time and the demands for more recreational facilities. A radical expansion in consumer credit was an immediate prospect. On top of all else, the domestic economy was stimulated directly or indirectly by conditions among other national economies. Directly, because American enterprises supplied food, raw material, and machine tools to foreign countries whose agriculture and industry had been enfeebled by six years of war. Indirectly, because until those countries could resume their exports on a major scale, the world markets they had traditionally served lay open to penetration by American-made products.

While all this was in motion, commercial bankers were, in a paradoxical sense, "actively passive." Their respective banks had ample reserves, a strong liquid position based on government securities acquired during wartime financing, and the environment was one in which low interest rates prevailed. When bankers, therefore, needed funds to meet increased loan demands, the need was met either through the deposit inflow, or by the redemption at support prices of some of the government securities held in their bank portfolios. Loans were made on the basis of funds in hand, and bankers rarely fished for more resources in streams lying beyond the familiar realm of demand deposits or the traditional boundaries for time and savings deposits. The banking accent of the day was on "assets management"— another name for the *funds using* side of a bank's balance sheet. "Liability management"—another name for an active *funds seeking* or *funds buying* side of that balance sheet—was not a predominant concern of bankers.

THE TURNING POINT

The general picture just sketched began to change after the early 1950s, and radically so in the 1960s. Bankers could no longer passively await the influx of deposits for conversion into loans and investments compatible with traditional standards of safety. Nor could they readily finance loan expansions as before, simply by drawing on their accumulations of liquid assets. The accumulations had been gradually consumed by the rising loan demand in the economy. At the same time, the concurrent rise in interest rates on government securities and the fall in their prices—following the Treasury–Federal Reserve Accord of March 1951—made bankers think twice before they would unload these securities to acquire more funds for more loans. Nor could they expect monetary authorities to supply all the reserves banks needed. To the contrary, bankers could never be certain when and how far Federal Reserve authorities would shift from a policy of monetary and credit expansion to one of restraint—or the other way around. A wrong judgment on this point could have awkward consequences for bank-loan policies.

On another front, the competition for time and savings deposits was no longer a contest where commercial banks were the rivals of other commercial banks. It was now a contest between commercial banks and newly invigorated financial intermediaries—pension funds, mutual investment funds, credit unions, and savings and loan associations. Between 1945 and 1960, for example, though commercial bank savings increased 116 percent, mutual funds channeling private savings into equities increased 661 percent. Pension funds, a form of involuntary savings, increased 826 percent. Credit unions, starting from a very modest base, increased 1,005 percent. And deposits in savings and loan associations—which had always led the mortgage field—increased 641 percent.

Still other events on the move between the mid-1950s and early 1960s accounted for practices, financial inventions, and institutional developments that would presently change the face of commercial banking. It was a period, for example, that saw a shift in the cash management practices of major corporations, a general decline in the importance to firms and households of the cash reserves they held in the form of bank demand deposits, and the advent of new money market instruments such as the negotiable certificate of deposit (CDs). It was also a period that saw the rise of the Eurodollar, the swift growth in the market for federal funds and repurchase agreements, and the exploratory application to banking of the revolution in computer technology.

All these concurrent events laid the basis for the development of what is now known as liability management—a judgmental art that puts the perceptions of a commercial banker to a supreme test. But what needs to be sketched right here concerns the political and legal responses to the new wave of bank mergers.

IV

THE CHANGING WORLD OF BANKING

12. The Bank Holding Company Act of 1956

A new wave of bank mergers began to roll over the American financial landscape starting in the early 1950s, for reasons stemming from the conditions sketched in the preceding chapter. As the merger movement gained momentum, government regulatory agencies, Congressmen, and private interests tried to curb it by rules, restrictive legislation, or by antitrust suits. Many bank holding company bills were introduced into the Senate and House, but all foundered on the rocks of old questions. Should any enacted legislation be only precautionary in nature? Were bank holding companies to be abolished outright, frozen, or merely controlled? How should bank holding companies be defined? Who should supervise the administration of any enacted legislation? What controls should be laid out for the guidance of state officials? What organizations should be exempt? It seemed impossible to reach a consensus on these matters among unit banks, bank holding companies, and federal and state supervisory authorities.

Meanwhile, mounting pressures for some kind of legislation, and the continued doubts about the specifics of any measure Congress might pass, spurred a "second generation" growth of bank holding companies unlike the process that had peaked in 1928–29. The second round entailed not the organization of new companies, but the acquisition of more banking affiliates by existing companies while they still had a chance to expand before Congress lowered the boom.

Between 1949 and 1956, fifteen bank holding company bills were introduced in Congress, but it was not until May 1956 that Congress finally approved and President Eisenhower signed what is now known as the Bank Holding Company Act of 1956.[1] The new law, unlike its aborted predecessors, was neither a freeze nor a death sentence. Its stated purpose used the word *control,* not *prohibit* or *prevent.* In other words, the way was clear for the expansion of bank holding companies subject to the regulatory provisions of the act. Among these, a bank holding company was defined as a corporation that controlled 25 percent or more of the voting shares of at least two banks, or otherwise controlled the election of a majority of the directors of the two banks. Excluded from the definition were hundreds of chains controlled by individuals or partnerships, corporations that controlled only a single bank, farm groups, labor unions, and the Coca Cola Company (by virtue of its tie-in with the Trust Company of Atlanta, Georgia).

In formulating standards for bank holding companies, the new law specified that such companies must confine their activities to banking and to closely related services. Existing companies were given two years—or until the spring of 1958, with the prospect for extensions—to divest themselves of ownership or control of enterprises not directly related either to banking, to management of banks, or to the extension of services to affiliated banks. Further, the law prohibited bank holding companies from acquiring more than 5 percent of the stock of a bank located outside the state of its principal operations, unless state law specifically authorized such acquisitions by an out-of-state company. While this curbed future interstate banking affiliations, twelve preexisting bank holding companies—including those that were foreign owned—were covered by a "grandfather clause" and were permitted to continue their operations in more than one state.

Congress designated the Federal Reserve Board as the federal agency to regulate bank holding companies, and all existing bank holding companies subject to the 1956 Act were required to register with it. New companies could not be formed without the Board's approval, and existing companies must have its approval before acquiring more than 5 percent of any nonaffiliated bank's voting shares. Finally, the Federal Reserve Board was to report to Congress on any problems it encountered in administering the new statute. It remains to be added that the results of periodic meetings held between the Board and a small advisory committee representing the nation's bank holding companies were subsequently reflected in the Board's annual reports. Though these continuously urged changes in the law, it was not until 1966 that Congress responded to the accumulation of the Board's suggestions over the previous decade.

FALLOUT

The effects of the 1956 legislation went beyond the divestiture by bank holding companies of their nonbank assets—and beyond the further fact that the Federal Reserve Board approved the formation of only a few new bank holding companies. For one thing, a number of existing companies changed their corporate structure to avoid being subject to the new law. This explains why, at the end of 1965, only fifty-three bank holding companies were registered with the Board—a figure that was virtually the same as the number that had registered with it in 1956.[2] In the intervening nine years, however, existing holding companies grew internally along four lines—in the number of banks they controlled, in the expansion of their banking offices, in the growth of their total deposits, and in their percentage of all U.S. commercial deposits.

For another thing, the fact that one-bank holding companies were exempt from the reach of the 1956 legislation amounted to a standing invitation where banking organizations used the device of a one-bank holding company to expand into new financial services not permitted them *as* commercial banks. The process worked like this. First the living bank became the cocoon out of which a one-bank holding company fluttered forth. The holding company then acquired control of the bank itself as one of its assets. After that, the holding company was free to seek new and profitable outlets for the investment of such funds as it could mobilize. It was not subject to direct supervision by any federal banking agency, and there appeared to be virtually no legal restrictions on the kind of affiliates it could acquire. This permissive arrangement was, from the start, the object of protests by bankers at the helm of multibank holding companies—who had been forced to divest themselves of the kind of nonbank assets and affiliates one-bank holding companies could acquire. It was not until 1968 that one-bank holding companies proliferated to an extent that the scope of their activities pierced the consciousness of Congress and evoked a legislative response to it.

THE COMMISSION ON MONEY AND CREDIT

Other developments affecting banking will be returned to in a moment. But for two reasons this seems to be an appropriate point to comment on the work of the Commission on Money and Credit, extending from the last years of the 1950s to the start of the 1960s. In the first place, the troubled birth of the Commission sheds light on the kind of sharp political infighting which often rages over the seemingly neutral question of how to structure a public inquiry into monetary and credit systems and policies. Second, when the Commission's findings, recommendations—and dissents—were presented in a published report, the results were promptly assailed by opinion-makers, condemned by many bankers, and ignored by the public at large. Yet when the Commission's report is revisited today, the text reads like a prophecy of much that was in store for American banking.

The genesis of the Commission was this.[3] As far back as 1950, a subcommittee of the Joint Committee on the Economic Report under the chairmanship of Senator Paul H. Douglas recommended a "thorough and complete study of the monetary and credit system and policies of the United States." The immediate response was silence. Five years later, or in December 1955, Allan Sproul, the president of the Federal Reserve Bank of New York, suggested a "renaissance in the study of money and banking in general and of central banking in particular." Again nothing happened. But the next spring, when Sproul was due to retire to private life, he returned to the point of his December remarks when he delivered a "valedictory address" at a meeting of the New Jersey Bankers Association. He called for "an inquiry into the whole intricate and complicated arrangement of financial institutions which has developed during the past forty years, and particularly during the latter half of the period."

We cannot [he said] afford much longer—or we can only afford it because we are rich—to go ahead not really knowing what to expect of our central banking system, of our commercial banking system, of our savings banks and building and loan associations, of our insurance companies and pension trusts, and of all the other bits and pieces we are using to try to keep our production facilities and credit facilities in balance. The task would be a difficult one. The rewards would be commensurate with the difficulties.

The impact Sproul's plea had on most bankers and businessmen seemed not to exceed the dent of a withered rose petal dropped into the Grand Canyon. His call, however, stirred much interest in academic and governmental circles—up to and including President Eisenhower. The president saw the need for the proposed reappraisal and followed through with a suggestion contained in his State of the Union message on January 10, 1957. It was that Congress authorize a "broad national inquiry into the nature, performance and adequacy of our financial system, both in terms of its direct service to the whole economy and in terms of its functions as the mechanism through which the monetary and credit policy takes effect."

The Senate and the House were Democratic, and the Democrats feared that if the president were free to appoint a commission he would choose men who shared his own political outlook. There were other complications. Some congressional leaders held that the proposed inquiry was by right a legislative prerogative. Others saw a chance to amass some political capital by conducting their own investigation. President Eisenhower's request was turned down by Congress, followed by a clash among congressional committees with each claiming an exclusive right to stage-manage the proposed inquiry.

Amid the commotion, Senator Harry Byrd had an announcement to make. The Senate Finance Committee, of which he was chairman, had unanimously agreed to assume responsibility for a complete study of the full range of matters bearing on the financial condition and financial institutions of the United States. It turned out, however, that the committee lacked a supporting technical staff competent to dredge up and give coherence to the material that was needed. What had been initially billed as "serious investigation" quickly degenerated into a political firefight with the weapons of rival economic theories. Little new information was developed, and Senator Byrd's investigation died an unlamented death in April 1958.

In the interval, White House spokesmen for President Eisenhower quietly voiced the hope that once the Senate Finance Committee had finished its work, an independent nonpolitical group would assume responsibility for the kind of inquiry that was needed. Perhaps by prearrangement, the Committee for Economic Development (CED) was poised to respond to the quiet voice. On November 21, 1957, the CED announced that it was forming a special committee of presidents of universities and major research organizations which would be responsible for choosing highly qualified and objective-minded members of a privately financed Commission on Money and Credit.

As originally conceived, the commission was to consist of nine to eighteen expert members, ranging in outlook from conservative to liberal. It would not, however, include organizational representatives who most likely would be bound to take doctrinaire positions. But the original plan was derailed when most of the invited conservatives accepted an offered place on the commission, while many of the invited liberals declined. To redress the imbalance, the selection committee issued a second round of invitations. The commission membership was now expanded to twenty-five. It also included individuals prominently identified with the institution of organized labor. It was explained that, unless professional labor representatives served on the commission, any report it eventually issued would simply be "thrown in the waste basket at the White House and in Congress."

This is not what Allan Sproul had in mind. He agreed that the collective wisdom of a large committee drawn "from all walks of life" could be helpful in such varied causes as "improving schools, raising money for cancer research, and fighting urban blight." But he did not see how such a committee could collectively produce an incisive report on the highly technical and emotionally divisive issues of monetary and credit policy. Sproul, who was to have been a commission member, severed his connection from the enterprise at an early hour.

In May of 1958, the CED announced the creation of the Commission on Money and Credit with Frazier B. Wilde, president of the Connecticut Life Insurance Company, as chairman. The costs of the three-year study—$1.2 million—were covered by grants from the Ford and Merrill foundations. Professors with impeccable academic credentials were chosen to direct the research, and these in turn mobilized 110 more professors who eventually supplied the commission members with 11,000 pages of research paper.

The commission's own job was not to try to make intellectual history with magisterial pronouncements on matters lying in the realm of theoretical economics. Its job was to make wise choices among existing and conflicting views, and to convert the choices into practical proposals about how monetary and fiscal policies would help attain the goals of national economic policy. This would have been difficult even for a small group of "disinterested" experts. It was all the more difficult for a large and diverse group containing spokesmen for entrenched institutional interests. In fact, the sharp divisions of opinion were flagged by footnotes containing individual dissents which almost eclipsed what was affirmed, as in the instance of a member who presented a 12,000-word footnote, which eventually fissioned off into a separate pamphlet.

The official release date for the final report was set for June 19, 1961, when a copy was formally presented to President John F. Kennedy in the White House. But instant criticism of its contents began several days earlier, when *Business Week* broke the embargo on the release and rushed into print with an appraisal of the 285 pages of text. Other publications followed, and the result of "wolf pack" journalism was a fandango of howling tongues from the camps of the political right and the political left. In the absence of a clear view of what was being decried, the press attacks fostered a negativist climate and the work of the commission was generally rejected out of hand by people who did not bother to read the text of the report.

Of the commission's eighty-five definite recommendations, some pointed to greater "centralism," some were neutral in that respect, and some pointed to greater freedom for competitive enterprise. But among all these, there is space here to note only the recommendations which either prefigured the intense disputes of recent years, have lately been settled, or remain the subject of disputes to the time of this writing.

The report, among other things, recommended that all insured banks be required to be members of the Federal Reserve System; debt ceilings and interest rate ceilings be eliminated; changes in tax structures and expenditure programs be timed to coincide with stabilization needs; interest on demand deposits be prohibited; FDIC and FSLIC insurance be standardized and administered by one agency; all eligible institutions be encouraged to become members of the Federal Home Loan Bank System; forms of consumer credit controls be investigated in case of need; the Federal Reserve not regulate mortgage credit; interest rates on government-guaranteed loans be varied in accordance with monetary policy.

Other recommendations included the following: reserve requirements be identical for all banks; reserve requirements be repealed against savings and time deposits; the investment of such reserves be permitted pending repeal; there be no extension of direct Federal Reserve control over nonbank financial institutions; savings banks and savings and loan associations be permitted to acquire a wider range of long-term debt instruments; commercial banks be allowed the same flexibility in investing in time and savings deposits; less restricted and more equal lending power be secured for all financial institutions; the limitation on maximum interest rates payable on savings be removed, but authorities have the power to reimpose such ceilings if necessary; branch banking be allowed within a "trading area," even though this might cross state lines; commercial banks be granted a greater freedom to invest in equities.

BANK HOLDING COMPANY ACT AMENDMENTS

The legislative restraints of the 1956 Bank Holding Company Act were forced to give ground before the continuing pressures of economic realities that could not be legislated out of existence. In 1966, therefore, Congress proceeded to incorporate into amendments of the Bank Holding Company Act many of the changes the Federal Reserve Board had been urging in its annual reports during the previous decade. Among other things, restrictions on some intra–holding company transactions were lifted. Affiliated banks were permitted to sell loans among themselves on a nonrecourse basis. Bank holding company affiliate provisions of the Banking Act of 1933 were repealed, eliminating some of the confusion and administrative burdens resulting from two sets of laws—one a banking law, the other a holding company law—dealing with the same subject.

Another element of the 1966 law, and perhaps its most important, concerned bank acquisitions and the antitrust laws. The basic goal of the amendment, which paralleled action taken by Congress when it passed the Bank Merger Act of 1966, was to establish uniform standards for bank agencies and courts in evaluating the legality of bank holding company acquisitions. Any previous acquisitions not already subject to antitrust litigation became immune from future antitrust challenges. Future acquisitions of bank holding companies could be challenged on antitrust grounds, but in most cases only if the Justice Department brought suit within thirty days after the Federal Reserve Board approved the acquisition.

The 1966 amendments to the Bank Holding Company Act, however, continued to be silent on one-bank holding companies. These would remain unregulated until Congress was galvanized into action by the one-bank holding company boom that swept across the nation after mid-1968. Of this, more later.

13. The Currents of Electronic Banking

ACCOMMODATIONS TO NOVELTY

The role of computers in banking is now so extensive that it is often hard to grasp the fact that this has been the case since only yesterday.[4] They were first applied toward the end of the 1950s to high volume clerical operations, and then to credit card operations in the 1960s—but in both cases chiefly by large banks. It was only from 1973–1974 onward that computers were pressed in every direction by financial institutions across a wide front of banking, and with major consequences.

Among other effects, the electronic computer spawned new banking services—often at substantial costs to banks, and with no certainty of accrued benefits greater than the costs. It became a battering ram against the ramparts of legal restraints on the territorial expansion of banking enterprises. It stimulated the rise of new kinds of nondeposit funds, and helped expand the global reach of banking. It was among the factors that forced a redefinition of "money." It posed new problems of security for financial transactions, and engendered new controversies over the rights of privacy. It created subsets of new professions within the profession of banking. Its very existence inspired more demands for more information from banks by private financial analysts, more demands by government regulatory agencies for more reports, along with more regulations bearing on the accuracy and disclosure of transactions between banks and their customers.[5]

The way some of these effects actually came about will be noted in due course. What is offered immediately below is an overview of the current technology of electronic banking, as well as a line of comments on the kind of problems electronic banking poses for bank executives.

A SYSTEM OF SYSTEMS

Electronic banking is not just one system. It is a system of systems, covering a range of banking operations. The systems which replace the paper and metal of the conventional payments process with electronic impulses whereby funds are transferred, once gave buoyancy to the inflated vision of a "checkless society"—a vision that has since been anchored to earthbound realities. In today's grammar of electronic banking, the phrase checkless society has been displaced by the awkward but more accurate phrase "less check society." More accurate, because of the statistics of the case.

Specifically, despite the systems for electronic funds transferral (EFT), the volume of checks cleared by the nation's check-processing system has increased over 7 percent every year since the end of World War II. At present, the annual volume cleared is about 40 billion checks—which criss-cross the country through an intricate network of people, machines, buildings, trucks, aircraft, railroads, with tens of millions of people and a mass of private and governmental institutions sending out and receiving the checks. The growth is all the more striking when viewed in conjunction with a parallel development—namely, that an estimated 586 million credit cards are in current use in the United States today. (It is not uncommon for individual business people to use an average of 11.3 credit cards—the bulge of which sometimes suggests that they are carrying concealed weapons on their persons.) The volume of checks is bound to grow still larger as depository institutions, besides commercial banks, offer checkbook facilities under the permissive features of the Depository Institutions Deregulation and Monetary Control Act of 1980.

The efficiency of the electronic transfer systems notwithstanding, check-collection costs continue to be staggering. Federal Reserve data indicate that in 1978 alone, American financial institutions spent $11 billion for check handling. Different studies differently compute the average costs to the banking system as a whole for processing and collecting a single typical transit check. Federal Reserve estimates place average costs at fifty cents, while other studies place costs at roughly half that amount. But give or take the nickels and dimes in dispute, not all checks in transit in the banking system *are* typical. To process a returned check on which payment has been stopped costs about five times more than what it does to process a check paid upon being presented. Exclusive of clearinghouse checks, approximately 160 million "return items" are now annually processed by the Federal Reserve System alone, and their volume is still growing.

Despite these sobering figures, or better, because of them, two important claims can be made on behalf of electronic banking. One is that the steady increase in the volume of checks would have overwhelmed the nation's check-processing system were it not for constant technological improvements in the digestive system of electronic banking. The other is that the labor-intensive costs of processing a tidal wave of checks would have sharply undercut banking system profits if it were not for the laborsaving devices of electronic banking.[6]

A SHORT LEXICON

As is true in other professions and crafts, bankers have a code language of their own comprised of meanings intelligible only to member-practitioners. This is particularly true when banks use the acronyms of electronic banking in their advertising—often to the confusion of the very customers they hope to hold or win by offering them the new services the acronyms represent. If so, there may be a gain in clarity if the acronyms are decoded before turning to the policy questions electronic banking has posed for bank executives.

ON-LINE

The term on-line is a shorthand expression for on-line inquiry response system. Prior to its development, tellers needing information about a customer's account got it by poring over ledger sheets to the rear of their cages or by telephoning another person—providing the number was not busy—who then leafed through even larger ledger sheets. While papers rustled and numbers were dialed, the irritated customer waiting at the teller's window, and those waiting further down the line, might toy with the idea of an assault and battery. Today, a teller taps a few keys on a miniature on-line keyboard, thereby reaching into a central file for information about the status of deposit or loan accounts. The answer, whether it is a "clear," "hold," or "stop payment," quickly pops up on a computer screen. In branch banking networks, on-line linkages between distant branches work the same way as they do in the unit bank.

It is hard to gauge the extent to which on-line processing has eased the signs of psychological distress—nervousness and truculence—that often mark the act of cashing a check or withdrawing funds from a savings account. Yet any banker familiar with odd patterns of human behavior in banking transactions knows that no technological advance will quiet the distressed depositor such as the one who, fearing a bank run, rushed to a teller's window and shouted: "If my money's still here, I don't want it. But if it isn't, then by God, I want every penny of it right now!"

ATS

The acronym ATS stands for automatic transfer service. Opinions are divided as to whether ATS should be classed as an electronic banking system, or as being more of a banking product than a system. In either view, ATS is a substitute for a NOW account—itself the acronym for negotiated order of withdrawal—a process in which a depository institution automatically transfers funds from a customer's savings account to his checking account, or makes payments from either source to designated third parties. In contrast to a NOW account—which is a single interest-bearing transaction account—ATS entails the use of two accounts: a demand deposit account and a savings deposit account.

Any innovation in banking is almost invariably challenged in the courts by financial interests who see their competitive position threatened in a real or obscure way. The predictable happened when the Federal Reserve Board and the Federal Deposit Insurance Corporation respectively authorized commercial banks and thrift institutions to offer ATS and several other kinds of transfer services to their customers. Suits were filed against both regulatory agencies on the ground that their grants of authority violated the 1933 Glass-Steagall bill which banned the payment of interest on transaction accounts. The trial court upheld the regulatory agencies, but on April 20, 1979, was itself overruled on an appeal to the U.S. Court of Appeals for the District of Columbia.

It was the opinion of the appellate court that ATS's combined checking and savings accounts with their automatic transfer services were not permissible under the Glass-Steagall bill. It recognized that the restrictive features of that measure which barred interest payments on demand deposits were at odds with the fact that in the everyday world of finance, three million customers were already using ATS accounts. Yet it maintained that it had no choice except to construe the forty-six-year-old Glass-Steagall bill as though it still expressed the intent of Congress. The appellate court, however, did not order an immediate suspension of the ATS system. It stayed its judgment until January 1, 1980, to give Congress time to decide what it wanted to do in the matter at issue. As it happened, the court's opinion intersected with other events in motion, and with interesting legislative consequences.

TCS

The acronym TCS, standing for telephone computing services, is derived from an experiment conducted a few years ago by the Seattle First National Bank, with some 170 depositor institutions elsewhere subsequently following the Seattle bank's lead. TCS initially involved interest-bearing savings accounts from which a depositor could pay bills by touch-tone telephone instructions directly to a bank computer, or by talking to a bank teller from any phone. Funds were then withdrawn from the customer's account and credited to a participating merchant or corporation to whom the bill or bills were owed. More recently this telephone form of bill paying has been superseded by "bank by phone" which allows bill payment, but no cash-disbursing transactions from the individual's bank account. As telecommunications grows in sophistication, its application to banking is likely to see a greater resort to the telephone. Extensive and complex systems of telecommunications are not as cost-effective for small banks as they are for large banks. This helps explain why small banks on the average spent only $12,000 on telecommunications in 1977 and only $14,300 in 1978. But as every bank already has a telephone, voice telecommunications banking functions are economically within the means of small as well as large banking institutions.

ATM

The acronym, ATM, stands for automated teller machines—customer-activated terminals usually available twenty-four hours a day, seven days a week. They can be placed in a bank office to relieve peak loads on human tellers, on sites adjacent to a bank, or in heavy traffic areas such as shopping centers and airports. Wherever installed, ATMs provide most of the services available at a manned teller window. These include cash deposits or withdrawals from checking or savings accounts, transfer of funds between accounts, advances drawn against a line of credit, and responses to balance inquiries. The machines are activated by inserting a plastic card along with a PIN—meaning, personal identification number. A simpler version of ATMs takes the form of a dispenser, generally limited to paying out cash to the customer who activates it, again with the plastic card and PIN.

POS

Point of sale terminals, represented by the acronym POS, vary greatly from one system to another, depending on the design of the particular system. Some use a plastic card and PIN, some use neither, and some use only the plastic card. Starting in 1974, federally chartered savings and loan companies, with the approval of the Federal Home Loan Bank Board, took the lead in deploying POS terminals. Wherever local law allowed, commercial banks subsequently did so as well.

ACHs AND NACHA

Except that the transfer of funds takes the form of electronic impulses on magnetic computer tapes, ACHs—meaning automated clearinghouses—parallel the conventional functions of a check clearinghouse. The first ACH was formed in 1972, but there are now thirty-two across the nation, organized by regional groups of financial institutions that establish the operational procedures and responsibilities of the members. With one privately operated exception, regional Federal Reserve Banks provide the facilities for ACH operations. This was done without charge to users until the Depository Institutions Deregulation Act of 1980 authorized the imposition of a schedule of fees for all Federal Reserve services. Payroll payments, preauthorized billings, and points of sale transactions are settled through ACHs. Economies are particularly evident in the case of repetitive and regular transfers such as payroll deposits, mortgage payments, insurance premiums, and utility bills.

The federal government itself has actively pushed the development of the ACH, especially since the spring of 1978 when a presidential directive urged all federal agencies to use direct electronic deposits whenever feasible.

At present, about 85 percent of the volume of ACH's clearance work consists of Treasury payments made by the electronic movement of funds from the Treasury's deposit account directly to the deposit account of millions of recipients nationally.[7] The advantage to the recipient—who actually has a bank account—is that payments by electronic transfer eliminate the ever-present danger of loss in the mail or theft from a mail box. On the governmental side of things, the advantage lies in reducing the labor-intensive costs of handling payments by mail.

NACHA

The acronym NACHA—national automated clearinghouse association—stands for an interregional automated clearinghouse after the model of Europe's Common Market highly efficient payments system known as GIRO. Starting in February 1977, two test pilot projects were launched to determine the feasibility of interregional exchanges among regional ACHs. One was hinged to the existing Treasury program for direct deposits of recurring federal payments. The other entailed the activities of ten ACHs in six Federal Reserve districts. The tests, completed in December 1977, confirmed the fact that a nationwide automated clearinghouse was both useful and technically possible. Expansion was recommended and NACHA was formed based on the interaction of existing ACH organizations covering thirty-seven Federal Reserve offices—twelve head offices and twenty-five branches.

As of this writing, however, the Federal Reserve Board has found it hard to formulate guidelines for automated clearinghouse operations that are generally acceptable to bankers. Some bankers believe that the ACH system is still in its infancy, and should be allowed to mature before any decisions are made regarding the need for regulations and their nature. The New York Clearing House Association, for its part—which provides for the only ACH regional facility not operated by the Federal Reserve System—has led the crusade for free enterprise and against central bank control. In a statement filed with the Federal Reserve Board in March 1980 on behalf of New York's twelve largest commercial banks, the New york Clearing House contended that the Federal Reserve's latest operating guidelines worked "against the development of the ACH payments system in the private sector."

It remains to be seen how the development of ACH systems in the private sector will be affected by the schedule of charges the Federal Reserve has been authorized to make under the 1980 Depository Institutions Deregulation Act for the services it had previously rendered without cost. Of the more than 15 million transactions which passed through the interconnected networks of thirty-two ACHs in November 1979, 11.7 million were credits initiated by federal government agencies, and 3.4 million were credits and debits initiated by private concerns. Though more than 10,000 commercial banks, 2,500 thrift institutions, and 8,700 corporations are currently listed as ACH participants, the number of private sector debits and credits carried over the ACH systems, compared with total check volume, is microscopically small. Displacement of checks by ACH items is estimated at one-tenth of 1 percent—which is another way of saying that there is immense room for growth.

CHIPS

As the acronym for clearinghouse interbank payment system, CHIPS was developed for and by the New York Clearing House Association mainly to handle international interbank payments. As such, it is one of several such systems, the others being BankWire I, BankWire II, and SWIFT. Subject to technical wrinkles which remain to be worked out, CHIPS points to an interesting possibility. It is that an electronic transfer network, carrying 90 percent of the dollar flows in international commerce, will see network participants making their transactions final on the day they occur, rather than on the following day. The change in settlement method from "next day funds," known as "clearinghouse funds," to "same day" or "federal funds," may tell on the structure and procedure planned or initiated by CHIPS in preparation for the expected demands of the 1980s. A given day's transactions are presently conditional on funds being in participating banks at settlement hour the next day; new policies being formulated are designed to bring CHIPS international operations into line with the instantaneous nature of electronic fund transfer domestically.

IMPACT ON BANK MANAGEMENT

In 1960, *Business Week* placed a $2 billion value on the time invested since 1951 in the development of computer programs. Considering the proliferation of users and uses since then, a similar estimate today covering only their application to banking would probably blow the fuses on the best computer available. When computers first came on the market, chief executives of banks that could afford to acquire them paid a large tuition to learn what computers were all about. They continued to pay it each time a new computer system came on the market to the sound of coronation fanfare about how it would multiply bank profits. In the beginning, no one doubted that computers could churn out data, but what the data actually meant was often left in doubt. When a bank's chief executive asked a question to which a telephoned word or a five-line letter was once an adequate reply, he got back a fanfold of computer printout paper he tripped over while walking back to his desk.

Along with automation came built-in problems of continuing staff training, personnel turnover and hiring, and, not least of all, morale. Old-time bank officers, for example, were often baffled by the computer and mourned its invention. They saw it as an enemy alien in their midst, hostile to the "human touch" of loans made face-to-face with applicants whose character could be judged. They felt helpless before the language barriers raised by "Management Information Systems" experts who talked to themselves in obscure soliloquies. They also feared the power of these experts to "louse things up," in view of the many times a bank's routine operations were stalled because "something went wrong with the computer."

Old-time bank officers had their natural allies in old-time rank and file employees, bound to the time-tested routines of their sometimes considerable experience. If these employees were to sell computer-related services to bank customers, they must themselves be "true believers," and this was far from being the case. They were ready to blame every error and discrepancy in a customer's account on the electronic scapegoat down at the operations center, and they also believed that automated gadgetry would lower their wage scale and shoot jobs out from under them. The computer did in fact reduce the ranks of low-echelon bank employees engaged in clerical routines. In offset, however, it created more and better paying jobs, especially *if* and when it increased business volume and profits. It opened up challenging, new professional skills which placed their proud possessors on a plane coequal in importance with senior loan officers.

In between the old-time officers on the one side, and the old-time rank and file employees on the other, young M.B.A.'s increasingly being employed by banks rejoiced in the presence of the computer to whose technology they had been introduced while still in college. They often saw it as a magical instrument that could solve all problems and could enhance their own effectiveness. Through it—provided they could work in an atmosphere of relative "academic freedom"—they could not only discharge the specific projects assigned to them by senior management, but could also work on elective projects of their own. Perhaps they could even explore new possibilities for profitable products and services linked to computer technology. Time, experience, and the all-too-lamentable human shortfall between the ideal and the real eventually imposed its own sobering constraints on the enthusiasm of the young M.B.A.'s.

IMPACT ON THE CHIEF EXECUTIVE

As for the chief executive officers of banks and their flanking executive committees, the early questions they faced—when and what to computerize, and where and how to computerize—are still current questions. Today, as in the beginning, the search for answers to these questions is tied to factors of cost, need, return, changing legislation, changing regulation, changing judicial opinions regarding the changing legislation and regulation, staff capability, staff training programs, and market competition.

The dollars and cents of investments in computer system hardware are very large, and the issues of when to acquire new equipment, and of what type and magnitude, are not easily answered. To buy prematurely can lead to unwarranted spending that would miss the most efficient methods of operation, or the equipment could be rendered obsolete by a major new breakthrough in technology. If a purchase is postponed beyond the prime time for an acquisition, more than operating efficiencies may be lost to the bank. Its standing in a market area may suffer if a competitive institution were the first to introduce a computer-related new service which attracted more customers with more deposits, on the basis of which more loans could be made with more profit to the pioneering organization.

What to computerize

When computer technology first became available to banks, the possibilities of what to computerize were largely confined to a single objective—to relieve clerical problems and to provide for a swifter and more accurate system for the internal accounting of deposits and withdrawals. Beforehand, a balance sheet showing the deposit picture at the start of a banking day was the work of bookkeepers who began their tasks at the end of the regular banking hours on the previous day and made their entries item by item on a ledger of deposits and withdrawals. The work often extended well into the night, with no time off for Christmas or for New Year's Eve. Home life was often a casualty of the schedule, though bank executives were thought to be generous if they adhered to the tradition in which bookkeepers who worked the Christmas and New Year's Eve shifts were rewarded with a steak dinner at the expense of the bank. It was to deal with the clerical problem entailed in bookkeeping and balance sheet entries that the larger banks began to introduce computer technology into their operations, starting in 1958 when the Bank of America led the way with the purchase and installation of the IBM computer magnetic tape system.

A second objective—the pursuit of new sources of profits by offering new computer-related services to consumers—subsequently surfaced in response to postwar changes in the social and economic environment. Without getting into the details, it is enough to say that the early search for new sources of profits entailed two related lines of activity that were initially pursued only by the more adventuresome among the larger banks, but have since become common throughout much of the banking industry.

One new line of activity saw banks expand their consumer credit loans in response to a reassertion of effective consumer demands after the austere years of the Depression and the Second World War. Until then, consumer loans were in large part a monopoly either of independent finance companies, or of captive finance companies such as those controlled by automobile manufacturers. Even before computer technology was generally available, some bank executives had moved past the confines of "wholesale credit"—meaning credit to business and industry—and had pushed their banks into the field of "retail" or consumer credit. With computer technology, however, the money and time saved in billings worked in ways that spurred further advances in retail credit.

Second, some commercial banks explored the field of credit cards to meet new demands born of mobility, anonymity, and consumption—demands that were particularly pronounced in California, the sunbelt mecca of the postwar years. So here, by means of available computer technology, the Bank of America in 1959 introduced a statewide credit card operation. The initial results, though problematic, pointed to the existence of a new tributary stream of consumer dollars from which banks could profit through the issuance of credit cards. Early results also pointed to the utility of widening the network of bank credit card operations beyond California to cover the nation. Twelve computer-equipped banks located in other states joined with the Bank of America in pioneering the work entailed in laying down the lines for such a national network. The first fruits, however, were scarcely tantamount to the discovery of El Dorado. Losses were high. But by the end of the 1960s, there was a turn for the bettter, and BankAmericard became an established credit instrument in the banking world. It remained so until its name was changed to Visa as a member in a proliferating family of computer-related credit cards such as Master Charge, and of nonbank credit cards such as American Express, Diners Club, Sears, Penney, oil company credit cards, and so on. Under the permissive authority of the Depository Institutions Deregulation Act of 1980, thrift institutions such as mutual savings banks and savings and loan associations may now issue credit cards of their own.

QUESTIONS

With each advance in computer technology making possible new computer-related services banks can offer the public, chief executives of banks are confronted with a fishhook tangle of prickly new questions. Is the new service actually wanted by people in the bank's marketing area? Is it a permissible activity under existing law? Will the costs of installing the new service be substantially offset by bringing into the bank new deposits—or by holding existing deposits—in forms that would serve as the basis for new bank loans, and hence for profits to itself? Should the costs in any case be viewed as a "loss leader" that will, in marketing terms, attract or hold customers to the profitable services the bank offers?

Another major concern of bank executives is how they can best provide for the security of the depositor who uses a computer service, and how such a depositor's right of privacy can be safeguarded. Present devices where banking or transfer payments are made through automated instead of live tellers seem to appeal mainly to young people, perhaps because they have not been conditioned to personalized banking as much as have older customers. But bank executives have discovered the existence of a large group of customers who see in the new machines a threat to their security and privacy. They may like the speed with which they can check their balances or withdraw cash merely by inserting a plastic card into a machine and punching in their PIN. They may appreciate the convenience of being able to dispense with cash or checkbooks when they buy at stores having POS terminals. They may also like the convenience of being able to have their bills paid to third parties by touching a dial on a telephone linked to a computer in their depository institution. But with each transaction, they may also wonder if some unauthorized individual, faking the plastic card and knowing the PIN, might not do the same.

Bank executives have also discovered that the automatic deposit of paychecks has not as yet gained the popularity they expected. Some workers prefer to keep their paychecks to themselves without disclosing the amount even to their spouses or to other family members. When a significant number are jealous of their privacy in banking matters even within their own homes, their fear of unauthorized disclosures to outsiders is all the greater.[8]

There is also the question of fees to be charged. Here the practices may vary from one bank to the next. Some banks charge a fee for every automatic transfer of funds, while others charge for every transfer over a certain number allowed free every month. Still others charge by the check rather than the transfer. Yet again, many banks levy monthly charges for maintaining automatic transfer accounts instead of levying the charge on a specific check or number of checks. In some cases, both the monthly charge and the transfer charge are waived if the savings balance is high enough—usually between $1,000 and $5,000. In the overall, many banks are evidently using the introduction of automatic transfers as fluid contexts in which they can revise their schedule for the pricing of other retail services.

TRANSITION

All that has been said so far about electronic banking focused mainly on mechanics of computer technology. What needs attention next is the way computer technology merged with other developments—economic, political, legal—to alter the traditional nature of financial institutions, and to erode existing boundary lines among them.

14. *Erosion of Boundary Lines*

The 1966 amendments to the Bank Holding Company Act were silent on the one-bank holding company, but in mid-1968, Citibank of New York, the second largest commercial bank in the nation, suddenly announced it was forming a one-bank holding company. The pack followed. Many other large banks—with combined deposits of some $100 billion—about 25 percent of all U.S. commercial bank deposits at the time—organized themselves into one-bank holding companies. Not being subject to any of the regulatory restraints on multibank holding companies or to direct supervision by any federal banking agency, they were free to acquire or establish almost any kind of business—financial, commercial, industrial.

As the one-bank holding company boom swept across the nation after mid-1968, a transcontinental chorus of voices decried both the total volume of deposits involved in the boom and the green light flashing go-ahead signals to one-bank holding companies and their vehicles. Congress could no longer ignore the protests. New amendments to the Bank Holding Company Act of 1956 were now dropped into congressional hoppers, leading to hearings that began on April 15, 1969 and that extended over the next twenty months. Over that period, they amounted to a battlefield for all the clashing interests, private and public, that touch on or are touched by banking. Testimony was offered by officials of unit banks, chain banks, branch-banking systems, multibank holding companies, one-bank holding companies, savings and loan associations, mutual savings banks, credit unions, mutual funds, officials of federal and state bank regulatory agencies, officials of the Securities Exchange Commission and their counterparts among the states, spokesmen for insurance companies, American Express, and finance companies seeking to bar bank holding companies from entering their respective fields of business. Statistics contradicted statistics, charts charts, and prophecies prophecies in what seemed at times to be a war of all against all. Out of the tumult there nonetheless emerged the Bank Holding Company Amendments of 1970 which cleared Congress in December of that year and were signed into law by President Richard M. Nixon on New Year's Eve, December 31, 1970.

The measure ended the exemptions that one-bank holding companies and partnership-owned banks enjoyed under the 1956 Bank Holding Company Act. The new law also modified provisions of the 1956 law regarding the activities in which bank holding companies could engage. The Federal Reserve could henceforth permit a bank holding company to engage in activities that met two tests: first, "if the activities were so closely related to banking or managing or controlling banks as to be a proper incident thereto"; and second, if it could "reasonably be expected to produce benefits to the public . . . that outweigh possible adverse effects."

To flesh out the bare bones of the new law, the Federal Reserve Board announced a list of permissible activities, to give interested parties a chance to comment on its proposals before final regulations were adopted. Under the Board's rules which ultimately gave expression to the 1970 legislation, bank holding companies were permitted to have mortgage, finance, credit card, or factoring subsidiaries; industrial bank or industrial loan company subsidiaries; and subsidiaries that served loans, conducted fiduciary activities, or leased personal and real property. Other subsidiaries permitted to them included those that made equity or debt investments in corporations designed to promote community welfare; subsidiaries that provided bookkeeping or data processing services or that furnished economic or financial information; and insurance agency subsidiaries that underwrote credit life and credit accident and health insurance. Still others included subsidiaries that acted as investment or financial advisors to mutual funds and mortgage or real estate investment trusts; that provided portfolio investment advice to other persons, or that offered state and local governments financial advice on the issuing of securities. Bank holding companies were also permitted to have subsidiaries that engaged in the travelers' check business; that traded in arbitrage gold and silver bullion; and that provided management consulting services to nonaffiliated banks.

Another change set the stage for a sharp controversy regarding the advantages foreign-owned bank holding companies operating on American soil had over domestically owned bank holding companies. On the positive side, the Board's rules placed no geographical limits on activities of a bank holding company that were judged to be closely related to banking. Such activities could be carried on at will across state lines as in the case of nonbank subsidiaries, or of affiliates such as "Edge Act Corporations" formed to finance international trade. But there was also a restrictive side to the picture. A bank holding company, under the so-called Douglas Amendment, could not acquire *banks* located elsewhere than its home state, unless local law allowed bank acquisitions by an out-of-state bank holding company. The controversy alluded to a moment ago would be sparked when foreign-owned bank holding companies crossed state lines to acquire "distressed" banks—something which domestic bank holding companies were barred from doing.

There were other restrictive aspects to the rules laid down by the Federal Reserve Board in connection with the 1970 legislation. Its list of activities *not* permitted to bank holding companies because they were "not closely related to banking," included subsidiaries engaged in the savings and loan business, in insurance premium fundings (as in the combined sale of mutual funds and insurance), and subsidiaries engaged in real estate brokerage, land development, real estate syndication, general management consulting, and property management services. Included also were subsidiaries engaged in mortgage guarantee insurance underwriting, travel agency subsidiaries, and subsidiaries engaged exclusively in computer microfilm services.

Chief executives of bank holding companies often found that the Federal Reserve Board's final list of "Thou May" and "Thou Shalt Not" restored to legitimacy lines of activity in which their companies had engaged prior to the ban imposed on them by the 1956 Bank Holding Company Act. Now, at no small cost in time, energy and money—and a parallel reshuffling of personnel—they reabsorbed into their corporate structure some of the bank-related enterprises they had been forced to spill off or sell outright under the terms of the 1956 legislation. Affected stockholders sometimes found it hard to understand that these turns and turnabouts were not due to managerial aimlessness, but to congressional and regulatory reversals on where boundary lines should be drawn between the lawful and the unlawful.

On balance, the 1970 amendments to the bank holding company bill of 1957, as elaborated by Federal Reserve Board rules, so profoundly changed the terms for the conduct of banking as to create the need for a different type of bankers, and in many cases, for specialty types of banking. Stated in the present tense, bank holding companies—even those which are both small and located in the interior of the country away from the main money centers—now conduct many types of banking that previously would have been beyond their reach.

Thrift institutions that are the affiliates of bank holding companies can finance themselves through thrift certificates which are not restricted, as banks are, as to rates of interest and terms. Their industrial loan companies can offer deposit accounts on which they can pay interest not subject to Regulation Q restrictions. The parent bank holding company can issue different types of term financing and pass the money down to subsidiaries such as leasing companies and mortgage companies. The financing can entail floating rate notes, commercial paper, private placement, long-term convertible preferred stock or convertible debentures—convertible, that is, into the common stock of the holding company. Where commercial paper in particular is concerned, the parent company can arrange back-up lines with other banks for the total amount of the commercial paper issued. The meaning of these terms will be returned to in a later chapter.

The operations of the nonbank subsidiaries of the bank holding companies are in some cases the same as those of the bank, and in others are strikingly different. Mortgage company subsidiaries, for example, conduct the same type of operations as the mortgage divisions in the banks. The mortgage companies which originate the loans usually finance them from funds received downstream from the parent company. But unlike banks, they can operate across state lines.

Subject to the approval of the Federal Reserve Board, a leasing company subsidiary of a bank holding company can also operate across state lines. While its funds are usually provided by a downstream loan from the parent holding company, it can either mobilize the needed funds on its own, or handle leases financed and owned directly by a subsidiary bank. In the case of what is known as "leverage leasing," the leasing company or the affiliated bank would own the item to be leased—whether it was rolling stock, railroad cars, hopper cars, covered hopper cars, mining equipment, or aircraft for airlines or for other corporations. It would put up 25 to 30 percent of the cost of the item, and an outside investor would put up the balance.

The advantages of leverage leasing—whether in the form of investment tax credits or depreciation allowances—either can be retained by the leasing company or can be passed on to the lessee. When they are retained, they help the tax picture of the parent holding company and all its subsidiaries as they file a consolidated tax return. At the same time, the holding company gets the benefits of the depreciation allowances—up to 100 percent over the life of the lease—though the leasing company may have put up only 25 to 30 percent of the equity in the lease. When the leasing company sells a lease to an outside investor such as a pension fund, it receives a fee as the originator and manager of the lease over its 10-to-15-year duration. Also, in the form of a trusteeship, the lease can be funneled into the trust department of a bank.

Meanwhile, banks currently have NOW accounts which are interest-bearing checking accounts. They issue various types of of term instruments such as four-year or six-year certificates at a fixed rate. The variable rate time certificates of deposit which they issue in large denominations are sold in the public market either through a brokerage house, or, frequently, directly by the banks. If the 30-, 60-, 90-day or 1-year time certificates of deposit are over $100,000, the rates are not controlled under the Federal Reserve's Regulation Q. While the banks also get downstream money from the parent holding company in the form of term loans, they do not get the proceeds from the parent company's commercial paper. If they did, the proceeds—for reasons to be noted later—would be subject to reserve requirements that apply to other deposits. In addition to all else, banks now place money in the federal fund market overnight or for a longer period. They originate and handle the issuance of industrial revenue bonds which are term bonds. They buy Eurodollars which usually carry a higher rate than either direct domestic CDs or secondary market CDs. They buy short-term bonds from other holding companies. They buy governments and prime municipals, and they issue credit cards which provide for personal financing.

In all this, they try to match the maturity schedule of their liability side and their asset side so that they won't be loaning short-term money in long-term loans or taking long-term money and merely putting it in short-term loans. Yet the type of financing just sketched would be virtually impossible without branch banking where one can consolidate the deposit picture and participate in larger ventures. It would also be virtually impossible in the absence of the bank holding company which permits nonbanking types of operations. There is, however, a complicating element in the new picture, and it is this. The fact that banks are buying all types of liabilities in order to finance their operations is one of the leading reasons why the chief executive officers these days are having a hard time in keeping their capital ratios in balance with their liabilities.

It is enough to say here that banks usually have to restrict the scope of their operations to their capital ratios, but there is a difference in the way the rule of thumb here is applied to money center banks on the one side, and interior banks on the other. A 4 percent capital ratio is considered "good" for a money center bank, while a "good" ratio for an interior bank is set at a much higher figure. It is set somewhere in the range of 6 to 7 percent. While chief executives keep an eye on their capital ratios, they must decide—depending on the types of bank deposit liabilities—whether they want, for example, a short-term government bond portfolio or a medium-term government portfolio. They must decide on the extent to which they will invest in tax exempt securities, for if they are into the leasing business, their tax exempt securities cannot be very large. This is because a combination of such securities, coupled with the tax investment credits and depreciation allowances of their leasing operations, would place their bank holding companies in a negative tax position. More will be said in due course about the new faces of commercial banking, and especially about liability management. What follows immediately below is centered on other new aspects of banking.

ATTEMPTED REENTRY OF COMMERCIAL BANKS IN THE SECURITIES MARKET

The Banking Act of 1933, as noted, restricted the securities activities of commercial banks, but not to an absolute extent. Commercial banks were expressly permitted to underwrite the general revenue bonds of state and local governments, and to buy and sell securities, including equities at the order of customers for their accounts. In addition, they were allowed to buy some types of debt securities for their own portfolios and to underwrite Treasury issues.

In the three decades following the banking crisis of the thirties, bankers passively accepted the existing legal restrictions on their securities activities. Besides, they had no compelling motive to probe the gray zones of the 1933 legislation which amounted to a no-man's-land between the permissible and impermissible. Where municipal bonds in particular were concerned, the problems confronting chief executives of commercial banks were largely portfolio management problems. They entailed decisions on how best to arrange a municipal bond portfolio so as to gain simultaneously the benefits of maximum liquidity and profitability on the one side, and maximum security on the other. This is never easy. The management of a municipal bond portfolio is and always will be a taxing and time-consuming task.*

If a portfolio is not to become outdated as to security and vulnerable to market changes, its contents require constant attention and an intimate knowledge of individual credit and market conditions. These days, for example, a bank executive directly responsible for the management of a municipal bond portfolio must ceaselessly bear in mind all the recurrent threats to the financial stability of local governments. They include tax limitation measures, budget imbalances, growing pension fund deficits, the resort of unionized municipal employees to crippling strikes, increased vulnerability to reductions in state aid of federal revenue sharing, abandonment by private industry of obsolete facilities, poor fiscal administration, and the erosion of the local tax base by the migration of enterprises and people to other places. All such factors can reduce investment ratings and cause portfolio market losses to a bank owning bonds issued by the affected municipality.

After three decades of quiet, bank executives—starting in the first years of the 1960s—began to look longingly at the securities market. They were prompted to do so by the convergence of several factors—the search for new funds to meet a continued loan demand, an intensified competition among banks and between banks and nonfinancial institutions for profitable business, and a somewhat more relaxed regulatory environment. So now, some bank executives began to test the 1933 limits on their securities activities.

Of the tests, one of the first entailed an effort by national banks to underwrite municipal revenue bonds—meaning debts secured by payments that depend on a particular source of municipal revenues such as highway tolls, parking fees, or airport license revenues. In the national aggregate, the funds at stake in underwriting municipal revenue bonds are far from being penny ante stuff. In a representative year (1977), underwriters issued $20 billion in such bonds.

In 1963, the Comptroller of the Currency, in response to an application by national banks in the state of Washington, ruled that they could underwrite certain revenue bonds the state wanted to issue. His permissive view was based on the theory that the term "general obligation bonds" in the Banking Act of 1933 had not been used in a strict technical sense. That is, its meaning was not confined to the right of national banks to underwrite bonds backed

---

* The average municipal bond portfolio in a medium-sized bank will amount to about 12 percent of its assets. The executives of a medium-sized bank may be familiar with local bond issues. In the case of other bonds, however, they tend to rely on the investment evaluations of rating services such as Moody's and Standard & Poors. But this information does not tell the investment officer how best to combine in the bank portfolio the differently rated bonds so as to achieve the best mix of profitability, liquidity, and security.

by the general taxing power of the municipality. It also included the right to underwrite municipal revenue bonds secured by payments from a particular source of municipal revenues. As an auxiliary source of support for his ruling, the Comptroller cited studies showing that commercial bank entry into underwriting would increase competition and reduce borrowing costs for state and local governments.

An investment banking firm which underwrote revenue bonds presently sued the Comptroller. The litigation came to a head in 1966 when the courts held that the Comptroller's ruling three years previously was in violation of the Banking Act of 1933. That, however, did not put an end to all controversies over the rights of commercial banks to underwrite municipal revenue bonds. The controversy grew in intensity with the passing years and spilled over into Congress. In the late 1970s, for example, when Congress seemed poised to deal legislatively with the issue in dispute, the air overhead was thick with the smell of cordite as rival financial interests exchanged counter-battery fire over a statistical question. To what extent would the borrowing costs for state and local government actually be reduced by the increased competition that would follow from the entry of commercial banks into the underwriting of municipal revenue bonds?

Academic studies on the point, made either on behalf of the commercial banks or on behalf of established underwriting companies, were in sharp conflict. Amid the smoke of battle, Chairman Henry Reuss of the House Banking and Currency Committee observed: "One does not have to be convinced of any particular dollar amount of savings to recognize the public benefits of a congressional measure that would enable commercial banks to compete for the underwriting of revenue bonds. Competition is better than no competition in holding down costs."

COMMINGLED AGENCY INVESTMENT ACCOUNTS

The limits of the Banking Act of 1933 were again tested in 1963 when the First National City Bank of New York (the deposit bank of Citibank N.A.) applied to the Comptroller of the Currency for the right to serve as investment advisor to a commingled managing agency account. Such an account, in essence, is a bank-sponsored mutual fund operated by the bank's trust department. Bank executives previously had a well-established legal authority to commingle individual trust accounts, pooling their funds for investment purposes. Their management, in an agent's capacity, of large individual investment accounts was also universally accepted as being permitted under law. What had not been tested and tried before was the combination of these two powers—management on an agency basis of commingled accounts.

The Comptroller of the Currency approved the application of the First National City Bank in the matter at issue, and was promptly sued by the Investment Company Institute, the trade organization of the mutual fund

industry. In the litigation that followed, different courts at different tiers of
the federal judiciary reached different conclusions. First, the U.S. District
Court in New York ruled against the Comptroller. Then the U.S. Court of
Appeals for the Second Circuit reversed the district court. After that, the
U.S. Supreme Court in 1971 reversed the circuit court and upheld the district
court. It maintained that the Comptroller's grant of authority to the First
National City Bank of New York to offer a commingled agency account was
in violation of the 1933 Glass-Steagall Act which separated commercial from
investment banking.

Automatic Investment Services (AIS)

Yet another test of the limitations of the Glass-Steagall Act of 1933 flowed
directly from the search for new uses of computer technology in bank operations. One of the provisions of the Act was that a bank could buy and
sell securities "upon order, and for the account of customers." Some bank
executives who focused on these words construed them to mean that their
institutions could rightfully enter the retail securities brokerage business.
Presently, therefore, about two dozen banks applied for and secured permission from the Comptroller of the Currency to offer automatic investment
service accounts (AIS) to their customers. Under the terms of an AIS arrangement, customers authorize a bank to deduct regular amounts each
month from their checking deposits in order to buy a number of preselected
stocks—usually taken from a list of twenty-five stocks on the New York
Stock Exchange with the largest capitalization.

   To hold down commission costs, funds from all the bank's AIS accounts
are pooled so that stocks can be bought in large blocks. The price a customer
is charged for a stock is usually the average price paid for the stock that
month, and is not the price paid in any one transaction. AIS plans were not
as widely accepted as their sponsoring executives hoped, and several banks
dropped the service.

   Still, merely by offering AIS plans, the involved banks roused the fears
of the security industry that they would ultimately enter the brokerage business on a full-scale basis. Though all AIS sales and purchases were made
through established brokers and dealers, officials of the New York Stock
Exchange were stirred into action by the fears just mentioned. They publicly
appealed to the Comptroller of the Currency to withdraw from commercial
banks the authority he had granted them to offer AIS arrangements. In their
view, AIS accounts would lead commercial banks into abuses of power and
conflicts of interest by using checking accounts to buy stocks for their customers. The Comptroller, for his part, rejected the appeal in a public letter
of June 10, 1974, which read in part:

We do not believe that the mere possibility that conflicts of interest or other suggested abuses might occur provides a sufficient regulatory reason to abort in its infancy a legal activity with as much promise for the public good as the AIS. The mere potential for conflicts of interest exists in banking just as it does in virtually every other business endeavour. It is no more reasonable to assume that banks will violate the laws, regulations and policies which govern their conduct than it is to assume that brokerage houses will do so. There are numerous opportunities for conflicts of interest which arise in such brokerage firms where research, underwriting and merchandising often occur under one roof and in small houses, even under the supervision of one person.

The Comptroller went on to say that while such potential conflicts deserve examination, "unless there is an actual or immediate threatened abuse, regulatory prohibitions are not justified. Until such time as abuse actually develops, we should not stifle banks' competition in the free market for the patronage of American investors." The line of reasoning, however, did not satisfy the New York Stock Exchange. It brought suit against the Comptroller on the ground that he had exceeded his authority in the matter at issue. The trial court upheld the Comptroller in an opinion which stressed two points. First, deductions from checking accounts to buy stocks under AIS plans do not make security dealers out of banks any more than deductions for mortgage payments make them mortgage brokers. Second, nothing in the Glass-Steagall Act actually barred banks from being brokers as long as they did not themselves underwrite and deal in corporate securities.

THE SHAPE OF THE CURRENT ISSUE

Legal challenges by elements of the securities industry designed to stop the expansion of commercial banks into their markets is, to some extent, a predictable response when enterprises are threatened with new competition. But in the absence of strong reasons to the contrary, protection from competition is neither a defensible nor a suitable goal for legislation. To say this, however, does not end the argument. Involvements by commercial banks in the securities market *do* raise issues that cannot be ignored in any legislation framed to give expression to public policy.

The issues include the possible dangers of increased concentration of resources by banks exploiting competitive advantages of their exclusive charters; the likelihood of conflicts of interest when banks lend to companies in which they buy stock as agents for their customers or arrange private placements of securities for companies that use the proceeds to pay off loans to the bank; the effect on bank solvency if an investment company the bank serves as an advisor fails; the possibility of "voluntary tie-ins" where customers, to increase their chances of obtaining a loan, agree to use a bank's other services without regard to merit; the dangers to investors where banks are not subject to the broker examinations, "suitability" requirements, and prompt execution standards the SEC imposes on other brokers.

At the time of this writing, Congress has before it the latest of successive versions of a measure that would allow commercial banks to underwrite revenue bonds under specific conditions.[9] Yet without regard to the ultimate fate of the measure, it seems worthwhile to glance briefly at the data put forward by rival parties of interest in the protracted legislative contest.

Securities industry spokesmen agreed that 4,000 commercial banks among the 14,700 in existence already have fiduciary powers, and of these, 300 are registered as municipal bond dealers. Yet the top 60 banks among the 14,700 control about two-thirds of bank trust accounts nationally as well as over one-half of all deposits.[10] To spokesmen for the securities industries, these figures had an obvious implication, which was this. To allow commercial banks to underwrite revenue as well as general obligation bonds would serve only to assure a "monopoly position" for the top 60 banks in the security field, and to drive from the marketplace the many individual underwriters of municipal bonds. Even the small commercial banks, because of their close contacts and relations with municipalities, would acquire a monopoly position as against local investment bank underwriting, and thus reduce competition at the grass roots level.

Spokesmen for commercial banks, however, turned the argument around. They noted that the concentration of power in securities underwriting is even greater than it is in commercial banking. For example, in the brokerage area from which a securities firm may realize more than 50 percent of its revenues, the top twenty-five brokerage firms in 1977 earned almost 60 percent of the commission revenues earned that year by the entire industry. In the private placement area during 1975–76, five investment banks handled 44 percent of all advised placements. In the specific and rapidly expanding new issue market for revenue bonds there was a pronounced movement toward the contraction in the number of investment banks which underwrite and deal in these bonds. In the last decade, the number was reduced from about 470 in 1968 to about 370 in 1977.

Commercial bank spokesmen observed further that investment banks had contacts and relations with municipalities which were equally as long and as close as those of commercial banks. True, commercial banks provided deposit services to municipalities and held their securities. But this did not tilt the scales in favor of commercial banks in the underwriting of the general obligation bonds. Investment banks had long held the lead in providing general obligation underwriting services, and they were also the sole source of underwriting for revenue bonds since the latter came into widespread use. It was fair to assume, therefore, that if commercial banks were permitted to offer underwriting services for revenue bonds, the competitive pattern would roughly correspond to the one set forth in the SEC's 1978 analysis of the distribution pattern for the underwriting of general obligation bonds.

The analysis suggested that while the underwriting for the smaller issues would be well distributed between the large and small underwriters, banks and nonbanks, investment bankers would still maintain the lead position in the revenue underwriting field as they had done in the general obligation area.

THE SHAPE OF A LEGAL MISFIT

Back in 1963, at a time when the Comptroller of the Currency began to issue rulings designed to promote greater competition among financial institutions, a bank merger case reached the U.S. Supreme Court on appeal. The case— *United States* v. *Philadelphia National Bank et al.* (374 U.S. 321)—arose under the antitrust provisions of the Clayton Act which forbids mergers that may lessen competition "in any line of commerce in any section of the Country." The opinion of the Court comprised a fascinating exercise in judicial economics.[11]

In applying antitrust law to bank mergers, the Court concluded "that the cluster of products (various kinds of credit) and services (such as checking accounts and trust administration) denoted by the term 'commercial banking' comprised a distinct line of commerce." The Court acknowledged that savings and loan associations, mutual savings banks, and credit unions were "more or less in competition with commercial banks"—meaning that they were either in the same lines of commerce as commercial banks or offered potential substitutes for many bank services. But the Court maintained that for three important bank services it specifically cited, the potential substitutes were not effective. First, the checking accounts of commercial banks were "entirely free of effective competition from products or services of other financial institutions." Second, in competition with small loan companies in the personal loan market, commercial banks enjoyed "such cost advantages as to be insulated within a broad range from substitutes furnished by other companies." Third, while some were freely competitive in terms of cost or price with those provided by other financial institutions, with respect to savings deposits, they enjoyed "a settled consumer preference, insulating them, to a marked degree, from competition."

When the Court rendered its 1963 opinion in the Philadelphia case, its key point—that commercial banking was the relevant line of commerce for antitrust purposes—was dissected by a puzzled collection of chief executives of commercial banks, economists, and lawyers. They agree that commercial banks were multi-product firms offering a set of services, some of which were not offered by other types of financial firms. But they were baffled by the implication of the Court's "cluster argument." What did this mean?[12]

If it meant that commercial banks provided their services as joint products on an all-or-nothing basis, the view was doubly flawed. For one thing, all commercial banks do not offer the same services. They specialize. Large money center banks primarily serve major corporate accounts and provide correspondent banking services which differ fundamentally from small suburban and rural banks which primarily serve household and small businesses. It made no sense to lump them together for antitrust regulatory purposes simply because all were commercial banks. For another thing, no commercial bank could afford to offer its services on a restricted all-or-nothing basis, because other financial firms would grab at a chance to provide some of the same services.

At the time of the decision, critics observed that if commercial banks actually enjoyed a "settled consumer preference" which insulated them against competition from other financial institutions, they should have at least maintained their market share of total savings deposits. The opposite happened. In the eighteen years between the end of World War II and the 1963 Philadelphia Bank case, commercial banks' share of financial resources in all deposit institutions declined from 86 percent to 65 percent. Yet the conclusion the Court reached amounted to a directive to regulatory agencies and lower courts. When faced by antitrust issues in the banking field, they were to view the services commercial banks offered as though they were indivisible, a "one step" coverage which they alone provided customers. Second, in judging proposed mergers among commercial banks, they should ignore the competitive position of savings and loan associations, mutual savings banks, credit unions, personal loan finance companies, sales finance companies, and other nonbank financial intermediaries.

Post-1963 developments among nonbank financial institutions, coupled with radical changes in the bank deposit picture, compounded the doubts about the Supreme Court's view that commercial banking constituted a separate line of commerce. The Court itself, however, stood pat. In 1974, despite more than a decade of continued changes in the competitive picture, in a case involving the proposed merger of Connecticut National Bank and First New Haven National Bank, it reaffirmed its earlier view that commercial banks offered a "cluster of products" which were to be viewed as a single product distinct from those offered by other financial intermediaries. Events themselves, however, and not words, were in the saddle. They moved at an accelerating pace in directions which increasingly homogenized the activities of banks and nonbank institutions, as each offered competitive financial services to their customers.

BREAKTHROUGHS

The homogenizing process received its first powerful stimulus in 1971—or three years before the Supreme Court decision just mentioned—when executives of mutual savings banks in Massachusetts unveiled the NOW account, an invention that spread rapidly among other mutual savings banks in New England and in New York. The NOW account, to repeat, is a form of interest-bearing savings whose holders can make third-party payments by executing negotiable orders of withdrawal. Executives of commercial banks who felt the heat of the new competition from mutual savings banks in their service area proceeded—albeit reluctantly—to secure authority from regulatory agencies to offer their own form of NOW accounts. They did so reluctantly because of the explicit or implicit higher costs they incurred when depositors of interest-free checking accounts shifted at least part of their funds to the interest-bearing savings deposits under NOW account arrangement.

Subsequently, mutual savings banks began to offer conventional checking accounts in the manner of a commercial bank. They offered point-of-sale terminals for electronic transfer payments from savings accounts to merchants, as well as twenty-four-hour-a-day withdrawals through cash dispensing machines. They offered credit cards, an expanded range of consumer loans, family financial counseling, an opportunity for depositors to invest in securities through the purchase of shares in no-load mutual funds. In some states—New York, Massachusetts, and Connecticut—authority was granted the mutual savings banks to issue various types of low-cost, over-the-counter insurance, an activity barred to commercial banks. In virtually every other respect—far beyond their traditional involvement in mortgage loans—mutuals performed functions associated with commercial banks.

The same thing was true of the savings and loan associations. Aside from dramatically expanding the scope of the mortgage loan activities, they extended the range of their operations through the establishment of permanent branch offices and mobile branch offices. They adapted the new computer technology to their use by establishing "minibranches" located within other business establishments such as retail stores. They directly approached the functional character of commercial banks by offering time and passbook savings certificates in a wide range of size and varying maturities, and in interest-bearing NOW accounts on which depositors were permitted to write negotiable orders of withdrawal. In consequence of a regulatory decision effective on June 1, 1978, savings and loan associations—in common with mutual savings banks—were authorized to issue money market certificates.

Credit union officials were long concerned about their future ability to compete for consumer deposits if they were not able to offer accounts on which funds could be drawn through a check or check-like instrument. In August of 1974, the National Credit Union Association (NCUA) granted three federal credit unions temporary authority to begin offering share drafts—payable through drafts which could be drawn on the member's interest-bearing share account. Other credit unions soon joined the pilot program, at the end of which the share draft program became widespread, with competitive consequences felt by commercial banks.

One more point. While all the traditional financial intermediaries were invading each other's territory, all, in turn, faced stiff competition from institutions which were not banks in any conventional sense. Credit card companies and merchandizing establishments, such as Sears and Penney's, were giving their customers access to the "free money market," and inflation furnished the incentive to go there. In February 1979, Sears, Roebuck & Company, the world's largest retailer, informed its 26 million credit card-holders that it was offering them an opportunity to invest in a Sears-backed issue of $500 million 2-to-10-year notes in $1,000 denominations at attractive interest rates.

At the same time, the brokerage house of Merrill Lynch, Pierce, Fenner and Smith offered their customers cash management accounts allowing them to write checks against the balance of their account. In the case of money market mutual funds, the brokerage house allowed shareholders in the funds to redeem the shares by checks drawn on accounts established by designated banks, by wire or by mail. Walter B. Wriston, chairman of Citicorp, was not entirely engaging in hyperbole in late March 1980 when he remarked that "while commercial bankers squabble among themselves, their customers are being wooed away by 'the bank of the future'—which already exists. The bank of the future," Mr. Wriston said, "is called Merrill Lynch, Pierce, Fenner and Smith."[13] A stunning statistical fact buttressed his remark. It was that from March 1978 to March 1980, the ready assets of Merrill Lynch increased from $770 million to $10.7 billion—a two-year gain of 1300 percent.

The increased homogenization of functions performed by different financial institutions, along with their continued pressures to unshackle themselves from the juridical chains which confined them to specific territories and modes of conduct, plainly demanded a new set of ground rules to replace those which events had rendered irrelevant. The new ground rules, in the form of an omnibus legislative measure, would eventually be forthcoming—under the impact of other events which shook up the whole world of American finance.

15.   Concerning Liability Management

An earlier chapter briefly sketched the preconditions for the radical shift in the 1960s which saw bankers add to their concern with "assets management," (or the *funds using* side of a bank balance sheet) a new and all-consuming concern with "liability management," (or the *funds seeking* and *funds buying* side of the balance sheet). It was noted that as the 1950s gave way to the 1960s, bankers could no longer readily finance loan expansion as before, simply by drawing on their accumulations of liquid assets. Nor could they passively await the influx of deposits for conversion into loans and investments compatible with traditional standards of safety. The pool of liquid assets was absorbed by the rising loan demand in the economy, and the influx of deposits—demand, time, and savings—was being reduced by the "irrigation ditches" that diverted funds away from commercial banks.

Demand deposits, or transaction accounts on which banks were barred by law from paying any interest, were drained off by new cash management practices of major corporations. Corporation treasurers saw little point in maintaining large transaction accounts in banks, when they could use a substantial portion of the funds to buy highly liquid income-producing assets in the money market—for quick conversion into transaction account funds in case of need. A parallel development saw the general decline in the importance to households of the cash reserves they held in the form of bank demand deposits. They could profit if they diverted part of their cash reserves into highly liquid interest-bearing money market instruments, while they used their credit cards to finance from one month to the next many of their ordinary transactions.

As was also noted, the competition for time and savings deposits was no longer a contest in which commercial banks were the rivals of commercial banks. It was now a contest between commercial banks and newly invigorated financial intermediaries—savings and loan associations, mutual savings banks, credit unions, mutual investment funds, pension funds. Even the monopoly commercial banks had long enjoyed in the area of transaction accounts backed by demand deposits was being broken into by the inventions of competitive financial intermediaries, armed with the new computer technology. Inflation, Regulation Q ceilings on what commercial banks could pay for the time and savings deposits, and the higher interest rate that could be earned through the acquisition of money market instruments, combined with all the forces just mentioned to limit the growth of commercial bank deposit funds that could be used for loans. Bankers were thus compelled to cast off their former passivity and to seek and buy nondeposit funds for use in meeting a continuous loan demand.

The process calls for the description offered below. It concerns the dynamics of "liability management," as well as the origins and nature of the money market instruments that enter into that dynamics. It will be seen that though the term "money market" is used in the singular, it actually stands for a variety of markets, each serving and served by different client interests, each also subject to different regulations. The description itself can best start with a sketch of the markets for federal funds and repurchase agreements (RPs).[14]

Overview

The markets for federal funds and RPs are among the most important financial markets in the United States. Using either of these instruments, executives of many banks, large corporations, and nonbank financial institutions trade large amounts of excess funds with one another for periods as short as one day. The institutions involved provide much of the short-term credit available in the United States and, as such, manage their financial positions carefully and aggressively.

Federal funds transactions are often described as "the borrowing and lending of excess reserve balances among member commercial banks." This description was once true, but is now inadequate, or at least too narrow. In a larger sense, the phrase "federal funds" has come to mean overnight loans between financial institutions, whether or not they are member or nonmember banks.[15] The larger definition corresponds to the fact that market participants now include savings and loan associations, mutual savings banks, and the branches and agencies of foreign banks operating on American soil.

The interest rate on overnight (one day) federal funds measures the return on the most liquid of all financial assets, and is the chief determinant of the level of rates set on most short-term money market transactions. This rate, in other words, usually creates a base for determining the level of rates and the various maturities for certificates of deposit (CDs), commercial paper, bankers acceptances, and so on. Until early October 1979, the federal fund rate was the primary instrument used by the Federal Reserve Board in carrying out its monetary policies. By measures designed to confine changes in the federal fund rate to a tight fraction below 1 percent, the Federal Reserve believed it could more easily control the size of the monetary aggregates that would be available to the economy.

Because interest rates on other short-term financial assets such as Treasury bills and commercial paper usually move parallel with the federal funds rate—either up or down—the latter rate has also tended to influence the costs of credit, such as commercial paper obtained from sources other than commercial banks. Nor is this all. In addition to controlling monetary aggregates by controlling the level of federal fund rates, the Federal Reserve also influences short-term rates in connection with repurchase agreements (RPs), reverse repurchase agreements, and through the Federal Reserve's outright purchase or sale of U.S. Treasury and federal agency securities. Because federal funds transactions are unsecured—in the sense that lending institutions have no guarantee of repayment other than the promise of the borrower—transactions in federal funds are conducted only among institutions that enjoy a high degree of mutual confidence. There may be special circumstances—governed by state and federal regulations—where some collateral may be required for these transactions. In practice, however, this is not a common occurrence.

In addition to federal funds, a very substantial portion of short-term money market transactions are conducted—as noted a moment ago—by repurchase agreements. In essence, RP agreements involve transactions where at least one participant is *not* a financial institution as defined by Federal Reserve regulations. In fact, in many cases, repurchase agreements are conducted by Federal Reserve Banks themselves. When an RP is arranged, the acquirer of funds agrees to sell the provider of funds U.S. Treasury or federal agency securities in exchange for immediately available funds—named so, because they have been normally cleared through a Federal Reserve branch, and thus are immediately available to the recipient. At the maturity of the RP agreement, the transaction is reversed in a "buy back," again entailing the use of immediately available funds. In most cases, RP agreements are based upon the market value of the securities involved in the transaction; this helps protect the seller of the funds if the borrower should fail to repay the funds themselves. Given the nature of the RP instrument, large nonfinancial corporations, along with state and local governments, dominate the RP market as well as the Federal Reserve Banks themselves.

The main purchasers of funds in the RP market are large banks and government securities dealers. Banks using the market have a distinct advantage over other institutions because they hold large portfolios of U.S. Treasury and federal agency securities which they can use in connection with RP agreements. At the same time, because nonfinancial corporations and state and local governments which provide funds receive securities in return, the RP market attracts a wider array of participants than does the federal funds market. Where government securities dealers are concerned, they use the funds borrowed in the RP market to finance their holdings of U.S. Treasury, federal agency, and other eligible securities.

The federal funds and the RP market are distinct, but they also share common features. Both mainly involve transactions for one business day—though transactions with maturities of up to several weeks are not uncommon. In both markets, transactions are settled in "immediately available funds." Because transactions in both markets have for some time been free of reserve requirements, both have provided a larger base for the expansion of loans in response to credit demands. Precisely on that account, the Federal Reserve in periods of restrictive monetary policy has considered imposing reserve requirements on federal funds and RP transactions mainly in order to control excessive expansions of credit.

ORIGINS OF FEDERAL FUNDS

The federal funds market dates from the early summer of 1921 when large banks in New York City—as Reserve member banks—were differently affected by the painfully depressed economic conditions of the time. Some found that their reserves at the Federal Reserve Bank of New York had significantly increased. Others found themselves borrowing at the discount window. Chief executives of banks with surplus reserves, however, were not free of headaches on that account. They had trouble finding outlets in the usual channels for profitable reinvestment of the funds on hand.

By mid-1921, after months of diminished activity in the money market, money rates had declined from their 1920 peak to levels close to or even below the average discount rate in all Federal Reserve districts. In that context, executives of several leading New York banks, on both the "excess" and "deficit" side of the reserve picture, informally discussed their plight and agreed on an *ad hoc* solution to their respective problems. When the terms of the solution were presently put into effect, dual benefits followed for the parties to the agreement. Banks reporting excess reserves began to sell a portion of the balances to those reporting insufficient reserves. This enabled the sellers to realize a return on those excess reserves until the funds involved could be used as a basis for new loans, investments, or other outlets in the money market. On the other hand, banks with insufficient reserves that bought the excess reserves of other banks were able to reduce the level of their direct borrowing at the Federal Reserve discount window. As a related matter, in buying funds from other banks, the buyers spared themselves the expense and trouble of assembling collateral or customer's paper eligible for discount at the Federal Reserve Bank.

During the first year of the market in federal funds, the volume traded rarely exceeded $20 million a day. But as the decade of the 1920s progressed, trading within New York City itself broadened. Local markets appeared in cities such as Boston, Philadelphia, Chicago, and San Francisco. An interdistrict trading of funds, albeit on a limited scale, also began to take root. The typical unit of federal funds traded was $1 million, though with the growth of correspondent bank trading arrangements, transactions as small as $50,000 were common. The aggregate volume traded varied from one day to the next. The range of the normal daily trading was between $100 million and $250 million. The upper limits were reached on "reserve settlement days"—Fridays under the old system, Wednesdays at the present time—when banks made their last-minute adjustments in their reserve positions.

Interdistrict trading between the two coasts was stimulated by the time zone difference. When New York banks closed at 3 p.m., it was only noon in San Francisco, with its banks still open for business. This enabled eastern bank executives to estimate funds in excess or in deficit of legally required reserves. If funds were in excess, then before the wires closed in the East, about 2:30 p.m., they could sell the balances in the West. With the receipt of the funds around noon on the west coast, funds trading started immediately in connection with the adjustments of reserve positions. They were generally returned to the east by wire early the next day.

One should add that the factors of time zone differences continue today to influence interdistrict trading in federal funds. Thus bank executives in charge of a "money desk" may "follow the clock," buying or selling funds successively in New York and Chicago, occasionally in St. Louis or Kansas City, and finally in San Francisco or Los Angeles. "Trading westward" has become particularly significant for executives in mountain time banks and those in the contiguous central zone time. Though banks in these zones use the eastern market, an excess or deficit in the reserve position of a bank in Dallas, Denver, Phoenix, or Salt Lake City can be corrected by transactions with the San Francisco district after the eastern banks have closed.

THE ECLIPSE OF THE MARKET FOR FEDERAL FUNDS

During the Great Depression, the caution bankers showed about arranging trades of federal funds reflected their mutual uncertainties about each other. Bankers with excess reserves on hand in their respective institutions were increasingly fearful of selling them to other institutions—because if the latter failed, they could not get back the funds they had sold for short-run use. As the rate of bank failures increased, the volume of trading in federal funds dwindled, and especially so in the context of interdistrict trade. Except for random trading in instances where correspondent relationships were particularly strong, the funds market virtually dried up by 1933. Nor was it revived in the years that followed immediately. The reasons have been touched on in another connection. It is enough to repeat that loan demand remained small. Disturbed political conditions abroad caused a heavy movement of gold to the United States for safekeeping. Banks accumulated huge excess reserves which vexed both the Federal Reserve and the United States Treasury. With rare exceptions—such as the increased reserve requirements the Federal Reserve Board ordered in 1936 and 1937 to defuse any inflationary potential in the huge excess reserve—individual banks seldom faced any need to borrow federal funds.

CHANGES IN THE MONEY MARKET

Apart from what has already been said about the impact on the banking system of the way the Second World War was financed, the rapid postwar growth of population and production expanded the demand for banking services, while the growth in the size of business units created a demand for bigger banks and larger capital accounts to permit an increase in the size of individual loans. At the same time, the pattern of bank assets was affected not only by the absolute growth in population and incomes, but by changes in the way both were distributed. The greater diffusion of deposits throughout the United States, the shrinkage of business borrowing in the form of commercial paper, the decline in the acceptance volume, and the tremendous growth in the market for U.S. government securities altered the character of the money market. The funds market in particular began to develop a strong national character, and all the more so as the general economic environment changed as the postwar period wore on.

Financial institutions—bank and nonbank alike—became more closely interconnected. Mechanized arrangements for communication and the transfer of money market instruments followed rapid technological advances. Correspondent relationships among banks were broadened and increased in scope. Specialization of services was developed further to meet the particular needs of various lenders and borrowers, and transactions were more swiftly consummated at lower costs. Knowledge of markets was more widely diffused, and the link between the short-term money market and the long-term capital market grew stronger and closer as more financial and nonfinancial institutions began to conduct transactions in more than one market. In this way, influences affecting a particular group of institutions in one market tended to be more rapidly transmitted to other related markets or groups of institutions.

With significant increases in size, changes in composition, and broadening ownership patterns, the marketable portion of the public debt assumed a new importance. It emerged as a sensitive new medium for adjusting the cash positions of financial and nonfinancial institutions, and increasingly served as an immediate and continuing investment outlet. This was especially true after the Treasury–Federal Reserve Accord of 1951 was reflected in higher rates for government securities and a greater reliance on borrowing for reserve adjustments by individual banks. As bank reserves were placed under pressure, and as short-term rates rose with an increase in the breadth and depth of the securities market, assets and liabilities alike became rate sensitive, and the competitive search for funds intensified. Government security dealers found it necessary to step up their own activity in the funds market both as intermediaries and in some instances as principals.

Meanwhile, executives heading small banks were introduced to the federal funds market mainly through their correspondent relationships with large banks. It was their practice right after World War II to hold relatively large amounts of their assets in cash, and for two reasons. Interest rates at the time were very low, and still vivid memories of depression-time bank runs translated into the high value they placed on immediate liquidity. But when interest rates began to climb in the 1950s, some executives in small banks began to think anew about their practices. They saw that by holding large amounts of cash on hand at a time when large banks were willing to borrow in a market where interest rates were rising, they were forfeiting what their own banks could be earning but were not because of an addiction to large cash balances. Consequently, pioneering executives in a few small banks began to lend their cash balances to large banks in the form of overnight funds, thereby gaining the best of two worlds. The cash balances they loaned in the form of overnight federal funds were tantamount from the standpoint of liquidity to actual cash on hand, and they also earned interest.

By the early 1960s, executives in every type and size of bank had become familiar with the workings of the federal funds market. They were also directly encouraged to trade in federal funds in consequence of two rulings in governmental quarters—the kind which escape the attention of the general public. Both rulings emerged through the administrative procedures of federal banking authorities, and both had practical consequences for banking as great as any legislation enacted in full view of the nation.

As to the first of the two rulings, it is in point to explain that, prior to 1963, unsecured lending of federal funds to a single borrower had been restricted to 10 percent of the lending bank's combined capital and surplus. The limit applied to all nationally chartered banks, but the practical effects restricted the activities of only the small national banks. In 1962, however, the Comptroller of the Currency ruled that federal funds transactions were not borrowings and lendings, but purchases and sales. This ingenious distinction removed the restrictions that had kept small banks from placing relatively large amounts of funds in the federal funds market. That is, they could now be viewed as sellers of the funds rather than as lenders.

The Federal Reserve Board, for its part, followed the lead of the Comptroller. It ruled in 1964 that member banks could legally purchase correspondent balances of *nonmember* banks as federal funds. So now sales of federal funds by small nonmember banks began to accelerate. More than that, executives of small banks began to ask their correspondents to engage in federal funds transactions. If the latter refused, they faced the danger that the cash balances the small banks kept with them—and on which no interest could be paid under the 1933 Glass-Steagall bill—would be moved to a competitor.

Executives of large and small banks alike eventually came to view their correspondent relationships as a convenient basis for arranging federal funds transactions. In the practice of the matter, those who managed small banks intentionally accumulated large balances, and then sold off to their correspondent banks the excess they did not need for check clearing or for other purposes. The arrangement neither required an actual physical transfer of funds over the Federal Reserve wire transfer network, nor did it necessarily entail a legal change of ownership. The borrower and the lender both posted bookkeeping entries simply to show that a non-interest-bearing correspondent demand balance had been converted into a federal funds borrowing on which interest was paid.

To round out the sketch of how the market for federal funds was developed, mention should be made of a 1970 decision by the Federal Reserve Board. Prior to that year, executives of some banks had begun to borrow federal funds from nonbank institutions, but under the Federal Reserve Board's Regulation D—which specifies member bank deposits that are subject to reserve requirements—federal funds borrowings were exempted from reserve requirements only when the lender was another commercial bank. In 1970, however, Regulation D was amended and interpreted in ways which extended exemptions from reserve requirements to cover borrowings of federal funds and RP funds from nonbank institutions.

The aggregate effect of the three regulatory rulings—those made in 1963, 1964, and 1970—was this. In 1969, about 55 percent of all member banks either bought or sold federal funds. By 1976, the proportion who did so had climbed to 88 percent, with most of the new entrants being small banks. Later, under the terms of the 1980 Depository Institutions and Deregulation Act, it would be the rare financial institution of any description—bank or nonbank—that would not be a participant in the market for federal funds. On a daily average, the volume of trading in federal funds and RPs combined is well in excess of $50 billion—in contrast to the case in the 1920s when the daily average of trading in these funds peaked at between $100 and $250 million.

The market mechanism for federal funds and RPs

Each large bank has an executive—often called the money desk manager— who is responsible for the bank's having sufficient deposits at the Federal Reserve and cash vault to meet its required reserves—whose level is tied in with the lending policies of his institution, as formulated by its chief executive and other members of the executive committee.

The money desk manager of a lead bank starts each day with an analysis of his bank's reserve position, and then roughly estimates the net volume of federal funds and RPs he wants to buy or sell.[16] He also makes a rule of thumb judgment as to the net amount of such assets his small correspondent banks will supply or absorb. The difference between these two judgmental figures—one bearing on the affairs of his own institution, and the other bearing on the affairs of the small correspondent banks—serves as a basis for calculating the amount of federal funds and RPs he may want to buy or sell to *other* large banks. He then locates buyers and sellers of such assets either by telephoning other large correspondent banks or one of several brokers in New York. In the latter case, the money desk manager informs the broker of his own preferred purchase or sell position. As the day progresses, the broker matches buyers and sellers.

In the specific case of federal funds transactions, not all are initiated by a telephone call from a large bank to one of its smaller correspondents. Just as many are initiated the other way around, by a morning telephone call where the correspondent advises its lead bank of the quantity of federal funds it wishes to buy or sell. In many cases, a federal funds position is on a "rollover" basis—meaning that a lead bank continues to adhere to a previously agreed upon position until advised otherwise by the correspondent. When a lead bank buys federal funds from a correspondent by debiting the seller's correspondent deposit account, it sends the correspondent an "advice of debit" form on which the size of the federal funds transaction and interest rate payable are noted. Although no actual federal funds are transferred as a result of the transaction, and lead bank's required reserves are reduced— with a two-week lag—and, more importantly, a probable reserve drain is avoided. If the correspondent had drawn on its balances at the lead bank to buy Treasury bills or some other money market instruments instead of selling federal funds to its lead bank, the latter would have lost reserves— with a consequent reduction in its lending power.

It is not to be understood from anything so far said that the federal funds market is the only forum for reserve adjustments. Executives of banks who face the need for additional reserves can meet the need in alternative ways. They can sell Treasury bills or other marketable paper or borrow from the Federal Reserve discount window. They can call a loan with a government securities dealer, or raise dealer loan rates to encourage dealers to refinance their own operations elsewhere. To a large extent, the choice executives make among these options—whether singly or in combination—depends on their respective relative costs, on likely movements within money markets, and also on the length of time the additional reserves will be needed. If funds are needed for only a brief period, a bank executive may buy federal funds or borrow from the Federal Reserve discount window to avoid the costs of selling short-term assets one day and buying them back the next.

As with other free market rates, the rate on federal funds depends on supply and demand conditions in the market. To a greater extent than other money market rates, however, it is influenced by special considerations which cause it to fluctuate more widely than the rest. Reserve requirements, for example, must be met on a daily average basis over the statement week which runs from Thursday to Wednesday. Since excess reserves equal to only 2 percent of required reserves can be carried over from one reserve-averaging period to the next, bank executives tend to dispose of their excess reserves for whatever price they can get as the reserve statement week draws to a close. The pattern is not absolute, but it helps explain some of the sharp day-to-day movements in the federal funds rate even during "normal" periods when bank executives tend to hold on to excess reserves during the first part of the reserve period and release them toward its close.

THE REVOLUTION IN MONEY MANAGEMENT

Assets management traditionally tried to meet the liquidity needs of banks by building up short-term assets represented by savings and checking accounts in a bank, the investment portfolio, supplemented by occasional short-term borrowing at the Federal Reserve, and the use of overnight federal funds. Assets management still remains the way of life for small and medium-sized banks. In recent years, however, large money center banks, joined by large regional banks, have engineered the "liability management" revolution in the management of money.[17] Its emphasis is on techniques and instruments for raising short-term and long-term funds by borrowing in money markets. As for the money markets themselves, they are no longer purely domestic in character. To an ever-increasing degree, they are overseas money markets as well—as will be seen when these pages focus on the internationalization of banking.

The onset of the liability management revolution stemmed directly from the events previously noted—the intensified competition for funds among different kinds of financial intermediaries, and the handicap commercial banks faced in that competition because of the Federal Reserve Board's Regulation Q which set upper limits on what commercial banks could pay for various types of savings and time deposits. At a time when loan demands continued to be very strong, executives of major money center banks, joined by those at the head of important regional banks, cast about for ways in which they could secure "nondeposit" funds for profitable use in meeting the loan demand. They were using federal funds and RP agreements to adjust their reserve position in connection with their lending operations. But they were in need of a new source of funds, borrowed or "purchased," that could provide adequate funding and capitalization in order to honor loan commitments already made, or to meet anticipated future needs. the search for new sources of funds led to the invention of the certificate of deposit (CD). It also led to a new or increased resort to money market instruments such as commercial paper, floating-rate notes, bankers acceptances, term and tax-exempt notes, European CDs and Eurodollars.

DEFINITIONS

First, the certificate of deposit. Despite the restrictions the Federal Reserve Board had placed on interest rates commercial banks could offer for deposits, it had become apparent by the end of the 1950s that huge amounts of funds were available in money markets. They were ready to be tapped by commercial banks, provided a banking instrument was on hand for the purpose that could carry an interest rate above Regulation Q ceilings. The need for such a banking instrument was acutely felt by executives of New York banks in particular. Though faced by heavy loan demands, their proportionate share of total deposit funds was declining, and for reasons which went beyond the brisk competition of nonbank financial institutions coming on top of changes in the cash management techniques of major corporations. The added reasons included the shifts of population and commercial and industrial enterprises away from the New York area to other parts of the nation.

The desired instrument they looked for turned out to be the negotiable certificate of deposit, an invention of George Moore of the National City Bank of New York. It surfaced for the first time in 1961, and was destined for adoption nationwide not only by commercial banks, but, in time, by thrift institutions such as savings and loans associations and mutual savings banks. The negotiable CD was technically a deposit and carried a reserve requirement. In essence, however, it was a money market instrument because it could be resold in a secondary market. Subsequent to 1961, the CD was to have a stop-and-go career. Its use either fell off, increased, fell off again, or again increased, depending on changes in interest ceilings and on the intervention of Federal Reserve regulations.

Commercial paper, to speak of it next, is unsecured promissory notes, issued by finance, sales, and industrial companies to raise short-term funds. They can be sold with maturities from 5 to 270 days, generally in $100,000 denominations. The quality of such notes varies with the reputation of the company issuing the paper, and the way they are "rated" by private rating services goes far toward determining their marketability. Individual banks under existing regulations were barred from issuing commercial paper, but the prohibition did not extend to bank holding companies. Six of them began at roughly the same time to issue commercial paper, and to use the funds gained for short-term operations, such as the financing of construction mortgages. When construction was completed and permanent mortgages issued, the latter could be resold in the secondary market.

The Federal Reserve Board belatedly awoke to the fact that the commercial paper issued by a bank holding company for the acquisition of funds to be used by its banks amounted to an end run around Regulation Q. Accordingly, the Board amended its Regulation D—which concerns reserve requirements—and imposed reserve requirements on the funds banks used from commercial paper proceeds. But the cat-and-mouse game between banking needs and the regulatory rules of officialdom now took a new turn. Bank holding companies began to transfer the use of commercial paper proceeds from their constituent banks to their nonbanking affiliates, such as those engaged in the mortgage business. Commercial paper issued by bank holding companies has sharply increased in volume in recent years, and is sold not only to their individual customers, but in a general market with the aid of investment banking houses.

As for floating-rate notes, they are issued by banking holding companies to finance long-term lending operations such as those involved in the work of mortgage and leasing companies. The descriptive word "floating" is derived from the fact that the rate on these notes is often set under a formula tied to the average Treasury bill rate. Some bank holding company executives set the rate at a fixed level of 1 percent above the Treasury bill rate. Others set the minimum rate for floating notes at 1¼ percent above Treasury bills, or at a rate determined by the bank holding company itself, subject to a minimum rate base. Though these obligations have long maturities, holders can redeem them at six-month intervals at par if they are not satisfied with the varying rate. Initial differences in the judgmental decisions of bank holding company executives concerning the scheduling of rates on floating notes had different effects in the market place. Most holders of the first groups of notes—those whose rates were fixed at 1 percent above the Treasury bill rate—became dissatisfied with their return. They did not retain their investment at the six-month redemption benchmark, but returned their notes to the bank holding companies which issued them, thus drying up the greater part of their outstanding issue. In marked contrast, floating notes originally issued at a rate set higher than 1 percent above Treasury bills were in large part retained by investors.

It remains to be added that bankers acceptances are drafts or bills of exchange. They may be payable in the United States or abroad, in dollars or some other currency. In any event, they may be accepted by a bank, a trust company, or some other firm, but they take their name from companies which specialize in granting bankers acceptance credits. As for short-term tax-exempt notes, these are notes issued by local agencies and federal agencies, generally with maturities from three months to one year after issuance. The meaning and place of European CDs and Eurodollars in the pattern of money market instruments used in liability management will be noted, as was said a moment ago, in the larger context of the internationalization of banking.

THE DYNAMICS AND PERILS OF LIABILITY MANAGEMENT

Large banks set targets for the total liabilities they will try to borrow through money market instruments—depending on the total of the profitable loans and investments they think they can make in addition to those made on an existing base of deposit funds. Their profit depends on the spread between the costs of the funds they borrow through money market instruments, and the income from the interest they get on loans made with the borrowed funds. Some regional banks as well as major money center banks may on the same day borrow funds in the money market and then, as financial intermediaries, lend the same funds to other banks which need them to meet a loan demand. Some banks, mainly large ones, are continuous net borrowers of funds, while others, mainly small banks, are continuous net lenders. But the judgmental art and practice of liability management is not exercised in the context of just a single money market instrument. It is exercised in the context of a package of such instruments—depending on their rates and maturities, each within itself, and all in relationship to another.

In a larger sense, it is exercised with an eye to the fundamental long-range task of a bank's top management. That task, to restate it, is to chart the probable course of a bank's needs in the impending future—to allow for adequate funding and capitalization in support of commitments already made or in prospect. In that kind of "prediction planning" all the aspects of both assets and liability management come into play—investments, money market activities, customer deposits and loans, reserves against defaults on loans, analyses of trends in the economy as a whole, prospective action by Congress and by the regulatory arms of government, the shape of events on the move in the world arena.

Bankers comprising policy-making executive committees of their respective institutions understand—providing they were not born yesterday—that events will rarely, if ever, proceed exactly as planned. Lending opportunities may be greater or less than anticipated. Money market conditions may tighten or ease. Currencies may come under upward or downward pressures. The political and regulatory arms of government may alter their anticipated course, or both may be checkmated by a judicial decision. A bank's top management, therefore, must take care to position their institution so that it can adapt profitably to whatever conditions actually materialize. This means that they must always give due weight to the factors of capital, liquidity, market exposure, maturity mismatches, and—to an increasing extent today—foreign currency positions.

As to the first of these factors, when the ratio of assets to capital increases, the risk to shareholders also increases. Conversely, when the ratio declines, the rate of return on capital falls off. When a happy medium is found—to the extent that it ever can be—it is generally a blend of what competitors are doing, what supervisory authorities believe is appropriate, and what the bank's own management thinks is prudent in their service area. Where the factor of liquidity is concerned, the bankers' problem is always to be able to honor commitments to borrowers and to their own creditors at an acceptable payment cost without reliance on the Federal Reserve discount window. To that end, bankers chart foreseeable inflows and outflows of funds. They prepare for anticipated outflows by arranging to obtain funds at the time they are needed. They also try to reduce the likelihood of an unforeseen shortfall by using stable sources of funds, such as customer deposits and funds with long maturities. As a cushion on the assets side, they hold liquid assets.

Because a capacity to borrow in money markets is an important alternative to holding liquid assets, top executives of a bank must necessarily be concerned with the extent of their institution's "market exposure." To preserve a bank's borrowing capacity, its executives generally try to stay within the bounds of what they (and others) believe is its "proper" or "consensus share" of each segment of the market. They may need funds beyond the customary level to exploit a profitable opportunity; they may need funds to honor prior commitments to customers of long standing who, being hard pressed, are compelled to draw on a full line of credit. Yet they are sensitive to the high-tension risks they run when they borrow more than their consensus share of a market. Among others, financial analysts—instead of pinpointing the true reason—may construe the event to mean that the bank is experiencing serious internal problems. Conclusions to that effect, circulated by word-of-mouth or through cryptically worded reports, may be instrumental in closing all segments of the money market to the bank. To avoid placing a bank under a cloud of embarrassing suspicion, its top management will generally think twice before any borrowings they make exceed customary levels.

All such matters call for carefully balanced judgments by senior executives in a bank, and their decisions can miscarry even when made by bankers of wide experience at the helm of major money center banks. Among those that can miscarry, the one that bears hardest on bankers when they err in their judgments is a "maturity mismatch." On the one side, profits may be earned when unexpected changes in market interest rates find a bank in a position where its executives can borrow market funds at the maturity of its own debts below the rate the bank charged on the loans it made to its customers. On the other side, losses may result if a bank's loans are financed with relatively short-term funds or with long-term funds at fixed rates, only to find at the time of maturity of its own borrowings that the market rate is above the rates it set on its loans.

The process of trying to harmonize maturity structures with projected developments in interest rates is known in banking circles as "gapping." Thus if bankers expect rates to drop, they lock up their yield—go long on their loans at fixed rates, and shorten the maturity of their own borrowings. If, on the other hand, they think that rates are on a rising trend, they shorten the length of their loans and try to make them at rates that float with the money market costs of funds—and at the same time try to lengthen the maturity of their own borrowings at fixed rates.

Even when interest rate cycles behave normally, gapping is nervous work; to judge correctly the size of the gap to be filled requires a species of "divine madness." It is all the more nervous work when interest rates behave abnormally as they have in recent years, and when judgments in the size of the gap to be filled are as slippery as snakes in Vaseline. When interest rate cycles behave normally—that is, when they move up in the prosperity phase of an economy and fall back to previous lows during slack periods—the cheapest source of purchased funds, gauged over the entire business cycle, would be one-day federal funds. Concurrently, the most profitable assets, as confirmed by many Federal Reserve studies, would be long-term mortgages and bonds. In recent years, however, normal interest rate cycles have not been part of the real world of banking, though they may live on in textbooks. The simple facts of the complex case are these. Between 1965 and the opening months of 1980, four periods of declining business activity were marked by *rises* in interest rates, and by the tendency of short-term rates to move *above* long-term rates. Very able managers of major banks have been known to be tripped up by the maturity mismatches growing out of the wrong judgments they made about interest rate movements.[18]

CODA

In striking a balance between reserve requirements, investments, loans, and deposits, any well-run bank holding company needs to be in a net borrowed position—meaning that it can borrow more money than it sells. This, in turn, underscores the importance of its money desk and the talents of the individuals who manage it. They must bear in mind the reserve requirements which the banks of the system must maintain, and act accordingly in the market for federal funds and RPs. They must pay attention to the short-term investment requirements of customers of the banks such as correspondent banks, corporations, and local governmental units. They may have to act as advisors to municipalities in connection with their bond issues, as well as dealing in municipal securities and creating a market for them. They must weigh carefully all the factors entering into decisions regarding the rates for CDs above $100,000. They must work closely with the managers of bank holding company affiliates—such as mortgage and leasing companies—to determine *their* needs for funds, and with the advertising and marketing divisions in order to attract customers to the money market instruments issued by the bank holding company. They must also work closely with the executives in direct charge of the bank holding company's trust department.

The trust business itself is a tough one to engage in profitably. It is purely a personal service business utilizing relatively little capital investment—furniture and office equipment make up its capital assets. Its conduct nonetheless requires a staff whose expertness encompasses such varied fields as law, investments, taxation, accounting, and real estate management. Staff members must also possess extraordinary tact to meet the variety of needs of trust customers, toward whom the members stand as close personal advisors in what often amounts to a parental role.

It is no easy thing for a trust department to meet the challenges of the trust business—all of which depend on a staff that can provide superior trust services to customers at reasonable charges and with a return of profits to shareholders. A major segment of the trust industry in recent years has found these objectives beyond attainment, and in fact, trust departments in many major banks and bank holding companies tend to be "loss leaders"; the fees charged for trust services do not cover the salary costs of trust officers and their support personnel. This in turn explains why many bankers either have little interest in their respective trust departments, or view them as lemons with which they are stuck.

Others, however, have vigorously pushed the activities of their trust departments. They have introduced systems of cost analysis as a basis for scheduling fees that could be income earners instead of income losers. They have entered the corporate trust business as a trustees and paying agents under bond issues, and as transfer agents and registrars under stock issues. They have aggressively sought to have wills deposited in their banks on terms where the bank is named as executor or trustee. They have gone after pension and profit sharing trusts, and inaugurated a pooled fund for investment of these types of accounts. They have expanded the personal trust business by establishing common trust funds, one aimed at investments in common stock, and the other at fixed-income securities.

Some banks have established sub-units within the trust department to provide expert advise to small corporations and individuals who wish to provide retirement benefits for their employees and themselves. They have also established a trust fund for municipal bond investing for customers in need of the tax-exempt features of these investments. They have entered the world of equipment trust and leverage leasing. All such activities, or at least the majority of them, require a sensitive knowledge of money markets—which in turn, requires a close coordination of trust department activities with the work of money desk managers.

16. Redefining Money for a Changing Financial System

There was never a time when all actors in the nation's financial system were of one mind on issues of economic fact, or on the merits of particular economic policies. But all the historic debates in former years over issues of economic fact and of policy seem to pale when viewed alongside the debates engendered by the immense changes that altered the face of American finance as the 1960s gave way to the 1970s. Even commonplace terms such as "money" and "financial intermediaries" seemed to lose whatever stability they once had. In both cases, the loss was due to the way two decades of changes in the nation's payment mechanism changed the form in which money was held, where it was held, and for how long. It was due as well to the swift growth in various forms of highly liquid nondeposit assets, to the increased application of computer technology, to the electronic transfer of funds, and to the erosion of functional boundary lines among and between financial and nonfinancial institutions.

The classical definition of financial intermediaries covered a short list of institutions: commercial banks, mutual savings banks, savings and loan associations, credit unions, and insurance companies. These qualified as financial intermediaries because they transferred funds from the original saver (or ultimate lender) on one side of the counter to the ultimate borrower on the other. Yet if this middleman role defined a financial intermediary, by the 1970s those on the classical list could no longer comprise the whole of the story. The expanded list would have to include pension funds, mutual funds, brokerage houses, financing companies, leasing companies, factoring houses, and the extensive range of institutions issuing credit cards—oil companies, large department stores, Sears, Penney's, American Express, and the like. All these came to absorb funds from savers and ultimate lenders on the one side, and to channel them to ultimate borrowers on another side.

In addition, a great range of federal, state, and local governmental agencies engaged in activities that would also qualify *them* for places on a list of financial intermediaries. They, too, absorbed liquid savings at one end of a tap line and transferred the savings to borrowers at the other end—to themselves as borrowers, to private borrowers under direct lending programs, or in support of insurance programs that covered a variety of credits which private financial intermediaries themselves extended to borrowers. At the federal level of government, for example, the process entailed direct or federally sponsored agricultural credit programs—the land bank system, banks for cooperatives, farm mortgages, farm home mortgages, non-real-estate credit services. It entailed credits through the Veterans Administration and the Small Business Administration, an extensive array of housing bonds, along with direct lending by agencies such as the Atomic Energy Commission, Bureau of Indian Affairs, Export-Import Bank, Maritime Administration, and in time of war, the Defense Department. At the state and local levels of government, the middleman process entailed everything from student loans to pollution bonds, from subsidized mortgages to industrial revenue bonds, from general revenue bonds to municipal revenue bonds.

As of this writing, there continues to be a conceptual misfit between the meaning of financial intermediaries and the identity of the institutions and agencies that discharge functions associated with the term. The financial press, writers of textbooks, and speakers for financial organizations continue to confine their discussions of financial intermediaries to the institutions enumerated on the classical list. A concerted effort has been made, however, to redefine the meaning of money, and for reasons and ways to be treated in the remainder of this chapter.

THE IMPORTANCE OF ANY DEFINITION OF MONEY

The first dimension of money—the actual stock on hand—is central to the task of assessing the economy's liquidity. But the second dimension of money—the velocity or intensity of its use—is central to any monetary policy decision bearing on the likely impact a future growth in the money supply might have on the nation's economic activity.

Even under ideal conditions, it is no easy thing to gauge the economy's liquidity. Any estimate of the actual stock of money on hand would have to take into account what cannot readily be calculated—namely, the untold billions of dollars either held outside financial institutions in the secret possession of organized crime, or in the hands of private persons who wish to evade detection by Internal Revenue agents.[19] But this "lawless" dimension of liquidity has been further complicated by the way the radical changes in the nation's payment mechanism has impacted on the factor of velocity.

Day-to-day monetary policy decisions, for example, may be focused on quickly affected targets such as short-term interest rates, bank reserves, or the money supply. But these judgmental decisions are not self-limiting. They have long-range consequences for employment, production, inflation, or deflation. And this, in turn, introduces an eccentric variable in all such judgmental decisions. The variable, put in question form, is this. How long is long? Monetary authorities could amuse themselves by answering that it is twice the distance from the middle. But the answer would not carry the weight of the serious decisions entrusted to their care. They have to make some sort of calculation concerning the *economics of time*—namely, the number of months that would intervene between the decisions they made here and now and the time when the effects of such decisions would be fully felt.

Suppose, for example, they set the intervening period at six months. Then the stock of money needed to achieve the desired ultimate level of activity would depend on how intensively the stock was used during the subsequent six months. If the rate at which money was used was expected to change from what it had been in an earlier time frame, a different quantity of money would be needed in the six-month period ahead to maintain the past level of GNP economic activity. In other words, depending on whether a dollar was used more or less often than in the past, fewer or more dollars would be needed along the route of the six-month period to facilitate the same amount of transactions as in the past.

IMPLICATIONS FOR THE FEDERAL RESERVE SYSTEM

While the Federal Reserve has a mandated responsibility to regulate the available stock of money to meet public demands, it cannot regulate what it cannot measure, and it cannot measure what lies beyond its fingertips. If it is to measure what it can at least try to control, its definition of monetary aggregates must fit the form in which money (or its equivalent) is held, who holds it, where, in what amounts, along with its velocity.

Between 1960 and June 1978 when the aggregate deposits in all depository institutions reached $1.4 trillion, the Federal Reserve found itself compelled periodically to redefine monetary aggregates—to keep up with new forms of assets with different combinations of utility, safety, liquidity, velocity, and interest-bearing payments. In January 1979, after earlier definitions seemed inadequate in points of detail, the Federal Reserve *Bulletin* published for comment by bankers, professional economists, and other interested parties, a number of new definitions of monetary aggregates that had been proposed by the Federal Reserve Board's technical staff. The time was roughly ten months before the Board, under the new leadership of Paul Volcker, announced the strategic terms of its historic shift of policy in its struggle against inflation. But it was not until the early spring of 1980 that the Board subscribed to certain of the proposed redefinitions of monetary aggregates.

IMPLICATIONS FOR MONETARY THEORY

The same events which changed all aspects of money—with a consequent need to redefine monetary aggregates—reopened all the arguments among theoretical economists that were presumably conclusively settled and sealed in the textbooks of the past. They began to debate anew the old questions of what in the economy money affects, how the effects were transmitted, the strength of the effects, the length of time before the effects can be observed, the stability of the effects, and the relationship between money and real income.

They also began to debate anew a set of specific questions which over-printed the general ones just mentioned. What, for example, was the relationship between money payments and the level of employment and economic output? Was there an ideal for monetary spending at which the economy could be fully employed without being vulnerable to marked inflation or deflationary changes in prices? What *measurable* effects did the velocity of money have on both prices and the means for payments? How did interest rates in fact impact on the velocity of money? How did interest rates impact on other economic magnitudes—such as investments, the ratio of deposits at banks to their reserves, the ratio of the public's holdings of deposits to its holdings of currency, the ratio of corporate holdings of assets either in the form of securities or in bank balances, to the extent to which corporations financed their needs either by borrowing from banks or by borrowing from the security markets?

IMPLICATIONS FOR BANKS AND FOR OTHER FINANCIAL INTERMEDIARIES

Executives of banks and all other financial intermediaries could scarcely be indifferent to the controversies engendered by attempts to redefine monetary aggregates. They lived with the fact that the way monetary aggregates were redefined pointed to the prospect of new or altered monetary policies that could affect the relationship between public regulations and private economic decisions, as the weather affects farming. It could affect the way private financial intermediaries managed their short- or long-term investment portfolios, or the way they calculated the liquidity they must seek depending on whether they believed money would be "tight" or "easy" in the future. It could affect their judgements on how to manage their deposit liabilities, how to manage their assets, the "mix" and the levels of the loans they made, the "rationing of credit" among classes of borrowers, the funds they must themselves borrow—where, in what amounts, for how long, on what terms, at what cost. It could affect the nature of the internal budgets they set for the "profit centers" within their corporate framework as an instrument for corporate management.

So, from three perspectives—that of the Federal Reserve, monetary theory, and the operations of financial intermediaries—the question, "What is money?" was far from being academic. Immense practical consequences followed from the way the question was answered.

THE HISTORICAL DIMENSIONS OF THE QUESTION

Since the dawn of human history, there has never been a definition of money that has been true for all times and places. Money has had so many forms as to warrant the conclusion that what constitutes money is simply what has been accepted as money—whether through force of physical necessity, custom, or legal decree.

Copper, silver, gold, and paper are only a few among the long list of money forms that have included salt, feathers, water, cattle, elephants, pigs, skulls, leather, furs, iron, tin, palm nuts, corn, tobacco, cotton, and gunpowder. Even counterfeit money—known to be counterfeit—has been accepted as money in lieu of any better alternative, provided a second party was willing to accept it on the assumption that it could be passed on to a third party.[20]

In view of the way in which money appeared to have so many forms, economists surmounted the problem of coherence by defining money in terms of its functions—without regard to its specific character, but depending on the state of a society's development. In the functional definition, it was observed that money serves as a medium of exchange whereby goods and services are paid for, and debts and other contracts are discharged. It serves as a unit of account in which loans and transactions are kept, costs computed, values compared. It is a means for stating the prices of goods and services, and for expressing debts, wages, and comparative wealth. It serves as a store of value and as a reserve for ready purchasing power. It also serves the psychic need of people who want money for its own sake, for the self-esteem the successful pursuit of money gives them.

Still, it is one thing to define money. It is another thing to measure its stock. It is still another thing to measure its stock with an eye to the formulation and execution of monetary policy.

EVOLUTION IN THE FEDERAL RESERVE'S DEFINITION OF MONEY

Starting in October of 1960, the Federal Reserve Board began to publish a measurement of money based on an average number of days in contrast to its former practice of measuring money from one day to the next. Known as M-1, the definition of monetary aggregates it offered under the new system of averages did not cover all forms of financial assets. It was confined only to the public's holdings of financial assets that could be used as a means for payment in connection with transactions—namely, currency, coin, and demand deposits at commercial banks. Moreover, the "public" was itself confined in meaning only to the assets held by commercial banks and by the United States government. It did not cover financial intermediaries such as savings and loan companies, mutual savings banks, and credit unions.

When M-1 was first defined along the foregoing lines, it was recognized that savings instruments also provided potential purchasing power. But they were excluded from the measurement of money offered in October 1960, on the theory that they first had to be converted into cash or demand deposits before they could be used for transactions. In 1962, however, the Federal Reserve Board began to publish *separately* the data on commercial bank *time* deposits, and again excluded the savings on deposit in thrift institutions. It was up to an interested person to take the published figures of demand deposits covered by M-1, combine them with the separate figures of savings deposits at the commercial banks, and extrapolate from them a broader measure of monetary aggregates.

So things went until 1971 when the Federal Reserve Board, after much talk, formally published more than the single money supply measure represented by M-1. The convergence of at least four factors accounted for the decision. One was the decade-long development and use of the certificate of deposit. Another was the sign of marked advances in computer technology for the electronic transfer of funds. The third factor was the announcement by the Federal Home Loan Bank Board that, as of September 1971, savings and loan associations would be permitted to make preauthorized transfers from savings accounts for household-related expenditures; this was the forerunner of the permission later granted them to make preauthorized third party nonnegotiable transfers from savings accounts for any purpose. The fourth factor had not yet materialized in 1971, but was known to be in clear prospect—namely, the onset of the process in which state-chartered mutual savings banks would offer negotiable orders of withdrawal (NOW) accounts for payments to third parties.

The new additions to the money supply measurements published by the Federal Reserve Board were called M-2 and M-3. Then, as now, M-2 was defined as M-1 plus commercial bank time and savings deposits other than large negotiated CDs issued by major banks. M-3 included M-2 *plus* mutual savings bank deposits and savings and loan shares. All this, however, was only a beginning. The need for new definitions of money and monetary aggregates would continue to press hard on the Federal Reserve Board.

Prior to mid-1974, the Federal Open Market Committee (FOMC) of the Federal Reserve had been remarkably successful in setting, tracking, and attaining the policy targets for monetary aggregates. Its average error in predicting the quarterly growth rate of M-1 was only 0.2 percent from the first quarter of 1970 to the second quarter of 1974. The picture would change markedly in the next four and one-half years. The error in FOMC's predictions would increase sharply at the rate of 2.9 percent per quarter, resulting in a cumulative overprediction of $53.9 billion by the fourth quarter of 1978.

The poor performance after mid-1974 was due at least in part to continued changes in regulations governing deposits at commercial banks and thrift institutions, and to the widening adaptation of computer technology to the electronic transfer of funds. In this period, savings and loan companies expanded their check-like payments from savings accounts to third parties, and increasing numbers of mutual savings banks offered NOW accounts. Also, from January 1974 onward, savings and loan companies were permitted to establish point-of-sale terminals (POS) permitting the remote withdrawal of deposits from savings balances. Then again, it was from early 1974 onward that money market mutual funds came into existence on a large scale. As these funds were invested in money market instruments, shareholders could redeem the shares by checks drawn on accounts established at designated banks, by wire transfer, or by mail.

Further, it was in October 1974 that credit unions began to experiment with and then expand the practice of offering check-like share draft programs for third-party payments. Then in April 1975, commercial banks were permitted to offer programs where transfers from savings balances to checking accounts could be made by telephone. In September of the same year, commercial banks were permitted to make preauthorized third-party nonnegotiable transfers from savings accounts for any purpose. Three years later, or in November 1978, regulatory authorities allowed prearranged automatic transfer services (ATS) from savings balances at commercial banks and thrift institutions having transaction accounts. Finally, throughout this period, large banks intensified their use of "offshore" funds such as Eurodollars, while their increased reliance on repurchasing agreements (RPs) with their customers, gave customers a highly liquid earning asset as a safe alternative to holding deposits.

THE FEDERAL RESERVE BOARD'S RESPONSE—AND PROBLEMS

To keep pace with the foregoing development, the Federal Reserve Board in 1975 introduced and published two new monetary aggregates—M-4 and M-5—besides redefining M-3 by adding credit union shares to mutual savings loan deposits and savings and loan shares. M-4 represented public holdings of currency, coin, and all deposits at commercial banks—including for the first time large negotiable CDs. M-5 represented all public holdings of currency, coin, and all deposits at thrift institutions—again including for the first time large negotiable CDs. Meanwhile, because of the uncertainties associated with the introduction of prearranged automatic transfer from savings to checking accounts (ATS), a sixth monetary aggregate measure was introduced in late 1978. Known as M-1+, it included M-1 plus savings deposits at commercial banks and transaction accounts at thrift institutions.

The new definitions of monetary aggregates did not, however, resolve all problems of measurement. In theory, it was possible to develop concepts of money that satisfied the user's criteria. But in practice, lack of data or the availability of only poor data could hamper the construction of a series of monetary measurements corresponding to theoretical specifications. Besides, the construction of a series based on data that is not timely could limit its usefulness for policy purposes—as in the instance of the poor quality of the data on RP liabilities, on the movement of money market mutual funds, Eurodollars, and commercial paper. While an ideal measurement of money would cover all the functional purposes of money in a range from a medium of exchange to a store of value, no one measure could do so. *That* was the problem the staff of the Federal Reserve Board faced in 1978 when it was asked to consider anew how monetary aggregates should be redefined.[21]

Responses

All the redefinitions proposed by the Federal Reserve Board's staff pointed up the need to perfect or develop new information sources about monetary aggregates—because continued uncertainty about the amount of money actually available to the economy would clearly impair the execution of monetary policy. In the discussions and comments that followed the publication of the staff's proposals in the Federal Reserve *Bulletin* for January 1979, some people viewed them as being conceptually closer to theoretical money than any measures the Federal Reserve Board had previously used. Others criticized them as being wholly inadequate reflections of what was going on in the financial system. Still others voiced their despair over the possibility of ever getting a handle on a measure of monetary aggregates, given the elusiveness of the data, and the power of any official body to control monetary aggregates.

17. The Internationalization of Banking: Its Politics and Problems

DOUBLE VISION

To many American eyes, the dramatic surge of foreign banking activity on American soil in the 1970s—whether measured by "takeovers" of American banks, or by increases in the American-based assets held by U.S. offices of foreign banks—posed a grave threat to native control of American financial and industrial enterprises. The threat seemed all the more ominous when linked to two auxiliary facts growing out of the "energy crisis." For one thing, the $90 billion the U.S. spent on the import of foreign oil in 1980, alone, equalled in dollar value the entire assets of General Motors, General Electric, Ford, and the International Business Machines Corporation. For another, if that rate of expenditure continued, total payments for foreign oil by the end of the 1980s would equal in dollar value all the stocks currently listed on the New York Stock Exchange.

Hence the nature of the fears that followed. First, these billions of American dollars in foreign hands would enable their owners to buy up American enterprises which were among the key customers of American banks. Second, if a sizeable portion of these billions were redeposited in American banks, their foreign holders could threaten the depositor institutions with ruinous withdrawals of funds unless their executives collaborated with foreign depositors in an attempt to alter the course of American foreign policy. Third, to the extent that these billions moved into the vaults of foreign banks, they would enable foreign banks to increase the scope of their financial transactions on American soil and to buy up more American banks—with adverse effects on the ability of the Federal Reserve to conduct American monetary policy.

Of these fears, the third one in particular seemed to be confirmed by a glance at the upward moving curves on statistical charts, showing two concurrent developments. One was an accelerating rate of takeovers of American banks by foreign institutions since the early 1970s. The other showed that total claims on the American economy of U.S. branches and agencies of foreign banks rose from $23.4 billion in 1972 to $164 billion by the end of 1979—a 680 percent increase within the decade.

Meanwhile, in the eyes of people standing on the foreign side of the international financial fence, the great expansion of American offshore banking activity since the late 1950s posed a grave threat to the native control of *their* financial resources. Among other things, they noted that since the 1950s, American banks increased their foreign assets by 600 percent. They noted more pointedly that in the seven years between 1972 and the end of 1979, the claims by foreign offices of U.S. banks expressed in dollar terms rose from $70 billion to nearly $260 billion. Nor did these statistical facts stand alone. Foreign fears of American "domination" of local economies were compounded by the popular belief that the United States was the home of the greatest concentration of "world class banks," and that these could grab and get anything they wanted in foreign markets.

It is worth adding that this particular belief was wide of the mark. While Bank of America and Citibank are two of the largest banks in the world, the general picture has been radically altered since 1956 when 44 U.S. banks ranked among the top 100 banks in world markets according to deposit size. By 1978, only 15 U.S. banks were so ranked, and by 1980 only 12 were in the top 100. As of that time, France was the leader among the top ten banks in the world, having institutions that ranked third, fourth, fifth, and sixth among the very largest. London and Frankfort, Germany, each had two banks among the top ten. Taking the top 100 banks as a single whole, the leader was Japan with 24 banks, followed by Germany with 14, the United States with the previously mentioned 12, and the United Kingdom with 8. Switzerland, famous (or infamous) for its "gnomes" and "secret numbered accounts," had only 3 banks among the world's 100 largest, and the leading Swiss bank ranked only thirty-fifth in size. In the overall, 20 different nations (or city-states) were represented among the world's 100 largest banks.

THE LONG PROLOGUE TO A GREAT CHANGE

The framers of the U.S. Constitution contended that a "more perfect union" would stimulate international trade and the foreign inflow of capital vital to the economic development of the infant American Republic,[22] and their views were reechoed by later generations of American leaders. Yet with random exceptions, the financial and banking services necessary for the conduct of international transactions were provided not by American but by European-based institutions.[23] Part of the reason was the fact that most U.S. banks were fully absorbed in meeting the domestic needs for capital in cities or on the Western frontier. But a larger part of the reason sprang from the political and legal restrictions the U.S. government placed on the international activities of American banks. In the specific case of national banks, federal law prior to 1913 barred them from financing foreign trade through bankers acceptances, and from establishing branches overseas.

It was only when political attitudes began to change with the emergence of the United States as a major industrial power, that legislators were willing to ease the earlier legal barriers to international activities by American banks. Thus the Federal Reserve Act of 1913 contained a provision which permitted national banks with $1 million in capital and surplus to establish branches in foreign countries "for the furtherance of the foreign commerce of the

United States, and to act, if required to do so, as fiscal agents of the United States." It was assumed that if America's national banks were allowed to engage in business abroad, the effect would help promote U.S. exports and the extension of credits to friendly European governments. The hoped-for effect, however, was derailed by the outbreak of the First World War. Between 1913 and 1916, Chase Manhattan—then the leader in the nation—was the only bank that established overseas branches. The costs and risks of expanding abroad—even in neutral countries—were judged too great to be borne by any but the largest banks.

In 1916, therefore, an amendment to the Federal Reserve Act was adopted with the object of broadening the base and of increasing the number of American banks that might be willing to engage in international banking. By the terms of the amendment, national banks with a capital of $1 million or more could invest—individually or jointly with other banks—up to 10 percent of their capital and surplus in auxiliary institutions chartered by *state* banking authorities solely to conduct an international banking business. These state-chartered institutions were called *agreement corporations*, a name derived from the fact that they had to agree to observe any restrictions placed on them by the Federal Reserve Board.

In the practice of the matter, few restrictions were actually imposed. No minimum capitalization was required, and there were no constraints on the nationalities of the corporations' owners and directors. Yet the hoped-for results were so small as to be almost invisible. During the next two years—marked by America's entry into the World War, the Russian Revolution, the military defeat and collapse of the German and Austro-Hungarian Empires—only three agreement corporations were chartered by the states.

In 1919, though Europe was still in turmoil, another effort was made to stimulate the international activities of American banks by yet another amendment to the Federal Reserve Act. Known as the Edge Act after its sponsor, Senator Walter Edge of New Jersey, the new amendment empowered the Federal Reserve Board *itself* to charter corporations to engage in international banking. State-chartered *agreement corporations* remained in being, and several of these are still in existence at the present time. But those chartered by the Federal Reserve Board under the 1919 amendment came to be known as Edge Act Corporations, or simply as Edges, though the original Act distinguished between "investment Edges" and "banking Edges."

The original Edge Act opened more doors to corporations chartered to engage in international banking and financial activities. Either for the first time or beyond prior bounds, they could trade in foreign currencies and engage in foreign lending, acceptance financing, and foreign collections. They could accept time demand and time deposits in the United States (but not savings deposits) as long as the deposits were related to identifiable international transactions. They could accept deposits from foreigners, from foreign governments, and from businesses operating primarily abroad, provided the deposits were not used to pay purely domestic expenses. They could also be located anywhere in the United States, even though their parent banks were prohibited from establishing branch banks or from owning banks outside their home states.

The Edges held out many *potential* advantages to their parent banks. In the first place, though Edges could only service the foreign trade and other international banking needs of a parent bank's customers, they could help their parent banks compete for the domestic as well as the international business of firms far removed in space from the geographical location of the home office of parent banks. Secondly, though national banks were barred by law until 1966 from making equity investments in foreign corporations, Edges had the "general consent" of the Federal Reserve Board to invest up to $500,000 in foreign corporations not doing business in the United States, provided they did not hold more than 25 percent of their voting shares. The percentage could even be greater under two circumstances: if the Federal Reserve Board approved, or if the purchase of additional stock was necessary to prevent losses on existing loans. On the foregoing count, Edge Corporations could potentially improve the competitive position of their parent U.S. banks relative to banks in other countries which, typically, were permitted by their own national laws to make equity investments in foreign corporations. At the same time, the equity investments Edges could make in foreign corporations provided their parent U.S. banks with the only potential vehicle for investments in foreign banks in countries where they were barred by national law from establishing bank branches of their own.

In time, two Congressional measures eventually undercut the near monopoly the Edges enjoyed as a unique channel for equity investments by American banks. The first, a 1966 amendment to the Federal Reserve Act, permitted national banks, subject to Federal Reserve Board approval, to invest directly in foreign banks doing a substantive business in the United States. The second, a 1970 amendment to the Bank Holding Company Act, allowed bank holding companies to make equity investments in foreign corporations on terms coequal with the Edges. These two measures, however, left untouched a particular potential advantage the Edges had over other forms of international banking organization. Because the Edges were exempt from some of the restriction on loans to or investments in the foreign affiliates of their parent banks, parent banks could use them as "holding companies" for their foreign subsidiaries and affiliated companies.

Though all such possibilities were inherent in an Edge Corporation, American bank executives were slow to seize and use its mechanism to their own advantage. Even during the sunshine years of the 1920s, when it seemed that tomorrow would be automatically better than today simply because twenty-four hours had passed, only 20 Edge Corporations in all were formed by American banks. Of these, only five were still alive in the early 1930s, survivors of the fierce storms that broke thousands of banks starting at the end of the 1920s.

Subsequently, the worldwide depression of the thirties, followed by the war and reconstruction of the forties, made for an environment inhospitable to the growth of any form of international banking, including the establishment overseas of American bank branches. In the specific case of the Edge Corporations, only three new ones were chartered in the twenty-four years between 1932 and 1956. Aside from several existing agreement corporations, when the three newly chartered Edges were added to those which had been formed prior to 1932 and endured, the total in 1956 came to only eight in all.

THE GREAT CHANGE

The late fifties marked the onset of a dramatic increase in the international activities of American banks. The formation of the European Common Market, the expansion of world trade, and the increased investment abroad by American business, intensified the demands for international banking services. Increasing numbers of American banks established branches overseas and created international departments at their head offices. At the same time, increasing numbers of American banks formed Edge Corporations to complement the operations of their overseas branches, or to establish a "presence" in New York. But not in that city alone. With the growing importance of cities other than New York as international banking centers, banks elsewhere in the nation began to form Edge Corporations—as is suggested in the following detail. In 1966, 36 Edge Corporations were in existence, and half of these—or 18—were located in New York City. A decade later, when the number of Edge Corporations had grown to 122, only one-fourth of the total—or 38—were in New York. Significant concentrations of Edge Corporations were present in cities such as Los Angeles with twelve, Chicago with eleven, Miami with ten, and Houston with nine.

Yet the impressive growth in the Edges was eclipsed by two further aspects of the international activities of American banks. One saw the foreign assets of American banks increase from little more than $6 billion in 1957, to the previously mentioned figures of $70 billion in 1972, to nearly $260 billion in 1979. The other, which coincided with the rise of the Eurodollar market, saw the proliferation in the number of overseas branches of American banks which conducted a dollar denominated business on foreign soil. Toward the end of the 1970s, for example, London alone contained more than 50 branches of American banks—all primarily engaged in a dollar banking business, though some were engaged as well in a sterling banking business.

To cite this figure, however, is not to suggest that American branch banks rule the London roost. To the contrary, the intensely competitive picture of which they are a part can be seen in the City of London itself, the financial heart of the United Kingdom and its overseas possessions and client interests. The City of London contains 500 *separate* banks and representative offices, without taking into account the multiplicity of branches of banks such as National Westminster, Lloyd's, and Barclays; National Westminster, to cite but one example, has 500 branches in the London metropolitan area alone. The size and branch network of such English banks give them natural competitive advantages; the major Main Street sites they have long occupied give them an advertising edge; and their retail deposit base, especially during periods of high interest rates, enables them to price their loans aggressively.

Besides London, branches of American banks engaged in a dollar banking business have lately been established in newly emergent offshore financial centers such as Luxembourg, Singapore, Hongkong, the Bahamas, and the Cayman Islands—with 90 branches in the last two locations alone. All this in turn lies behind a recent estimate made by Professor Robert Aliber of the University of Chicago that a "minimum of thirty to fifty thousand positions in banking and bank related business have been exported from the United States to offshore financial centers." London, however, remains the primary offshore financial center, with 30 percent of the total offshore deposits for banks from all countries. France and Luxembourg are the next largest, while centers such as Singapore, Hongkong, the Cayman Islands, and the Bahamas are essentially relay points linked mainly to London.

As noted a moment ago, increased foreign investment activities of American firms spurred the establishment of offshore branches by American banks. Today, for example, one-fourth of all new investments by American firms occur overseas, and they also provide roughly one-fourth of the total profits earned by all American firms doing business abroad. But the development of offshore markets by American banks is not solely due to a natural interest in serving American firms doing business abroad. Another cause is of equal importance. It is that transactions denominated in various foreign currencies are less extensively regulated in their offshore than in their domestic markets. In particular, the principal costs advantage to a foreign bank in producing offshore deposits is that in an overseas location, it is not subject to the same reserve requirements as would apply if it were a domestic bank.

At the conclusion of these pages, notice will be taken of the major change in store for the international activities of American banks following the official introduction in early December 1981 of what is known as a "free zone" within the United States. Something else, however, is of immediate interest right here. It is the way the intense competition among banks in Euromarkets during 1979 resulted in a narrowing rate of international profitability for multinational U.S. banks.

As portrayed in a *Profile of Commercial Banking in the United States*, published by Salomon Brothers in June 1980, the volume of gross new Eurocurrency financing by U.S. multinational banks surged in 1979 to a record of $82 billion—an increase of $12 billion, or 17.1 percent from the previous year. But wait. The *profitability* on their average contractual spreads fell 31.3 percent. At the same time, while the average international loans outstanding for the ten largest American multinational banking institutions grew by 13.6 percent in 1979, this was a third less than the 38 percent expansion in the net size of the Eurocurrency marketplace. The downward trend in connection with borrowing by subgroups was even more marked. Thus U.S. multinational banks' share of net lending claims on oil-exporting countries dropped from 58 percent in 1976–77 to 5 percent in 1978–79, while, in the same period, the share of net lending claims held by U.S. banks on non-oil-producing countries fell from 46 percent to 15 percent.

THE CASE VIEWED THE OTHER WAY AROUND

The obverse side to the overseas activities of multinational American banks is comprised of the expansion of foreign banking activities in the United States marked, among other things, by the acquisition outright of American banks by foreign-based institutions.

The benchmark date for gauging the growth of foreign banking activity in the United States is November 1972 when the Federal Reserve Board began to issue fairly detailed data on the activity of foreign banks in the American banking system. Until that time, the scope of their activity was not quantitatively significant either through direct branches and agencies, the number of foreign banks involved, or the size and scope of their operations. The expansion that subsequently occurred appears in a comparative difference between the figures for 1972 and those for 1979.

In 1972, there were some 30 foreign-owned banks in the United States with 110 offices—though if one were to add bank subsidiaries such as investment companies, total foreign banking organizations came to about 54. Six years later, there were about 90 foreign-owned banks in the United States, while the total number of foreign banking institutions operating on American soil had grown to 305. The total assets of all foreign banking institutions in the United States in 1972 was the previously mentioned $24.3 billion, which came to about 0.6 percent of the total domestic assets of all U.S. banks. By 1979, the assets of the 90 foreign-owned banks in America had grown to 4 percent of the total domestic assets of all U.S. banks.

Out of the total assets in the hands of foreign banking organizations in 1972, the assets in their agencies—which may not accept domestic deposits but can hold credit balances—amounted to $13.6 billion, or over one-half of the total. The remainder was in branches and commercial investment companies. By 1979, their assets expansion, paced by commercial and industrial lending, equalled 29.5 percent of the total commercial loans at large weekly reporting banks. The growth in these business loans was more striking when they were viewed on a regional basis. In the single year 1978–79, foreign banking offices increased their business loans in New York by 43.1 percent, in Illinois by 52.6 percent, and in California by 89.8 percent.

In 1972, Japanese banks were dominant among the foreign banking institutions in the United States. By year-end 1979, however, Western European banks were in the ascendancy, and they controlled about half of the standard assets of foreign banks operating in America. There was more to this statistical picture—an element that set off alarm bells in American banking circles, among state regulatory agencies, and in the Congress. That added element entailed the swift change in the pattern of foreign ownership of U.S. banks. Specifically, since 1972, the number of banks acquired by foreign parties, either directly or through existing U.S. subsidiary banks, exceeded the number established *de novo* by almost 3 to 1. At the same time, the number of banks acquired by foreign individuals, rather than by foreign banking organizations, increased substantially.

The takeover process, starting in 1979, had pronounced features which differed from those of the immediately preceding years. Previous acquisitions of U.S. banks by foreign parties tended to involve relatively small-sized institutions. Alternatively, when they involved banks with domestic assets exceeding $500 million, the takeovers tended to be spaced out from the standpoint of time. In 1974, for example, foreign parties acquired two U.S. institutions. One was the First Western Bank & Trust, Los Angeles, Cal., whose assets, preceding an acquisition by Lloyd's Bank of London, were $1.3 billion. The other was the Franklin National Bank, N.Y., with assets of $3.8 billion. There was but one sizeable takeover in 1975—Southern California First National Bank, Los Angeles, with assets of $884 million. Again in 1976, the only sizeable takeover involved the Bank of California, San Francisco, with assets of $2.7 billion. The same was true in 1977 when the Bank of the Commonwealth, Detroit, Mich., with assets of $925 million was the only sizeable bank to be taken over by a foreign party.

Starting in 1979, however, and extending into 1980, the takeovers came in bunches. In the first seven months of 1979 alone five acquisitions of major banks by foreign banks were either consummated or proposed and soon consummated. Union Bank, Los Angeles, with $5.1 billion in assets was acquired by Standard Chartered Bank of London—which helped up Standard's rank from 74th to 59th place among the world's largest banks. National Bank of North America, N.Y., N.Y., with assets of $3.6 billion was acquired by National Westminster of London—which helped up its world rank from 21st to 17th place. La Salle National Bank, Chicago, Ill., with assets of $920 million, was acquired by the Algemene Bank Nederland—which helped up its world rank from 29th to 25th place. The proposed acquisition in 1979 by Hongkong and Shanghai Banking Corporation of the Marine Midland Bank, N.Y., with assets of $10.5 billion, was consummated in 1980—which helped raise Hongkong and Shanghai's rank among the world's largest banks from 79th to 44th place.

The takeover process was temporarily checked by a provision of the Depository Institution Deregulation and Monetary Control Act of 1980 which imposed a moratorium on foreign acquisitions of U.S. banks extending April to July 1, 1980. But when the moratorium expired, the Midland Bank Ltd. of London announced plans to acquire a majority holding in Crocker National Corporation of California whose end-1979 assets of $15.6 billion made it the 14th largest banking group in the U.S. The consolidation of the Midland Bank and the Crocker National Bank—the main asset of the Crocker holding company—would help make Midland the 13th largest bank in the world in terms of deposits.

SUMMARY OF CAUSES FOR FOREIGN ACQUISITIONS

Each foreign acquisition of an American bank has had its own distinctive features. But among the general causes at work in the picture, one has been the increased internationalization of the world's banking system as a whole, and the growing maturity of the international activity of many banks in different parts of the globe. Acquisitions which go with the process occur in many places on a trans-national basis involving a cluster of participating institutions.[24]

As for other factors influencing foreign acquisitions of U.S. banks: Because of the preeminence of the U.S. dollar in international trade and finance and the size of U.S. financial markets, foreign banks conducting an international business have found a need for a U.S. presence and consequent access to dollar clearing facilities. Their decisions to expand through acquisitions rather than through growth of existing facilities have reflected both the availability of U.S. banks on relatively attractive terms and the corporate strategy of acquiring foreign banks. In recent years U.S. bank stocks, like those of many other U.S. corporations, were at relatively low levels. Shares of banks with below-average earnings records have sold at especially deep discounts from book value. This has doubtless played a role in the acquisitions made by foreign individuals as well as by foreign banking institutions.

An added factor has been the availability for sale of a number of U.S. banks that were owned by nonbanking companies. The Bank Holding Company Amendments (BHCA) of 1970 required nonbanking owners of banking institutions to choose by 1980 to divest themselves of their banks or to limit their nonbank activities to those permitted by the BHCA. Faced with this choice, a number of American holding companies sold their U.S. banks, including the former owners of the National Bank of North America in New York, and the La Salle National Bank. The divestiture requirement increased the availability of several U.S. banks at a time when a number of foreign banks were seeking to expand their U.S. activities. Coincidentally, statutory restrictions on interstate banking, combined with Federal antitrust laws, effectively prevented large domestic banks from acquiring any sizeable U.S. banks and thus from competing with foreign parties in acquisition situations.

Beyond the foregoing, a Federal Reserve Board staff study of July 1980—based on an examination of 42 U.S. institutions that were eventually merged with foreign-owned institutions or acquired by foreign parties— underlined other characteristics common to many of the acquired banks.[25] The staff study noted that 18 of the banks had been experiencing losses or, as in the instances of Southern California and Franklin National, were in receivership immediately before changing ownership. The Bank of the Commonwealth was receiving direct financial support from the FDIC. Another six banks reported a very low return on assets—less than 0.2 percent. The Marine Midland was low on both capital and earnings. Compared to other banks, the acquired banks in general had a lower liquidity, a higher proportion of loans to assets, higher loan charge-offs, higher levels of nonperforming assets, below-average earnings, and lower capital ratios, and they relied more on money markets for their funding. The most tangible effect of foreign ownership, and indeed a condition of approval, was an immediate injection of needed capital.

U.S. LEGAL REACTIONS: FIRST ROUND

Though the Joint Economic Committee of Congress as early as 1966 indicated an interest in the competitive implications of foreign bank operations in the United States, it was not until 1973–74 that the Federal Reserve began to develop legislative proposals to deal with the regulation of foreign banks.

Congress, for its part, was uneasy over foreign investments in American banks, or for that matter, in any significant business or asset. Its unease increased to a pronounced degree after 1973 when the Arab boycott on oil shipments to the United States, and the quadrupling in the price of OPEC oil, was followed by an accelerating shift of billions of American-held dollars into the hands of foreign oil producers. At the same time, another factor compounded Congressional unease over foreign entry into the heart of the American financial and industrial structure. It was the general sense among legislators that they lacked full information about the actual extent of that foreign entry. In consequence, no fewer than four laws were put on the statute books between 1974 and 1978 having a disclosure purpose.[26]

While the disclosure laws were being enacted, banking posed fewer or more familiar problems to Congress than did foreign investments in the general run of American enterprises. Aside from the fact that foreign banking institutions had been in the United States since the 1880s, the banking industry itself was thoroughly regulated. The growth of a foreign banking presence, therefore, seemed at first to pose only another regulatory issue. How could foreign banking institutions be brought under better control? The provisional answer to the issue—forthcoming before the rash of foreign acquisitions of major American banks—was the International Banking Act of 1978.

THE INTERNATIONAL BANKING ACT OF 1978

Among the issues that measure purported to settle, the main one was "reciprocity" versus "national treatment."

The term "reciprocity," like "reciprocal trade agreements," besides being familiar, had a ring of fairness. Advocates of the concept argued that a foreign bank should be able to do the same kind of business in the United States that an American bank could do in the country where the foreign bank was headquartered. Its opponents argued that the contemplated trade-off would be extremely hard to administer. More than that, the United States would be required either to relax its own complex restrictions on domestic banks, or see them placed in a grossly unfair competitive position. The case against "reciprocity" was succinctly stated by Treasury General Counsel Robert Mundheim during his 1978 testimony before the Senate Banking Committee. Mundheim, who favored the "national treatment" concept, observed:[27]

Under a policy of reciprocity, we would allow a foreign bank to engage in the United States in all those activities in which American banks are permitted to engage in the home country of the foreign bank, even though we do not permit domestic banks to conduct such activities here. Since countries differ on which activities banks may engage in, the United States under a policy of reciprocity, would have to administer different sets of rules for various foreign banks operating in this country, depending on their nationality. . . . Furthermore, the advantages we would have to afford foreign banks under a policy of reciprocity—such as the ability to engage in interstate branching, and a broad range of nonbanking activities—would result in unfair competitive pressures on domestic banks. Under the national treatment approach, foreign banks would generally be put on the same footing and held to the same restrictions as domestic banks.

It was the "national treatment" concept that was eventually incorporated into the International Banking Act of 1978 (IBA). Thus foreign banks were given the right to branch into states other than their "home" states, but only if such out-of-state branches were permitted by the states in which they were to be located. They could also accept deposits, but only if they arose in the course of international banking operations. In this connection, the legislation permitted foreign banks to set up Edge Act subsidiaries. To maintain parity for domestic banks, however, the 1978 legislation also significantly liberalized Edge Act rules. It directed the Federal Reserve Board to remove unnecessary regulatory restraints, not only to facilitate competition with foreign banks, but also to enable the Edge corporations to become more effective providers of international banking services and to foster ownership of such corporations by small and regional domestic branches.

As to other features of the 1978 legislation: The Federal Reserve could henceforth impose reserve requirements on federally chartered branches and agencies of foreign banks in cases where the parent had worldwide assets of $1 billion or more. It could also exercise the same authority over state-chartered branches and agencies after consultation with state banking authorities. Further, while the Comptroller of the Currency, the FDIC, and state regulators were granted primary examining authority over foreign banks in their jurisdiction, the Federal Reserve was granted residual examining authority. Restrictions of the Bank Holding Company Act on activities not related to banking were extended to foreign bank operations in the United States, subject to two exemptions.

First, the Federal Reserve Board was granted the right to permit a foreign company to engage in any activity or to make an investment if it found that doing so was in the public interest. The object of this discretionary exemption was to avoid precluding investments in the U.S. for foreign non-banking firms simply because those firms owned foreign banks. The most frequently cited example involved Daimler-Benz, the German automobile maker. Without the indicated exemption, Daimler-Benz—which is more than 25 percent owned by Deutsche Bank—could not do business in the United States as long as the Deutsche Bank was also engaged in banking in this country. The second exemption permitted a foreign institution principally engaged in banking business outside the U.S. to hold shares of foreign nonbanking companies that do business here. Both exemptions, as will be noted in a moment, were to be tightened toward the end of 1980 by new ground rules issued by the Federal Reserve Board.

Foreign bankers, meanwhile, only grudgingly approved the "national treatment" approach that was incorporated in the International Banking Act of 1978. They had strongly urged that the reciprocity approach be adopted—because they saw that it would work to their advantage.

The issue of reciprocity, however, was not settled for good. It was bound to arise in different forms. Not the least of the reasons why was this: that while foreign interests had a wide latitude to acquire U.S. banks, U.S. banks generally found it difficult if not impossible to acquire major foreign banks with assets having the magnitude of a Marine Midland or a Crocker National Bank. The case here was delicately put by Paul Volcker when he was president of the New York Federal Reserve Bank. In addressing the International Monetary Fund Conference in London in early 1979 Mr. Volcker observed:[28]

I personally question whether open entry on a basis of national treatment in instances where the home country does not provide reasonably equivalent access to American and other foreign banks is equitable to U.S. banking interests. . . . I recognize that many foreign banking systems are much more concentrated than in the United States, and they are much smaller markets in the aggregate. Takeover of one or a handful of leading banks in those countries would have quantitatively and qualitatively dif-

ferent implications than a takeover in the United States—but the differences might
not be so great if analysis were directed toward regional sections of the U.S. market.

POLICY CONFLICTS

With the surge of foreign takeovers of American banks in 1979, Congressional
responses tended to differ from those of federal regulatory authorities. In
the Congress, serious concern was voiced not so much over the entry of
foreign banks on a *de novo* basis, but rather with the acquisition of major
American banks by foreign banks. At the federal level of government, the
Federal Reserve and the Comptroller of the Currency seemed reasonably
confident that they could handle any problems likely to arise from the foreign
takeovers. Both, in fact, struck a decidedly pro-international tone in their
public statements. Thus Paul Volcker on the eve of his appointment as
Chairman of the Federal Reserve Board:[29]

In broad principle, the United States accepts the market system. We like to see more,
not fewer competitors. In general we are content to see economic policy work its
way through relatively impersonal market incentives. And we have long supported
the free movement of capital, internationally, alongside trade, as being in the national
as well as the international interest.

Comptroller of the Currency John Heimann struck an even stronger
pro-international note. In testifying before a subcommittee of the House
Banking Committee in the mid-summer of 1979, he recalled Alexander Hamilton's statement that "rather than treating the foreign investor as a rival,
we should consider him a valuable partner." Then he went on to say:[30]

We recognize that foreign ownership of U.S. banks can pose special problems.
However, we believe that intervention or restrictions which are inconsistent with our
policies of national treatment and free and open markets should be adopted only
upon a clear cut demonstration that such intervention is in the national interest.
. . . Our capitalistic system, the freedom of private enterprise to make market-based
investment decisions with but few government restraints, has stood the test of two
centuries. Those who, by restricting foreign investments would tamper with the
underlying precepts of our system, must bear the burden of proof.

Federal Reserve Board Governor Henry Wallich, in testifying before
the same House subcommittee, dwelt on the benefits of foreign investments
in domestic banks. They included the transfusion of capital into enfeebled
banks, the positive impact foreign purchases would have on the undervalued
price of U.S. bank stocks generally, the likelihood that foreign investments
would "bring innovation and improved efficiency to U.S. banks," and their
role in acquiring "problem" banks. This last touched an exposed nerve.
Under existing U.S. law, a large American bank that was in difficulty could
not be acquired by a domestic bank headquartered in another state. The

constraints did not apply to foreign investors. They could acquire a "problem" bank wherever it was located.

MORE ACQUISITIONS

As noted earlier, the Depository Institutions Deregulation and Monetary Control Act of 1980 ordered a moratorium on foreign acquisitions of American banks until July 1, 1980, pending a report the General Accounting Office was directed to make and submit to Congress by that date. When hearings on the completed report were set before the Financial Institutions Subcommittee of the House Banking Committee, Chairman St. Germain indicated that the hearings, besides focusing on the effect of acquisitions of U.S. banks by foreign interests, would also consider the problems of interstate banking and related issues.

Meanwhile, with the end of the July 1, 1980, moratorium on the foreign takeover of U.S. banks, the takeover movement was resumed. The continued expansion of foreign banking activity in the United States exacerbated preexisting fears about how the effect would crimp the ability of the Federal Reserve to carry out its monetary policies. The fears revolved around two points in particular. One was that much of the growth of foreign banking activity entailed the establishment of branches and the formation or acquisition of nonmember banks whose operations were not subject to reserve requirements. The other was that foreign institutions would be less responsive than U.S. members to public statements and guidelines issued by the Federal Reserve Board—a policy tool often termed "moral suasion."

The two fears just mentioned, along with virtually all other aspects of the controversy over the increased scope of foreign banking activity in the United States, were examined in the previously mentioned Federal Reserve Board staff study of late July 1980. The staff observed that the reserve requirement issue had in effect been eliminated by the International Banking Act of 1978 (IBA), and by the Monetary Control Act of 1980 (MCA) with its linkage to the Depository Institutions Deregulation Act of that omnibus legislation. The IBA gave the Federal Reserve the authority to apply reserve requirements to agencies and branches of large foreign banks (over $1 billion in consolidated assets), and such reserve requirements on their liabilities were due to be introduced in a two-year period starting in September 1980. Similarly, under the MCA, the deposits of all nonmember banks, including U.S. subsidiaries of foreign banks, were subjected to Federal Reserve reserve requirements which were to be phased in over an eight-year period. Thus, in time, all the banking offices of foreign banks would be subject to the same reserve requirements as member banks.

The staff study observed further that foreign-owned banks were as responsive as U.S. banks to suggestions and guidelines issued by the Federal Reserve. Foreign banks, for example, cooperated with the Federal Reserve's request in mid-1973 voluntarily to maintain reserve deposits against increases in their Eurodollar lending. Again, when the Federal Reserve asked foreign banks to cooperate in support of its monetary restraint programs of October 1979 and March 1980—and to observe the same guidelines as U.S. member banks—they complied with the request to the extent equal to member banks. The staff study concluded: "In view of the impending application of reserve requirements to all depository institutions in the United States, foreign ac- quisitions of U.S. banks should no longer give rise to concern about the effects on the ability of the Federal Reserve to implement monetary policy."

In November 1980, or roughly four months after the staff study was published, the Federal Reserve Board did move to tighten the restrictions on outside business run by foreign banks in the United States. The restric- tions were addressed to the two previously mentioned exemptions from the nonbanking prohibitions to the Bank Holding Company Act which were carried over into the International Banking Act of 1978. One of the excep- tions, to repeat, gave the Federal Reserve Board discretion to permit a foreign company to engage in any nonbanking activity or to make an in- vestment in it if the Board concluded that approval was in the public interest. The second exemption permitted a foreign banking institution principally engaged in banking outside the U.S. to hold shares in foreign nonbanking companies doing business in America.

The Board originally took the position that a foreign organization could qualify for these exemptions if it had more than 50 percent of its worldwide business in banking, and if more than 50 percent of its banking business proper was conducted outside the United States. But after receiving com- plaints from Congress that an organization ineligible for the exemptions could qualify by increasing its banking business through the acquisition of a U.S. subsidiary branch, the Board tightened its approach. It ruled that an institution's banking business outside the U.S. must exceed its worldwide nonbanking business—though any foreign institution disqualified by the new test could apply to the Board for a waiver. The Board also unveiled a com- plicated new formula to be used in measuring an institution's business to see if it qualified for an exemption.

FUTURE PROSPECTS

Where will all the movements in the internationalization of banking lead U.S. banking itself in the years immediately ahead? Only a dogmatist would venture to answer that question in a flat-out way. "The trouble with our times," as Paul Valéry's paradox put it, "is that the future is not what it used to be." Yet it is reasonable to suggest that an important consequence of the penetration of the U.S. economy by foreign banks may be the one farthest removed from the conscious aims of the foreign bankers themselves.

It may be the impact foreign acquisitions will have on present geographical restrictions on commercial bank expansion in the United States.

As pointed out a moment ago, the "national treatment" approach adopted in the International Banking Act of 1978 purported to place all domestic and foreign banking institutions doing business in the United States on the same footing. But the approach left smouldering issues behind. Because extensive "grandfathering" was given foreign banks which were already in the United States when the law was enacted, a number of foreign banks had the right under the 1978 Act to branch into states other than their "home" states. These secondary branches, in turn, could make loans to the extent permitted by state law—a tilt favorable to foreign banks not paralleled in the instance of domestic banks. Further, foreign banking investors could cross state lines to acquire "problem" banks, something domestic banks were not allowed to do.

Interstate branching barriers were not only being undercut or seriously eroded by foreign institutions in the immediately foregoing ways. They were also being eroded by the liberalization of what used to be the obscure 1919 Edge Act. With liberalization—itself a continuing process—Edge Act Corporations have been brought to a point where they are no longer limited to financing transactions of an international nature, primarily imports and exports. They are within reaching distance of a title of right to offer *full* banking services to domestic customers primarily engaged in international business.

All such developments amount to an "end run" around the 1927 McFadden Act, barring interstate banking to domestic institutions. As a matter of equity, pressures mounted on Congress to reverse the policy where it withheld from domestic banks rights enjoyed by foreign banks. It seems that foreign banks would provide the ultimate shove that would help topple the geographical constraints imposed on banking by the McFadden Act and by the Bank Holding Company Act—constraints whose practical effect distorted the meaning of "competition." The current status of the issue here will be touched on in the last chapter of this book.

18. *The Management of International Assets and Liabilities*

Changed context

With the internationalization of banking, executives of U.S. multinational banks—and of other large U.S. banks as well—have had to reexamine the management of their assets and liabilities in concurrent international and domestic contexts. The need to do so first surfaced at the end of the 1950s when the resources of the fast-developing Eurodollar market became a significant factor in the mechanics of international financial transactions. But the need became irrepressible after the early 1970s when domestic and international events intersected to create new conditions for the transnational management of assets and liabilities. The picture, drawn in a few strokes, was this.

On the domestic side of things, the controls the U.S. government had previously imposed on capital movements—in response to persistent inflation and balance-of-payments deficits—were removed step-by-step as the 1970s wore on. On the international side, the tattered Bretton Woods formula for an international monetary system finally gave up its ghost in 1973 when central banks stopped pegging their exchange rates and allowed them to float. Soon afterward, the quadrupling in the price of imported Organization of Petroleum Exporting Countries (OPEC) oil radically increased the preexisting deficits in the U.S. balance of payments. With each subsequent price increase, the tidal flow of U.S. dollars into foreign hands swelled the volume of Eurodollars in international money markets that were readily available for lending and borrowing purposes. The aggregate effect these and other events had on management of assets and liabilities is treated below.

Increased risks

In the late 1960s, the U.S. government had imposed three controls on capital movements. First, the U.S. interest equalization tax (IET)—a tax on foreign equity and debt issues purchased by U.S. residents—was extended to cover long-term bank loans to foreigners. Second, bank lending abroad was limited by the Federal Reserve Board's "voluntary" foreign credit restraint program (VFCR). Then in 1969, the Board, as part of its tight money policy, applied its Regulation M—affecting reserve requirements—hoping to stem the inflow of funds into the U.S. from the foreign branches of U.S. banks. These three restrictions, taken together, drove an institutional wedge between the domestic and international activities of major U.S. banks.

As long as capital controls limited options, executives of multinational banks faced no great costs when they subdivided the decision process for managing assets and liabilities into domestic and foreign compartments. In early 1974, however, the IET tax and the VFCR restrictions on banks were removed, and the Regulation M reserve requirement was reduced in stages between 1973 and 1978. With these decontrols, the institutional factors that had previously segmented dollar financial markets were displaced by a significant increase in the degree of interdependence between domestic and foreign operations. Domestic funds of U.S. multinational banks could support foreign business, and foreign funds could support the domestic business of the multinationals and the primarily domestic banks alike. The price of errors in international financial transactions ceased to be hypothetical—or small. They were real, and large.

The price of errors was increased after foreign central banks, starting in 1973, stopped pegging their exchange rates and allowed them to float. Despite subsequent attempts within the European Economic Community (EEC) to provide a measure of cohesion in the EEC's internal currency arrangements, international exchange interest rates lacked their previous relative stability. They were unhinged by the radical increases in the price of OPEC oil, the impact of widespread inflation, recessions in industrial countries, their uneven recovery, and in many cases, their persistent trade imbalances. As exchange and interest rates moved by wider margins than in the past, they increased the risks to banks of foreign exposure and maturity mismatches in their international lending and borrowing.

All this alone would have forced activists in the world of U.S. finance to reexamine the internal control mechanism among banks as they related to the management of assets and liabilities—either domestically, internationally, or both together. Other events, however, played their own part in accenting the need to reassess the institutional management structures of banks.[31] In one direction, for example, stories in the financial press read like medical reports in an intensive care unit, regarding the way major U.S. multinational banks—acting alone or as members of a consortium—were badly hurt by their loans to less developed countries (LDCs) and to some tanker companies. In another direction, the price of bank mismanagement was cast into bold relief by the failure of large U.S. banks such as Franklin National and Southern California, by the near failure of First Pennsylvania, and by the reported fact that other important U.S. banks were on the Comptroller of the Currency's "sick list." Perhaps at no time since the Great Depression did the internal control mechanism among banks draw more concerned attention to itself.

Central coordination vs. decentralization

Ask any group of bankers how they think their work in any market can best be approached and organized, and you are sure to start an argument. That, after all, is what a market is all about. It is not a mathematical abstraction. It is part of the real world—a meeting place for a large number of people whose views and interests vary. They certainly vary in the case of the judgments bankers make when they assess the costs-benefits they see in the alternative models for managing institutional assets and liabilities in the new environment around them.[32]

Some bankers—and the immediate focus here is on those associated with multinational banks—strongly favor central coordination of responsibility. They claim that in this way they can better manage the *total* flow of their funds—can initiate profitable foreign and domestic transactions that would not be possible but for the ability of central headquarters to shift funds from one place to the next. On the other hand, bankers critical of central coordination claim that the arrangement tends naturally to shift responsibility for decisions to head offices, with cramping effects on the talents and morale of personnel in foreign branches. Instead, they strongly favor a decentralized management structure—organized by geographical areas. In their design, each geographical area is treated as an individual "profit center," whose executives have broad on-the-spot discretionary powers.

Whether bankers subscribe to a centralized or decentralized model—or to something in between—all are alike in one fundamental respect. All seek to increase the profitability of their respective institutions through a more effective use of funds in world markets, and particularly in world dollar markets. The divisive issue entails a disagreement over the best ways and means.

In developing their case, advocates of a centralized global management of assets and liabilities argue that the arrangement may help a bank fund itself at the lowest rates and lend at the highest. They agree that all banks compare rates in various markets when seeking or placing funds. Under usual circumstances, though, the advantages of centralized information may be small. Yet where timing is crucial—where market conditions, for example, unexpectedly change—the *authority to act* as well as the information prerequisite for action can make all the difference in the fruits of a transaction. They note that the officer responsible for the global management of assets and liabilities has far more flexibility in his choice of markets than does the officer in charge of an individual profit center. He also generally has a wide scope for the discretionary positions he can take, while the relative effectiveness of an officer in the individual profit center tends to depend on the speed with which he can get permission from the head office to exceed in special situations the fixed limits on his commitments. Through force of contrast, the factor of speed—call it "the economics of time"—favors the centralized management of global assets and liabilities.

Advocates of centralized management further argue that the arrangement, among other things, enhances a bank's ability to arbitrage favorable differentials in interest rates. If, for example, six-month dollar funds are available at 10.50 percent in the New York certificate of deposit market, but can earn 10.75 percent in the London Eurodollar market, then a bank which placed $1 million in the London market financed from funds raised in New York could earn a profit of $1,250, provided the process of bidding for funds in one market and offering them in another were closely coordinated.

Yet when banks are organized as separate profit centers, any manager may initiate an arbitrage transaction at arm's length from profit center managers elsewhere—while a decision to transact simultaneously in two markets would require an agreement between the managers responsible for each. Before such an agreement was reached, however, managers in New York and in London would each determine if the prospective transaction were in the interest of their respective profit centers; if the answer were in the affirmative, they would still have to decide how to split the profits.

All such problems are avoided by the centralized global management of assets and liabilities. The arrangement facilitates arbitrage transactions by establishing a clear management responsibility to exploit profit opportunities in the interest of the bank as a whole. At the same time, the ability of the parent bank to maintain close contact with the world market through the flow of information from its branches, materially aids the parent in spotting arbitrage opportunities.

Further, the global management of assets and liabilities enhances a parent bank's ability to net out opposing transactions before they reach a market. A branch in Paris, for example, may need funds at the same time that a branch in Frankfurt wishes to supply funds. If they recognized their offsetting needs, they would transact with each other. If they didn't, the transaction would be made in the market, potentially costing the bank the spread between the bid and offer rate for funds. But with the global management of assets and liabilities, the close communications between the parent bank and each of its branches facilitates, as in the Paris-Frankfurt case, offsetting internal transfers of funds. The parent bank can thereby avoid the potential market cost of the transaction in funds.

All such lines of argument, however, are met head-on by advocates of decentralized management. The latter, to start with, contend that there is no monopoly of information in the market; local managers are as likely to exercise good judgment as their counterparts in the head office. By managing individual parts of a bank's total portfolio, they enable the bank to respond to favorable local market opportunities. Further, while coordination at the center is crucially dependent upon information on conditions in diverse market locations, headquarters personnel are not preeminent candidates for a vacancy in the Trinity. They cannot and do not know everything about what is special to a local market—its tides, tensions, prospects for trades, loans, borrowings, the character of the parties to any and all transactions.

That kind of knowledge comes only with direct on-the-spot exposure to and activity in a local market. To supplant the judgment of a local manager by those made in the headquarters of the parent bank would pay homage to the abstract concept of global management at the risk of profits lost to the bank. On the other hand, the challenge to earn profits, the freedom to manage a department without daily yaes and nayes from superiors—and the sobering experience of being trusted with discretionary power—can be a source of long-range benefits to a bank far beyond the earnings from a cluster of transactions.

The mind, like a muscle, needs to be exercised, else it gets flabby. And the best exercise for training the mind of a banker depends on two conditions: the right to make discretionary decisions within his jurisdiction, coupled with his accountability for the consequences of the decisions he made. Those in the field who are blunder-prone can be spotted at a fairly early hour by the top managers of the parent bank. They can be shunted to one side before they are a matching piece in banking terms to what Marshall Foch said about the military: "It takes 14,000 casualties to train one major general." Those who do well in the context of decentralized organization can also be spotted by the top managers of the parent bank. They can become natural candidates for appointment to higher places of responsibility—and the training by top managers of able successors to their *own* posts is among *their* own major responsibilities.

INTERMEDIATE POSITIONS

Executives in some multinational banks have experimented with organizational forms intermediate between the global management of assets and liabilities, and decentralized decision-making. Those in command of a parent bank's headquarters do not interfere with the actual decisions of local managers. They do, however, require local managers to report daily to the head office, where executives may then hedge market positions that appear in the aggregate to be unsound. Through such offsetting transactions made at the center, the interests of the bank as a single whole are served, while the principle of local autonomy is upheld. Other larger multinational banks confine their centralized coordination of domestic and international money market trading to specific Euromarkets, such as London, Nassau, and the Cayman Islands, while allowing for local autonomy elsewhere. Still others have informal arrangements in which a supervisory unit in a parent bank oversees the way local managers coordinate their own activities. All such experiments reflect the felt need of bank executives to adapt to the realities of their larger institutional presence in world markets, the tighter interplay of domestic and foreign market transactions, the increased risks posed by the general economic environment, and by revolutionary ferments in the world arena.

CONGRESSIONAL RELIEF

It used to be possible for foreign creditors to seize a defaulted country, as the British and French did when they foreclosed Egypt in the 1860s during the reign of Ismail Pasha. They landed in Egypt, assumed control of the tax collection system, and paid themselves. But the fabled days of "gunboat finance" are long since over. Today—at least in the American case—the search for ways to cope with the consequences of debt defaults by foreign governments has led to two recent congressional enactments.

The first is known as the Foreign Sovereign Immunities Act of 1978. For the first time in American law, the bill—in theory—provides a statutory procedure "for making service upon, and obtaining *in personem* jurisdiction over a foreign state and its entities." If Zaire, for example, after defaulting on a $500 million loan to it by a consortium of New York banks, had willfully refused to consider a rescheduling of the defaulted debt, the creditor banks could go into a federal court in New York and get a judgment against Zaire in the indicated amount. But what if Zaire (unlike Iran) had no assets in the U.S. that could be attached? That's the rub. The creditor banks would have to send their agents to Zaire in order to collect on the judgment—a project, which in the light of Zaire's financial bind, would produce little more than a series of regrets.

The second of the two ways for handling the defaults of LDCs is by socializing any losses the banks suffered on their loans to the LDCs—this, by having the American taxpayer underwrite the costs of a bail out by the federal government. A representative bail-out device, known as the White-veen Facility, initially provided $10 billion for loans to LDCs hurt by the oil gouge, and the LDCs in turn could then pay off the New York banks.

The use of the phrase "bail out" in this connection met with heated objections from the banks that would be directly aided. At a Senate Banking Committee hearing, for example, John Haley, Executive Vice President of Chase Manhattan, denied that "a recommendation for increased official international credit is basically a plea for a 'bail out' of the major multi-national commercial banks. . . . What is at stake here is *not* the health of the major banks but rather the health of the world economy." The *Wall Street Journal,* for its part, was left dry-eyed by this eloquent disclaimer. It observed in an editorial that the honest name for the Whiteveen Facility of the IMF should have been "The Bankers' Relief Act of 1977." It went on to charge that the Whiteveen Facility was flying false colors: "American tax-payers, in other words, will be asked to cough up a few billion for the IMF to loan to the poor countries so that they can pay off the banks. The indirect approach was necessary to fool the taxpayers into thinking that they were thereby helping the poor."

Criticism of this kind from a leading organ of American capitalism struck exposed nerves—which were already throbbing from the pain experienced by the managers of multinational U.S. banks when they actually tried to collect loans made to the LDCs. When OPEC in late October 1979 again sharply increased the price of oil, David Rockefeller warned through the columns of *The New York Times* that U.S. multinational banks could not be counted on to play their previous part in recycling oil dollars by making loans on their own account. Nor have they done so. As indicated previously, while the share of net lending claims held by U.S. bank on oil-exporting countries dropped from 58 percent in 1976–77 to 5 percent in 1978–79, the net lending claims held by U.S. banks on non-oil-producing countries fell from 46 to 15 percent.

Previous stability in exchange rates

Between 1946 and the mid-1960s, the distinctive feature of the international monetary system—which contributed to the expansion of world trade—was a structure of par values designed to combine exchange rate stability with flexibility. After adjustments were made in 1949, most countries—at least most industrial countries—maintained their exchange rates very close to their par values, as prescribed by the Articles of Agreement of the International Monetary Fund.[33]

The United States held virtually all of its monetary reserves in the form of gold; other countries, at their option, held in their reserves both gold and foreign exchange (chiefly dollars, but also sterling and French francs). The system worked, notwithstanding periodic and sometimes severe speculative and other pressures on one or more currencies in the foreign exchange markets. Changes in par value did occur, but only infrequently. Exchange rates for the leading currencies were held firmly within the prescribed narrow margins by official intervention. But if the system thus served the cause of exchange-rate stability, after the mid-1960s, it became increasingly apparent that it was failing to serve the companion cause of flexibility.

Until that time, foreign commercial bankers knew that, whenever they wanted to, they could take their dollars to their central banks and get their own or other currencies at fixed rates. Besides, foreign commercial banks were able to lend dollars at higher rates than they could lend their own currencies. This was particularly true in 1969 when the Nixon Administration, as a first gesture in its stop-and-go economics, briefly instituted a restrictive monetary policy. When the supply of funds became tight in the United States, Americans borrowed great blocks of these dollars owned in Europe—the Eurodollars.

In the spring of 1970, however, the Nixon Administration, with its eye on the congressional elections, shifted from a restrictive fiscal and monetary policy to one of fiscal expansionism and monetary ease. More funds for loans now became available in the United States and interest rates went down. Americans to a large extent repaid their Eurodollar borrowings, and as Eurodollar interest rates dropped, foreign commercial banks no longer wanted to hold as many dollars. They began to channel the dollars to their central banks and obtained other currencies in exchange.

Foreign central banks, on their part, had long been quite willing to accept dollars. Since the 1930s, they had been assured by U.S. law, tradition, and repeated statements of policy that the U.S. Treasury would buy dollars and gold at fixed prices—$35 per ounce of gold—any time a foreign central bank so desired. But by December 1970, foreign central banks held $20.1 billion in short-term dollar claims, and the U.S. government held only $11.1 billion in gold. Other reserve assets available—convertible currencies and drawing rights on the International Monetary Fund—amounted to only $3.4 billion. Under the circumstances, if foreign central banks pressed for payment, the U.S. Treasury would have been unable to redeem its obligations as they were presented. In a sense, the nation was insolvent, and only through the forbearance of the creditor central banks was the U.S. Treasury spared the humiliation of a presentation and confessed inability to pay.

Meanwhile, inflation-driven American goods became less competitive in world markets, and American exports continued to suffer—though more was imported than ever before, with continuing adverse effects on trade balances. Some seventy-seven years of U.S. trade balance surpluses were displaced by sustained deficits in the balance of trade. By 1971—or two years before a bad case was made worse by the actions of the OPEC oil cartel—the accumulated deficiency in the American international balance of payments over the immediately preceding years reached $73 billion. Concurrently, foreigners accumulated dollars in amounts that rose from $7 billion in 1950 to $43 billion in 1970.

The seriousness of the problem lay in the fact that the dollar had been viewed as the versatile workhorse of the international monetary system, hinged to the International Monetary Fund. The dollar, for example, was the *key* currency, because the United States was the sole country which still pegged its currency to gold. It was the primary *intervention* currency, because other countries pegged their own currency to the dollar, either directly or indirectly. Further, because the dollar was widely used by central banks as an international asset—more useful than gold because of the interest to be earned on it—the dollar was the primary *reserve* currency. Because it was widely used for trading operations as a currency of *contract,* the dollar (along with the pound) was the primary *vehicle* currency. Because it was widely used as the *currency of quotation,* the dollar was the main currency serving as a *unit of account.* By 1971, however, it was as if mice suddenly began to chase cats. The dollar buckled, slid, and groaned, crushed between the overload of internal and external stresses it had long carried.

Government officials in the United States, like those abroad, met the strain by patchwork expedients. Alone or after international consultations, they confined their efforts to papering over the most immediately visible cracks in the inflexible international monetary system. But once a seemingly localized crisis had passed, they took their bearing from the demands of domestic politics. They would not risk reprisals from an electorate by advocating and *persisting* in measures—requiring domestic discipline—to infuse the dollar and the international monetary system with vital new strength.

They would not risk reprisals from an electorate by appreciating their undervalued currencies when doing so—as in the case of the German deutsche mark, the Japanese yen, and the Swiss franc—implied a concealed loss of some trade advantages in world markets.

In 1970–71, growing payments and imbalances, increasingly centered on the U.S. dollar, generated heavy speculative pressures on the dollar and very large losses of U.S. reserves—leading to the collapse of the system of fixed international exchange rates, all pegged to the U.S. dollar. On August 15, 1971, President Nixon announced that the U.S. would no longer freely buy and sell gold and that, for the time being, it would not maintain the parity of the dollar. At the same time, he instituted a sweeping new economic program entailing an immediate wage, price, and rent freeze, and a 10 percent import surcharge. Other leading countries, most notably Germany and Japan, were not prepared to hold the dollar within prescribed narrow margins by official intervention with no assurance that they could convert excess dollar holdings into gold. So there followed a period during which leading currencies floated, with the dollar depreciating.

If the agreement reached at the Smithsonian Conference in December 1971 had been followed by a termination of nontariff barriers (NTBs) against American goods, the devaluation of the dollar and the appreciation of other currencies announced at the time might have sustained the new structure of par values. But no significant NTBs were lowered and none removed. American authorities repeatedly called for a return to the agreed principles of nondiscriminatory trade. They also repeatedly called for further upward revaluation of the deutsche mark and yen. But there was no cooperative response—only demands that the U.S. make the dollar convertible into gold. In the absence of any discernable signs of cooperation, the U.S. balance of payments picture worsened, and a further devaluation of the dollar appeared likely. U.S. corporations and banks doing business abroad, foreign corporations doing business in America, all sought to sell dollars and buy foreign currencies, especially deutsche marks and Swiss francs. Dollars continued to flow abroad and soon reached a flood stage under the pressures of massive speculations.

So things went until January 11, 1973, when President Nixon ordered an end to the mandatory wage and price controls which had been in formal effect for the previous seventeen months. They were to be replaced by a "voluntary" program to permit greater flexibility in wage and price administration. The Federal Reserve Board signaled its resolve to press its battle against the domestic forces of inflation that were weakening the dollar. It announced an increase in the rediscount rate from 5 percent to 5.5 percent, representing a further extension of the new tight money policy it had recently put into effect.

Many commercial bankers believed that a swift solution had been found for a crisis whose combined domestic and international elements put at hazard any economic decisions they made. They hoped that a period of relative calm would now ensue when economic decisions could be made within fairly stable boundaries. But this was not to be. In baffling ways, loans to foreigners on the books of U.S. banks continued to increase. Even overnight federal funds found their way into the Eurodollar market at what was then the high rate of 7 percent. Speculation continued unchecked. With the principal attention focused on the deutsche mark, a point was reached where the Bundesbank was forced to close the market on March 1, 1973. Most other European central banks followed suit by closing the market for their respective currencies. An emergency meeting of Europe's finance ministers and central bankers was held in Brussels. But the only agreement they reached was to keep the money market closed for a week, and at the end of that time to reconvene in Paris where they would be joined by representatives of the United States, Japan, and Canada. In Paris, more patchwork decisions were made on the international monetary front—and the consequent uncertainties haunted commercial bankers in the conduct of their own business.

Within the European Economic Community proper, successive attempts were made to stabilize internal exchange rates among the member nations. But the attempts were periodically unhinged by the disproportionate economic strength of some member nations as against others. In any realistic view of the foreign exchange picture, foreign exchange rates worldwide have been floating ever since the end of 1973. That fact, in turn, has massively complicated the task of managing international assets and liabilities insofar as they entail foreign exchange operations.

THE MECHANICS OF THE FOREIGN EXCHANGE MARKET

Academic literature overflows with articles on one or another aspect of foreign exchange, often using highly sophisticated mathematical and econometric techniques to lay bare its mysteries. Corporate treasurers have written books explaining how and when they hedge their position. Central bankers and finance ministers follow foreign exchange movements with close interest. And of course, newspapers regularly report on these movements—and in stories which often couple bullish comments on a currency from a trader in Frankfurt with bearish comments from another in London. Yet what is missing from much of this discussion is a grasp of how practitioners in the trade—the foreign exchange dealers themselves—actually work in the exchange markets, and the problems they encounter.

The comments which follow immediately below are addressed to that subject, and in doing so, they largely draw on what was recently written by a practicing expert in the field of foreign exchange—Mr. Scott E. Pardee, senior vice president of the Federal Reserve Bank of New York.[34]

IDEALS AND REALITIES

To start with, the foreign exchange market in some respects closely resembles the ideal of a perfectly competitive market. There are many participants, as well as actual and potential buyers and sellers in both the interbank market and the market between banks and their commercial customers. Rates for all major currencies are widely quoted, communications are extensive and swift, and deals can be made virtually around the clock. Each day billions of dollars of transactions are smoothly conducted through a set of conventions utilizing trading terminology common among people of many national languages. Confirmations and payments are regularly made through procedures consistent with national regulatory structure and legal codes. Mistakes sometimes occur, but when they do, are generally resolved amicably.

Still, despite these resemblances to the ideal of a perfectly competitive market, what happens in actual practice may be at odds with the ideal. To put the case more directly, what Mr. Pardee has called "the factors of depth, breadth and resilience"—which should be present in a smoothly functioning market—are not always present in the foreign exchange market. The realities of the case come into view when the ideal form of each of these factors is placed alongside the course of events as they actually unfold.

DEPTH

In ideal terms, depth means that a sizeable amount of business can be transacted without having a significant impact on the exchange rate. That is, market makers in the interbank market can ideally absorb temporary excesses of supply and demand into their own positions.

While this may be generally true in practice, there are many instances when it is not. Occasions arise when market makers in the interbank market for foreign exchange feel inhibited about taking large orders, and for three main reasons. They are, first, the volatility of exchange rates which increases the risk of loss in covering positions later on; second, internal limitations on positions previously taken which may leave no room for traders to absorb sizeable transactions; and third, the presence of external limits which exchange controls impose on a bank.

The problem of depth has another aspect. The days are past when market-making banks were prepared to deal in perhaps several hundred millions of dollars against major currencies and to carry the position overnight—if not longer. Today, they are likely to give ground after doing ten million dollars of foreign exchange business, lest they get stuck with a position that cannot unwind quickly. In fact, as Mr. Pardee has observed, there are times when the market is so thin that the mere hint of a large potential transaction coming on stream will cause traders to shrink back from enlarging their own position. The effect of their retreat will then tell on the foreign exchange rate structure even if the potential transaction hinted at does not actually materialize.

BREADTH

The ideal of breadth means that many traders are willing to make a market at any particular time, so that a participant who doesn't like one trader's rate can shop elsewhere. In that sense of the term, however, occasions arise where the foreign exchange market—and particularly its "forward" market—lacks depth. Some traders acting on behalf of banks may be willing to make commitments where they accept both the risks and the substantial booking the forward market entails. Others, however, pull back to concentrate on dealing spot.

This does not deny that exchange markets *do* have a greater and more sustained breadth today than in a former day. More banks than ever before are prepared to deal within individual money centers as well as between centers or through international brokering. There has also been a sharp increase in the number of corporations, individuals, and even official institutions which have turned to the exchange markets for their needs either as buyers and sellers of goods internationally or as managers of funds.

The factor of breadth, however, is not without its problems. For one thing, the increasing cost of staffing and equipping a modern trading room and back office can give banks at the core of the market such a competitive edge that others retrench into correspondent banking relationships. For another, the proliferation of institutions related to the market—banks, brokers, advisory services—has already stretched thin the available pool of foreign exchange talent, especially in the United States which is a latecomer on the scene of large-scale foreign exchange activities by many market participants. The pressures on available talent heightens the risks of serious mistakes, either through a flaw in internal management control systems, overwork, or inexperience.

RESILIENCY

The ideal of resiliency means that a large order to buy or sell a particular currency can be absorbed in the market without generating a cumulative movement in the rate. The assumption here is that if a currency declines, it will recover on its own to a condition of equilibrium, and will not continue to drop as a result of internal market dynamics.

This ideal view of resiliency, however, is not supported by the performance record of recent years. While the most visible swings in rates have occurred under floating exchange regimes, substantial one-way pressures have been built up under fixed rates as well. In fact, so Mr. Pardee has remarked, "the lack of resiliency in exchange markets appears to be one of their inherent characteristics—partly due to the speed of communications, and the number of people who are prepared to act at a given moment through readily available facilities for trades.''

On the latter count, as soon as a currency comes under, say, a selling pressure, the pressure feeds on itself. Within seconds, the fact that a currency is declining is flashed around the world. Market commentators and the news services provide instant explanations for the decline. They may ascribe the cause to a statement by a government official, the release of an economic indicator, a large sell order, or a rumor. Even when the explanations are farfetched, the dry fact of a decline—coupled with a plausible explanation of the event—can trigger a widespread reaction as many market participants respond virtually at once.

With hundreds of millions of dollars suddenly on the move, the sellers may be risk-taking speculators who thrive on volatility where they are the first to sell on the way down and the first to buy on the way up. The sellers may also be risk-avoiding hedgers who, when they see a wide movement against them, hasten to cover their exposures; they fear that the longer they wait, the greater the losses they would take. When the risk taker and the risk avoider are suddenly on the same side of the market, they compound the one-way pressures on the rate, and add to the general volatility once profit-taking sets in. The less the depth and the breadth of the market, the wider the scope of the swings. What has been said about a bearish market applies as well to one that is bullish. Either way, the one-way pressures may push rates to levels that may overshoot by a large margin any rational equilibrium rate based on broad economic considerations, such as trade, current account or basic payments balances, relative rates of inflation, or even relative interest rate differentials.

EQUILIBRIUM

From the standpoint of economic policy, exchange rates should reflect a broad economic equilibrium within and among countries. If they do not, policy adjustments have to be made, and policy decisions are not easily made—given the trade-offs among different economic objectives within a country and between domestic and international objectives. In fact, there are compelling examples which go to show the dangers that are invited when policy makers react to every swing in the exchange rate, without thought of how the volatility of exchange market sentiment can project some un-welcome feedbacks into the domestic economy. One among such examples is the way in which domestic inflation leads to an exchange rate depreciation which generates such a bearish exchange market atmosphere that the rate is pushed even further than could be explained by inflation differentials. The persistence of this excessive decline of the rate ratchets up the cost of both imports and domestic substitutes for imports, and thereby aggravates domestic inflation all the more.

CENTRAL BANK INTERVENTION

But there are some conditions when the exchanges are so disorderly that only central bank intervention can counteract them. The conditions include those already mentioned—but carried to an extreme. Market makers may be unwilling to cushion the pressures hitting the market by absorbing buy and sell orders into their carrying position overnight or merely for a few hours. A trader may quote the same bid-asked spread to a good customer and then unload his position in the market as quickly as possible, or he may go the other way and effectively refuse to quote at all. When many traders shrink back, the market loses depth, breadth, and resiliency. One-way market pressures increase, and rate movements become cumulative and volatile. Traders, including corporate treasurers, portfolio managers, and even the man on the street, begin to respond to the rate movement alone as though the whole of the world was absorbed into it, and they do not take into account the medium- or long-term outlook for a currency.

At a time when exchange market matters are unusually politically sensitive, or when tensions are high, ill-advised actions by some market participants may not only be costly to themselves but also to the market as a whole. The growing recognition that only with the cooperation of private participants can the inherent instability in the exchange markets be held within manageable bounds accounts for several positive developments. Where the commercial bank trader is concerned, there are now various codes of ethics and internal management manuals to guide his conduct—though the extent to which he abides by them depends on the attitudes of the bank's top management, or on the private "penal powers" of other traders who see themselves harmed by any violation of the code. At the same time, at both the national and international levels, FOREX—the trade organization for foreign exchange dealers—is seeking to improve the professionalism and expertness of its members.

But this does not absolve central bank authorities from their own responsibility to maintain close contact with the market, not only for carrying out intervention policy but also for gauging how well the market is functioning. Intervention *per se* is best considered as a limited act, reserved mainly for calming nervous markets and smoothing excessive fluctuations in rates. Intervention in the form of direct controls may be necessary *in extremis,* and may work well in the short run. But over time, the controls may create serious distortions and trading problems, even to the extent of favoring some market participants over others—or what is just as bad, encouraging their systematic evasion by some participants. This is another way of arguing that when such controls are used, they should be relaxed at the first opportunity.

V

THE STRUGGLE TO GOVERN

19. *The Changed Face of Inflation*

INITIAL STABILITY

Between the end of World War II and the mid-1960s, overall economic developments were, in the main, satisfactory. By prewar standards, for example, recessions both in the United States and in other countries were brief and mild. World trade expanded rapidly under the previously noted regime of fairly stable exchange rates, and living standards rose impressively throughout the developed world. Inflationary pressures did make themselves felt in most industrial countries—acutely so in the immediate postwar years, during the Korean hostilities, and for several years after the mid-1950s. In some countries, moreover, the pressures were more substantial than in the United States. But in none did inflation appear to be entirely out of control. In the six years between 1958 and mid-1964, the United States itself enjoyed an unusual degree of price stability. The wholesale price index rose at the rate of a little more than 1 percent annually.

THE ONSET OF INSTABILITY

Starting in mid-1964, however, the picture changed into a pattern of accelerating price increases annually: 3 percent from 1964 to 1968, 4 percent from 1968 to 1972, and 10 percent from 1972 to 1978. By the fall of 1979, the rate had reached 12 percent, and by the first months of 1980, it had soared to 18.9 percent.

The pattern of acceleration was by no means unique to the United States. It was true of many other countries as well, starting typically in 1969 and 1970. That fact, in its own way, underlined a new characteristic of inflation and its dilemma. Inflation, which was traditionally viewed as being primarily a national phenomenon subject to national control, came to exhibit international traits with regard to both its causes and consequences. Hence a dilemma. While the containment of inflationary pressures continued to depend on national policy measures, national measures taken in the face of the internationalized aspects of inflation tended to be less effective than under traditional conditions where inflationary factors could be isolated within a single country.

DEGREES OF DIFFERENCE

Though inflation is now a worldwide phenomenon common to all industrial societies, its manifestations differ from one place to the next. So do the methods of dealing with them, and the degrees of success that go with the methods. It is important to note the causes for the difference, starting with the celebrated—and generally misunderstood—instance of Germany.

While Americans remember the Great Depression, Germans remember their Great Inflation of the 1920s which shattered the middle class, divided society between the propertyless on the one hand and the rich speculators on the other, and thus helped pave the way for fascism. Not even the runaway inflation in Greece after the end of the Second World War, where 15,000 drachmas were worth no more than one dollar, was as devastating as the Great Inflation in the Germany of the 1920s. Because of the deep scar the event left on the memories of the German people, they were more prepared than Americans in the mass to accept tight monetary and fiscal constraints designed to hold inflation in check—even at the price of some unemployment. From the same cause, German trade unions when they bargained were—at least until recently—more inclined than their American counterparts to accept arrangements in which their demands for wage increases were weighed in the context of their increased productivity. These conditions prevailed in Switzerland as well.

Furthermore, in both Germany and Switzerland, the control of work permits for "foreigners" were among the key tools of economic management. Germany, for example, drew on workers from Italy, Spain, Yugoslavia, and Turkey; Switzerland drew nearly 25 percent of its labor force from Southern Italy (while France drew on workers from Algeria, Tunisia, Morocco, and Portugal). By allowing in roughly the number of workers for whom there were jobs, and by refusing entry to workers when there was a surplus, Germany and Switzerland could keep their unemployment at relatively low levels. There was no large "voting constituency" of unemployed German and Swiss citizens that could effectively demand public expenditures to "cure unemployment" without regard to its inflationary effects. People who did not get in were counted as unemployed not in Germany and Switzerland, but rather in Italy, Spain, Yugoslavia, and Turkey.[1]

In the United States, however, the unemployed were and are within the country. They are counted *here*. They cannot be kept out by visas and work permits. Most of the unemployed are American citizens with all the political rights that inhere in citizenship. They can be vocal. They can organize themselves politically. They can *vote* their versions for the relief of unemployment, without regard to the inflationary implications of the relief measures they favor.

The USSR and the socialist countries of Eastern Europe, being still predominantly agricultural countries, presently do not have much open unemployment. In their case, disguised unemployment—where people divide up what work there is and work less hard—replaces the open statistical unemployment of a fully developed industrial economy and factory system. But they have persistent inflation, even though the coercive power of the state is used to control wages. As in the dramatic recent case of Poland, people press for higher wages, more consumer goods, and more public services. There is a continuing excess of demand in relation to the available supply of goods and services. Because costs press on prices that are generally fixed, controlled, and cannot be bid up, inflation wears a different external face than it does in the West. It shows itself not in more consumption at higher prices, but in quotas for available goods, and in longer queues of people waiting for scarce goods.

ASPECTS OF THE CONTEMPORARY AMERICAN PROBLEM

In the United States during the 1950s and the first half of the 1960s, consumer price increases were barely noticed, or if noticed, did not seem ominous. Americans, with their high discretionary income and immense choice of goods—which cushioned the impact of inflation—could take comfort in the notion that the savage side of inflation was an experience reserved for Latin Americans and other foreigners.

Besides, not every price increase was due to inflation. The higher price of wheat, for example, could be due to a crop failure. The higher price of meat could be due to a severe drought in livestock areas, where the size of herds exceeded available water supplies, and where a sharp reduction in the size of herds reduced the supply of meat that reached the market months later at increased prices. The higher price of office space could be due to a shortage that appears at a given phase of a business cycle. The higher price of homes in some areas could be due to zoning requirements.

Each of these may in fact increase living costs, but none by itself comprises inflation—no more than inflation is a one-shot spurt in a given set of prices. Inflation is a sustained and accelerating escalation in the general price level over a protracted period. It was in that sense of the term that inflation began its remorseless course in American life, starting in the mid-1960s.

Of the factors that launched that inflation, one was the "guns and butter" policy for financing the Vietnam War. On the butter side of that policy—and it extended from the Johnson to the Nixon presidencies and beyond—incumbent administrations faced a society that was in turmoil. In part, the unrest of the time reflected discontent by blacks and other minorities with prevailing conditions of social discrimination and economic deprivation—a discontent that erupted during the hot summers of the middle 1960s with burning and looting. In part, it reflected the growing feeling of injustice by or on behalf of other groups—the poor, the aged, the physically handicapped, ethnics, farmers, blue collar workers, women. In part, it reflected a rejection by a segment of middle class youth of prevailing institutions and cultural values. In part, it also reflected the belated recognition by broad segments of the population that the economic reforms of the New Deal and the more recent rise in national affluence had left untouched irrepressible problems in various areas of American life—social, political, economic, environmental.

Meanwhile, incumbent presidents tried to respond to all these ills of society while waging war in Vietnam on a rising scale. In doing so, however, they repeated the financial pattern of the Second World War. They did not meet the greater costs of the war effort by increased taxation. To do so could have added to the unpopularity of a war that was being opposed by a growing proportion of the population on nonfinancial grounds. Only one-third of the cost of the war—estimated at roughly $150 billion as of May 1972—was covered by taxation. The remaining two-thirds was covered by borrowing. The aggregate federal deficit during the years of America's direct involvement in the Vietnam conflict up to May 1972 was approximately $90 billion— a deficit that radically inflated the money supply. Without Vietnam, there could have been an aggregate budgetary surplus of around $60 billion.[2]

Budgetary deficits continued to be run in consequence of the government's efforts to reduce fractional unemployment, eliminate poverty, widen the benefits of prosperity, and improve the quality of life. Many of these efforts were long overdue, and many proved wholesome. Their cumulative effect, however, was to impart a strong inflationary bias to the American economy. That is, they awakened new ranges of expectation and demand which incumbent administrations did not resist because the political costs for doing so were "unacceptable." Once it was established that the key function of government was to solve problems and relieve hardships—not only for society at large, but also for troubled industries, regions, occupations, or social groups—a great and growing body of problems and hardships became candidates for governmental action. New techniques for bringing pressure on Congress—and also on state legislatures and other elected officials—were developed, refined, and exploited. Congress responded by pouring out a broad stream of measures that involved government spending, special tax relief, or regulations mandating private spending—which increased budgetary deficits and increased costs in the private sector.

The pursuit of costly social reforms often went hand-in-hand with the pursuit of full employment. In fact, much of the expanding range of government spending was prompted by the commitment to full employment. Inflation came to be viewed as a temporary phenomenon—or, provided it remained mild, as an acceptable condition. "Maximum" or "full" employment, not price stability, became the nation's major economic goal. Fear of immediate unemployment, rather than fear of current or eventual inflation, came to dominate economic policy making.

But as inflation continued to accelerate, it posed a real threat to basic economic and political freedom—by becoming a source of social conflict between its beneficiaries and victims.[3] It fostered a capricious redistribution of income and wealth—one in which there was no reward for hard work, or for savings, or for risk taking in connection with new ventures. With raging inflation, units of value which once served as standards for decisions were set on their head. In an economy where everything from human behavior to the worth of money was distorted and warped by inflation, corporations were less inclined to build a plant whose payoff could be a gamble even in normal times—and bankers thought more than twice before saying yes to corporate loans for such purposes. The radically heightened uncertainty of how much more inflation there might be—or whether it would be reduced in the impending future—made businessmen more cautious, more reluctant to employ labor, more inclined to buy or merge with an existing enterprise, and less inclined to make capital investments in the creation of new productive facilities.

The opportunity to escape the constraints of the marketplace was generally limited to people who could control their own income because they were in a position to enjoy or to enforce some kind of monopoly. This was true of corporations which felt free to raise prices without regard to costs. It was also true of union labor which could secure wage increases without regard to productivity. What each gained by way of increased prices and wages was then passed along in the form of added costs to someone else with scant regard for the linkage between the domestic course of inflation, deficits in the U.S. balance of payments, and the international position of the dollar in the foreign exchange market. There were moments when the price spiral within the United States seemed to be temporarily checked. If so, the event was followed by a slackening in the will to persist in the inflation fight until a secular breakthrough had been achieved—meaning, a basic lowering of the inflation profile for an extended period, not just a temporary cyclical decline in it.

As costs pushed up prices, banks and other enterprises faced increased costs in every aspect of their operations, not the least of which was the cost of compensation for employees. Firms that operated on borrowed money needed to borrow more if they were to do the same volume of business at higher prices, including higher interest rates. When they borrowed from the banks, they increased the supply of money, added more fuel to the inflationary fires, to increase the push in the cost-push equation. At the same time, with more money in circulation, bank deposits increased at a rate faster than the banks could build up their capital ratio. When banks themselves were "loaned up" from their own deposit sources, the borrowing continued from other financial intermediaries with other cost-push inflationary consequences. As the wage and price spiral continued upward, fewer goods were sold, leading to a drop in employment and production. The worst of two worlds—inflation and unemployment—thus bore hard on the life of individuals, families, and firms that could not escape the constraints of the marketplace.

THE RECORD OF THE FORD ADMINISTRATION

The stop-and-go attempts of the Nixon Administration to bring inflation under control has already been touched on, albeit in the context of the remarks focused on the post-1970–71 instability in foreign exchange rates. It is enough to add that when Gerald Ford succeeded to the presidency in July 1974, inflation was running at the rate of 12.2 percent annually.

To bring inflation under control, the Federal Reserve Board used the weapons of "monetarism" at its disposal. The Board focused on the interest rates for short-term borrowing of federal funds, and on the interest rates charged at the Reserve System's discount windows. Its operations were designed to curb banks' access to reserves on which to expand their loans, to increase the costs of borrowed money to banks, and thus to increase the costs of money to the public. To the extent that this would curb the public's demand for credit, pressures on prices would thereby be curbed.

The Ford Administration did not eliminate inflation, as was later claimed. Inflation was merely slowed down to an annual rate of 7.2 percent. Divorced from all else, the decline from the inflationary high of 12.2 percent at the outset of the Ford presidency was no small achievement. It would certainly look good in the textbooks. In the real world, however, it did not look good at all to people who were subject to market forces and could not control their own income.

The monetary brakes on inflation were governed by the principle of undernourishing the inflationary process while still accommodating a good part of the pressures of the marketplace. Yet the undernourishment led to abnormally high interest rates, to a steep drop in consumer buying, a deep slump in housing construction, hectic efforts by businessmen to reduce their inventories, hard blows to the revenues of state and local governments, major losses to major banks along with the failure of the Franklin National Bank in October 1974. In an earlier case—namely, the failure of the Penn Central Transportation Company in June 1970 due to its inability to refinance its outstanding commercial paper—the Federal Reserve had put aside its monetary targets for a while. To prevent a financial panic among holders of commercial paper generally, the Federal Reserve opened the discount window wide and changed its regulations so that commercial banks could raise funds in the open market to finance firms unable to renew their maturing commercial paper. Four years later, or in 1974, to prevent a panic that could have been triggered by the failure of the Franklin National Bank, the Federal Reserve again put aside its monetary targets for a while. It loaned that troubled multinational bank almost $2 billion, and while these advances were outstanding, it was possible to arrange a takeover by another bank that protected the interests of Franklin's depositors and customers.

But in the economy as a whole, the policy of undernourishing inflation reduced the nation's gross national product at a record annual rate of 10.4

percent during the first quarter of 1975. Along with this went an unemployment rate of 9.2 percent, the highest rate of unemployment since the 1937 recession, and the worst general slump since the Great Depression. A great cry went out to reflate the economy by more deficit spending, by tax cuts, and by a general easing of monetary policy. All these things came to pass.

By August 1975, unemployment was decreasing, but prices began to rise again. In the months leading up to the 1976 presidential election, and afterwards in the Carter Administration, two economic factors—the level of employment and inflation—seemed bound together in a common and ill-fated destiny. From the look of things, it seemed impossible to reduce inflation or even to have it "level out" without reducing the growth rate in the gross national product, and unemployment with it. It seemed impossible to stimulate economic growth and increase employment without also stimulating a spurt in the rate of inflation. It also seemed politically impossible for an incumbent administration to pay the price for a sustained anti-inflationary policy when even the slightest intimation of a possible downturn in the economy, as in 1977, generated political pressures for an expansionist fiscal and monetary program.

THE FDIC COMES OF AGE

Between 1973 and 1976, the number of significant bank failures increased from six to sixteen. While other failures were in immediate prospect, the existence of the FDIC and its effective intervention as a safety net for depositors removed the grounds for panic in the street.

All this stood to the credit of the FDIC. Yet the sense that all was well in the world of American banking was deceiving. The list of insured banks that failed—or, in the descriptive language favored by the FDIC, "were closed because of financial difficulty"—was confined to institutions in which a deposit assumption was made by the FDIC or by some other institution. The list did not include distressed banks which received financial help from the FDIC, and were not recorded as "closed" or "failed." The list, for example, did not include the Bank of the Commonwealth of Detroit which received substantial assistance from the FDIC in 1972, or the Farmers Bank of the State of Delaware which received equally impressive financial aid from the FDIC in 1976—institutions with combined deposits of $1.3 billion at the time the FDIC came to their aid. It did not include the distressed Security National Bank on Long Island which involved no FDIC disbursement, but was saved in 1975 through its acquisition by the Chemical Bank of New York. Nor did the list include the direct assistance the FDIC rendered First Pennsylvania Bank—whose $5.3 billion in deposits were almost equal to all the deposits combined in the 548 insured banks that failed over the forty-five years between 1933 and the end of 1978.

As the erratic, wrenching problems of the 1970s and early 1980s compounded the strains for various banks and for depository thrift institutions,
the way bank failures were handled began to engross the attention of financial
analysts. More than that, as steep recessions followed by partial recoveries
were followed again by steep recessions, demands were heard for the first
time since the early 1930s for the enactment of new emergency legislation
for handling large bank failures. Whether or not such legislation is enacted,
it seems worthwhile to pause long enough at this point to sketch the way
in which bankruptcy in banking is currently handled.

BANKRUPTCY IN BANKING

A bank, like any other business, can voluntarily place itself in bankruptcy
or can be sued by creditors who are refused repayment. But this is generally
true in theory alone. It rarely happens in actual practice. In practice, a bank
can be placed in receivership—or the equivalent of bankruptcy—only by a
regulatory authority, and then only by the authority that issued its charter.
Thus, though the Federal Reserve and the FDIC are both heavily involved
in bank supervision and regulation, they lack the legal power to close a
financially distressed bank, because they are *not* bank chartering agencies.
As chartering authorities within their respective realms, only the Comptroller
of the Currency can legally close a distressed national bank, and only a state
bank supervisor can close a state bank in financial distress. The fact that the
chartering authority—which represents neither the bank itself nor the creditors of the bank—alone has the legal power to force a bank into bankruptcy
proceedings is among the important distinctions between banks and other
commercial businesses.

Bank supervisors have fairly wide latitude in determining whether a
bank should be placed in receivership. If a bank is insolvent, if its capital
is impaired, if its practices are likely to result in substantial financial losses
to depositors—or if it is about to engage in such practices—the supervisor
may take control of the bank and place it in receivership. A bank is insolvent
when its assets, though liquidated in an orderly and prudent manner, would
not be enough to pay off its noncapital liabilities. A bank's capital is "impaired" when charges against the capital account—as, for example, in writing
off losses or uncollectable debts—exceed the sum of contingency reserves,
undivided profit, and surplus. Because of a supervisor's wide latitude, a
bank is usually closed long before it actually defaults on its debts.

When a bank is declared insolvent, it is taken over by regulatory authorities and closed to all business. The Comptroller of the Currency or state
bank supervisor places the bank in the hands of a court with jurisdiction in
such matters. This is usually a federal district court. The court then appoints
and oversees a receiver, whose job is to examine the books and accounts
of the bank to verify assets and liabilities, to collect interest and principal

due on outstanding loans and investments, to notify all creditors of the failed bank to present proof of their claims, and to judge the validity of all claims presented. In the vast majority of failure cases, the Federal Deposit Insurance Corporation is appointed receiver for a state bank that has failed, and it must be appointed the receiver for all failed national banks.

Unlike other business failures which can be wound up only by a debt restructuring or by a liquidation, bank failures can be handled in five distinct ways, with the FDIC intervening in all but one. In a "purchase and assumption" arrangement, negotiations are entered into between the FDIC and sound banks interested in acquiring the business of the failed bank. The acquiring bank must assume all deposit liabilities of the failed institution and may choose to assume other liabilities as well. In offset, it will acquire some but not all of the assets of the failed bank. Potential assuming banks bid competitively for the opportunity to acquire the sound and ongoing business of the failed bank. Each competing bank submits a bid to the FDIC, which includes a promise to pay the corporation a specified sum of money called a "premium" if the bid is accepted. The payment entailed in the premium is the willingness of the assuming bank to accept a lower cash advance from the FDIC to make up the difference between the liabilities assumed and the assets taken, plus the premium.

The second way the FDIC handles a bank failure is by the liquidation or "deposit payoff" method. Secured or preferred depositors, such as political subdivisions, have a first claim on the failed bank's assets. Other depositors who have valid claims receive the value of their deposits from the FDIC, up to the insured maximum. If the depositor has received a loan from the failed bank, the amount of the loan may be offset against his deposit. As the assets of the bank are liquidated, general creditors are compensated *pro rata* from the proceeds. This includes depositors whose accounts exceeded the insurance maximum, suppliers of business forms or office equipment, and similar other parties to whom the bank owes money.

The third way the FDIC handles a bank failure is by temporarily setting up a new bank in the place of the failed bank, and titled Deposit Insurance National Bank (DINB). As such, it is chartered by the Comptroller of the Currency, has no capital, is automatically granted deposit insurance, and makes no loans. It holds only U.S. Treasury securities or other securities guaranteed as to principal and interest by the U.S. government, or cash assets. In essence, it only conducts a payments business, because all insured deposits in the failed bank are transferred to accounts in the DINB and depositors can withdraw from it the amount of their deposits in the bank that failed. The DINB method is used only where no other banking facilities are available in a community, in the hope that local people will be encouraged to organize a permanent bank for themselves. The FDIC has the discretionary right to sell the business of the DINB by accepting bids to capitalize the bank.

Fourth, when a bank becomes insolvent before any actual default on obligations occurs, the FDIC has the discretionary power to make long-term loans to the institution if the chartering regulator agrees that the survival of the distressed bank is necessary to the economic well-being of the community or, alternatively, that its demise would cause an excessive concentration of banking resources in the existing banks. The most recent example of this type of assistance involved FDIC loans to the Bank of the Commonwealth of Detroit, Farmers Bank of the State of Delaware, and the First Pennsylvania Bank. Such loans, coupled with close supervision and perhaps mandatory changes in operating personnel and procedure, can help restore a distressed bank to a sound condition.

Finally, state and national banking laws provide that a failed bank can be reorganized, presumably with reduced capital and other liabilities to reflect the reduced market value of its assets. The arrangement does not require FDIC intervention. It may be invoked when liquidation of the bank will result in large losses for all classes of creditors. To invoke the reorganization procedure requires the concurrence of creditors holding claims to 70–80 percent of the bank's nonequity liabilities. This method of disposing of failed banks, however, is seldom if ever used. Financial aid is used more often to prevent actual failure than to dispose of a failed bank. Deposit Insurance Banks are used infrequently and are really only an alternative means of paying off depositors.

PROTESTS

As the 1970s wore on, all the factors that threatened the survival of an increasing number of weakened banks bore hard on bank executives whose own institutions were in no way candidates for FDIC life preservers. The same factors also enlarged the grounds on which bank executives protested the costs of compliance with a growing mound of new-style federal regulations piled on top of those inherited from a different or remote past.

The costs of compliance included the disruptive effects of duplicate bank examinations by state and federal regulatory authorities—whose different policy objectives engendered contradictory rules. They included the need to provide regulatory authorities with an endless stream of mandated reports and extensive record-keeping on the minutiae of bank decisions. As a related matter, intricate regulations rising from new legislation—such as "truth in lending," "equal opportunity," and "community reinvestment"— were not only difficult to construe even on the advice of high-priced legal counsel; they also multiplied lawsuits which put banks to the expense of defending themselves even when the suits were void of merit.

Bank executives subject to Federal Reserve Board regulations in particular had three added reasons to raise their voices in protest. First, in the intensified competition for funds, they were discriminated against by differentials in the lower ceilings on the interest rates they could pay on deposit funds, as against the higher interest rates thrift institutions could pay. They chafed under the restrictions which barred the payment of interest on checking accounts. Then again—and this was of overriding importance—they protested both the explicit and the opportunity costs of the idle, non-interest-bearing reserves they were required to hold at Federal Reserve Banks. More about the regulatory picture in the next chapter.

20. The Regulatory Picture on the Eve of a Revolution

THE SCOPE OF REGULATIONS

The supervisory regulations federal and state authorities issue and enforce—as part of our "dual banking system"—have always had an extensive reach. They control the right of entry and the locations for a banking enterprise—by controlling the chartering and branching of banks. They control the growth or death of a banking enterprise—by controlling mergers, acquisitions, and consolidations. They control the kind of business in which banks can engage—by the legal distinctions they draw between permissible and impermissible activities. They also control the portfolios of banks—this, through the formulation and application of rules regarding reserves, assets, liabilities, and capital.

Leaving other regulatory agencies out of account, the Federal Reserve Board alone administers more than two dozen regulations designated by alphabetical letters. When regrouped according to subject matter, the letters cover four general matters. The first, designated specifically as *bank regulation,* governs the relationship between the central banks and commercial banks. The second governs *consumer credit;* the third, *monetary policy;* and the fourth, *securities credit.* Each regulation designated by a letter itself subdivides into detailed provisions, legal "interpretations," and amendments, themselves largely the work of the permanent staff of the Federal Reserve Board.

When changes are contemplated in the regulatory harness fashioned by any bank regulatory agency, staff recommendations are broadcast through organs of the financial press, and comments from financial institutions are invited by a set date, followed by public hearings. The aggregate reactions are then reviewed by the staff of the agency, with variable effects on the form in which changes become "official" by their publication in the *Federal Register.*[4]

The flow of "exposure drafts" into the regulatory pipelines is seemingly endless, as is the outpouring at the other end of the official regulations. A summary of "coming regulatory attractions" published on February 8, 1980, in *Pratt's Letter,* a reporting agency on Washington-based banking and finance, outlined the subjects of new Federal Reserve regulations that were being proposed for comment as of that moment. The subjects included the creditor extension of the holder-in-due-course trade rule; permissible nonbanking activities for foreign bank holding companies; expansion of Edge Act Corporations' powers; higher ceilings on the amounts businesses may hold in savings accounts. Also, new public disclosure rules affecting the Board's own disclosure practices; rules forcing banks to disclose their policy on commissions paid in connection with accounts over which they have investment discretion; and mandatory disclosure rules for deposit accounts. Further, as part of the Board's Project Augeas—suggesting the Augean stable which needed a cleaning out in connection with an anti-inflationary program—the Board was expected to review its regulations under ten different letterheads for possible clarification and simplification.

By the near end of February 1980, *Pratt's Letter* had more "coming regulatory attractions" to report—this time, covering changes in the new regulations the Comptroller of the Currency indicated he would probably propose in the next six months. They included general guides on the eligibility of investment securities; changes in the rules on the disposition of credit life insurance income; changes in procedures and forms related to corporate applications; application of lending limits to standby letters of credit; and revision of the rules on other real estate owned and investment in bank premises. Also, rules on providing pension plans for the indemnification of bank employees and officers; review of the rules on national banks' role as guarantor or surety on an indemnity board; national banks' powers to contribute to charity; application of generally accepted accounting principles to national banks that lease bank premises; minimum security devices and procedures; and a review of Community Reinvestment Act regulations. All this came on top of the existing regulations.

THE BANK EXAMINATION

The bank examination is the best known form of supervisory activity, whether conducted by the Comptroller of the Currency, the Federal Reserve Board, the Federal Deposit Insurance Corporation, or by state banking authorities. A bank examination, however, is not an audit. It does not include a detailed study of itemized entries on the bank's records. Banks themselves, as noted already, generally provide such audit facilities through internal audit departments of their own or through the services of public accountants. The purpose of a bank examination is to develop information that will disclose the current financial condition of the individual bank, ascertain whether a bank is complying with applicable laws and regulations, and indicate the bank's operating prospects. The bank examiner in the field is primarily a fact-finder and appraiser. He or she analyzes and appraises the bank's assets and liabilities, capital structure, liquidity, and operating trends, along with its position and plans in the context of general business conditions and of those special to its service area.

THE BENEFIT SIDE

Examinations have a benefit side and a cost side.[5] On the benefit side, examination information lends itself to five purposes. It may be used by the directors and officers of an examined bank to strengthen the institution as well as to prevent further difficulties. It may serve as the basis on which banking authorities decide whether or not to approve the branching or merger of particular institutions, or to grant a competing bank charter to a new institution. The data distilled from many examinations may guide banking authorities in framing or revising regulations, in shaping supervisory policies, and in recommending changes in banking laws. Then again, the "economic intelligence" gleaned through the examinations may provide monetary authorities with a better "feel" of prospective shifts of attitudes and expectations of bankers and businessmen.

THE COSTS SIDE

A survey of bankers, regulators, and consumer specialists conducted in mid-1979 on behalf of the FDIC underlined the costs side of bank examinations.[6] In response to a questionnaire, bankers noted that the examination visits disrupted bank operations and pulled employees away from their regular work. They did not discount the benefits of a trade-off. In particular, many bankers associated with small institutions—state or nationally chartered—recognized that governmentally conducted examinations helped them reappraise loan quality and the merits of institutional policies. But the common cry of bankers who managed small and large institutions alike was for a reduction in the burdens of the examinations, from the standpoint of their frequency, duration, and duplication. One out of five bankers cited specific "problems" they encountered during the examinations of their institutions. These included the demeanor and methods of the examiners, inexperienced examiners, requests for information "that was not needed," conflict between or delays caused by the state and federal agencies involved, differences over interpretations of laws and regulations, differences over credit appraisal, and differences over the definition of terms such as "capital."

TENSIONS AMONG REGULATORS

With many different federal agencies actively engaged in supervising banks and thrift institutions—the Comptroller of the Currency, the Federal Reserve Board, the Federal Home Loan Bank Board, and the National Credit Union Administration (NCUA)—the cross-winds whirled by their different needs and purposes often buffeted the financial institutions subject to regulation by multiple agencies. Complaints on this score were not confined to the financial institutions directly affected. They were also voiced by the regulatory agencies themselves. The Federal Reserve in particular often decried the way its responsibilities regarding monetary and credit policies were adversely affected by the examination or other policies of the Comptroller of the Currency.

Since at least 1938, periodic efforts were made to coordinate the supervisory responsibilities of federal and state banking agencies.[7] Sometimes the efforts were initiated by the agencies themselves; at other times, Congress tried to impose uniformity on them. Sometimes the steps taken were simply interagency agreements; at other times, formal organizations were established. Sometimes the steps were limited to federal regulatory agencies, and sometimes they also entailed agreements with the Conference of State Bank Supervisors. In addition, they might include attempts to coordinate the work of the Federal Trade Commission and the Securities Exchange Commission with all the bank regulatory agencies.

In an extension of this process, when Congress in 1978 enacted the Financial Institutions Regulatory and Interest Rate Control Act, it authorized the creation of a Federal Financial Institutions Examination Council (FFIEC) consisting of the three federal banking agencies, the Federal Home Loan Bank Board and the National Credit Union Administration, and with liaison members from state banking departments. The FFIEC was not meant to be a "sixth" regulatory agency in addition to the Federal Reserve, FDIC, Comptroller, Federal Home Loan Bank Board, and NCUA. In fact, when Comptroller John C. Heiman became chairman of the FFIEC, he tried to manage its affairs by using the staff resources of the existing regulatory agencies instead of building a new staff. Yet it soon turned out that the only way the FFIEC could comply with all the stringent demands of the law which gave it birth was by means of a staff larger than the one put together *ad hoc* from the staffs of existing regulatory agencies. Even so, the coordination of the activities of all the regulatory agencies remained as illusive a thing as the search for the Holy Grail. The case here has been complicated by the intersection between the traditional regulations focused on solvency and financial probity and the new kinds of regulations that are the carriers of social policy objectives.

EQUAL OPPORTUNITY AND AFFIRMATIVE ACTION

In times past, the personnel departments for medium and large banks, like those for other corporations, tended to be the end of the line for officers who had outlived their usefulness where functional operations were concerned, but had not yet reached retirement age. The practice was all the more odd when viewed alongside the fact that since the mid-1930s, over 100 federal laws (not to mention state laws) were enacted bearing on employer-employee relationships. If the practice remained "tolerable," the reasons included slack enforcement of the laws by government agencies and the lack of knowledge on the part of employees as to the existence of these laws and the nature of their rights under them.

Today the picture is altogether different. The personnel department of any sizeable bank can no longer be a place into which misfits can be side-tracked, or exhausted officers can mark time until their retirement date. Personnel departments of banks are expected to make Equal Opportunity and Affirmative Action programs not merely sonorous words, but facts of life. That means giving concrete substance to the various congressional acts designed to prevent discrimination in every aspect of employment under the following measures: Title VII of the Civil Rights Act of 1964, Equal Pay Act of 1963, Age Discrimination Act of 1967, Vocational Rehabilitation Act of 1973, and the Vietnam Era Veteran's Readjustment Act of 1974. Through this legislation, qualified employees are entitled to equal employment opportunities regardless of race, creed, color, religion, national origin, age, sex, or handicapped status.

In addition, by Executive Order 11246 addressed to the Labor Department, employers are required to carry out a written result-oriented affirmative action program; the U.S. Treasury Department is the designated agency to secure compliance by banks and other financial institutions. The larger the bank, the more likely it is to be singled out for a stiff Treasury audit—or for suits initiated by employees as in the case of the Bank of America, Crocker's Bank in San Francisco, and the Harris Trust in Chicago. A bank now invites embarrassing trouble if its personnel division is not armed with a clearly identifiable authority with supporting procedures to receive complaints about discrimination, to investigate them, and to correct such wrongs as may come to light—before the wrongs become the subject of litigation in the courts.[8]

COMMUNITY REINVESTMENT ACT OF 1977 (CRA)

Under the terms of this Act, the respective government agencies which regulate commercial banks and thrift institutions must examine the institutions in their jurisdiction to determine if they are meeting the needs of the community or communities where they are domiciled. Moreover, such assessments must be taken into account when the regulating agency evaluates any application by a financial institution requiring its approval—as in the instance of branches, mergers, charters, or insurance. A judgment regarding an institution's past failures to meet the credit needs of its community or communities may be the grounds on which all such applications can be denied.

The detailed provision of CRA regulations approved by the agencies are meant to assist lenders in complying with the Act, to inform the public of existing rules, and to help regulators discharge their responsibilities. Yet the Act and the regulations are perhaps unavoidably vague and in any case hard to administer. In the language of jurisprudence, they tend to belong more to the "morality of aspirations" than to the "morality of duties." For example, lenders subject to the Act are required to prepare and review, at least annually, a map delineating the local community or communities comprising the lender's entire community without excluding low and moderate income neighborhoods. A local community consists of the contiguous areas around each office or group of offices of the institution, but need not take account of off-premises electronic facilities that receive deposits from more than one deposition.

Lenders subject to the Act are required to adopt a Community Reinvestment Act Statement for each delineated local community, including the identified boundaries of the community, a list of the principal types of credit the lender is prepared to extend in the local community, and a copy of a standard Community Reinvestment Act Notice for display in the lobby of the lending institution. At the same time, the lender is required to maintain files, readily available upon request for inspection by any member of the public, of all signed written comments received from the public within a previous two-year period referring specifically to any CRA Statement or to the lender's performance in helping to meet the credit needs of its community or communities.

Complaints under CRA so far have been brought by community groups, by local merchants, by a state banking commissioner, by other banks—*and* by a savings and loan association which apparently feared competition from a commercial bank if its application to establish a branch were granted. Mortgage lending is the prime source of complaints, but other loans such as home improvement loans also generate complaints. At the time of this writing, regulatory agencies had denied only two bank applications where CRA was listed as the reason. But aside from the possibility that other applications may be denied outright, CRA has been instrumental in producing a number of indirect or low visibility actions on the part of institutions.

So far, approximately 1,700 banks have been examined by regulatory authorities to determine how well they are complying with the Community Reinvestment Act. Where the Federal Reserve Board is concerned, its tendency has been to encourage voluntary settlements under CRA complaints because of its conviction that no one would be happy with any decisions it made as a regulatory agency. As to bankers, whether in connection with CRA or any other matter, no guitarist has strummed a tune to the lyrics: "I hanker for a banker." Yet it is no special pleading to take judicial notice of the dilemma they face. In a period when they must pay a high price for the funds they use, and hence may have strong motives to reduce their lending operations straight across the board, how can they be secure against punitive action if they fail to make CRA loans? Their banks would be less vulnerable to attack if they shut off loans *completely* than if they set down restrictive standards. This would be an ironic effect of CRA—to provide no credit at all to a depressed community so as to escape the penal aspects of a measure whose animating aim was to stimulate widespread credit allocations.[9]

CONSUMER CREDIT

In the past decade, the protection of consumers who deal with banks and other sources of credit has not only assumed a position of prime importance as a regulatory activity of government, but has also brought bankers and consumer advocates into sharp conflict.

Four regulations of the Federal Reserve Board—designated by the letters B, C, Z, and AA—deal with consumer credit. Each is the common carrier for some kind of "social policy" legislation enacted since the start of the 1960s—as in the instances of Equal Credit Opportunity Act, Truth-in-Lending, the previously mentioned Community Reinvestment Act, Fair Debt Collection Practices Act, and Fair Housing (under the Civil Rights Act of 1968). All haunt banking practitioners with costly consequences if they err in judging what they can or cannot do under the regulations.

Regulation B was issued by the Federal Reserve Board under the authority of the Equal Credit Opportunity Act of 1975. The intent of the act is to prevent creditors who regularly extend credit from discriminating against an individual on the basis of the applicant's sex or marital status, race, color, religion, national origin, age, receipt of income from public assistance programs, or the good faith exercise of rights under the Consumer Protection Act of 1968.

As applied to bank officers or to any other kind of creditors, Regulation B allows a loan application to be taken orally as well as in writing, but any information or action that is prohibited in writing is banned in an interview as well. That is, a lender may not ask any questions verbally that would not be permissible on a written application. Each applicant must be advised that courtesy titles such as "Miss," "Mrs.," "Mr.," and "Ms." are optional. Unless requested by the applicant, they cannot be used in the application or in the debt or security documents. All other words and terms on printed forms must be neutral as to sex.

The notice of credit approval may be delivered orally or in writing. But when credit is denied, the applicant must be notified in writing—stating the reasons for the rejection or calling the applicant's right to request the reasons under the Equal Credit Opportunity Act of 1975. By the terms of that Act, the creditor must retain for 25 months from the date the final action is taken all forms, written information, or statements concerning an application. Further, if a creditor is notified of an investigation by an enforcement agency for violation of the Act, all forms, notices, written information, or statements concerning the application must be retained until final disposition of the matter. Penalties for violations of the Act include civil liability for the creditor for all *actual* damages, plus punitive damages up to $10,000 per violation if the suit is brought within one year. In a class action suit, the creditor may be liable for punitive damages up to $500,000 or 1 percent of its net worth, whichever is lesser. Penalties may be avoided if the actions were taken in good faith in reliance on a regulation of the Federal Reserve Board, even if the regulation is subsequently changed.

Regulation C carries out the Home Mortgage Disclosure Act of 1975, which seeks to provide citizens and public officials with enough information to determine if depository institutions are fulfilling their obligations to meet the housing credit needs of their local communities. While the Board of Governors is charged with the responsibility to write the regulations that conform with the purposes of the Act, enforcement is left to the appropriate Federal Financial regulatory agencies depending on their jurisdiction over commercial banks, savings banks, savings and loan associations, building and loan associations, homestead associations, and credit unions which make federally related mortgage loans. All these institutions must disclose annually the number and total principal amount of residential first mortgage loans originated or purchased, and home improvement loans originated or purchased during the most recent fiscal year.

Regulation Z was issued by the Federal Reserve Board pursuant to Title I (Truth in Lending Act) and Title V (General Provisions) of the Consumer Credit Protection Act. It applies to all persons who in the ordinary course of business regularly extend, or offer to extend, or arrange, or offer to arrange for the extension of consumer credit. It applies to any transaction that is primarily for personal, family, household, or agricultural purposes and either for which a finance charge is or may be imposed, or which, pursuant to an agreement, is or may be payable in more than four installments. The purpose of Regulation Z is to let borrowers and customers know the cost of credit. It does not fix maximum, minimum, or any charges for credit. The maximum charges are still governed by applicable state law. The regulation prescribes uniform methods of computing costs of credit, disclosure of credit terms and lease terms, and procedures for resolving billing errors on certain credit accounts.

Regulation Z requires that records be maintained for at least two years in order to supply evidence to any enforcement agency that the required disclosures have been made, and that a bank has also actively tried to verify all disclosures on the paper it has purchased—medical-dental-hospital notes, vehicle dealer papers, equipment sales, and so on.[10] Any creditor who fails to disclose the required information is liable to the customer for an amount equal to twice the sum of the finance charge, with a minimum of $100 and a maximum of $1,000, plus court costs and attorneys' fees. In addition, a willful violation is subject to a criminal penalty of a $5,000 fine or one-year imprisonment or both. If a bank is the assignee of notes or contracts from a dealer or institution with which the bank has a continuing relationship, the bank becomes subject to liabilities in credit transactions where a security interest in land is involved, unless it can prove it had no reasonable grounds to believe the original creditor was violating the Act and it maintained procedures reasonably adapted to appraise it of the existence of violations.

COSTS OF COMPLIANCE

It would take the equivalent of a law library to enumerate in analytical detail the sweep of things bankers must bear in mind in order to comply with the great mass of regulations to which they are subject. This is so much the case that even the heads of medium-sized banks who used to rely solely on "outside legal counsel" for guidance in connection with the ebb and flow of cases and controversies, now face so many legal questions as a matter of daily routine, that some among them feel compelled to do what they have never done before. They feel compelled to provide themselves with a regular "in-house" legal counsel after the manner of large money center banks.[11]

The previously mentioned survey conducted in mid-1979 on behalf of the FDIC elicited the attitudes of bankers, regulators, and consumer specialists on the importance, costs, and enforcement of consumer protection laws and regulations. In the aggregate, bankers perceived the laws and regulations as being costly, actively enforced—and not very important in protecting consumers. Consumer specialists took a diametrically opposed view. Regulators and examiners, for their part, adhered to a "middling view" on the importance of the regulations, but leaned toward the banker attitude on the matter of costs. The survey, however, reached but very little in banker attitudes toward a more fundamental aspect of the regulatory picture. As the inflation-driven 1970s wore on, increasing numbers of bankers "voted with their feet" regarding membership in the Federal Reserve System. The next chapter deals with the manner of the matter up to the time in October 1979 when the Federal Reserve Board initiated its new policies to control a spiralling inflation.

21. The Issue of Federal Reserve Membership

THE CASE FOR MEMBERSHIP

National banks always had an avenue of escape from their obligatory membership in the Federal Reserve System. They could return their charters to the Comptroller of the Currency and then reincarnate themselves as state banks under readily available state charters. Prior to the 1970s, however, it seldom happened that member banks, state or national, contracted out of the System.

Managers of member banks accepted the costs of membership, and these were not small. Under the Federal Reserve Board's Regulation I, each member bank was required to hold the stock of a Federal Reserve Bank in an amount equal to 6 percent of its own capital and surplus. Of the total, half must be paid in, with the remainder subject to call. Moreover, unlike other corporations, there were limits on the dividend which a Federal Reserve Bank could pay its members. The maximum was 6 percent per annum, while 90 percent of a Reserve Bank's earnings after dividends went to the U.S. Treasury as an interest charge on outstanding notes. Above all, each member bank bore the costs of holding a required non-interest-bearing reserve with the Federal Reserve Bank of its district.

The costs of membership, however, were offset by direct and indirect benefits whose scope went beyond a general commitment by leading bankers to the concept of an independent central banking system. The effective power of member banks to choose a majority of the board for each Federal Reserve Bank, who in turn set its policies and chose its chief executives, was not something to be given up lightly. More immediately, the Federal Reserve Banks, as "bankers' banks," performed important services for member banks. Under the terms of the Federal Reserve Board's Regulation J, they cleared the checks of member banks free of charge and made coins and paper money available to them without handling or shipping costs. Also free of charge, or at only a nominal cost, they collected notes, drafts, and maturing securities for member banks, and credited the proceeds to their respective reserve accounts with the Federal Reserve Banks. Nor was this all. Under the Federal Reserve Board's Regulation A, Federal Reserve Banks served as a "lender of last resort" to member banks. The latter could borrow funds at the "discount window" when they were faced by a temporary need to augment their reserve accounts in order to support a given volume of loans and deposits.

In addition to all else, a psychological benefit of no small importance went with membership in the Federal Reserve System. It was that the fact of membership, publicized in all bank advertising, conveyed a felt sense of institutional safety and stability. Few bank managers would lightly give up that psychological benefit by withdrawing their institutions from the System. Least of all would they do this when the traumas caused by the waves of bank failures of 1920–30 were still alive in public memories. Most of the 3,604 state banks that failed at the height of the crisis between January 1932 and March 1933—with aggregate deposits of $2.03 billion—were nonmember banks. The security attached to membership in the System was thus firmly fixed in the minds of many depositors, and it would be a rash management of a member bank that would subsequently take it out of the Federal Reserve. Depositors would construe such an act to be a sign of weakness or an omen of trouble to come, and hence would move their funds elsewhere. They would be disposed to do just that, even after the FDIC demonstrated its own ability to protect depositors against losses.

Pressures on member banks

Starting at the end of the 1960s, all the old and divisive questions about membership in the Reserve System came to be asked with increasing urgency. The reasons were due to the convergence of factors that have run like a *leitmotif* through many of these pages. They included sustained inflation, high interest rates, and differentials in the interest rates different kinds of deposit institutions could pay. They included changes in the nature of the deposit base, changes in the mobility of bank funds, and the radically intensified competition for funds which banks faced from nonbanking institutions and from arms of the government. Above all, they entailed the way sustained inflation and high interest rates affected the explicit costs of banks, and the "opportunity costs" to member banks represented by the idle non-interest-bearing reserve they were required to hold at the Federal Reserve Banks. Bank managers were squeezed on the one side by an inflation process that remorselessly devalued the idle dollars in the required reserve, and on the other, by the increased costs of their own borrowing to meet the sustained loan demand on their institutions. They also lived with the depressing fact that they were forfeiting business opportunities to nonmember banks or other financial intermediaries not subject to the same constraints on required reserves.

Focal points for controversy

A critical point of departure and return for controversies about all such matters was the Federal Reserve Board's Regulation D. The regulation established differentials in member banks' required reserves according to deposit categories—demand, savings, and time—and according to the size and geographical location of member banks. Besides, Regulation D worked in its own way to promote a double disparity adverse to the competitive position of member banks; first, between them and nonmember banks because of the differential in their reserve requirements; and second, between member banks and other depository institutions not subject to comparable reserve requirements.

The controversy over reserve requirements *per se* extended over the length of a century preceding the end of the 1960s. On various grounds, uniform reserve requirements, for example, were expected to follow from the National Bank Act of 1863, from the Federal Reserve Act of 1913, and from the 1933 legislation that created the Federal Deposit Insurance Corporation. But the expected didn't happen. Subsequently, uniform reserve requirements were recommended in 1950 by a subcommittee of the Joint Committee on the Economic Report under the chairmanship of Senator Paul H. Douglas—and again in 1952 when the chairmanship of that subcommittee passed by rotation into the hands of Rep. Wright Patman. The same recommendation was subsequently urged by other high sources as time went by. It was urged by the 1961 report of the National Commission on Money and Credit, by the 1963 "Heller Committee" report, by the 1971 report of the Commission on Financial Structures and Regulations, and by the 1976 report of what was known as the "FINE" study. All such recommendations came to nothing. They were stopped dead by the countervailing thrust of those financial interests which were determined to preserve for themselves the special benefits they saw in non-uniform reserves or no reserves at all.

Beneath the roof of the long and protracted controversy over reserves in general, a critical dispute centered on the differences between member and nonmember banks concerning the nature of the assets they could count as required reserves; and secondly, the way the Federal Reserve and state regulatory agencies defined the deposit base against which legal reserves must be held. For although reserve requirement ratios in most states having them were generally similar to the Federal Reserve ratios, they tended to be tilted in ways that favored nonmember as against member banks. For example, the assets which member banks could count in satisfying their reserve requirements were determined by a specific percentage of their demand and time deposits in the form of vault cash and balances at the Federal Reserve—neither of which earned interest. On the other hand, with the exception of Illinois which had no statutory reserve requirement, all other states allowed nonmember banks to satisfy reserve requirements with their vault cash, and demand balances at correspondent banks.

Earnings on cash assets that member banks had to forgo, but nonmember banks did not, represented a "cost burden" of membership which became more pronounced as the 1970s wore on. It became more pronounced not only because of the impact of inflation and the associated rise of interest rates on the funds banks borrowed, but for other factors as well, starting with the impact of the Federal Reserve Board's Regulation Q. To repeat, member banks were subject to lower ceilings on the interest rates they could pay on their time and savings deposits, as against the higher ceilings on rates thrift institutions could pay. Where banks were directly concerned, the regulation restated the statutory prohibitions of the Glass-Steagall Act of 1933 against the payment of interest on demand deposits (besides prescribing rules governing advertising of interest on deposits). Commercial banks had long protested the competitive advantages the regulation gave to thrift institutions. But the protests were amplified to a roar by the thrust of the events in the 1970s.

For example, with the limitation on the rates of interest banks could pay on their time and savings deposits, this class of funds increasingly flowed out of the banks into money market mutual funds with their higher yields. This not only limited the lending capacity of the banks. It also forced their executives to "buy deposits" in the money markets at rates which narrowed the spread between the interest on their own loans and what they had to pay for the funds *they* bought on order to make the loans. At the same time, the brokerage houses and other firms which offered money market mutual funds to investors did not have to hold any reserves against the investments that were made, yet began to offer them the equivalent of bank accounts.

In a second but related direction, still other institutions besides banks began to provide third-party payment services. As noted elsewhere, the share draft offered by credit unions, and the negotiated order of withdrawal (NOW) accounts offered by mutual savings banks and savings and loan associations, worked much like bank checking accounts. None of these, however, had to hold non-interest-bearing reserves against such check-like deposits as did member banks. At the same time, under Regulation Q, both the mutual savings banks and the savings and loan associations retained the right to offer rates on their time and savings deposits that were higher than the rates allowed member banks.

THE EROSION OF FEDERAL RESERVE MEMBERSHIP

All the negative realities so far sketched began to tell on the management of national banks and state member banks, to set in train their secession from the Federal Reserve System. Increasing numbers among them began to trumpet the fact that they were quitting the Federal Reserve, and that local funds which "used to go to Washington" in the form of reserves were now being "kept home" to help the local economy. What would once have been a public relations disadvantage was thus turned into an advantage. In fact, some bank managers who led their institutions out of the Reserve System viewed the event as being so commonplace, that they failed beforehand to inform even their own employees of what was in prospect.

In 1967, the percentage of commercial bank deposits held by member banks stood at 82.5 percent. By the end of 1977, the percent had dropped to 73 percent. By the start of 1980, they had declined further to 70 percent. In that same period, though the total number of commercial banks in the United States increased by 985, the total number of banks in the Reserve System *declined* by 403. During the fourth quarter of 1979 and the first weeks of 1980, 69 banks with about $7 billion in deposits—including two very sizeable Pennsylvania banks with more than $3 billion in deposits between them—gave notice of their intention to withdraw from the Federal Reserve System.

Meanwhile, there was a close and ominous accord between the findings made in mid-1979 by the FDIC survey previously alluded to, and a separate survey made by Reserve Banks half a year later. In dealing with the issue of Reserve System membership, the FDIC survey put a leading question to the chief executive officers of banks and bank holding companies: If you were deciding today, which class do you feel would be best for your bank? National, State member, or State nonmember? The answers had the aspect of a giant sheet of litmus paper bringing out the acids in the soul of many bank managers.

About three-quarters of the chief executive officers of banks and two-thirds of holding company executives selected state nonmember status as best for their banks. The most commonly mentioned reason was "reserve requirements." By class of banks, almost half of the national banks and more than half of the state member banks chose a class different from their own, the bulk of them preferring state nonmember status.

A later survey by Reserve Banks, based on information volunteered by members in the normal course of business, found that 320 member banks would certainly or most likely withdraw from the system. Another 350 were actively considering withdrawing. These 670 banks—some of which had already initiated withdrawal procedures—represented more than 10 percent of the System's membership and had in excess of $71 billion in deposits. If these banks in fact withdrew, deposits of banks holding federal reserves would decline to 64 percent—and the momentum would build for other banks to withdraw.

IMPLICATIONS FOR THE CONDUCT OF MONETARY POLICY

A moment's reflection could light up from within the way in which the loss of membership would have adverse effects on monetary control, the soundness of the banking system, and the strength of the Federal Reserve. As attrition caused the total amount of reserves held at Federal Reserve banks to decline, the "multiplier" relationship between reserves and money would increase and tend to become less stable. Fluctuations in the amount of reserves supplied—and these fluctuations inevitably have a range of uncertainty—could cause magnified and unintended changes in the money supply. As attrition increased, the proportion of deposits held by nonmember banks would increase—as would the possibility of unanticipated shifts of deposits between member and nonmember banks—with a consequent destabilization in the relationship between reserves and money.

As banks left membership behind, they would also lose ready access to the Federal Reserve discount window, along with its benefits. At the same time, the Federal Reserve would lose the intimate supervisory contact with individual institutions important to the administration of the discount window and the effective discharge of the Reserve System's regulatory responsibilities. Finally, as ever larger segments of the banking industry came to hold their entire operating and liquidity reserves at other commercial banks instead of with the Federal Reserve banks, localized strains and individual failures would be transmitted to other banks, in a widening arc of serious repercussions.

THE STRUGGLE TO GOVERN

Starting at the end of 1977, various proposals were advanced within the Congress, by the Federal Reserve Board, by the American Bankers Associations, and by the Independent Bankers Association of America,[12] to deal with the questions of membership in the Reserve System and/or uniform reserves for all depositor institutions. But the struggle to reach an agreement on what should be done resembled at times another familiar war of all against all—within the banking industry, within the Congress, within the Executive branch of the government, and between all these elements. Alliances or agreements reached one day became unstuck the next, only to reform a day later. So it went from one season to the next, with great commotions followed by twilight pauses, followed again by commotions, and again by pauses.

The questions at the heart of the shifting firefights were not easily answered. For example, should membership in the Federal Reserve System be compulsory for all depositor institutions? As of the near end of 1977, there were 42,000 depositor institutions in the United States. Viewed from the standpoint of their subdivisions, 14,701 were commercial banks. Of these, in turn, 5,800 were national banks for whom membership in the Federal Reserve System was obligatory. The other 8,919 commercial banks were state-chartered institutions, for whom membership in the Reserve System was voluntary. Only the larger of the state-chartered banks were members of the Federal Reserve, but from the standpoint of numbers, they were eclipsed by nonmember state banks, generally small institutions. In addition to commercial banks, there were 4,047 savings and loan companies, 407 mutual savings banks, and 22,249 credit unions.

Should all these be compelled to join the System? Should membership be voluntary for some of them—considering that their deposit asset size ranged from $5,000 for a credit union to over $80–90 billion for institutions such as Bank of America and Citicorp? Were the costs of membership— principally in the form of idle, non-interest-bearing reserves held in the Federal Reserve—greater or less than the benefits of the services the Federal Reserve provides its members without charge? Should there be a legal reserve requirement for all depositor institutions whether or not they were commercial banks? Should the reserve requirements the Federal Reserve set for member banks be duplicated by those other regulatory agencies set for savings and loan associations and for credit unions?

The controversies among the rival parties at interest did not stop with the disputes over reserve requirements or the erosion of Federal Reserve membership. In due course they extended to differentials in Regulation Q interest rate ceilings, and interest-bearing transaction accounts such as the NOW accounts. Every design for an omnibus measure embracing these issues was cut down at some point by conflicts not only within private financial camps but within the governmental camps. On the governmental side of things, the rival camps included the House and Senate Banking Committee, state banking authorities, the Federal Reserve Board, the Treasury, the Department of Housing and Urban Development, the Home Loan Bank Board, and the National Credit Union. Each of these, as was true of the private camps involved in the contest, approached the issue in dispute from its own institutional perspective. On top of all else, the political and legislative contest spilled over into the courts where competitive financial institutions assailed each other with lawsuits alleging unlawful invasions of their respective markets.

AGREEMENTS IN PRINCIPLE

Regarding the membership issue itself, all rivals in the contest were agreed "in principle" on three general points. First, the attrition in Federal Reserve membership should be halted and hopefully reversed. Second, the main cause for that attrition was the excessively high financial burden of membership. And third, the chief financial burden of membership was the required reserve ratios of member banks—that is, the ratios of idle, non-interest-bearing funds member banks had to keep at Federal Reserve banks. Agreements "in principle" on these three points, however, were not self-executing. They did not set in motion any ready agreements on the specifics of what should be done to halt the attrition in Federal Reserve membership.

The case was complicated by the fact that the membership problem *per se* did not stand on an autonomous plane of its own. Aside from those already mentioned, the membership issue was entangled with many other sensitive matters. Some went to the heart of the existing division of federal and state regulatory powers which accounted for the nature of the "dual banking system." Others bore directly on the future of the correspondent relationships among major member banks and small nonmember banks—with implications for their reserves, earnings, services, loan participation, and the management of their assets and liabilities. Still others went to the heart of the Federal Reserve's functions as an institution, and their interaction with the institutional interests of other agencies and departments of the federal government.

QUESTIONS WITHIN "THE FEDERAL RESERVE ISSUE"

If membership in the Reserve System was to be compulsory for all commercial banks and thrift institutions, how would this affect the balance between federal and state power in the regulation of banking and other depository institutions? To what extent, if at all, would it disrupt the subtle but complex pattern of bank correspondent relationships? Did all member banks regardless of size benefit equally from the Federal Reserve's cost-free services—as in the instance of the check-clearing process—or did the benefits accrue mainly to the large member banks?

If the main cause for the attrition of the Federal Reserve was the high costs to the banks of their idle, non-interest-bearing reserves, would the attrition be checked by the payments of interest on those reserves? If such payments were made, how much revenue would the Treasury lose in the form of the earnings it received on the Federal Reserve's portfolio? Could the loss of revenue be offset by income Treasury would redeem if the Federal Reserve charged explicit prices for its services? Should *all* depository institutions, regardless of their parent regulatory agency, be subject to uniform and universal reserve requirements under schedules set by the Federal Reserve? Should anything be done to simplify the requirements ratio for demand deposits which rose in five steps from 7 percent to 16.25 percent depending on deposit amounts—with even more complex ratio schedules on time deposits depending on the maturity and class of deposits as well as on their amounts?

Again: Should access to the Federal Reserve's discount window be confined to member banks, or should the right of access be extended to all depository institutions? Should the right to offer interest-bearing transaction accounts of various kinds be confined to particular depository institutions in particular regions of the country, or should the right be extended to all depository institutions nationally? What should be done about the competitive advantages thrift institutions such as savings and loan associations enjoyed over commercial banks under the terms of Regulation Q? Should that regulation be scrapped in the name of equitable competition? Should it be preserved on the theory—favored by the Department of Housing and Urban Development—that the regulation enabled the savings and loan associations to attract more deposit funds for conversion into home mortgages? Finally—and this question was the subject of earnest argument prior to

October 1979—were reserves actually indispensable to the conduct of monetary and credit policies, or could the object of those policies be attained only by open market operations?

It would be a fatiguing task to trace the way every event, starting in the fall of 1977, caused another turn and turnabout in the long dispute over these questions. But to keep the general picture in focus, it must serve here to say that from January 1979 onward, the events included the interaction between the inflationary spiral and the constraints on lending under state usury laws, the surge in the foreign takeover of American banks, and the rising chorus of protests over the costs of complying with new layers of banking regulations piled on top of preexisting ones.

ORDER OF BATTLE

Though skirmishes over "the Federal Reserve issue" began in late 1977, the battle over it was fully joined at the start of January 1979. At that time, Chairman Henry Reuss (D-Wis.) of the House Banking Commitee introduced two companion measures—the Monetary Control Act of 1979 and the Reserve Requirement Simplification Act of 1979.

In broad outline, their terms conformed in some respects to the position previously taken by Federal Reserve Board Chairman G. William Miller, while differing from it in other respects. Mr. Miller, on behalf of the Federal Reserve Board, proposed to arrest the attrition of Federal Reserve membership in ways which combined the persuasive powers of sticks and carrots. First, under his formula, the system of required reserves would be extended from member banks to all federally insured thrift institutions above a certain size that offered transaction accounts. That is, the system would be extended to savings and loan associations, mutual savings banks, and credit unions—because all these had come to offer various forms of transaction accounts: demand deposits, negotiable order of withdrawal accounts (NOW), automatic transfers from savings deposits, and in the case of credit unions, share drafts.

The carrots Chairman Miller offered along with the coercive stick initially took the following form. The first $10 million in transaction deposits would be exempt from any reserve requirement. But the next $40 million would be backed by reserves held in an "earnings participation account" with the Federal Reserve—a portion of which would earn interest at a rate equal to the average return on the System's portfolio, the estimated rate being 6.5 percent. Further, all depository institutions subject to the required reserve, whether they were nonmember banks or thrift institutions, would have equal access with member banks to the Federal Reserve's discount window. At the same time, the Federal Reserve would charge explicit fees for the services it previously provided without charge to member banks, and thereby offset the Treasury's loss of income because of the interest to be paid on the mandatory reserves of the depository institutions.

The legislation introduced by Chairman Henry Reuss of the House Banking Committee would extend the system of required reserves to all commercial banks above a certain size and to all federally insured thrift institutions offering transaction accounts. It also contemplated the opening up of the Federal Reserve discount window to all depository institutions subject to the new system of required reserve. The important points of difference between Chairman Reuss's draft measure and that of Chairman Miller were these. First, no interest would be paid on the required reserve. Second, "to ease the burden on small banks," banks having less than $50 million in each class of deposits would be exempt from the reserve requirement. As for the banks with deposits in excess of $50 million, they would be subject to a simplified schedule of reserve requirements which reduced the previous 14 categories to the following four: an 8–10 percent reserve against demand deposits, 1–2 percent on savings accounts, 3–8 percent on short-term certificates, and 1–3 percent on long-term certificates of deposit.

In the hearings on the "Reuss bill" before the House Banking Committee, the Treasury Department, through its spokesman, Deputy Secretary Robert Carswell, stressed the urgent need to pass some kind of legislation that would stop the attrition of the Federal Reserve System by relieving the burdens of Federal Reserve membership. Carswell predicted that if nothing were done to that end, the Federal Reserve within five years would lose about 20 percent of its existing membership—with a consequent sharp loss of income to the Treasury from earnings on the Federal Reserve's portfolio. He supported the concept of universal and uniform reserve requirements for all federally insured depository institutions, but feared that interest payments on reserves held in each deposit category would entail an "unacceptable" loss of income to the Treasury—a loss it could "ill afford because of the budget stringency it faced in the years immediately ahead." He doubted whether the loss—the estimated figures ranged from $200 to $600 million— would be materially offset by income to be earned if the Federal Reserve began to charge explicit prices for the services it rendered.

If Washington officialdom could not agree on the details of what should be done about "the Federal Reserve issue," the American Bankers Association scarcely comprised an Amen Chorus. Starting in midsummer of 1978, it was riven from within by the different stands taken by major money center banks, "lead" regional banks, one-bank holding companies, multibank holding companies, branch-banking systems, and small unit banks on Main Street. If all belonged to the same financial planet, each class of institutions, according to its own kind, lived in a different world. The protracted backstage duel among spokesmen for these rival interests came to a provisional head in the ABA's Leadership Conference held during February 13–16, 1979. The resulting "consensus statement" issued at the end of the conference amounted to a fragile cluster of *ad hoc* compromises among representatives of three groups: major member banks, small member banks, and small non-member banks.

The consensus statement, upon being unveiled before the Reuss Committee, made manifest an attempt to gain all possible advantages for the different constituent interests of the ABA at the least cost to all. It opposed a universal reserve requirement on the ground that such an attempt to bring nonmember banks under Federal Reserve control would seriously weaken the "future vitality of the correspondent banking system." It opposed the extension of mandatory reserve requirements to nonmember banks because doing so would do violence to the "long established principles of the dual banking system and of voluntary membership." Rather, the Federal Reserve "should seek to strengthen the voluntary basis of membership by making membership less financially burdensome and by improving the benefits of members." To that end, an earnings participation account "which provided a riskless, assured source of income at market rates, could make it attractive for new and small banks to join the Federal Reserve even if their deposits were under $10 million."

IMMOBILITY

The order of battle just sketched in broad outline ended in a stalemate on March 21, when the House Banking Committee by a 20–21 vote rejected Chairman Reuss's bill which would lower required reserves starting with a $50 million exemption, and would extend the system of non-interest-bearing reserves to all depository institutions that were not already members of the Federal Reserve System. Republicans on the Committee voted in a block against the measure, and for reasons which echoed the position taken by the ABA. It was that the measure would *de facto* mandate membership in the Reserve System by requiring reserves from all banks above a certain size without paying interest on them—and further, that this involuntary membership would destroy the "dual banking system" by creating an incentive for state banks to switch to national charters.[13]

IN DUBIOUS BATTLE

Subsequent to the March 20 vote, the Reuss Committee argued over the terms of the revised bill designed to reduce the burdens of Federal Reserve membership and to strengthen the levers of monetary policy by imposing reserves for the first time on transaction accounts at federally insured thrift institutions. A little after mid-April, Chairman Reuss appeared to have formed a coalition within the committee with enough strength to vote out a redrafted bill which covered thrift institutions, imposed required reserves on all commercial banks, and with no bows to the principle of "voluntary membership." Several concurrent developments, however, caused Chairman Reuss to cancel a committee meeting set for April 25 in order to "mark up" the text of the proposed revision.

First, the U.S. Court of Appeals for the District of Columbia, in a decision rendered five days previously, construed the Glass-Steagall Act of 1933 in ways which outlawed interest-bearing transaction accounts, remote service units, and share drafts. At the same time, the court suspended the application of its decision to give Congress time—that is, until January 1, 1980—to decide whether it wished to legitimize such accounts by amending the 1933 Act which prohibited them.

The immediate effect of the decision was to unhinge the features of the draft legislation before the Reuss Committee which called for the imposition of reserves on all transaction accounts. Rep. Thomas Ashley (D-Ohio) spoke for others on the committee in saying that "as the definition of transaction accounts [had] suddenly been turned into a wild card," he would "feel very uncomfortable about proceeding with a mark-up of the revised legislation." Rep. Fernand St. Germain (D-R.I.), Chairman of the Subcommittee on Financial Institutions, also urged the full banking committee to hold off any decisions on the Federal Reserve membership problem until the transaction account issue was clarified in the light of the Court's decision. His own subcommittee, said he, would quickly move to consider legislation that would authorize nationwide interest bearing.

Besides, another Leadership Conference of the ABA was being held at that very time. So it made sense to wait until the Conference could analyze the U.S. Court of Appeals decision, and, in its light, review the ABA's opposition to the "mandatory" aspects of bank membership in the Federal Reserve System. It was argued that the judicial decision which undercut the legality of interest-bearing transaction accounts also flung open the door to legislative horse-trading over many issues of immediate importance to diverse financial institutions—Regulation Q, Federal Reserve membership, reserve requirements, and the heavy investments thrift institutions had made in the technology of their transaction accounts.

The "consensus statement" that emerged from the Leadership Conference at the end of April was described by *Pratt's Letter* as being "a lot more statesmanlike—and more politically saleable—than the group's previous effort of February 13–16." While the Conference supported transaction accounts for *all* depository institutions, it also insisted on total rate equality between banks and thrifts which offered them. Only so, could the process be stopped which saw the savings and loan lobby continuously nibble away at banking's checking account monopoly on a state-by-state basis, without ever squarely facing the rate differential issue in Congress. The conference also endorsed the concept of uniform reserves for all "intermediaries" offering transaction accounts—even for nondeposit intermediaries such as money market mutual funds.

SUSPENDED ANIMATION

No immediate reaction from the House Banking Committee was forthcoming to any of this. Of the constraints in the way, the first was this, that the progressive worsening of the inflationary environment was hardly a congenial time to make wholesale cuts in member bank reserves. Secondly, relationships between some influential members of the House Banking Committee and Federal Reserve Board Chairman G. William Miller deteriorated to a point where they discounted the worth of any recommendations he might personally make.[14]

Further, the House Banking Committee as a whole could not act on the membership problem until its Subcommittee on Financial Institutions reported out legislation designed to clarify the transaction account issue, and perhaps authorize various forms of interest-bearing checking accounts nationwide. Then again, the legislative machinery in both chambers of Congress as it bore on banking matters was put on "hold" in September 1979, until Paul Volcker, the newly appointed chairman of the Federal Reserve Board, could define where he personally stood on various aspects of "the Federal Reserve issue."

The machinery began to move again following his confirmation by the Senate. Under questioning by members of the Senate Banking Committee at his confirmation hearings in September, he dismissed the "principle of voluntary membership" as an irrelevant clinging to nostalgia for a past that had ceased to exist. He backed off, as his predecessor Mr. Miller had already done, from the payment of interest on the required reserve. But he urged that Congress give the Federal Reserve Board authority to impose a supplemental reserve on transaction accounts—within a given range—if the Board found that monetary policy could not be effectively carried out on the basis of a regularly required reserve. These matters rested until the full meaning packed into Mr. Volcker's request exploded—as it did on October 6, 1979.

22. The Anatomy of the Federal Reserve Board's Revolution

ITEMS IN THE NEWS

In the first days of October 1979, coincident with the Belgrade Conference of the International Monetary Fund (IMF), the American press featured commemorative articles about the impending fiftieth anniversary of the Great Crash on the New York Stock Exchange. At the same time, reporters filed stories out of New Orleans where the American Bankers Association (ABA) was holding its annual convention. As was true elsewhere in the nation, financial analysts and managers of financial institutions gathered in New Orleans agreed that the Federal Reserve Board must inevitably respond to the spiralling domestic inflation and to the flight from the dollar in international money markets. The only question was the actual timing of the response.

Existing doubts on the point were resolved for those who could read between the lines of a press bulletin for October 5. It reported that Paul Volcker, who had recently succeeded G. William Miller as Chairman of the Federal Reserve Board, had abruptly left the IMF's Belgrade Conference for Washington where he called a special meeting of the Federal Reserve Board and the Federal Open Market Committee (FOMC). That meeting, set for Saturday, October 6, could only mean one thing. The Board, after consultation with the FOMC, would presently decide how it should deal with an increasingly acute domestic and international monetary crisis.

EXPECTATIONS

Within the financial community, expectations about what the Board would actually do were mainly based on past history. Since at least 1974, the Board's "practical monetarism" focused on an attempt to control and stabilize short-term interest rates. This was in line with the Board's theory that by influencing the public's demand for money and the monetary aggregates available to the economy as a whole, the rates would exert a controlling influence over inflationary pressures.

Financial analysts, however, had noted several recurrent features in the pattern of the Board's practical monetarism. First, the *gradualism* of the pattern predictably led to only relatively small interest rate adjustments in a range from a quarter to a half of a percent for federal funds. Second, when short-term interest rates were incompatible with monetary growth targets, the Board tended to sacrifice control over the monetary supply in favor of a stable federal fund rate. Then again, whenever a restrictive monetary policy caused significant increases in unemployment, the politics of the case generated pressures either for an expansionist fiscal policy or for an easing of restrictions on monetary growth before secular inflation was actually brought under effective control.

A typical case involving the first two of these recurrent phenomena occurred in the spring of 1979 when an inflationary surge in monetary aggregates—and particularly in the basic M-1 money supply—climbed at a 14.1 percent annual rate. Administration economists, in their alarm, began to pressure the Federal Reserve Board to raise the federal fund interest rate as an anti-inflationary step. But in a spirited show of independence, Board Chairman G. William Miller led a well-orchestrated media campaign to resist the claim of the administration's economists. Both before and after a critical April 17 meeting of the Federal Open Market Committee, he reaffirmed his loyalty to a "steady as you go" monetary policy. So did the FOMC itself at the April meeting. It voted against a tighter monetary policy.

Ten days later, however, there was a change of front. Faced by a continuing surge in monetary aggregates, the Federal Reserve—having previously avoided the appearance of a "cave-in to outside political pressures"—reversed its April 17 stand. It actively intervened in the money markets to push up the federal funds interest rate—but only by a quarter of a percent. While some financial analysts believed that the reversal "weakened" Mr. Miller's "credibility," others applauded his "moderate restraint as an appropriate policy choice." Still others, who zeroed in on the statistics of the case, produced figures which showed that the tightening action would not materially affect credit availability. In the previous twelve months, so they noted, the Federal Reserve had boosted the federal funds rate by 600 basis points (6 percent). The April 25 increase of another 25 to 50 basis points, therefore, would have little impact on the growth of monetary aggregates.

The Federal Reserve Board, at its own discretion, could legally increase the reserve requirements of member banks in order to restrain their lending activities. Yet bankers at the ABA convention in New Orleans and elsewhere in the nation reasoned that the Board would avoid that kind of direct action, lest it drive even more member banks out of the Reserve System. They had previously tracked the many public statements made by Chairman Miller and other Federal Reserve authorities on the subject of reserve requirements. But as of January 1979 forward, the statements bore on the Federal Reserve's legislative proposals "to put more precision and predictability" in the Federal Reserve's "control of the federal fund rate through open market activities." In line with that objective, the Federal Reserve wished to extend reserve requirements to all commercial banks above a certain size and to transaction accounts of thrift institutions also above a certain size. This, however, was not the same as a bid to increase their required reserves. The opposite was true. The Federal Reserve's legislative program during the months in question called for a *lowering* of the required reserves on trans-action accounts.

With the whole of the foregoing in mind, bankers and managers of other financial institutions shared a widely held assumption. It was that the decisions the Federal Reserve Board would make known after its October 6 special meeting would not differ radically from those that were part of its previous policy initiatives. The Board, as in times past, would concentrate on the federal fund rate, and would adjust it upward in a range from a quarter to one-half of a percent. It would perhaps also make a modest adjustment upward in the rate it charged at the discount window of the Federal Reserve Banks when member banks applied for loans. If so, money would be available in the economy at a price not very far removed from previous price levels. Financial institutions could thus continue to press ahead with aggressive lending policies—though these could be sustained over a long period only by inexorable increases in the money supply.

JOLTS

In Washington on the night of October 6, Paul Volcker held a special press conference to reveal and explain the decisions the Federal Reserve Board had reached after a day-long meeting. Divorced from all else, there was nothing new in his announcement that the Federal Reserve meant to reduce the growth of the money supply toward levels consistent with price stability. That objective squared with previous Federal Reserve positions and was also in line with the old perception that the process of inflation is intimately related to an excessive growth of money and credit. This did not mean that the Federal Reserve viewed the relationship to be so close, or that economic realities were so simple, that the Federal Reserve Board could set a monetary dial on a computer and then relax. As Paul Volcker himself later explained:[15]

Changes in spending and savings habits, the shifting characteristics of different financial instruments having some of the characteristics of money, and the inflationary process itself, all affect the observed relationship between money and economic activity. The increased openness of our economy in general, and the growth of international financial markets in particular, has long since ended illusions of autonomy in policy. Spending, the tax policy, and the behavioral patterns of business and labor all affect the performance of the economy, and the relationship between money, inflation and economic activity. But with all the complications, I do believe that moderate, noninflationary growth in money and credit, sustained over a period of time, is an absolute prerequisite for dealing with the inflation that has ravaged the dollar, undermined our economic performance and prospects, and disturbed our society itself.

The jolt in what Paul Volcker had to say about the Federal Reserve Board's decisions concerned the *method* the Board would use in trying to control the growth of monetary aggregates. It would focus on the level of member bank reserves, and thus on their ability to make loans that affect the money supply. While it would not use its legal powers to raise the level of required reserves, it would seek to influence member bank reserves—and their relationship to loans and the money supply—by means of the following actions.

First, the Federal Reserve would abandon the policy of gradualism even with respect to a traditional instrument of control, such as the rate at the discount window which Federal Reserve Banks charge on the loans made to member commercial banks. In times past, increases in the discount rate had been generally confined to a fraction of 1 percent. But the fact that the October 6 announcement entailed a sharp increase from 11 percent to 12 percent in the costs of member commercial banks for borrowing funds from the Federal Reserve Banks meant that the discount rate was to have an enhanced role in the operating strategy. It was to be not just a symbol but a key regulatory device, and it would be set at levels that would materially affect the judgmental decisions of bank managers.

Second, the new monetary strategy would allow the federal fund rate to fall if excess reserves exerted a downward pressure. Gyrations in the rate would still be subject to Federal Reserve control, but without being pegged as before to within a predictable quarter or half a percentage range. The range would vary, according to circumstances.

Third, while the regular reserve requirements would not be affected, the new monetary strategy would entail the creation of a special 8 percent reserve requirement for designated types of funds, such as large short-term certificates of deposit and Eurodollar borrowings. The object in view here was to enable the Federal Reserve to convert "nonborrowed reserves" of a particular size into an instrument for use in making the money supply "dance." To illustrate, if bank demand deposits in excess of $400 million were subject to the special 8 percent reserve on top of the regular required reserves so that the total equaled 16.5 percent of the demand deposits, the Open Market Desk could better control the money supply by adding reserves to or draining them from the Reserve System as a whole, depending on need.

TURMOIL

By the time the media began to broadcast the substance of Paul Volcker's announcement, bankers at the New Orleans convention of the ABA had either retired for the night or were out on the town, enjoying its nocturnal divertissements. The next morning when they picked up the Sunday newspapers or switched on television sets for the latest news, they were shaken by the reports of the Board's decisions.[16]

Some bankers who where contacted by reporters on the scene of the ABA convention admitted that they did not grasp the full implications of the Board's new policies. Others were quoted as saying that while the terms of the new policies were "painful," they were "long overdue" and for "the first time signaled a serious attempt by the Federal Reserve to bring inflation under control." Paul Volcker himself flew to New Orleans where he appeared before the ABA on Monday to explain the technical details of the Board's anti-inflation program. "No part of it," said he in a model of understatement, "will make the life of bankers any easier."

Elsewhere, ardent "monetarists"—they included central bankers such as those at the helm of the St. Louis Federal Reserve Bank, directors of research in major money center banks such as the Harris Trust and Savings Bank in Chicago,[17] and noted professors of economics—hailed the new turn of events as a triumphant vindication of their own cause. They believed that if the Federal Reserve courageously adhered to its newly announced policy in defiance of all the slings and arrows that might be hurled at it, the effects would help lift the siege of inflation. Many central bankers overseas were of the same mind. The more so in the days immediately after October 6 when they were treated to early signs that the dollar gained strength in foreign exchange markets.

Foremost among the early critics of the Federal Reserve Board's new anti-inflation program were dedicated "fiscalists" in Congress, in the research departments of major labor unions, and in the ranks of noted professors of economics. Among the latter, those on the faculties of Harvard, MIT, and Tufts—the academic counterpart of the "Bermuda Triangle"—would soon make their views known in an ambiguous context. They arranged a publicized social event ostensibly to celebrate the fiftieth anniversary of the Great Crash on the New York Stock Exchange, but they converted the occasion into one in which the Federal Reserve's initiatives were the object of derisive songs, skits, and mocking laughter.[18]

Monday, October 8, was Columbus Day, and was observed in many places as a legal holiday. This fact delayed the full response of the money markets and the stock exchanges to the Federal Reserve's new policy. Starting on Tuesday, however, the reaction that got underway was presently called the "October Massacre," and gave wide currency to the saying that "it was the Great Crash of October 1929 all over again." Stock prices were overwhelmed by a tidal wave of selling, with a consequent slash of an estimated $30 billion in equity values.[19] The bond market caved in, with particularly heavy losses to underwriters who were engaged in offering new issues to the market. Interest rates on federal funds rose by several critical points. Prime rates of interest—reflecting what major money center banks ostensibly charge their best corporate customers—began a remorseless ascent above the level they had attained by the end of September 1979. Predictions of a sharp recession filled the air, though the time of its onset was a subject of conjecture.

The turmoil attending the October Massacre eventually quieted down— for a brief while. The stock market began to recover from its shambles. The rate of federal funds was stabilized. The bond market, with its many walking wounded, stirred with new signs of life. Early signs also indicated that the Federal Reserve had slowed down the rate of growth in the money supply—to 4.4 percent, which was within the targeted 4.5 percent or below. But the sighs of relief were premature. The spiral of inflation was not checked. International uncertainties about the worth of the dollar were not laid to rest. Their reemergence was reflected in further foreign exchange pressures on the dollar and in the hectic buying of gold and silver at fanciful speculative prices. In many places, the costs to banks of borrowed money continued to exceed the ceilings state usury laws set on the interest banks could charge—to dry up bank consumer loans to people who needed them the most. The market for new or old homes, and the building trades industry as a whole, remained precariously balanced on the razor's edge of high interest rates for mortgage money and for construction loans. So, too, in the case of the automobile industry. The high interest rates for automobile loans saddled dealers with new cars—especially the large gas-guzzlers—they could not sell.

In defense of the Federal Reserve, it could be said that lags in turning price statistics around were to be expected. Price data were bound to reflect trends built into the economy prior to October 6. In particular, they were bound to reflect a drastic 60 percent price hike in OPEC oil made in the fall of 1979, and the level of fixed mortgage rates prevalent at that time. They were also bound to reflect the international uncertainties that swirled around the course of events in Iran before and after the seizure of American hostages, and the course of events in Afghanistan following the Soviet invasion of that country. Besides, one could not quickly uproot deep psychological doubts regarding the Federal Reserve's determination to stick with its new policies until inflation was actually brought under effective control. Despite the reinforcing assurances by President Carter that his Administration firmly supported the Federal Reserve's new effort, doubts were nurtured by re-membrances of things past—by previous instances when stern anti-inflation measures had foundered on the rocks once unemployment generated coun-tervailing political demands for monetary ease and for an expansionist fiscal policy.

CRISIS

If the regulation of the money supply held the key to the Federal Reserve's anti-inflation policy, how was money to be defined? Could the reality of money be captured and compressed into a simple statistic in the midst of profound institutional and technological changes? As noted in a former place, the staff of the Federal Reserve Board had previously wrestled with the problem and had issued for comment in early 1979 a proposed new list of monetary measurements. With the October 1979 shift away from a preoccupation with the federal funds rate to a stress on the control of monetary aggregates, decisions regarding a redefinition of monetary measurements became all the more urgent. In the first days of February 1980, Federal Reserve Board Chairman Paul Volcker, while claiming success for the latest policies to control the nation's money supply, announced a new set of money measurements designed to help maintain control.

The new measurements were: *M-1A*, representing currency demand deposits at commercial banks. It was essentially the same as the old M-1, except that it excluded demand deposits held by foreign banks and official institutions. *M-1B*, which included M-1A and other checkable deposits at all depository institutions—including NOW accounts, ATS, credit union share drafts, and demand deposits at mutual savings banks. *M-2*, which included M-1B, savings and small denomination time deposits at all depository institutions, including overnight repurchase agreements at commercial banks, overnight Eurodollars held by U.S. residents other than banks at Caribbean branches of member banks, and money market mutual fund shares. *M-3*, which included M-2 plus large denomination time deposits at all depository institutions and term repurchase agreements at commercial banks and savings and loan associations. *L*, a broad measure of liquid assets, equaling M-2, plus other liquid assets not included elsewhere—such as term Eurodollars held by U.S. residents other than banks, bankers acceptances, commercial paper, Treasury bills and other liquid Treasury securities, and U.S. savings bonds.

Information on the two key measurements—M-1A and M-1B—was to be released on Friday of every week. Information on M-2 and M-3 was to be released monthly, in mid-month for the previous month.

The redefinitions of monetary aggregates did not, however, insure the success of the Federal Reserve's attempts to slow down the rate of growth in the money supply to a targeted 4.5 percent or below. To the contrary, despite claims to that effect voiced by Paul Volcker at the start of February 1980, the basic money stock grew at almost a 10 percent annual rate by the first days of March. Total bank lending was not held in check. It grew at an annual rate above 20 percent, while key interest rates such as the prime rate traveled the distance from 14 percent to 20 percent. Worse, the inflation rate was not arrested. It reached 18 percent annually. A crisis atmosphere gripped the nation and its monetary authorities.

Meanwhile, operating managers of most banks continued to be hit on both the assets and liabilities side of their balance sheet. They could not insulate themselves from the vagaries of movements in interest rates by making their loans at floating rates. They were forced to borrow shorter and to lend longer than in the past, with the result that they were increasingly exposed to the ravages of a negatively sloped yield curve.

In several respects, the complex legacy of the post-1975 recovery left them no choice except to borrow shorter and lend longer. Specifically, because that post-1975 recovery was a consumer- instead of a business-impelled expansion, it biased banks' balance sheets toward fixed-rate rather than variable-rate loans. And while bank balance sheets were changing, so were those of nonfinancial corporations. In their desire to avoid their previously excessive reliance on short-term debt, nonfinancial companies trekked to the capital markets to a record extent. To the degree that they continued to borrow short, it was increasingly in the commercial paper market.

At the same time, the European economies failed to sustain any sort of capital-spending recovery—a phenomenon widely attributed to the success of most European trade unions in raising the level of real wages above its equilibrium level. While this shortfall in overseas business lending weakened the demand for variable-rate loans, new actors in the form of German and Japanese banks became more aggressive in global lending. The supply of funds from these sources relative to an already foreshortened demand for loans greatly eroded spreads. They also caused U.S. money center and regional banks to concentrate still more of their resources on the domestic market, where the dominant form of incremental assets was the fixed-rate consumer loan.

Just as there were new actors abroad, there were new or more active participants at home. The strong cash flows of domestic insurance companies, for example, enabled them to invade both the medium- and the short-term market for corporate loans. In doing so, the insurance companies possessed a competitive advantage over banks, in that their liabilities are denominated in nominal rather than in real terms. Hence the insurers could satisfy the borrowers' demand for a fixed-rate credit without unbalancing their own assets-liability structure. Banks, whose liabilities were becoming increasingly real—that is, variable in cost—could not satisfy customers without seriously distorting their maturity structures.

Meanwhile, the new participants at home included increasing numbers of foreign banks operating on American soil. To consolidate the toeholds they had gained, they began to cut price, thereby forcing American banks to make rate concessions that often took the form of fixing the yield on credit. Among other things, they increased the number of their "capped loans"—a peculiarly troublesome kind of fixed loan that can mislead bank analysts and perhaps the top operating managers of banks as well. In an attempt to placate clout-heavy corporate borrowers seeking predictability in money costs, bank lending officers might say: "We will make you an ostensibly prime-related loan, but we will stipulate that the rate cannot exceed a certain percent *below* prime." Such a loan continues to show up on the books as a sensitive asset whose yield is subject to change within a year or so. In point of fact, the loan has stopped floating, and its yield is fixed.

By the first days of March 1980 when the prime rate reached 20 percent annually, capped loans to important corporate borrowers—as the Federal Reserve belatedly disclosed several months later—were around 6 percent under prime. This left a very sour taste in the mouth of executives of smaller firms who knew what was afoot, yet could not get any capped loans for their own enterprises. Indeed, they were fortunate to get loans at prime or even a percentage over prime.

It was against this dim and afflicted background, with its inflation rate of 18 percent annually, and prime rate of 20 percent, that President Carter announced a new anti-inflation policy on March 10, with the details following on March 14.

MORE TURMOIL

The new program called for an increased discipline in the federal budget, wage and price action, restraint in the growth of monetary aggregates, greater energy conservation, and economic structural changes to encourage production, savings, and research and development. Divorced from practice, the aims of the new program were commendable. Taken as a whole, they respected the proposition that economic stability depended not on just a single line of action, but on the coordination of concurrent actions.

Yet it was not long before some of the central props of the new venture caved in. To start with, the Administration's program for increased discipline in the federal budget called for a $14 billion cut in expenditures for fiscal 1981 to bring the budget into balance. Still, in a budget of over $570 billion in an economy of $2 trillion, there was no evidence that such a cut could reduce the rate of inflation by even half a point. Available evidence ran the other way around. At budget-making time a year previously, the Congressional Budget Office had estimated that expenditure cuts of $25 billion would be required if the rate of inflation was to be lowered by as little as less than a point.[20] With the subsequent growth in inflation in the year that followed, the effects on inflation of a $14 billion cut in expenditures would be below the estimated effects of a $25 billion cut had it been made in early 1979.

According to press reports, President Carter believed a balanced budget would have a profound psychological impact on the American public, and presumably on financial markets. As part of a comprehensive program for economic stability, a balanced budget was a useful symbol. But it was one thing to use symbols in conjunction with substance, and quite another thing to use symbols instead of substance. The impact of a budget that was actually balanced would first be reflected in a falling output, and only then would there be any impact on prices. Yet precisely on this ground, congressional veterans, joined by veteran managers of financial institutions, predicted that the attempts to balance the budget in fiscal 1981 would fail.

And so they did. Once output and demand slowed to the point of a recession, the event triggered all the things associated with a recession—

large increases in transfer payments, larger counter-cyclical spending, and large shortfalls in revenue. The initial aim of a balanced budget disappeared in a recessionary deficit in excess of $50 billion.

In connection with the credit restraint features of the new anti-inflation program, President Carter invoked the Credit Control Act, a measure that had not been used after it was enacted in 1969 during the Nixon Administration.[21] The Act granted the President permanent authority to authorize the Federal Reserve Board to "regulate and control any or all extensions of credit." It also listed eleven specific areas where the Board could issue regulations upon being authorized to do so by the President; they included licensing credit transactions or persons involved in credit use, setting maximum limits for any type of loan, setting limits on loan terms, or the outright prohibition of certain kinds of credit extensions.

It so happened that a month before President Carter invoked the Credit Control Act, Federal Reserve officials had publicly stated their opposition to credit controls and questioned their value. Federal Reserve Board Chairman G. William Miller observed that credit "controls are unacceptable except under the most exigent circumstances. . . . The shortcomings . . . are so well known as to assure that they would be used only in an emergency situation." He defended the existence of standby legislation for mandatory controls only on the grounds that if an "emergency situation arose, and selective credit controls appeared to be necessary, it would be helpful to have the authority for such controls already in place. Moreover, the fact that mandatory controls could be imposed may well contribute to the success of voluntary guidelines."

But with the President's March 10 decision in the matter at issue, the Federal Reserve Board moved quickly, though perhaps not enthusiastically, to outline the terms for credit controls. Their sweep exceeded anything the Congress had granted even during World War II, or at the peak of the postwar boom when credit controls were imposed under conditions where business was operating at close to capacity, and where shortages of consumer goods led to excessive demands that stoked the fires of inflation.

The March 14 terms for credit controls left everyone in doubt about what could in fact be done under them.[22] Anxious calls lawyers for banks made to members of the Federal Reserve Board's legal staff were met by admissions that even *they* didn't know the answers to the regulatory questions put to them.[23] There were also instances where some legal staff members spoke in code language to convey their personal opposition to imposing credit controls because controls resulted in the "reallocation"—or rather "misallocation of credit" and "could be readily evaded." For example, if auto loan terms were tightened, there might be a slowdown in auto loan credits until consumers adjusted to that tightening. Thereafter, they would begin to borrow ostensibly for nonregulated transactions, or they might take out second mortgages to get cash, and then pay cash for cars instead of financing their purchase under the new credit regulations.

On the face of things, the Federal Reserve's credit control program consisted of the following elements. First of all, banks were advised to hold loan growth within the 6–9 percent range previously targeted for total bank credit by the Federal Reserve. Banks were also encouraged to hold back on lending considered to be unproductive, inflationary, or of low social priority—such as unsecured consumer lending, financing of corporate takeovers or mergers, and financing of speculative holdings of commodities. At the same time, lenders were urged to make "special efforts" to maintain credit flows for farmers, home buyers, and small businesses.

Further, restraint was advised on certain types of consumer credit, including credit cards, check credit overdraft plans, and unsecured personal loans. The Federal Reserve established a special deposit requirement of 15 percent for all lenders on increases in these types of credit. Still further, marginal reserve requirements were increased from 8 percent to 10 percent on the managed liabilities of major banks—their large time deposits, Eurodollar borrowings, and repurchase agreements against U.S. government and Federal agency securities. Again, restraint on the amount of credit raised by large nonmember banks was sought through a special deposit requirement of 10 percent on increases in their managed liabilities. The rapid expansion of money market mutual funds was to be restrained by a special deposit requirement of 15 percent on increases in their total assets above the level of March 14. Finally, to discourage the use of the discount window and to speed bank adjustments in response to restraints on bank reserves, a surcharge of 3 percentage points was applied to discount window borrowings by large banks.

In theory, the Federal Reserve could decree that a patient could not go to a doctor unless he paid cash. The actual administration of the new program exempted loans for housing, automobiles, furniture, and appliances, and was confined instead to selected private credit markets. Even so, in a vast, complex economy, credit controls—with their elaborate rules, interpretations, and exceptions—were bound to cause confusion and uncertainties. This was particularly true of the effects of wide-scale controls on consumer credit which blanketed banks, credit unions, thrift institutions, finance companies, retail stores, oil companies, and travel and entertainment credit card concerns.

The immediate reaction of consumers was to retrench. Credit card usage dropped off dramatically. So did demand for loans to buy autos, furniture, appliances, and other credit-sensitive durable goods. In some cases, consumers were merely confused about what they should or should not do under the program. Other consumers, in their bewilderment over the hastily drafted decrees, apparently stopped using credit almost as a patriotic gesture. Consumer debt nose-dived. Installment credit contracted at a seasonally adjusted 7.5 percent annual rate in April, and 13 percent in the months of May and June. By the end of June, the monthly volume of new credit was 28 percent below the peak in September 1979. All told, the second quarter decline in outstanding consumer debt amounted to almost $9 billion—the largest drop in percentages as well as dollar terms since World War II.

As for business credit, a major aim was to limit its expansion and to provide that, within a reduced volume of total credit, certain borrowers—particularly farmers, home buyers, and small businesses—would have preferred access to loans. There were no penalties or inducements to accommodate those borrowers who were to be favored. Bankers were simply admonished to make such loans. The admonishment, however, was beside the point in the case of home buyers and small businesses who were reeling under the impact of a disrupted economy.

The whole of the credit control effort, coming on top of a recession that had begun in January 1980, may have played a key role in lessening a rampant inflation psychology, and in reducing the annual rate of inflation to 10–11 percent by the midsummer of 1980. But the long-range feasibility of the allocative features of the Federal Reserve credit control program—with their arbitrary quantitative limitations on economic activity—was never fully tested. For aside from the credit controls and the conventional fiscal measures taken in mid-March, the Federal Reserve—with its eye on the jaundiced view foreign bankers had about the U.S.—tried to "defend the dollar" by increases in the discount rate higher than domestic needs actually warranted. The combined effects transformed what was already a fragile economic situation into a sharp decline. As effective demand for new bank loans slumped, bankers could accommodate aggregate credit demands within the limits of the restraint program. In any event, with the collapse of economic activity, the credit control program was partially rescinded on May 22 just nine weeks after it was launched. It was fully terminated on July 3 when the recession was in full swing.

APPRAISALS

To judge from the picture that prevailed by the year-end of 1980, the Federal Reserve's new policy of monetarism did not stabilize the money supply. Though its targets called for a money supply growth of between 4 percent and 6.3 percent in 1980, the money supply was full of volatile bounces. After President Carter imposed credit control during the spring of the year, for example, the money supply declined sharply and interest rates plummeted when the recession slammed the country. But when spring faded into summer and the recession apparently reached its bottom, the opposite occurred. The money supply exploded, rising to a rate over 10 percent, while interest rates headed back up again.

While the Federal Reserve could claim that the explosion of the money supply in mid-1980 accounted for the subsequent signs of an economic recovery, in the fall of the year it was subject to new attacks when it began to tighten the supply of credit by increasing the discount rate. It was accused of choking off an incipient revival of the housing industry, disrupting the mortgage market, retarding job-creating investments, and remaining insensitive to extensive unemployment in the manufacturing belt. President Carter, Treasury Secretary G. William Miller, and leaders of union labor did not exhaust the list of vocal critics. Participants in money markets just as loudly complained that lenders no longer had a beacon light to guide them as was true when the Federal Reserve used to set the rates for federal funds. Now they could only watch the weekly release of money supply figures for clues about how tight or loose the Federal Reserve meant to be.

The phenomenon of "overshooting" followed in consequence of the uncertainties about the money market's actual direction. Lenders, in setting their own interest rates, had no way of knowing whether the rates accurately reflected market conditions. To be on the safe side, they tended to overshoot market conditions, and then make their adjustments afterward. The immediate effect was to make the market as unstable and nervous as "a drunken driver in a car with a loose steering wheel." The larger effect was to discourage corporations from borrowing for new job-creating investments— thereby frustrating the Federal Reserve's major aim to encourage improved productivity as a compelling anti-inflation measure.

Federal Reserve authorities did not directly respond in public to their critics, but privately, they stressed the need to keep the whole picture in perspective. They ran through an inventory of unhinging events in the world arena since October 1979 that were beyond their control, and insisted that their own policies were the only way to manage the money supply. They also insisted that their performance record over a twelve-month period was better than it appeared to be when viewed from one moment to the next. Specifically, despite extreme ups and downs, the money supply over the year following October 1979 averaged out at the top range of the Federal Reserve's targets.

What is beyond dispute is that inflation itself is the long-run consequence of short-run expediencies. The benefits of a tax cut, of increased public spending, are felt within a few weeks or quarters. The penalties in terms of inflation may not come until after a couple of years. "Life, to be sure," as Henry C. Wallich of the Federal Reserve Board observed, "is a succession of short-runs, but every moment is also the long-run of some short-run expediency of long ago." We have been experiencing the long-run consequences of the short-run policies of the past. If we continue to meet current problems with new short-run devices, the bill will keep mounting. If we always take the short view, we will find that the cost of fighting inflation is always too high, the short-run loss of output and employment too great.

What also came to be recognized, amid the twists and turns of the struggle against inflation, was that the establishment of a high-growth, low-inflation economy would be facilitated by extensive reform of costly government regulations. Regulatory activities in the health, safety, and environmental protection areas had not always achieved the desired outcome at minimum costs, and were in need of review with that thought in mind.

Where banking itself was concerned, extensive market and price regulation programs were in need of careful reexamination to ensure that their benefits outweighed their costs. In the same vein, it was important to consider carefully the alternatives for programs that limited competition and raised prices. It was particularly important to come to grips with the way mandated deposit rate differentials between banks and thrifts led to competitive inequities counter to the interests of small savers and economic efficiency. It was also particularly important to come to grips with the way the national policy of barring interstate banking, as embodied in the Mc-Fadden Act, worked in ways that were unfair to domestic banks while foreign banks were allowed to continue their expansion across state lines. Some of these matters, and a number of others, were addressed in the Depository Institutions and Deregulation and Monetary Control Act of 1980—as indicated in the chapter following next.

23. A Bill is Born

If you had been the chief executive officer of a commercial bank in the months between October 1979 and the end of March 1980, how would you have described the financial world you faced? The likelihood is that you would have been strongly tempted to describe it in the words ancient cartographers used when they exhausted the knowledge of the charted world, and covered the unknown by a notation in the margin of their maps: "Beyond this point lies nothing but sandy wastes, frozen bogs, wild beasts, and Scythian ice." In any event, wherever you looked before making your judgmental decisions about what to do or not to do, you would have encountered conditions where the known was overprinted by the uncertain.

The Federal Reserve Board's new-style monetarism, with its emphasis on measures designed to influence the level of bank reserves, merged into the new spurt in the inflationary spiral triggered by a 60 percent hike in OPEC oil prices, followed in turn by a new flight from the dollar in international money markets. The seizure of American embassy hostages in Teheran merged into the fears that the Soviet invasion of Afghanistan would lead to a major Middle East war or to the denial of Middle East oil to Western nations. At the same time, the quadrennial "War of the Presidential Succession" was being heated up in the United States, marked by doubts as to the identity of the 1980 Republican challenger to President Carter—and in what respects the program of the challenger might differ from that of the incumbent president.[24]

Where your own operations were concerned, the high costs of borrowing funds in money markets might have pushed the interest rates you were forced to charge on your own loans smack up against the state usury ceiling on consumer credit. At the same time, the ambiguous terms of the Administration's credit control program would have carried you into a ceaseless round of conferences with legal counsel to determine what you could rightfully do or must refrain from doing. In virtually every copy of the financial press, you would read reports about the woes of Job that were afflicting many thrift institutions that were losing depositor funds to high-yielding money market instruments, while their own investments were tied up in lower-yield long-term mortgages. You would also read another report about another foreign takeover of a U.S. bank in this or that corner of the nation. On top of all else, there were the uncertainties about how Congress would deal with the issue of interest-bearing transaction accounts as it was invited to do by the U.S. Court of Appeals for the District of Columbia.

Yet amid all the confusion, one thing was clear enough. It was that the Federal Reserve's new emphasis on measures designed to influence the level of bank reserves was bound to drive more member banks out of the System if the burdens of the Federal Reserve's anti-inflation policies fell in the first instance and mainly on member banks. To the extent that more of these left the System, the capacity of the Federal Reserve to carry out its new policies—let alone actually attain the objectives for which they were framed—would be correspondingly reduced.

In the clarity of crisis, it was obvious that there could be no further delay in coming to grips with the "membership issue" and with all other matters impacted within it—issues of politics, equity, competition between diverse financial institutions, relations among regulatory agencies, federal-state relations as they bore on the dual banking system, usury laws, the deepening penetration of American financial markets by foreign banks, and so on. The events that brought *you* under siege besieged the managers of a diverse range of other financial institutions, along with Congress and the political executives at the head of federal and state regulatory agencies. There must be a serious exercise in group diplomacy out of which at least some agreements could be reached about divisive issues that had long been in the air. And so it happened.

GROUP DIPLOMACY

At the bargaining table, none of the rival parties at interest—private or public—got all that they wanted, and none gave up all that they had. Everyone took a little and gave a little. The results fell short of the ideal, and some matters were left hanging in an unresolved state, though they would be returned to and become the centerpieces of a new round of controversies and bargainings during the Reagan Administration. The intermediate agreements that were reached were sealed in the Depository Institutions Deregulation and Monetary Control Act of 1980, passed by Congress on March 30 of that year, and signed by President Carter the next day. The Act materially changed the competitive relationship among diverse financial institutions. It altered the inherited accumulation of regulations for the governance of commercial banks and for all other depository institutions. It gave a new turn to the dual banking system and moved the Federal Reserve further along the road toward an old goal where it would become "a central bank" in fact and not in ambiguous name only.

The terms of the new legislation were grouped by subject matter under nine titles. Taken in sequence, the first dealt with reserve requirements; the second with the deregulation of depository institutions; the third with consumer checking account equality; the fourth with the powers of thrift institutions, as well as with other matters; the fifth with state usury laws; the sixth with truth in lending; the seventh with amendments to national banking laws; the eighth with regulatory simplification, and the ninth with foreign control of United States financial institutions.

TITLE I

As addressed to the relationship between reserves and monetary control, this title set certain Federal Reserve requirements for *all* depository institutions, but without mandating their membership in the Federal Reserve. Thrift institutions, for example, were authorized to use balances maintained in Federal Reserve Banks to satisfy their liquidity requirements under either the Federal Home Loan Bank Act or the National Credit Union Act.

All transaction accounts over $25 million were subject to reserve requirements ranging from 8 percent to 14 percent, with an initial rate of 12 percent. A 3 percent reserve requirement was set for transaction accounts below $25 million. Either way, the base level of $25 million was to be indexed to change each year by 80 percent of the changes in the total transaction account. Where nonpersonal time deposits were concerned, the initial rate of required reserve was set at 3 percent—regardless of maturity—with a range of 0–9 percent. The Federal Reserve, in applying the schedule or reserve requirements mandated by the Act, was explicitly directed by Congress to use open market operations in order to offset any changes in reserve availability.

Reserve requirements were to be put in place over an eight-year period for nonmember institutions and over four years for member banks following April 1, 1980. Any bank that was a member of the Reserve System as of July 1, 1979, even though it left the System after that date, would be subject to reserve requirements as if it were a member bank. There would be no phase-in period for reserve requirements for either member banks or nonmember depository institutions which were authorized to provide new types of deposits or accounts after the reserve provisions became effective. This would apply to NOW accounts, except for the eight states in which such accounts were authorized by law prior to April 1, 1980.

At the same time, the Act gave the Federal Reserve Board something like the safety net Paul Volcker had requested in his appearance before the Senate Banking Committee in September 1979. Thus, under extraordinary circumstances, the Board was authorized to impose supplementary reserves on transaction accounts—within a range of 0–4 percent—outside the statutory limits, and for a period limited to 180 days. The supplementary reserves would be uniform for all depository institutions, and would earn interest for them at a rate up to the average rate of earnings on the securities portfolio of the Federal Reserve System. Before the supplementary reserves could be imposed, however, five or more members of the Federal Reserve Board must cast affirmative votes in support of a proposal to do so. In other words, a majority of the Board must find that the statutory levels of reserve balances are inadequate for purpose of monetary policy, and that supplemental reserves are needed to change the condition for the better.

Among the other provisions of Title I, any depository institution holding transaction accounts—be it a bank or thrift institution—would henceforth have access to the Federal Reserve discount window under the same terms and conditions as member banks. Further, within 18 months after the Act went into effect, the Federal Reserve Board was authorized to charge explicit prices for its services, as in the instance of floats on checks within the system. In doing so, it was to include, as part of its annual report to Congress, a detailed account of the costs of providing each its services, the basis on which the fees charged for each service were determined, and the impact of its service offerings and fees on competing or potentially competing services providers, on depository institutions, and on commercial and private consumers. Title I also included a provision which expanded the types of Federal Reserve assets that could be used to collateralize Federal Reserve notes, and removed the requirement that Federal Reserve notes in the vaults of the Federal Reserve banks be collateralized.

TITLE II

Among the main features of Title II, bearing on the deregulation of depository institutions, the Act provided for a six-year phasing out of Regulation Q limitations on interest rates. The indicated ways and means were designed to permit thrift institutions to organize themselves to compete for dollar savings in a market environment, and to ensure equity for depositors with small savings, among depository institutions and between them and non-depository institutions. As part of the process, the Act transferred the authority to set interest rates on deposits from the Federal Reserve Board, the FDIC, and the FHLB to a six-member Depository Institutions Deregulation Committee comprised of the heads of these agencies, plus the Secretary of the Treasury and the Chairman of the National Credit Union Association, with the Comptroller of the Currency as a nonvoting member. The Committee was to meet in public sessions at no less than three-month intervals, and was to make its decisions by majority vote of the voting members.

Title II set forth specific targets for increasing rate ceilings to market rates—this, to make sure that the committee would in fact initiate such increases. But while the targets were set, the Committee was granted the discretionary authority either to exceed any one of them if economic conditions warranted, or, on the same grounds, not to increase them at all. It could selectively increase or decrease permissible rates on any particular class of deposits, or lower permissible rates on any and all accounts. Its authority in the matter, and its own existence as well, would expire at the end of the six-year period.

TITLE III

This was separately named the "Consumer Checking Account Equity Act of 1980." Its terms, effective on December 31, 1980, authorized a nationwide extension of negotiable order of withdrawal accounts (NOW accounts) to federally insured commercial banks, savings and loan associations, mutual savings banks, and savings banks. As of March 31, 1980, the Act granted permanent authority to commercial banks to offer automatic transfer accounts (ATS), to federally insured savings and loan associations to offer remote service units (RSU), and to credit unions to offer the equivalent of checking accounts in the form of share drafts. Where ATS accounts in particular were concerned, the permissible rate of interest on them was left to the discretion of the deregulation committee, but the latter was also expected to provide competitive equality between ATS and NOW accounts.

At the same time, the Act permitted Federal Home Loan Banks to process NOW account drafts and other instruments issued by their members. The provision expanded the Federal Home Loan Banks' existing authority to engage in the processing and settlement of negotiable orders or other instruments of payment. Such services were to be priced in line with the pricing principles applicable to the services rendered by Federal Reserve Banks. Similarly, the Central Liquidity Facility (CLF) of the National Credit Union was authorized to process share drafts and other instruments issued by CLF members—again in line with the pricing principles applicable to Federal Reserve Banks.

TITLE IV

While this title increased the limits of FDIC insurance on deposits from $40 thousand to $100 thousand, its main provisions gave new investment authority to federally chartered savings and loan associations, to mutual savings banks, and to credit unions. Savings and loan associations, for example, could invest up to an aggregate limit of 20 percent in assets in unsecured or secured consumer loans, commercial paper, and corporate debt securities. They could invest in, redeem, or hold shares of certificates of open-end investment companies. They could make residential real estate loans to the same extent as national banks. They could exercise trust and fiduciary powers and offer credit card services.

The provisions in question also removed the geographical restrictions on the residential real estate loans the associations could make, authorized them to make second trust loans, expanded their authority to make acquisition, development, and construction loans, and substituted a 90 percent loan-to-value ratio requirement in place of the preexisting dollar limit on residential real estate loans.

Further, the Act authorized federal savings and loan associations to issue mutual capital certificates which would pay "dividends" rather than "interest," but dividend payments would not be allowed until the requirements for federal insurance had been met. The legislation also called for the early completion of a study of ways in which the Federal Home Loan Bank System and other federal agencies could assist all thrift institutions overcome their economic difficulties in periods of rapid inflation and high interest rates—difficulties which inhered in their portfolios bulging with low-yield mortgages, and in their attempts to pay market rates of interest.

The provisions of Title IV that were applicable to Federal Mutual Savings Banks (MSBs), permitted them to invest up to 20 percent of their assets in loans or investments without regard to any limitations of federal or state law, provided that 65 percent of such investments were made within the state where the bank was located or within 50 miles of such a state. They were also permitted to accept demand deposits from any source, and to hold up to 5 percent of their assets in commercial, corporate, or business loans provided that such loans were made within the state in which the MSB was domiciled or within 75 miles of the MSB's home office.

As applied to Federal Credit Unions, Title IV amended the Federal Credit Union Act in a number of signiifcant ways. It permitted federal credit unions to make loans on individual cooperative housing units, removed the limitation on the contract authority of the CLF which required appropriations, and allowed an agent member of CLF to charge its member more than 12 percent in interest if the CLF itself charged more than that figure. Federal credit unions were also allowed to raise their loan rates up to an annual rate of 15 percent subject to rules issued by the National Credit Union Association. The NCUA itself could raise the loan ceiling above 15 percent for periods not exceeding 18 months, after consultation with appropriate Congressional committees, the Department of the Treasury, and other federal financial regulatory agencies.

TITLE V

By its terms, federal authority overrode state usury ceilings on business, agricultural, and mortgage loans. State usury ceilings on first mortgage loans made by banks, savings and loans, credit unions, mutual savings banks, mortgage bankers, and HUD approved lenders under the National Housing Act were permanently preempted—subject to the right of affected states to override the preemption if they acted within three years. For another thing, state usury ceilings on business and agricultural loans above $25 thousand made by any person were preempted for three years, subject to the right of the affected state to override the preemption. A ceiling of five percentage points above the discount rate in the Federal Reserve district where the lender was located would apply to such loans. To one side of the foregoing, separate usury limits, administered by the Small Business Administration, would apply to small business investment companies. State usury ceilings on their loans would be permanently preempted subject to the right of affected states to override at any time.

When a state overrode any federal preemption of state usury laws as provided in Title V, whether by means of a statute or constitutional provision, the state's proposal must explicitly declare that it is overriding the federal preemption. It must also explicitly identify the specific preemption it was overriding—whether it concerned loans on home mortgages, on business and agricultural loans over $25,000, or on loans made by small business investment companies. It remains to be added that manufactured home financing—that is, the financing of mobile homes—was also made subject to the mortgage usury exemption as long as such financing complied with the consumer protection provisions specified in the regulations of the Federal Home Loan Bank Board (FHLBB). But any provisions of the FHLBB regulations bearing on consumer protection in manufactured home financing would not preempt any state law which provided the consumer with stronger protection.

TITLE VI

The object here was to simplify truth-in-lending, by amending the Truth-in-Lending Act in many ways. Among other things, the Federal Reserve Board was authorized to establish tolerance for numerical disclosures. If a creditor made a mistake in quoting the monthly payment, the Board could determine that the mistake was so small that it would not affect the consumer's right, and hence would not be in violation of the Act. Further, the preexisting requirement of an automatic itemized disclosure of the amount financed was removed in favor of itemization at the request of the borrower. The consumer, on the other hand, was to be informed of his rights to obtain additional information regarding the components of the amount financed, and the terms of a statement informing the consumer of such a right was outlined in Title IV. The Federal Reserve Board, for its part, was authorized to establish appropriate disclosure categories that would conform with a Congressional interest in providing coherent information to borrowers, in facilitating lender compliance with the disclosure categories.

TITLE VII

Title VII contained a number of amendments to national banking laws. One among these removed the 6 percent limitation on national bank stock preferred stock dividends. Another authorized the Comptroller of the Currency to establish the timetable for the examination of national banks, and to examine the foreign operations of state member banks upon request from the Federal Reserve Board. At the same time, the Comptroller was authorized to formulate regulations to carry out his responsibilities under the Financial Institutions Supervisory Act of 1966, but the rule-making provision carried no right to permit otherwise impermissible activities of national banks under provisions of the McFadden Act of 1927 and the Glass-Steagall Act of 1933 that were not amended. As a related matter, the legislation placed a moratorium until October 1, 1981, on the direct or indirect establishment, acquisition, or operation of a trust company across state lines, unless the trust company was acquired and in operation on or before March 5, 1980.

In another direction, Title VII allowed national banks to invest in the stock of federally insured banks, owned exclusively by other banks and engaged exclusively in servicing the investing banks, their officers, directors, or employees. The total stock owned could not exceed 10 percent of a national bank's capital account, and no national bank could own more than 5 percent of the voting securities of the institution in which the investment was made.

TITLE VIII

As expressly addressed to federal financial institution regulatory agencies, the language of the title breathed at least the spirit of the mounting complaints depository institutions voiced about the costs and burdens of over-regulation. Accordingly, federal agencies regulating financial institutions were directed to make sure that their regulations were needed; that the public and interested parties had an opportunity to air their views; that alternatives to the regulations were considered; that costs and burdens were minimized; that regulations were written clearly and simply; and that conflicts, inconsistencies, and duplications were avoided.

Congress recognized that there could be emergency situations or special circumstances where regulatory agencies could not comply to the letter of its foregoing directive. Examples included technical or clarifying amendments, regulations designed to eliminate a loophole or reduce a burden, regulation that would reformulate a proposal previously issued for public command, and regulations subject to a short cut-off point. Except in such limited contexts, Congress expected all federal agencies regulating financial institutions to comply with the terms of Title VIII "to the maximum extent practicable."

TITLE IX

The subject dealt with the foreign control of U.S. depository institutions. Without prejudicing any pending case one way or another, it was designed to provide a breathing spell during which the Federal Reserve, the Administration, and Congress could study and review that problem. Thus it provided a moratorium on foreign acquisition of U.S. depository institutions to July 1, 1980. Along with this went a number of exemptions from the moratorium. Acquisitions of under $100 million were exempt as were corporate reorganizations and transfers of ownership interest already under foreign control. Applications pending on or before March 5, 1980 were exempted from the moratorium provisions, but continued to be subject to existing statutory standards. Also exempt were acquisitions of a financial institution which were subsidiaries of bank holding companies under orders to divest by December 31, 1980.

MEANINGS

If you were a commercial banker on the morning after the foregoing legislation became law, you would have revealed an engaging innocence if you thought that the legislation was like a rainbow painted across the sky, promising an end to all the conflicts and storms in the financial world of which you were a part. On the other hand, even a banker who was a battle-wise apostle of the bitter truth would recognize in the legislation a counterpart to what geologists call "posthumous faulting"—meaning that a break in the earth's crust can extend its line forward long after the explosion that caused the break had spent its force. So, too, the legislation, by its break with the crustations of the past, opened the way to further reshuffling in the relationships among financial institutions. The concluding chapter touches on that prospect in the politics of banking.

24. *Future Prospects*

ON A NOTE OF CAUTION

Mark Twain once observed that as the Mississippi River had been shortened by floods by 150 miles between Cairo, Illinois, and New Orleans in the 18th century, it was safe to conclude that the Mississippi would continue to shrink 1.5 miles per year indefinitely. In 800 years, therefore, Cairo and New Orleans would be a single municipality, with a single city council and a common utility company.

The comic invention was Mark Twain's way of sounding a warning note regarding the all-too-human tendency to extract an immense speculative conclusion from a trifling amount of information. It is a warning that applies with special force to predictions about the future of American banking. Special, because it so often seems that the first law of life in banking is the law of surprise. No one can really be certain how the conduct of banking in the remaining years of the 1980s will be impacted by events that are quietly germinating right now out of our common sight. But *if* trends currently visible *do in fact* continue along their present line, some of the future traits or aspects of banking might resemble the sketch drawn below.

MANAGEMENT STYLES

Chief executives of banks most likely will reflect the management styles that will prevail throughout American business generally. It will be a trend away from the formal emblems of status and rank, and toward more openness and egalitarianism in interpersonal relations. Chief executives will have to exhibit a capacity to live with complexity, a tolerance for ambiguity, and a high order of skill in "getting everyone into the act and still get the action that is needed." To these ends, they will have to be, paradoxically, more systematic than any earlier generation of leaders of banking enterprises. They will be faced by a ceaseless need to make clear distinctions between matters that must of necessity be subject to central direction and decision, and those which can and should be decentralized. This, in turn, will entail actions where they clearly define goals and targets, while they allow different levels of their subordinates more latitude in the ways for attaining them.

Chief executive officers will still have to manage the entire situation—the physical setting, group team work, information flow, face-to-face discussions with personnel, as well as the formulation of policies, rules, and regulations to steer action in the desired direction. But it will be imperatively necessary for chief executives to arouse in their subordinates a commitment to the task set for them. Though the phrase, "Do this," or "Don't do that," will still be part of their vocabulary, it is likely to be preceded by an explanation: "This is the situation, and these are the reasons for the bank policies designed to meet it." The desired commitments on the part of subordinates will be more readily forthcoming if the latter understand and accept the tasks set for them because they have previously had some sort of voice in formulating the decisions affecting them.

Effective executive management will heavily depend on the skillful management of information as a *resource*. People in charge must know what is expected, must know how well they are performing, how well they have done in the past compared with coherent standards of performance, what is impending. Insight into what lies ahead, based upon a clear definition of the present situation, calls for more rapid and accurate information getting to the right place at the right time. The skills of managers in the communications process will be essential. The so-called "communication gap" in management will be subsumed under the new rubric of the "information revolution" which is already underway. If so, it will mean that an ever higher premium will be placed on the judgmental aspects of banking—to know how best to use to a good account the swift flash floods of information that can inundate the bank manager by the mere touch of the fingers on a few keys.

THE REGULATORY PICTURE

Despite the deregulation legislation of April 1980, the regulation of financial institutions will remain a fact of life, and, so such, will continue in the future as in the past to be a source of controversies.

Right now pressures are building up for a resolution of a long-standing dispute between bank managers and regulators regarding criteria for adequate capital, appropriate capital ratios, and, indeed, what capital actually *is*. Bank managers want a clear definition of the difference between the debts they have on the books and the deposits they have in the banks. One could argue that a five-year capital note is little different from a five-year deposit, yet regulators seem to make a distinction between the two.

In the practice of the matter, the definition of capital has tended to be a product more of indecision than of a clear-cut decision. As noted by indirection in an earlier place, regulators have allowed money center banks to run their capital ratios down to where they can be competitive with foreign banks, while retaining the pressure on regional banks to maintain higher capital ratios. The disparity here is bound to generate ever stronger demands that regulatory decisions should be more precise, thereby allowing banks and investors to make more rational decisions as to the underlying strength of individual banking institutions.

The internationalization of banking

Barring a collapse of the world order, it seems likely that American and foreign banks will increasingly leap over national boundary lines and expand their financial operations in each other's "back yard." For the time being, however, the restrictive structure of banking in the U.S. is still offering attractive opportunities to foreign institutions to acquire U.S. banks while no comparable opportunity exists for American banks to acquire the same U.S. institutions. The *political* question to be answered is whether you break down the domestic structure of bank restrictions and bank regulations to allow banks within the United States to merge or buy each other across state lines—despite the long-standing opposition of unit banks—or whether you allow the competitive advantages now possessed by foreign companies to continue.

Some legislative and regulatory moves have been made of late to equalize the competitive conditions among U.S. and foreign banks in the case of "distressed" institutions. Pressures are now mounting to bring these competitive conditions still more in line with each other. But in the period immediately ahead, all such attempts seem likely to be met by the continued resistance of those banks who see in the terms for equalizing the conditions for a takeover of a "distressed" bank, by either a U.S. or foreign bank, a "Trojan Horse" potential for interstate banking which they strongly oppose.

Meanwhile, after almost two years of staff studies and public discussion, the Federal Reserve Board on December 3, 1981, gave a major spur of its own to the internationalization of banking.[25] It faced up to the fact that multinational U.S. banks had been conducting an extensive dollar-denominated business in offshore locations. To bring this business back to the U.S.—and the banking jobs with it—the Board agreed to permit the nation's banks to set up international banking facilities (IBFs) which would be free of domestic reserve requirements and interest rate ceilings. An IBF could accept only foreign deposits and extend credit only to foreign banks and corporations, and would otherwise be limited to international banking in ways where they would not be used to evade controls on domestic banking. In effect, an IBF would act as a conduit for foreign funds, and its activities would not impact U.S. money and credit flows.

An IBF would be, in essence, a "booking office" using the offshore rules that prevailed in places such as Nassau and Grand Cayman. The rationale for the IBF was that the business was going to be done some place one way or another, and it might as well be done in the U.S. right under the eyes of senior management.[26] Also, it was believed that some banks and some customers, other things being equal, were more comfortable having their assets within U.S. jurisdiction. At the same time, the big New York City banks, which pushed the hardest and longest for the change, had an additional argument: jobs. The City of London had obviously benefitted enormously from the job creation that went with the steady growth of Euromarkets. Why not give New York City—a place that was losing jobs—a chance to get back the benefits of international banking?

The State of New York passed appropriate enabling legislation, while an IBF can be set up in any state that permits them. At the time of this writing, Florida has already enacted enabling legislation, and both Illinois and California are on the verge of doing so.

Some U.S. bankers expressed disappointment over several features of the IBF regulations issued by the Federal Reserve Board. They approved of the provision which set a deposit minimum of $100,000 (or its equivalent in foreign currency), and a one-day minimum deposit maturity for interbank transactions. But they feared that the two-day minimum for transactions with nonbank customers would inhibit the kind of fast, in-and-out transactions that many corporate treasurers favor for cash-management purposes. Secondly, subject to changes in existing legislation, some U.S. bankers pointed to the drawback they saw in an FDIC ruling (in the wake of the Federal Reserve's authorization of IBFs) that because IBF deposits are on shore (or at any rate on the books of an on-shore entity), they are subject to deposit insurance. The imposition of deposit insurance raises the costs of the funds by several basis points, and this fact—during a period of narrow margins on much foreign business—reduces the appeal of using an IBF instead of an existing offshore unit. On balance, however, a great number of bankers, whether associated with the "money center" banks or with the "regionals" see in the IBFs a major breakthrough in the internationalization of banking.

INTERSTATE BANKING

As noted at many points in these pages, interstate banking has been debated for a long time. What makes the current explosion of talk about the subject different from the case in the past is the way the debate has been sharply focused by an event that marked the last days of the Carter Administration—namely, President Carter's transmittal to Congress of a report on geographical restrictions on commercial banking.

The report defined the purposes of the McFadden Act and distinguished it from the Douglas Amendment to the Bank Holding Company Act. The importance of this starting point lay in the fact that operations of interstate branch offices are often confused with bank holding company acquisitions across state lines—though there is a world of difference between the two. On the basis of the difference that was seen and drawn, the report of the Carter Administration made three recommendations for priority action. They were: A phased liberalization of the Douglas Amendment to permit bank acquisition across state lines on a regional basis; a modification of the McFadden Act to permit electronic fund transfer terminals on a statewide basis and within standard metropolitan statistical areas (SMSAs) which cross state lines; and enactment of the emergency bank acquisitions bill which was previously submitted to Congress.

The first recommendation was the most important, and while it was strongly resisted in many quarters, it was just as strongly endorsed by the Association of Bank Holding Companies (ABHC)—whose members believed that their own proposed Regional Banking Deregulation Act was the ideal vehicle to carry out the White House recommendation. The ABHC plan would amend the Douglas Amendment to permit a bank holding company to acquire another bank holding company in each contiguous state during the first five years of the new law. Companies with less than $500 million in assets would be exempt from the time limit. In addition, bank holding companies of all sizes would be prohibited from "leapfrogging" from one to another state, which was not contiguous to the home state of the acquiring holding company. Each acquisition would be subject to approval by the Federal Reserve Board and to review by the Antitrust Division of the Justice Department.

The ABHC believed that its proposal carried out the basic concepts of the Carter Administration's recommendation—this, by continuing the process of deregulation on a phased regional basis while fully protecting the dual banking system and guarding against any undue concentration of banking assets. Limiting acquisitions to *existing bank holding companies*, and not permitting *bank* acquisitions was of fundamental importance to the ABHC plan. Bankers who were not interested in operating a bank holding company, nor in banking across state lines, could maintain their status quo simply by not organizing a bank holding company.

This line of argument has not swept everything before it.[27] Opponents of the effort to liberalize geographic restrictions on banking usually argue that only a handful of money center banks—50 at the most—are interested in changing the status quo. Others, taking a different tack, argue for a level playing field among financial service competitors. They contend that it would only be equitable to grant savings and loan association holding companies the authority to acquire other savings and loan association holding companies in contiguous states on a comparable basis as the ABHC proposal allows for bank holding companies.

The clash here is likely to continue for some months ahead—until competitor interests having a stake in what is done about the geographical restrictions on commercial banking negotiate the terms for possible trade-offs. Judged in current political terms, all parties at interest still seem "too weak to advance, too strong to surrender, and too proud to ask for mercy."

MORE HOMOGENEITY

In the immediate future, the focus for controversy among competing financial institutions promises to be the wide-ranging Financial Institutions Restructuring and Services Act introduced in the Senate by U.S. Senator Jake Garn (R-Utah) along with the supplementary bill he introduced into the Senate incorporating features of "The Regulators Bill" as crafted by the House Banking Committee. Senator Garn's measures bypassed for the time being the general prohibitions against interstate banking in the McFadden Act and the Douglas Amendment. They also bypassed a broad review of the issues carried over from the 1933 Glass-Steagall bill. Yet the sweep of the measures was very great. The increased homogeneity among financial institutions they pointed to could not but help set the stage for an industry donnybrook—or horse trading, depending on one's choice of imagery. Leaving fine points of detail out of account, Senator Garn's major proposals would: (1) Combine the insurance funds of the FDIC, the FSLIC, and the National Credit Union Share Insurance Fund into a single fund. (2) Increase FSLIC and FDIC flexibility in assisting troubled institutions, including the permission of interstate and cross-industry mergers, "but only after reasonable efforts are made to find intra-industry and in-state merger partners," and allowing the FDIC to approve an interstate acquisition of a bank with $2 billion in assets, but "only after exhausting the possibilities of an in-state or adjacent-state merger." (3) Permit member banks to deal in and underwrite municipal revenue bonds. (4) Permit banks, thrifts, and credit unions to operate investment companies, including money market funds. (5) Preempt both state due-on-sale clause restrictions and usury ceilings, though states would have three years to override these preemptions. (6) Grant broader lending and investment powers to national banks, including an increase from the present 10 percent to a prospective 15 percent of the capital and surplus lending limit to a single borrower. (7) Increase the deposit insurance on IRA/Keogh accounts to $250,000. (8) Subject to some exceptions, including a "grandfather provision," generally prohibit bank holding companies from providing insurance as principal, agent, or broker. (9) Expand the savings and loan powers as they apply to checking accounts, commercial lending, and corporate debt investment—as well as grant them the right to make a wide variety of nonresidential real estate loans, or secured or unsecured loans for corporate, commercial, business, or agricultural purposes.

If the traditional financial intermediaries eventually agree on some of the trade-offs built into the Garn proposals, the reason may well be due to the hot breath of competition they are feeling from "outside sources." For even as the two chambers of Congress were debating the pros and cons of the Garn proposals, Sears Roebuck & Company, the nation's largest retailer, announced two major steps of expansion in the financial services it offered. It announced that it had agreed to purchase Coldwell Banker & Company, the nation's largest real estate brokerage of wholly owned offices, in an exchange of cash and stock valued at nearly $179 million. It also announced its bid to buy Dean Witter Reynolds, Wall Street's fifth largest brokerage house, for some $600 million.

Sears had previously unveiled its U.S. Government Money Market Trust. The acquisition of Dean Witter itself added yet another major cubit to its "financial services group." Other elements in its group included Allstate's savings and loan network in California with assets around $2.3 billion, the Allstate insurance group, and the Seraco group, which involves real estate. In these respects, Sears laid its cards on the table face-up for banks, thrifts, and credit unions to see. Its president and chief executive officer plainly and explicitly said that Sears "planned on becoming a leading national provider of consumer financial services."

THE NUMBERS GAME

A young person embarking on a career in the banking business today might very well be haunted by a question that is the subject of intense speculation wherever experienced bank managers gather. The question is this. In years ahead, if the present barriers to geographic expansion were eased, and if the economic environment continued to be marked by high-rate inflation, how many banks and of what size would emerge from deregulation? To the young novitiate banker, the answer to the question has an obvious bearing on his career prospects. It is conceivable that the conclusions now drawn from events on the move may prove to be dead wrong if events themselves undergo an unexpected change of front. Yet one of the more compelling forecasts of what lies ahead—all based on probable reasoning—appears in a report issued in late 1980 by Golembe Associates, and prepared by Professor Harry Guenther of Georgetown University in Washington, D.C.[28]

The report, in brief, distinguished between the previous impact of deregulation on the securities industry, and that on the savings and loan industry, once more liberal statutes and rules were adopted as these affected their physical locations. The report then went on to argue that the impact of deregulation on the savings and loan associations best served as the model on which one could predict the likely effect of deregulation on the number of commercial banks.

If so, there could be a 30 to 50 percent decline in the number of commercial banks between the start of the 1980s and the start of the 1990s, though that kind of decline would raise the mean level of assets based on 1979 year-end aggregates to just over $200 million. Also, the natural internal growth due to the growth of the economy and inflation could push these figures considerably higher. Thus if commercial bank assets were to double during the 1980s (they grew by some 270 percent in the 1970s) a reduction from the present 14,701 banks to 10,000 would result in mean assets of nearly $300 million per bank; a reduction to 7,000 could result in an average bank size of $400 million in assets.

Average size, of course, does not reveal a great deal about banking structure. What if one half of the nation's banks were to disappear through merger or acquisition? Would the result be a banking structure such as in California, which has 252 banking organizations—of which the largest, BankAmerica Corporation, holds 35 percent of total domestic deposits, while the next two largest hold 11.5 and 10.8 percent respectively? It does not necessarily follow that geographical deregulation would lead to a California-like banking structure throughout the country. For one thing, bank mergers and acquisitions would still have to meet the competitive tests of the Bank Merger Act or Bank Holding Company Act, as well as the possibility of Justice Department challenge. Thus the largest banks could not expand geographically except *de novo* or by foothold acquisitions. Second, several states have enacted "cap" legislation which sets a limit on the share of state deposits a single banking organization can hold. The Golembe Associates report concluded on the following note:

It seems far more likely that the major structural shift would involve consolidation among small- and medium-size banks, with the very smallest seeking survival, those somewhat larger seeking regional status, and some of the regionals becoming truly regional, that is, multi-state among contiguous states. Judging from the California experience, new banks would continue to be chartered, albeit at a much slower pace until the dust settles. The net result of this would probably mean greater domestic competition for money center banks in the wholesale market and greater competition among all banks in retail markets. A substantial number of additional foreign acquisitions would also seem likely. In those states where two-to-five leading banks have a large share, the preponderance of structural shift would more likely be among the "second tier" of banks, as they sought to become viable competitors of the largest in the state.

ECONOMIC STABILITY

Arguments over President Reagan's program to restore the national economy to a condition of orderly growth at stable prices are not likely to diminish in the impending future. There will be sharp differences of opinion on how the economy will be affected in the long run for better or for worse by a tight money policy, a reduction in the size of the budgetary deficit, a further reduction of corporate taxes, and an accelerated depreciation plan to revive lagging corporate investments.

Given the sharply increased tax bite of recent years, there were very few who would argue against the notion of a substantial tax cut. But underlying this conceptual agreement in principle were marked differences of views as to the proper timing of the tax cut. Some believed, as did Paul Volcker, Chairman of the Federal Reserve Board, that with a projected federal budget deficit in the $65 billion range and inflation continuing at double-digit rates, the economy simply could not afford a tax cut at this time. Under this line of reasoning, federal expenditures should first be reduced, and when the forces of inflation began to subside, a tax cut would then be appropriate. Chairman Volcker in testimony before Congress pointedly said that "budget cuts must be in place before any tax reduction takes effect."

While the Reagan Administration, for its part, moved to reduce spending programs even in sensitive social areas, it held to the view that tax cuts could not be delayed until the budget outlays were significantly reduced. The conceptual basis for the administration's tax cut proposals was known as "supply-side economics." It asked the question of how national production could be stimulated in a tight money climate to fight inflation. It observed that restrained money creation meant that you could not stimulate production by boosting aggregate demand. But "supply siders" believed that production could be increased by changing incentives within the economy, by cutting taxes where marginal tax rates are so high as to create disincentives to production and supply. If so, then an immediate tax cut accompanied by reduced spending and monetary restraint would stimulate the economy in a noninflationary manner. More specifically, a strong, growing economy would help immeasurably in achieving a balanced budget, for the basic budget program would be solved when the economy started to grow faster than the government.

Even under favorable circumstances, however, real progress was bound to be slow. Until the financial markets were convinced that the administration and the Federal Reserve were firmly committed to their respective roles in an anti-inflation program, the expectations of future inflation were not likely to be broken. Perhaps one of the most serious aspects of the federal budget deficit was its impact on the credit markets. For example, in the first quarter of 1981, the Treasury faced the need to raise approximately $38 billion in new money. This, by itself, cut into the funds available in money markets to private financial institutions, besides adding to the significant portion of the aggregate federal debt represented by interest payments on past borrowings. Yet this prospect did not stand alone. Salomon Brothers estimated that the federal government's net demand for credit in 1981 would be a record $96 billion. To mobilize this sum, the Treasury would have to keep its interest rates high, leading to corresponding high or higher rates of interest private financial institutions would have to pay for funds in competition with Treasury borrowing. On the other hand, sharp reduction in government expenditures in the realm of social welfare programs carried with it the prospect of increased strains among rival camps each striving for a share of a diminishing pie.

ON A NOTE OF ENCOURAGEMENT

When Alexander the Great was but a youth in Macedonia, he wept each time he received the news of another victory won by his father, Philip, King of Macedonia. He bewailed the fact that by the time he came of age and was the successor to his father's throne, nothing great would be left for him to do. The moral of the story here is that no novitiate banker need fear the immediate prospect that all that needs to be done in the economic world of which he is a part will be done by the time he becomes a commander of significant banking resources in his own right. It should be obvious from even the brief summary of events touched on in this concluding chapter, that a new world in banking remains to be created and mastered.

NOTES

Notes

Part I. THE ENVIRONMENT OF BANKING

1. Even John Maynard Keynes of Cambridge was hard hit in his pocketbook because he clung to the belief—shared by another distinguished economist, Irving Fisher of Yale—that the worldwide collapse of stock prices in the fall of 1929 was but a temporary adjustment along familiar lines; once the adjustment was completed, stock prices would continue their jubilant upward course.

2. The reference is to the Franklin National Bank of New York.

3. Professor J. Sterling Livingston of the Harvard Business School brought together the findings of numerous studies which show that there is no direct relationship between performances in school or training programs and subsequent records of success in management. He observed that schools give instruction in "problem solving," whereas the real issue is often "problem finding." See his article, "The Myth of the Well-Educated Manager," *Harvard Business Review*, January–February, 1971, pp. 79–89.

4. Cited by John Maynard Keynes in *The End of Laissez-Faire*, lectures delivered in 1924 and 1926 (London: Irvington Publishers, 1926).

5. Cited in a report by Golembe Associates Inc., Washington, D.C., 1979, no. 2.

6. I have drawn on the writings of Kenneth Boulding for this suggestive figure of speech.

7. The aggregate figures tend to change from month to month. While this manuscript was under preparation, for example, Bank of America and Citicorp played "tag" with each other, with Bank of America holding the No. 1 spot, only to be displaced by Citicorp.

8. Cited in *Pratt's Letter*, Washington, D.C., October 11, 1981.

9. The Carter Administration, in response to the complaints that over-regulation added to inflationary pressures by adding to the costs of doing business, established a Deregulation Commission to study and recommend ways to deregulate aspects of American business. This work is currently going forward during the Reagan Presidency under the chairmanship of Vice President George Bush. It is worth noting that every major move to deregulate an important aspect of an industry is often met by protests from within the industry itself by interests which see themselves adversely affected by the restoration of a free competitive market.

10. Cited in the *American Banker*, October 11, 1981.

11. The Financial Standards Board is the professional body that establishes standards for certified public accountants. It ventured to establish standards for "inflationary accounting" under an apparent veiled threat from the Securities Exchange Commission that the Commission itself would establish such standards unless the Board did so.

12. The figures cited are taken from a report by Golembe Associates Inc., 1980, no. 1.

13. Here, as elsewhere, I have drawn heavily on the periodic reports prepared by Henry Kaufman of Salomon Brothers of New York.

14. Professor Robert Aliber, of the University of Chicago Graduate School of Business, and a respected authority on international banking and monetary structures, is the source of these figures.

15. The judgment is based on a personal conversation with Alan Greenspan during his 1978 visit to Utah State University in Logan, Utah, where he delivered a lecture under the auspices of the Distinguished Economic Lecture Chair I had established at that university.

Other leaders of economic thought brought to Utah State University under the same auspices included Milton Friedman, Walter Heller, Irving Kristol, Murray Wiedenbaum, Gary Becker, Daniel Bell, Herbert Stein, Henry C. Wallich, and Paul McCracken.

16. In ancient Babylon, religious temples controlled by certain priestly families performed the equivalent of banking services. Clay tablets on which their transactions are recorded indicate that they lent money to farmers at the start of a planting season and collected the loans at harvest time. They also indicate a concern over the effects of inflation on the value of the loan at payment time.

17. Solon, the Athenian lawgiver, as part of his reforms, paid attention to the relationship between the quantity of money in circulation and price levels. He undertook to reflate a deflated economy by measures that virtually doubled the stock of money in Athens. See Plutarch, on Solon.

18. Readers of Adam Smith's classic work sometimes overlook the very nature of its title. The title was not *The Wealth of Men*. It was *The Wealth of Nations*. As a moral and political philosopher, Smith was concerned with the well-being of the nation as a whole, and hence with the means by which it could best be promoted.

19. Once again, I have drawn on the writings of Kenneth Boulding for this particular line of commentary.

20. The comparisons and differences here have often been stressed by Professor Gary Becker, one of a long line of theoretical economists that have added distinction to the Department of Economics at the University of Chicago.

21. It was Professor Frank Knight of the Department of Economics at the University of Chicago who warned his fellow economists *not* to succumb to "an irrational passion for dispassionate rationality." Knight, in his writings, seemed always to pay a decent respect to the political and ethical judgments that bore on the ends of economics and on economic calculations.

22. The various statistical models used have often produced surprising results. Depending on the factors measured, say, in "a universe of 20 banks," some of the leading banks in that universe have ranked toward the bottom of the list.

Part II. THE INVISIBLE HAND OF HISTORY:
THE PAST AS PRESENT

1. Even before the First Bank was launched, Thomas Jefferson, as Secretary of State, and Edmund Randolph, as Attorney General, advised President George Washington that Congress had no constitutional power to grant the bank a charter. Moreover, at Washington's request, James Madison prepared the draft text of a veto message for Washington's use. The veto message, however, was pocketed under the force of Treasury Secretary Alexander Hamilton's argument that the creation of the First Bank, by being indispensable to the general welfare of the "more perfect Union" the Constitution had been designed to promote, was within the constitutional powers of Congress.

2. President Andrew Jackson had vetoed the renewal of the charter on the ground that its original charter, granted by Congress, was in violation of the Constitution—even though the constitutionality of the measure had been previously upheld by Chief Justice John Marshall.

3. The motive of the Suffolk Bank did not spring from philanthropy. It was aimed, at least in part, at improving its own position under conditions where "country banks" sent their representatives to Boston where they made loans to local merchants at rates lower than those the Suffolk Bank charged. To induce the "country banks" to join the Suffolk System, Suffolk made a practice of accumulating large bundles of notes the "country banks" issued and then, without forewarning, presenting them to the issuing banks for redemption in specie. Since the latter could never be certain when they would be faced by a demand for redemption, they were forced to maintain a large and idle reserve of specie.

4. A number of leading New York banks strongly objected to the creation of the Fund on grounds that would find a far-off echo in the objections some banks raised at the time the

Federal Deposit Insurance legislation came before Congress in 1933. It was that the insurance scheme would foster conditions where well-managed conservative banks would have to pay for the follies of the profligate banks.

5. It was argued at the time that if there had been a national currency before the Civil War which everywhere had the same value, it would have helped put a brake on the movement toward secession.

6. The panic had its genesis in what was known as the "Harriman Boom," a reference to Edward H. Harriman of the Union Pacific and Southern Pacific Railroads. For a number of years after Harriman gained control of these two bankrupt railroads, the task he set of rebuilding them from the ground up went hand-in-hand with scanty dividend payments even after they began to operate in the black. The bulk of the profits earned were poured back into the "betterments" of all aspects of the two railroads. Suddenly, however, in 1907, Harriman announced that the roads would be paying an extraordinarily high dividend to their stockholders. This triggered a speculative boom in other stocks as well, and the speculative fevers rose to the pitch of delirium within a few months after Harriman was locked in battle with J. J. Hill for the control of the Great Northern Railroad.

7. In his book, *An Adventure in Constructive Finance*, Carter Glass recalled that when the Reserve Act of 1913 was being drafted, its terms were kept secret from everyone except President Wilson and Secretary of the Treasury William Gibbs McAdoo. He explained that the "currency measure was so closely guarded" because "every other currency bill had been battered to pieces by hostile interests before it could get a start." He assumed that the "Federal Reserve Bank bill would be subjected to the same kind of attacks should its revolutionary provisions be prematurely disclosed."

8. The attachment to the Gold Standard dates from the 1870s when most of the leading nations of continental Europe changed from a currency system based on bi-metalism (and a ratio between the price of silver and the price of gold) to a single gold standard. It was at that time, as well, that the United States by law established a single gold standard as a basis for its currency. The undisputed dominion of the gold standard, however, was very brief. Various nations began to make pragmatic compromises with its simon-pure dictates—even before the outbreak of the First World War prompted virtually all of the belligerents to abandon the standard. There has been a current revival of interest in the mechanics of the Gold Standard as a means for keeping inflationary pressures under control. But the interest seems to be more of an exercise in romantic economics than in the economics of real possibilities.

9. The history of these three institutions has been reconstructed from materials brought together by Federal Reserve research divisions. Supplemental material has been drawn from *Freeman of First Chicago*, a two-volume collection of the writings of Gaylord Freeman, formerly the CEO of the First National Bank of Chicago, edited by Sidney Hyman (Chicago: R. R. Donnelley 1976).

10. For the history of the FSLIC creation, see *Beckoning Frontiers: Public and Personal Recollections of Marriner S. Eccles*, edited by Sidney Hyman (New York: Knopf, 1950).

11. State departments of financial regulation are also among the leading defenders of the dual banking system, and for reasons which go beyond any substantive merits of the case. They have a natural interest in preserving the jobs that go with state banking regulatory activities.

12. "I remember many times walking up Main Street with a black bag containing from fifteen to twenty thousand dollars worth of gold handcuffed to my wrist—almost more than I could carry." C. G. White, in *Branch Clearings*, First Security Corporation, June 1957.

13. When the value of the first mortgage collapsed in times of depression, the value of the second and third mortgages were naturally wiped out.

14. In the Intermountain West, for example, the ecological disaster of the "dust bowl" coincided with a disease carried by the "white fly" which imperilled the entire sugar beet crop industry.

15. For a vivid picture of the Federal Farm Loan Board and the agricultural conglomerate it was supposed to supervise, see *Eugene Meyer*, by Merlo Pusey (New York: Knopf, 1975).

16. Secretary Houston was in a position to have his way because the Treasury department had to give its approval of the issuance of any new offerings of WFC bonds. By vetoing a proposed new offering to help continue the underwriting of insurance against loss in overseas trade, Houston forced Meyer to comply with his wishes.

17. See *George N. Peak and the Fight for Farm Parity*, by Gilbert C. Fite (Norman, Okla.: University of Oklahoma Press, 1954).

18. "Problems of Unprofitable Business," by George S. Eccles, Western Regional Convention of the American Bankers Association, Salt Lake City, Utah, May 23, 1930; "Chain Stores, Railway Express Company, and Similar Accounts," by George S. Eccles, Bank Management Conference, Portland, Oregon, March 8, 1930; circular letter, "Credit Studies," sent to all bank managers of the First Security System, dated December 1929; "Handling Credits in Group Banking System," by George S. Eccles, American Institute of Banking Convention, Denver, Colorado, June 18, 1930.

19. "The advantages of the holding company type of organization were observed not only by the banker but by the speculator as well, for he saw in this development a splendid opportunity to gain a considerable profit. Country bank shares were selling at prices usually considerably below book value, whereas the stock of banks in major cities often sold at twice their book value. The price-earnings ratios were about equally disproportionate. Herein a promoter might profit in several ways. At least in theory, the banks under group supervision could be placed under better management, and larger earnings would result. Furthermore, since holding company stock was more marketable than local bank stock, the total of the prices of the individual bank shares before consolidation would often be much less than the market price of a share of the resulting holding company. This was an instance where the whole did not always equal the sum of its parts." *Bank Holding Companies*, by Gerald C. Fischer (New York: Columbia University Press, 1961), p. 26.

20. For a cogent description of the picture here, see *A Monetary History of the United States: 1867–1960*, by Milton Friedman and Anna Jacobson Schwartz (Princeton: Princeton University Press, 1963). In addition, see Charles S. Hamlin, Diary, Volumes 5–6, Hamlin Papers, Manuscript Division, Library of Congress; also, Lester V. Chandler, *Benjamin Strong, Central Banker* (Washington, D.C.: Brookings Institution, 1958).

21. In September 1931, Britain abandoned the gold standard after runs on sterling precipitated by France and the Netherlands. Anticipating similar action on the part of the United States, central banks and private holders in a number of countries—notably France, Belgium, Switzerland, Sweden, and the Netherlands—converted substantial amounts of their dollar assets in the New York money market to gold between September 16 and October 28. From the week of September 16, the unloading of bills onto the Federal Reserve assumed panic proportions. The gold stock declined by $275 million, and from then to the end of October by an additional $450 million.

22. *The Hoover Administration, A Documented Narrative*, by William Starr Myers and Walter H. Newton (New York: Charles Scribner's Sons, 1936).

23. *Challenge and Response: The First Security Corporation, First Fifty Years*, by Sidney Hyman (Salt Lake City: Graduate School of Business, University of Utah, 1979), pp. 100–102.

24. The South Sea Bubble was the name given to the historic speculation and collapse of a British corporation in the early 1700s, designed to provide the same kind of profitable outlets for investment in the South Seas as did the British East India Company and the Hudson Bay Company elsewhere. It was the collapse of this venture which prompted the British Parliament to pass restrictive legislation against the formation of any new corporations of any kind, though existing corporations were not disturbed. The history of the South Sea Bubble seems to have been among the factors that influenced President Andrew Jackson's hostility to the Second Bank of the United States *as* a corporation.

25. Hyman, *Challenge and Response*, p. 101.

26. *Ibid.*

27. *Ibid.*

28. See *The Fiscal Revolution*, by Herbert Stein (Chicago: University of Chicago Press, 1969).

29. Cited in Pusey, *Eugene Meyer.*

30. The grant of a very large RFC loan to the Continental Bank of Chicago was much criticized at the time because of Dawes's association with the bank. On the surface, Dawes himself, as Chairman of the RFC, appeared vulnerable to a charge of conflict of interest. Yet in a closer view, the grant of the RFC to the Continental Bank was preceded in mid-1932 by a wave of failures in Chicago which closed the doors of over 40 banks. The RFC loan to the Continental did not by itself stop the wave of bank failures, but it was instrumental in preventing the total collapse of the banking system as a whole in Chicago, the capital city of a Midland Empire.

31. The law specified only that the RFC make monthly reports to the President of the United States and the Congress on all loans granted the previous month. It was John N. Garner, the then Speaker of the House, who in August instructed the Clerk to make the reports public. The Democrats claimed that the publication of RFC loans served as a safeguard against favoritism in the distribution of loans. See Jesse Jones, *Fifty Billion Dollars* (New York: Macmillan, 1951), pp. 72, 82–82, 517–520.

32. See the chapter titled "The Great Contraction" in Friedman and Schwartz, *A Monetary History of the United States.*

Part III. THE CONTINENTAL DIVIDE OF TIME

1. Hyman, *Beckoning Frontiers*, p. 170.

2. The summary account presented here closely follows the one set forth in "Historical Background of Federal Regulation of Bank Affiliates" by William F. Upshaw (*American Banker*, April 16, 1973). It should be noted that in addition to extensive Senate hearings into the conduct of holding companies, the collapse of some of these companies was followed by extensive civil litigation, and, in particular instances, by Grand Jury investigations conducted with an eye to potential criminal indictments. In three cases of failure of major bank holding companies in the 1930s, the Courts held the holding company stockholders liable to assessment. On the other hand, the judge who conducted the Grand Jury investigation concerning the Michigan bank failures stated that there was no evidence of criminality on the part of the bank's officers. The court decisions were cited in news items in the *Commercial and Financial Chronicle* for September 23, 1933; March 10, 1934; November 21, 1936; and March 13, 1937. Of a piece with this, the Detroit banking collapse has been the object of numerous special studies. One of these, by Dr. Howard R. Neville, argues that "it is entirely possible to believe that if Henry Ford and Senator Couzens had been more cooperative and if the RFC loan had been made, the Michigan banking holiday might never have been proclaimed." "The Detroit Banking Collapse of 1933," Bureau of Research, Michigan State University, Occasional paper no. 2 (East Lansing, Michigan, 1960).

3. See Hyman, *Freeman of First Chicago.*

4. At the 1954 ABA convention, as president of the Reserve City Bankers Association, I teamed up with Harold Amberg, chairman of the Reserve City Bankers legislative committee and also chairman of the ABA resolutions committee, in working the lobbies of the ABA convention. The result was the adoption by the ABA of a new resolution which voiced support for bank holding companies subject to proper restrictions. A similar resolution had been previously passed by the Reserve City Bankers Association.

5. For a review of multiple unit failures between 1920 and 1930, see "Branch, Chain, and Group Banking," Board of Governors, Federal Reserve System, vol. VII.

6. "Historical Background of Federal Regulation of Bank Affiliates," by William F. Upshaw.

7. The data here is taken from a history of bank holding company legislation prepared in memorandum form by Bray Hammond of the Research Division of the Federal Reserve Board and submitted to the board on March 11, 1947.

8. *The Registered Bank Holding Company: Its History and Significance in Modern America*, The Association of Registered Bank Holding Companies, February 1969, Washington, D.C.

9. Hyman, *Beckoning Frontiers*, p. 260.

10. The conduct of banking was, of course, both directly and indirectly affected by supervisory powers over bank securities vested in the newly created Securities and Exchange Commission.

11. Gaylord Freeman of the First National Bank of Chicago, in a review of the self-defeating conservatism some bankers exhibit, was once brave enough to remind a wide audience of bankers of their original opposition to the FHA measure.

12. Originally in New Deal circles, the idea of "housing" was largely confined to "public housing" and to "slum clearance." This would have entailed heavy governmental expenditures, albeit for a desirable social end. But from the standpoint of a program of general economic recovery, it was indispensably necessary to stir the pools of idle private funds for investments in private housing.

13. The insurance scheme was the invention of Winfield Reifler, who presently became an intimate staff associate of Marriner S. Eccles when the latter was appointed Chairman of the Federal Reserve Board in November 1934.

14. Hyman, *Beckoning Frontiers*, pp. 150–52.

15. When Mayor Richard Daley was approached by a group of leading Chicago bankers for political help in securing the enactment by the Illinois State legislature of a measure that would permit statewide branch banking, he reminded them of a disconcerting fact. It was that when he was newly married and went to a local bank to secure a mortgage loan for a home, his application was refused by the bank. On the other hand, he secured a mortgage loan from a savings and loan association. It was Mayor Daley's way of making it clear that in any conflict between commercial banks and savings and loan associations, he had strong emotional reasons for siding with the associations against the banks.

16. The dominance of Main Street is visible as well in the case of the U.S. Chamber of Commerce and the National Manufacturers Association.

17. For a succinct discussion of the issue here, see Harold Barger, *The Management of Money: A Survey of American Experience* (New York: Columbia University Press, 1956), pp. 123–139.

18. In the 1939 budget message, a balanced budget was envisioned as a possibility when the GNP reached the neighborhood of $80 billion—or what it had been on the eve of the Great Crash.

19. Hyman, *Beckoning Frontiers*, p. 400.

20. *Ibid.*

21. Even Allan Sproul, the distinguished president of the New York Federal Reserve Bank, voiced his opposition to the special reserve plan.

Part IV. THE CHANGING WORLD OF BANKING

1. Fischer, *Bank Holding Companies*, pp. 102–20.

2. *Ibid.*

3. I have drawn on the account which appears in Hyman, *Freeman of First Chicago*. Gaylord Freeman was a member of the Commission, having been appointed to it in order to fill a vacancy created by the death of Beardsley Ruml.

4. As recently as the early 1970s, the leading textbooks on banking were virtually silent on the application of the new computer technology to banking transactions.

5. The application of computer technology to banking figures in virtually all discussions of what is now called "the post-industrial society," or "the information society." See Daniel Bell, *The Coming of the Post-Industrial Society* (New York: Basic Books, 1973); James Martin, *Future Developments in Telecommunications* (Englewood Cliffs: Prentice-Hall, 1977); Colin Cherry, *World Communications: Threat or Promise* (New York: John Wiley & Sons, 1978); John and Magda Cordell McHale, "Exploiting the Resource of Information," *Intermedia*, March 1979; Office of Technology Assessment, *Computer-Based National Information Systems*, (Washington, D.C.: U.S. Government Printing Office, 1981); Fritz Machlup, *Knowledge: Its Creation, Distribution and Economic Significance* (Princeton: Princeton University Press, 1980); B. T. Feld, "Secrecy and Development," in *Meeting on the Knowledge Industry and the Process of Development*, OECD, Document No. 37 (Paris, 1980); Marc C. Porat, "Communication Policy in an Information Society," in Glen O. Robinson, ed., *Communications for Tomorrow* (New York: Praeger, 1978); *Personal Privacy in an Information Society*, Report of the Privacy Protection Study Commission (Washington, D.C.: U.S. Government Printing Office, 1977).

6. In the last half of the 1970s, publications issued by regional Federal Reserve Banks began to bloom with informative articles on various aspects of the electronic transfer of funds. See "Electronic Funds Transfer and Monetary Policy," in *Review*, Federal Reserve Bank of Dallas, August 1977; "Why Bankers Are Now Concerned about NOW Accounts," *Business Review*, Federal Reserve Bank of Philadelphia, November–December 1977; "The Impact of NINOWs on Deposits in Illinois," *Economic Perspectives*, Federal Reserve Bank of Chicago, September–October 1977; "Fed Takes Steps to Improve EFT," *Voice*, Federal Reserve Bank of Dallas, May 1978; "Exception Items Processing to be Improved," *ibid.*, June 1978; "The Diffusion of NOW accounts in Massachusetts," *New England Economic Review*, Federal Reserve Bank of Boston, November–December 1976; "Checking vs. Savings: The Lines Blur," *Economic Review*, Federal Reserve Bank of Atlanta, May–June 1978.

7. For a related aspect, see "Changes in the Treasury's Cash Management Procedures," *Economic Review*, Federal Reserve Bank of Atlanta, January–February 1978.

8. Current concerns over the "right of privacy" go beyond the issue of the physical security of computer records. The relative ease with which information stored in a bank can now be retrieved lay behind several critically important cases in criminal justice where prosecutorial agents secured information from banks which might have been denied them through direct questioning of suspects under the Fourth and Fifth Amendments to the Constitution.

9. The reference is to the legislation introduced into the Senate in 1981 by Senator Jake Garn (R-Utah).

10. The argument here synthesizes the thrust of successive articles in the *American Banker*.

11. The economic impact of U.S. Supreme Court rulings is by no means a recent phenomenon. It dates from the economic-political opinions of Chief Justice John Marshall who used the judicial power of the Court to advance his commitment to an American future where the United States would comprise a single and great Common Market. The frequency with which cases were brought into the Federal courts for adjudication that would have been adjudicated elsewhere in political forums inspired the celebrated insight of Alexis de Tocqueville in the 1830s, to the effect that in the United States, political cases tend to come before the courts in the guise of legal cases.

12. The bewilderment had its echo in a number of articles of the period which appeared in the monthly publications of the regional Federal Reserve Banks.

13. Quoted in the *American Banker*, December 7, 1979.

14. See "Federal Funds and Repurchase Agreements," *Quarterly Review*, Federal Reserve Bank of New York, vol. 2, no. 2, summer 1977. See also *Federal Funds Market: Origin and Development*, by Parker B. Willis (Boston: Federal Reserve Bank of Boston, 1970).

15. Willis, *Federal Funds Market*.

16. The description here has been provided by George Denton who has ably managed the money desk of the First Security Corporation, Salt Lake City, Utah.

17. *Ibid.*

18. Errors of judgment in the realm of liability management proved very costly at the end of the 1970s to two major banks—First Pennsylvania of Philadelphia, and First National Bank of Chicago. In both instances, their respective CEOs misread the course of inflation and of its impact on the price of the funds they borrowed and what the price would be when the loans matured.

19. Various attempts have been made by detective-minded economists to determine "the money supply" that does not appear in any M-1 reports, but fuels "the underground economy." One such estimate, arrived at by ingenious calculations, places the stock of money in the hands of organized crime—and in the form of cash income individuals do *not* report to the IRS—at $150 billion.

20. At an early hour in the history of the Virginia colony in America when wampum, along with tobacco, was used as money, a colonial governor is said to have imported a glass blower from Italy in order to counterfeit the beads used in wampum.

21. See "Defining Money for a Changing Financial System," *Quarterly Review*, Federal Reserve Bank of New York, vol. 4, no. 1, spring 1979.

22. The theme here was expressly developed by Alexander Hamilton in various numbers of *The Federalist* ascribed to his pen.

23. Correspondent relationships existed between U.S. commercial banks and European banks by the 1860s, in connection with the financing of American agricultural products that entered into world trade. One of the earliest among these relationships was the one forged in the 1860s by the First National Bank of Chicago and correspondent banks in England, France, Holland, and Germany. But the dominant institutions in the financing of the movement of American agricultural products such as wheat and cotton to European markets were largely the American-based branches of European-headquartered private investment banking houses such as Lazard Frères.

24. At the end of the 1970s, for example, when Chase National sold its share in a German private investment banking house, the purchaser of the share was the Midland Bank of London.

25. Cited in *Washington Financial Reports*, no. 28, July 14, 1980.

26. The disclosure laws were not confined to reports on foreign ownership of U.S. banks, but covered a range of other economic matters—from holdings in real estate to farm lands. As such, they amounted to the first attempt since the eve of Pearl Harbor to determine the extent of foreign ownership and investments in the American economy.

27. Cited in a report by Golembe Associates Inc., Washington, D.C., 1979, no. 2.

28. *Ibid.*

29. Cited in a report by Golembe Associates Inc., Washington, D.C., 1979, no. 7.

30. *Ibid.*

31. For a balanced discussion of the general subject, see "Commercial Bank Lending to the Developing Countries," *Quarterly Review*, Federal Reserve Bank of New York, vol. 2, no. 2, summer 1977.

32. I have drawn heavily on "Global Asset and Liability Management at Commercial Banks," *Quarterly Review*, Federal Reserve Bank of New York, vol. 4, no. 1, spring 1979.

33. For a luminous discussion of the subject as a whole, see Robert Z. Aliber, "Stabilizing World Monetary Arrangements," Trade Policy Research Centre, Thames Essay No. 18 (London, 1979). Professor Aliber is, to use a sporting term, "a world class" economist, specializing in international trade.

34. Mr. Pardee's treatment of the subject appears in his article "How Well Are the Exchange Markets Functioning?" *Quarterly Review*, Federal Reserve Bank of New York, vol. 4, no. 1, spring 1979.

Part V. THE STRUGGLE TO GOVERN

1. I am indebted to Professor John Kenneth Galbraith for this insight—and language.

2. Even so, the end of the fighting in Vietnam did not mark the end of the costs of the war. The continued costs were in the form of the care of the disabled and of death benefits to the families of the deceased soldiers. As is true at the end of every war, these represented fixed charges against the government's treasury which go on and on for decades after the shooting stops.

3. The German economist Werner Günther observed, in a study of the new nations that emerged in the world arena in the decades after 1945, that, of those which originally embarked on careers as constitutional democracies, the greater number lapsed back into totalitarian or authoritarian regimes—many dominated by the military—once their inflation rate exceeded 15 percent annually.

4. The importance of the *Federal Register* as the official repository of Executive Orders and rules issued by the various regulatory agencies dates from the years of the New Deal.

5. See "A Banker Looks at the Examination Process," *Quarterly Review,* Federal Reserve Bank of New York, vol. 4, no. 1, spring 1979.

6. The survey was conducted by a private research agency, commissioned for the task by the FDIC.

7. The process began with an attempt to coordinate the policies of the Federal Reserve, the Comptroller of the Currency, the Treasury Department, and the FDIC, so that each would apply the same standards in assessing the "liquidity" of banks and the volume of commercial paper in their portfolios that was "eligible" for discount privileges at the Federal Reserve discount window. The imperative need for such coordination came to a head in the context of the 1937–38 recession.

8. During the years of the Nixon Presidency, the Treasury Department tended to confine its auditing procedures regarding compliance with equal opportunity legislation to "educational" objectives. There were no publicized instances where sanctions were applied for noncompliance with the terms of that legislation. Direct governmental pressures to secure compliance, coupled with privately initiated lawsuits, date mainly from the Carter Presidency.

9. For the discussion of type-cases where commercial banks were denied the right to establish branches on a finding of fact that they had not met their responsibilities under the Community Reinvestment Act, see *Washington Financial Reports,* no. 29, July 21, 1980.

10. As is true of all mandated record-keeping touched on here, the existence of the computer, which facilitates the retrieval of information, has no doubt played a part of its own in shaping the terms for the lengthy retention of detailed records.

11. It remains to be seen whether this arrangement in the case of medium-sized banks will lead to the same pattern of promotion that has often prevailed in the large money center banks—a pattern where a succession to the position of chief executive officers has often gone to bank officials originally associated with the institution's legal department.

12. The membership of the Independent Bankers Association of America is comprised of unit bankers. Within the American Bankers Association—of which they are also members—they represent the largest single "voting bloc," and exert a potent influence over the policy stands taken by the ABA.

13. The "Reuss bill" might still have been reported out of the House Banking Committee but for the defection of two Democratic members who objected to its terms on various grounds of their own. One of these, Rep. Thomas Ashley (D-Ohio) was also a powerfully placed member of the House Rules Committee, and, as such, was in a position to block placing the bill on the House calendar even if the measure had been voted out by the House Banking Committee.

14. Several members of the House Banking Committee were so hostile to Chairman Miller that they threatened to initiate a move looking to his "impeachment."

15. The occasion was an address before the National Press Club, Washington, D.C., in the early weeks of 1980.

16. Some veteran bankers at the ABA convention in New Orleans recalled that the Great Crash of October 1929 occurred at a time when the ABA was meeting in San Francisco.

17. One of these, Beryl W. Sprinkel, the chief economist of the Harris Trust and Savings Bank, had done his graduate work at the University of Chicago under the direction of Professor Milton Friedman. It was Friedman who also wrote a laudatory preface to Sprinkel's book, published during the 1970s, which argued the case of "monetarism" as the balance wheel of the economy—the same case he made in March 1976 when he appeared at Utah State University in connection with the George S. Eccles Distinguished Lecture Series, to speak on "The Challenge of Managing Economic Expansion." During the Reagan Presidency, Sprinkel has held a high post in the Treasury Department.

18. As reported in the *New York Times*, participants in the ironic celebration included Professors John Kenneth Galbraith and Paul Samuelson, both long-standing "intellectual adversaries" of Milton Friedman's "monetarism."

19. The source of this estimate is Professor Robert Z. Aliber of the University of Chicago.

20. The estimates made by the Congressional Budget Office may have entered into the calculations of the Reagan Presidency when it unveiled its own budget-cutting proposals.

21. The history of the Credit Control Act seemed to write large the sense of a cartoon which appeared some years previously in the *New Yorker*. It showed two members of the U.S. Senate standing in the well of the chamber, with one saying to the other: "I don't know what's in this Act, but let's vote for it and find out." The proposal for credit controls was tacked on to a House bill dealing with an entirely different subject. It was voted on virtually without debate in the House, and this was true as well of the vote in the Senate. See "Looking Back on Credit Controls," *American Banker*, September 8, 1980.

22. The texts of Federal Reserve Board releases on rules that would govern credit controls were brought together in the *American Banker* for March 17, 1980. Other releases followed on the subject. But those brought together for the March 17 issue ran to eight full pages.

23. The *American Banker* for March 21, 1980, tracked the steps taken by the Federal Reserve "to soothe bankers on rules." In a story out of Washington, it reported that "agency officials said they would allow for different accounting systems in determining levels of consumer credit as long as those systems were consistent. The message during a meeting here this week was that the Fed does not want to interrupt normal business procedures; it just wants an accurate reporting of monthly consumer credit levels."

24. The contest in the Republican camp was originally a four-way affair, involving the campaigns for the party nomination waged by Senator Howard Baker, Governor John Connolly, George Bush, and Governor Ronald Reagan. When Baker and Connolly dropped out of the race, Bush and Reagan squared off for the final rounds of the pre-convention campaign. The momentum for a while seemed to favor Bush who had called Reagan's approach to the economy "voodoo economics," but Reagan regained the momentum and won the party nomination at the convention with little serious difficulty. Though he appeared to excellent advantage in his post-convention debate with President Carter, the extent to which he actually had a "mandate" for the economic program he later brought to the White House remains a subject of intense controversy among political scientists. No one can say for certain what the outcome of the election might have been if it were not for the long traumas caused by the events surrounding the U.S. embassy personnel in Teheran, held captive by the Iranian militants.

25. It was in December 1980 that the Federal Reserve Board requested public comment on a proposal to amend Regulations D and Q in order to authorize the establishment of International Banking Facilities (IBFs). Commentators were overwhelmingly in favor of the concept of the IBF, but most—and especially non–New York institutions—urged either some modification in the proposal or would favor it only in conjunction with other changes in the circumstances under which IBFs would operate. Non–New York institutions, noting the importance of a New York presence for international business, felt that they would be placed at a competitive disadvantage if they could operate IBFs in New York only at their New York Edge offices. In

considering the proposed limitations on the lending and deposit-taking activities of the IBFs, U.S. bank commentators generally urged that they be permitted the maximum flexibility to compete with offshore banking offices. Commentators differed considerably with regard to their preference for the effective date of any IBF regulation. The date eventually decided on was December 3, 1981. Office of Staff Director for Monetary and Financial Policy, "International Banking Facilities and Related Issues" (Washington, D.C.: Federal Reserve Board, June 4, 1981).

26. "Offshore Banking Can Come Home," *ABA Journal*, June 1981.

27. See "Interstate Banking—The Topic of the 1980's," *Banks in Perspective*, The Robison Humphrey Company Inc., August 6, 1980; *Washington Financial Reports*, no. 19, May 11, 1981; *Perspective*, American Bankers Association, May 19, 1981; "Deregulating Interstate Banking—Pro and Con," *American Banker*, March 6, 1981; *Bulletin*, Association of Bank Holding Companies, vol. 24, no. 19, May 15, 1981.

28. "How Many Commercial Banks in 1990?" Golembe Associates, Inc., Washington, D.C., 1980, no. 6.

INDEX

Index